Information Exchange and EU Law Enforcement

Presenting an integrated approach to information exchange among law enforcement institutions within the EU, this book addresses the dilemma surrounding the need to balance the security of individuals and the need to protect their privacy and data.

Providing the reader with a comprehensive analysis of information exchange tools, exploring their history, political background, the most recent legal modifications and the advantages and disadvantages of their use, it includes a comparison between different information exchange tools.

Written by an author who has worked as a police officer, Home Affairs counsellor and academic, this is an important read for scholars working with EU Law, Criminal Procedure Law, and International Law as well as for practitioners who directly deal with international police cooperation or who perform criminal investigation both within and outside the EU.

Anna Fiodorova is Professor of Procedural Law at Universidad Carlos III de Madrid, Spain.

Information Exchange and EU Law Enforcement

Anna Fiodorova

Routledge
Taylor & Francis Group
LONDON AND NEW YORK

First published 2018
by Routledge

2 Park Square, Milton Park, Abingdon, Oxfordshire OX14 4RN
52 Vanderbilt Avenue, New York, NY 10017

Routledge is an imprint of the Taylor & Francis Group, an informa business

First issued in paperback 2020

British Library Cataloguing in Publication Data
A catalogue record for this book is available from the British Library

Library of Congress Cataloging in Publication Data
Names: Fiodorova, Anna, author.
Title: Information exchange and EU law enforcement / Anna Fiodorova.
Description: Abingdon, Oxon ; New York, NY : Routledge, 2018. | Based on author's thesis (doctoral – Universidad Carlos III de Madrid, 2015) issued under title: Information exchange efficiency in criminal investigation in European Union. | Includes bibliographical references and index.
Identifiers: LCCN 2018000131 (print) | LCCN 2018004826 (ebook) | ISBN 9781351240260 (Master ebk) | ISBN 9781351240246 (ePub3) | ISBN 9781351240253 (Web PDF) | ISBN 9781351240239 (Mobipocket/ Kindle) | ISBN 9780815375272 (hardback)
Subjects: LCSH: Law enforcement--European Union countries-- International cooperation.
Classification: LCC KJE5977 (ebook) | LCC KJE5977 .F56 2018 (print) | DDC 363.25094--dc23
LC record available at https://lccn.loc.gov/2018000131

ISBN: 978-0-8153-7527-2 (hbk)
ISBN: 978-0-367-59039-0 (pbk)

Typeset in Goudy
by Taylor & Francis Books

To my mom and Vicente, for being the greatest source of inspiration and indispensable support.

Contents

Tables

Foreword

The influence of globalization has brought significant changes to the paradigm of criminality in the modern world, as well as new challenges to the work of law enforcement authorities. As a result, an effective response to security threats has become impossible without police involvement, which, in one way or another, "crosses" national borders and requires transnational coordination and cooperation. The key and primal element for cooperation is a proper and efficient exchange of information. This makes the subject of this book especially relevant and timely.

This book originates from a PhD thesis the author wrote under my own direction and which finally received the 2016 Outstanding Thesis Award from the University Carlos III of Madrid, one of the leading Spanish universities in law studies.

As a result of the police and academic work experience of the author, gained through her career as a police officer, a national Home Affairs Counsellor to the European Union and a university professor and researcher, this book presents the reader with a perfect balance between academic research and a pragmatic approach on information exchange among law enforcement authorities of the EU Member States.

The book which the reader has in his or her hands provides a multidisciplinary view of this complex topic.

Firstly, it encompasses three perspectives of EU information exchange for the purpose of crime investigation:

- Political: explanations for the reasons and processes of the development of law enforcement cooperation, in particular, information exchange within the framework of the European Union;
- Practical: analyses of the advantages and disadvantages of existing information exchange mechanisms for the end user (i.e. law enforcement authorities) and how to make the best of them;
- Academic: studies of possible legal problems with the current information exchange systems, in particular, data protection questions.

Secondly, the author addresses the issue of the line between the limitation and the violation of Fundamental Rights (in particular, the right to privacy and the right to data protection) in the exchange of personal data; moreover, she draws attention to a current dilemma about the balance between the security of individuals and the need to protect their privacy. She provides the reader with a comprehensive analysis of the carefully and well selected information exchange tools.

In addition to the multidisciplinary approach and perfectly balanced academic and professional experience, this book offers further added value by dealing with the significant legislative changes related to the police cooperation that took place in the European Union in 2016, as well as addressing the issue of the effects of so-called Brexit on law enforcement cooperation and analysing possible scenarios.

In conclusion, it can be said without doubt that very rarely can we find such equitable, up-to-date and thorough research on police information exchange. Research which definitely enriches the readers' knowledge of the subject and highlights the many facets of the topic.

Before bringing this foreword to an end, let me ask for the reader's indulgence to finish my words with very sincere congratulations to the author for the wonderful work she has produced. I met Anna in 2010, when she decided to leave a really successful and promising career in the public service back in her homeland, Lithuania, to move to Spain for one of the few reasons (if not the only one) somebody can undertake such a crazy challenge: love. Since then, we have been working together very closely and I never regretted having offered her the opportunity to join University Carlos III. During all these years I saw her grow from a part-time lecturer, through a PhD candidate, to an experienced post-doctoral researcher and professor who has become today one of the main pillars of my team. This book indeed represents a key milestone in Anna's academic life, but I am more than sure it will be just one of many more to follow in the future.

Dr. Helena Soleto Muñoz,

Associate Professor of Procedural Law at Universidad Carlos III de Madrid, Program Director of the Master in Criminal Justice

Acknowledgements

The path of our lives is made up of a maelstrom of events, accidents, people and occasions. Some of them just stay as a record and pass through imperceptibly, but some determine its course, or at least influence its changes.

The path leading to this book and its research began in 2002 when Mr. Kestutis Lančinskas (at that time commissioner of the International Cooperation Board of the Lithuanian Police Department) entrusted me with responsibilities related to cross-border police cooperation. It was my first incitement to start discovering the shades of these rapidly developing areas and, in particular, their role in the exchange of information.

A decade later, in Spain, on the other side of the European Union, Dr. Helena Soleto Muñoz and Dr. Victor Moreno Catena encouraged me to take an academic approach to my professional and practical experience, and to convert it into research. Dr. Helena Soleto Muñoz extraordinarily and patiently guided my PhD research (the background of this book) for more than three years.

Without these people, my life's path would probably never have led to the development of this book.

I would also like to express my gratitude to the practitioners and researchers who have contributed to this work with their comments: Mr. Vicente Corral Escariz, Dr. Sabela Oubiña Barbola, Dr. Luís Manuel Vallés Causada, Mr. Artūras Šimelionis, Ms. Audronė Sviklaitė and Ms. Asta Norkūnaitė.

And last, but not least, I would like to express my appreciation and respect for all EU police officers, the guardians of our security.

Abbreviations

AML/CFT	Anti-Money Laundering/Counter Financing of Terrorism
ARO	Assets Recovery Office
AWF	Analysis Work File
CARIN	The Camden Assets Recovery Inter-Agency Network
CEPOL	European Police College
C-SIS	Central Schengen Information System
CISA	Convention implementing the Schengen Agreement of 14 June 1985 between the Government of the States of the Benelux Economic Union, the Federal Republic of Germany and the French Republic on the gradual abolition of checks at their common borders
CJEU	Court of Justice of the European Union
DAPIX	Council Working Party on Data Protection and Information Exchange
EC	European Communities
EC3	European Cybercrime Centre
ECHR	European Convention for the Protection of Human Rights and Fundamental Freedoms
ECtHR	European Court of Human Rights
EDPS	European Data Protection Supervisor
EDU	European Drug Unit
EEC	European Economic Community
EIS	Europol Information System
ENISA	European Network and Information Security Agency
ENU	Europol National Unit
EPE	Europol Platform for Experts
EPRIS	European Police Records Index System
EU	European Union
FIU	Financial Intelligence Unit
FRA	European Union Agency for Fundamental Rights
INTERPOL	International Criminal Police Organization
IOCTA	Internet Organised Crime Threat Assessment

LIBE	Civil Liberties and Justice and Home Affairs Committee of the European Parliament
OCTA	Organised Crime Threat Assessment
PCCC	Police and Customs Cooperation Centre
PIU	Passenger Information Unit
PNR	Passenger Name Record
SIENA	Secure Information Exchange Network Application
SIRENE	Supplementary Information Request at the National Entry
SIS	Schengen Information System
SIS II	Second generation of the Schengen Information System
SOCTA	Serious and Organised Crime Threat Assessment
TEEEC	Treaty Establishing the European Economic Community
TE-SAT	Terrorism Situation and Trend Report
TEU	Consolidated version of the Treaty on the European Union[1]
TFEU	Consolidated version of the Treaty on the Functioning of the European Union[2]
USA	United States of America

1 OJ C 83, 30.3.2010, p. 13–46.
2 OJ C 83, 30.3.2010, p. 47–199.

1 Introduction

Information is a primary and indispensable background to any conclusions, whether of scientific research, business plans, political decisions or the performance of justice.

Except on those occasions when the offender is caught in the act, the starting point of any police investigation is obtaining information about the crime, and on this basis making deductions, as glorified by Sherlock Holmes. It is also one of the main elements in crime prevention, given that its timely possession precludes damaging consequences and contributes to the legitimate interests of individuals and society.

Information is obtained from different sources, beginning with inquiries to victim and witnesses, and finishing with the inspection of crime scene, reviewing surveillance camera records, consulting databases or carrying out other operational or prosecution activities. It is very seldom that one piece of information is just one link in a chain, which guides competent authorities to the next links; and there is no certainty that this chain will end in the same country where the investigation is taking place.

Cross-border information exchange became more relevant a few decades ago, when organised crime, moving "in the rhythm of time",[1] identified globalisation and the facilitated movement of persons as an opportunity for new criminal markets. It was especially perceived in the EU and the Schengen zone with the establishment of the free movement of persons, goods, capital and services, the abolition of controls on internal borders and the introduction of a single currency in the majority of EU Member States (hereinafter – Member States).

Notwithstanding, such negative side effects of these undeniable values have not been led automatically by their antidote – the free movement of investigation and prosecution. Actions of law enforcement, prosecution and judicial authorities remained limited to state territory; this meant a high probability of impunity of increasing transnational crimes.

1 STORBECK, Jürgen, "La cooperación policial europea" in MONTERO, Julián, ROMERO, Francisco and VALIENTE, Elena, *¿Hacia una Policía Europea?*, Madrid: Fundación Policía Española, 2002, p. 155.

In these circumstances, when EU policies had endangered security by unintentionally giving wider possibilities to criminals than to prosecuting authorities, a need to introduce effective cooperation tools that would overcome the obstacle of the existence of border in investigation and prosecuting criminal deeds (including measures for information exchange) emerged.[2]

As a result of this in general and of some other incidents (mostly terrorist attacks) in particular, the EU has developed a wide range of mechanisms for information exchange that include databases, networks of experts or contact points, agencies and a purely legal basis for the information exchange process.

As shown by a study carried out by the International Centre for Migration Policy Development, in 2009 countries exchanged approximately 13 million messages[3] (requests and transmissions of information) through INTERPOL and within 5 years, in 2014, this number increased to 17 million.[4] INTERPOL's databases (such as those on suspected or wanted persons, on dactyloscopics, on DNA profiles, and stolen and lost travel documents) were consulted 1.7 billion times in 2014.[5]

Within the EU, in 2009, one quarter of all investigation information requests were sent to other Member States.[6] Comparing only information submitted to EIS in 2009 and 2014, a number of records were doubled.[7]

2 Only CISA has established at the same time abolition of the border controls and compensatory measures to it.
3 See INTERNATIONAL CENTRE FOR MIGRATION POLICY DEVELOPMENT AND EUROPEAN PUBLIC LAW ORGANIZATION, "Study on the status of information exchange amongst law enforcement authorities in the context of existing EU instruments", European Commission, 2010, p. 45, accessed August 20, 2017, https://ec.europa.eu/home-affairs/sites/homeaffairs/files/doc_centre/police/docs/icmpd_study_lea_infoex.pdf.
4 See INTERPOL, "Annual Report 2014", p. 13, accessed May 17, 2015, http://www.interpol.int/News-and-media/Publications.
5 Ibid, p. 14.
6 See INTERNATIONAL CENTRE FOR MIGRATION POLICY DEVELOPMENT AND EUROPEAN PUBLIC LAW ORGANIZATION, "Study on the status of information…", loc. cit., p. 46.
7 COUNCIL OF THE EUROPEAN UNION, "General Report on Europol's activities in 2014", document 8082/15, p. 42 and 43, accessed August 20, 2017 http://data.consilium.europa.eu/doc/document/ST-9219-2015-INIT/en/pdf.

As revealed by the International Centre for Migration Policy Development, the most frequent exchange data categories are:

"Data about persons; perpetrators, suspects, unidentified persons (name, date of birth, jobs, identification data of fingerprinted criminals for true identification, confirmation of identity, residence, DNA, fingerprints, verification of personal data, criminal convictions, passports, IDs, photographs);

Data about vehicles; vehicles used to transport suspects, perpetrators; vehicles located at the crime scene or recorded by surveillance cameras, registration details, owner and operator of a vehicle, chassis numbers, purchase documents, export and import documents;

In this way cross-border information exchange became a very dynamic field of EU policy and new initiatives, but sometimes it lacked consistency and clear indications of use of developed instruments. As a consequence, police officers face plurality of legal basis, channels, procedures and tools for different categories of information. In addition, the European legislator has established a variety of regulations for the storage of information, its transmission to third states and onward transmission, as well as for data subject rights towards the processing of their personal data.

For example, data such as fingerprints can be introduced and found in SIS, Europol's EIS, Europol's AWFs, national dactyloscopic databases which are accessible on the basis of Prüm Decisions, but subjects' data and the purposes for which it is stored can be different or overlapping. Information on suspicious financial transactions or bank accounts can be requested through Europol, a network of FIUs, bilaterally between competent authorities on the basis of Swedish Initiative, or found in AWFs.

It throws law enforcement officers into confusion: which mechanism should be used? How should it be used? Will it result only in cross-checks or direct access to information? How long will it take to get information? Is it possible to request or submit information directly or should it be done through the designated authority?

Facing such babel, the aim of this book is to analyse: Which information exchange tools can be used and under what circumstances? Do they overlap? How are they compatible with human rights?

Having said that, it is not less important to highlight the limits of this research; it addresses information exchange between law enforcement authorities while performing one of the core functions – the investigation of a crime. For this purpose, information exchange in crime investigation will be understood as its processing in pre-trial investigation, operational

Financial data; company information, banking information, property relationship, bank accounts, transaction details, account holders, company board of directors, share capital, income and wealth information, unusual or suspicious money transactions, asset tracing data payment cards, data for POS terminal device;

Communication data; subscribers' details (particularly for mobiles), IT addresses, billing details, outgoing/incoming calls, emails, wiretapping, interceptions;

Data about objects, confiscated objects, objects related to committed crimes are often exchanged while data about firearms (licensing data, lost weapon, weapon used for crimes) and other 'explanatory' data are seldom exchanged (e.g. interrogations, home searches, seizure of evidence, trends, statistics, customs documents, modus operandi, and fines)."

Source: INTERNATIONAL CENTRE FOR MIGRATION POLICY DEVELOPMENT AND EUROPEAN PUBLIC LAW ORGANIZATION, "Study on the status of information…", loc. cit., p. 49.

activities, as well as within the stage of traditionally understood investigation, as a stage of the penal process when pieces of exchanged or transmitted data do not involve the authorisation of a judge or a prosecutor.

In any case, information exchange between judicial authorities through Eurojust on the basis of rogatory letters, mutual recognition of evidence or other tools of judicial cooperation remains out of the scope of this research.

Summarising, it can be defined as the analysis of the mechanisms to exchange "raw material" for police investigation, which at the latter stage, and when it is necessary and following relevant procedure, can be converted into evidence.

From geographical perspectives, only the EU tools and those applied to the Schengen area are discussed; the book does not enter into detailed comparisons of international information exchange tools.

The book analyses circumstances that led to the necessity of law enforcement authorities to look for information beyond state borders, and how European politics evolved in this respect. It also scrutinises the impact of information exchange on fundamental rights and marks the difference between their limitation and violation. Special attention is drawn to the right to data protection and its regulation, as this is an inalienable element of any piece of data and largely exposed to violation.

It is devoted to the analysis of different information exchange tools between law enforcement authorities. A selection of tools has been created by basically applying two criteria: to analyse each type of information exchange mechanisms, and when there is more than one of each type, to analyse at least the most important or the most controversial one. On this basis, SIS and SIS II have been chosen as the centralised database, Europol as agency, Swedish Initiative in general as the legal basis for any information exchange, FIUs and AROs as networks, Prüm Decisions as decentralised databases with direct access and PNR as the most recent and controversial decentralised databases. A slight deviation from these criteria makes it necessary to analyse the entire part of the CISA which corresponds to information exchange, i.e. liaison officers, police and customs cooperation centres and the regulation of cross-border assistance foreseen in Articles 39 and 46. This was carried out taking into account that not only SIS and SIS II, but all the mechanisms envisaged in CISA are compensatory measures for the abolition of internal borders within the Schengen area, and represented the first appearance of real police cooperation tools. Besides, study of the Swedish Initiative would not be comprehensive without its comparison with the regulation, foreseen on Articles 39 and 46 of the CISA.

It would be inexcusable not to analyse the tools under development (European Information Exchange Platform and European Police Index System) and not to draw attention to the possible consequences of Brexit in relation to information exchange.

Bibliography

COUNCIL OF THE EUROPEAN UNION, 2015, "General Report on Europol's activities in 2014", document 8082/15. Available at: http://data.consilium.europa.eu/doc/document/ST-9219-2015-INIT/en/pdf (accessed August 20, 2017).

INTERNATIONAL CENTRE FOR MIGRATION POLICY DEVELOPMENT AND EUROPEAN PUBLIC LAW ORGANIZATION, 2010, "Study on the status of information exchange amongst law enforcement authorities in the context of existing EU instruments". Available at: https://ec.europa.eu/dgs/home-affairs/doc_centre/police/docs/icmpd_study_lea_infoex.pdf (accessed August 20, 2017).

INTERPOL, 2014, "Annual Report 2014". Available at: http://www.interpol.int/News-and-media/Publications (accessed May 17, 2015).

STORBECK, J., 2002, "La cooperación policial europea" in MONTERO, J., ROMERO, F., and VALIENTE, E.; *¿Hacia una Policía Europea?*, Madrid: Fundación Policía Española, p. 155–169.

2 Police and information exchange: European Union information exchange policy

1 Territorial limits of law enforcement institutions' competence and the need for cooperation

Guarantees of security (both internal and external) and justice are the core functions of any modern state[1] and so-called state monopoly.[2] As in the case of any public institution within any state, the competence of law enforcement institutions is pre-established by national law and as a global rule "do not generally transcend national borders."[3] It means that other persons or entities than the state constitute institutions (for example, private parties or institutions of other states) are not allowed to enforce the law.[4]

There are not so many sources referring to territorial limits of law enforcement institutions' competence as those dedicated to the same topic in relation to judicial jurisdiction. In any case, the scope of competence of the law enforcement authorities in crime investigation is closely linked to the scope of jurisdiction as crime investigation does not have an end in itself, but is an indispensable step in performing jurisdiction.

1 See ALMAGRO NOSETE, José, CÓRTEZ DOMÍNGUEZ, Valentín, GIMENO SENDRA, Vicente et al., *Derecho Procesal. Parte general proceso civil (1)*, Valencia: Tirant lo Blanch, 1989, p. 47; MONTERO AROCA, Juan, *Introducción al Derecho Procesal. Jurisdicción, acción y proceso*, Madrid: Tecnos, 1979, p. 18; MONTERO AROCA, Juan, GÓMEZ COLOMER, Juan Luís and BARONA VILAR, Silvia, *Derecho Jurisdiccional I. Parte general*, 20th ed., Valencia: Tirant lo Blanch, 2012, p. 85; MITSILEGAS Valsamis, MONAR, Jörg and REES, Wyn, *The European Union and Internal Security: Guardian of the People?* Hampshire: Palgrave Macmillan, 2003, p. 8.

2 See DE LA OLIVA SANTOS, Andrés and DÍEZ-PICAZO GIMÉNEZ, Ignacio, *Derecho Procesal. Introducción*, 3rd ed., Madrid: Ramón Areces, 2004, p. 164–165.

3 MITSILEGAS, Valsamis, BANTEKAS, Ilias and NASH, Susan, *International Criminal Law*, 2nd ed. Coogee: Cavendish Publishing Limited, 2003, p. 265.

4 See MONTERO AROCA, Juan, *Introducción al Derecho Procesal*..., op. cit., p. 35.

The main elements that determine limits of judicial jurisdiction and law enforcement competence are sovereignty and the principle of territoriality.

Penal law is an essential piece of classical understanding of sovereignty.[5] National sovereignty grants its jurisdiction exclusively to its judicial power and no other power (neither other branches of power, nor the judicial power of another state) can legitimately perform justice.[6] A judgment by a foreign tribunal admitted without any previous verification on the basis of the international agreement in force, would mean cession of sovereignty.[7] It also establishes what has to be treated as a criminal act on its territory and foresees sanctions. These limits are also reflected in crime investigation. This results in the principle of "no intervention" (or in other words, non-application of national *ius puniendi*) beyond its borders, as it would be an infringement of the sovereignty of another state.[8]

The principle of territoriality implies that national judicial and law enforcement authorities are the only ones that are able to implement their judicial, administrative and coercive powers within the territory of the state to which they pertain, and, "Country borders normally provide a sufficient signal that one legal order is being left and another is being entered."[9] As judicial and law enforcement authorities are submitted to their national law (with some exceptions foreseen in international conventions or agreements), their actions on the territory of another state would be lacking legality.[10]

Nevertheless, due to the facilitated movement of persons and goods over the last 30 years, as well as other factors that will be discussed in the following section, frequently investigative or preventive measures of one state

5 See ARNÁIZ SERRANO, Amaya, "Evolución de la Cooperación Judicial Penal Internacional: en especial, la Cooperación Judicial Penal en Europa" in CARMONA RUANO, Miguel, GONZÁLEZ VEGA, Ignacio U, and MORENO CATENA, Víctor, *Cooperación Judicial Penal en Europa*, Dykinson: Madrid, 2013, p. 10.

6 See GIMENO SENDRA, Vicente, *Manual de Derecho Procesal Penal*, Madrid: Colex, 2008, p. 9.

7 DE LA OLIVA SANTOS, Andrés and DÍEZ-PICAZO GIMÉNEZ, Ignacio, *Derecho Procesal: Introducción*, op. cit., p. 165.

8 See AMBOS, Kai, *Temas de Derecho Penal internacional y europeo*, Madrid: Marcial Pons, 2006, p. 80. This general rule has an exception which is admissible by international society in the form of universal jurisdiction, but it is not treated equally all around the world, not even in the countries with strong Rule of Law.

9 DE HERT, Paul, "Division of Competencies between National and European Levels with regards to Justice and Home Affairs" in APAP, Joanna, *Justice and Home Affairs in the EU. Liberty and Security Issues after Enlargement*, Cheltenham: Edward Elgar, 2004, p. 57.

10 See GARCÍA BORREGO, José Antonio and FERNÁNDEZ VILLAZALA, Tomás, *Introducción al Derecho Procesal Penal*, Madrid: Dykinson, S.L., 2007, p. 21.

require some investigative activities in another; or are related to an investigation held by competent authorities of another state. For instance, when a perpetrator has moved to another country or has contacts with its residents and they are suspected to be involved in the commission of or occultation of a crime or the laundering of criminal actives. In Spain, few of the last well-known examples are the escape of Sergio Morate (a suspect in the murder of two girls) from Spain to Romania,[11] the dismantling of Chinese criminal network that was involved in smuggling illegal immigrants from China to Spain and then onwards to Canada, Switzerland, the United Kingdom and other countries.[12]

In both cases, internal security of Spain was affected, but bearing in mind the territorial limits of the competence, its law enforcement authorities had not been authorised to perform any investigative activities on the territory of other countries and therefore needed the assistance of Romania, China, Canada and other countries in order to apply Spanish *ius puniendi*. At the same time, the application of *ius puniendi* in Spain contributed to the security of those countries by allowing the prevention of the criminal activities of the above-mentioned persons on their territory.

In these examples, the countries involved could either have performed all the necessary actions themselves, or their national laws could have allowed Spanish competent authorities to act within their territory. This would have meant limiting their own sovereignty and permitting the expansion of Spanish sovereign powers on their territory. Any of the two options would first require contacts between competent authorities of the countries involved (providing information about committed crimes, movements of suspects, their detection on the territory of the other state) and then interaction in performing necessary procedural actions. All these elements together form a cooperation or engagement to assist.

The origins of police cooperation can be found in the middle of the nineteenth century, with the aim of keeping travelling political agitators under surveillance. It intensified at the end of the nineteenth century after the assassinations of the Russian Emperor Alexander II in 1881, the President of France, Sidi Carnot in 1894 and Austrian Empress Sissi in 1898.[13]

11 See "La Justicia rumana aprueba la entrega definitiva a España de Sergio Morate", Europapress, September 3, 2015, accessed September 7, 2017, http://www.europapress.es/nacional/noticia-justicia-rumana-aprueba-extradicion-definitiva-espana-sergio-morate-20150902172359.html.

12 See ORTEGA DOLZ, Patricia and CONGOSTRINA, Alfonso L., "Detenidas 80 personas de una red de tráfico ilegal de ciudadanos chinos", *El País*, May 4, 2015, accessed May 15, 2015, http://politica.elpais.com/politica/2015/05/04/actualidad/1430738360_410640.html.

13 See MADSEN, Frank G., *Transnational Organised Crime*, New York: Routledge, 2009, p. 65.

The first attempts at legal regulation and institutionalisation of police cooperation took place at the beginning of the twentieth century. Thus in 1905, an International Police Convention between the authorities in Buenos Aires, La Plata, Montevideo, Rio de Janeiro, and Santiago de Chile was signed. In 1914 the first international police meeting in Monte Carlo took place, where an idea to establish a cooperation institution was raised. But due to the First World War this was postponed until 1923, with the establishment of the International Criminal Police Commission that in 1956 was transformed into INTERPOL – nowadays with 190 states as members.

Currently, cooperation and its different mechanisms are widely used both at regional and global levels and they cause the gradual softening of the principles of sovereignty and territoriality.[14]

2 Crimes and factors that gave rise to international police cooperation

As stated by Rebollo Delgado, any regulation emerges from already existing conflict or social necessity.[15] Thus, the state's response to any new criminal phenomenon is also re-active, i.e. first it occurs and only then legal, organisational, technical and other necessary measures to combat it and to prevent its recurrence in society are taken. One of the latest examples in this respect is cybercrime that only originated with the introduction of the World Wide Web which besides leading to enormous facilitation of communications, became a tool of unfair trade, access to information or accounts belonging to other persons, radicalisation and other criminal offences.[16] As stated in the report published by the Computer Science and Telecommunications Board of the USA in 1991, "The modern thief can steal more with a computer than with a gun."[17]

The same philosophy can be applied to international cooperation, where first a need occurs and then corresponding measures are developed. Besides,

14 See LLORENTE SÁNCHEZ-ARJONA, Mercedes, *Las garantías procesales en el espacio europeo de justicia penal*, Valencia: Tirant lo Blanch, 2014, p. 76.

15 See REBOLLO DELGADO, Lucrecio, *Vida privada y protección de datos en la Unión Europea*, Madrid: Dykinson S.L., 2008, p. 83.

16 The first computer-related infringements of privacy appeared in the sixties, but were a matter of civil and public rather than criminal law. In the seventies computer manipulation, sabotage, espionage became known and in the eighties – illegal copies of software, music and movies. But the development of the internet in the nineties became really attractive for those offering illegal or harmful content, radicalisation, gambling, etc. See COUNCIL OF EUROPE, *Organised crime in Europe: the threat of cybercrime*, Strasbourg: Council of Europe Publishing, 2005), p. 84–85.

17 COMPUTER SCIENCE AND TELECOMMUNICATIONS BOARD, "Computers at Risk: Safe Computing in the Information Age", The National Academies Press, 1991, accessed January 21, 2015, http://www.nap.edu/openbook.php?record_id=1581.

such a need or a reason must be very significant and cooperation indispensable in order to convince independent countries to take common measures that, to some extent, affect their sovereignty.

Before continuing the analysis, the terms "transnational" and "international crime" deserve a special mention. In this work the theory that transnational and international crime are different terms with different content will be followed.

Thus international crime will be understood as crime foreseen in the Rome Statute of the International Criminal Court, i.e. genocide, crime against humanity, war crime and crime of aggression.[18] The international community considers these crimes to be violations of the highest values of mankind and expresses global interest to repress them. Some authors[19] believe that several forms of terrorism and torture also have to be treated as international crime as they are included as subcategories of four international crimes covered by the Rome Statute.[20]

During the negotiations of the draft of the Rome Statute, the proposal to endow the International Criminal Court with jurisdiction on terrorism had been considered; but finally, due to opposition from some countries, for example Belgium, Brazil, France, the Netherlands, Norway, Spain, Sweden, the United States of America, it was left aside.[21]

Some international treaties establish other crimes (explicitly providing with their elements) that have to be criminalised in the national law of participating states. One of the best-known examples is the United Nations Convention against Transnational Organized Crime. Some authors (like Bassiouni, Bantekas and Nash) also ascribe them to international crimes, equally as those established by the Rome Statute.[22] Nevertheless, in this

18 See Article 5 of the Rome Statute of the International Criminal Court.

19 See CASSESE, Antonio, *International Criminal Law*, 2nd ed., New York: Oxford University Press, 2008, p. 11–13; MITSILEGAS, Valsamis, BANTEKAS, Ilias and NASH, Susan, *International Criminal Law*, op. cit., p. 1–21; VACAS FERNÁNDEZ, Félix, *El terrorismo como crimen internacional. Definición, naturaleza y consecuencias jurídicas internacionales para las personas*, Valencia: Tirant lo Blanch, 2011, p. 254–255; SANDOZ, Yves, "Lutte contre le terrorisme et droit international: risques et opportunités" in *Revue suisse de droit internationale et de droit européen*, 2002, No. 2, p. 347; PAULUSSEN, Christophe, "Impunity for international terrorists? Key legal questions and practical considerations" (research paper, International Centre for Counter-Terrorism, 2012), p. 7, accessed January 21, 2017, http://www.icct.nl/download/file/ICCT-Paulussen-Impunity-April-2012.pdf.

20 For instance torture as an element of crime against humanity (Article 7(1)f) as well as of crime of war (Article 8(2)a(ii)). Terrorism is not directly mentioned in the Rome Statute, but Vacas Fernández understands that it could have consequences foreseen in its Article 7, for instance such as assassination, grave deprivation of liberty or other inhuman acts. See VACAS FERNÁNDEZ, Félix, *El terrorismo como crimen internacional…*, op. cit., p. 223.

21 Ibid, p. 60.

22 BASSIOUNI, Cherif, *Introduction to International Criminal Law*, Ardsley, New York: Transnational Publisher, Inc., 2003, p. 114–118.

research they will be understood as transnational (or cross-border) crimes, i.e. that they cross the border of one country and require measures of global governance.

Thus, the focus will be on transnational or cross-border crime that affects more than one state by its preparation, direction or commission, by involvement of international organised crime[23] as well as by nationality of active and passive subjects or proliferation of the effects of crime.[24]

2.1 Reasons for the rise in cooperation within the European Communities

Although the original policies of the European Communities had not included security and justice topics and were purely oriented to post-war economic growth and the development of Europe, some global and regional factors as well as socially important events impelled its Members to start cooperation in these matters, and to adjust it to socially determined necessities. Over 40 years, an evolution took place from an informal cooperation through an intergovernmental one and finally with the Treaty of Lisbon became supranational.

Circumstances that urged Member States of the European Community towards closer cooperation can be conditionally divided into three groups that are presented below.

2.1.1 Socially relevant milestones

The first informal and intergovernmental forum for cooperation on security between some Member States of the European Communities was created in 1975; this was a consequence of the terrorist attack during the Olympic Games in Munich on September 4, 1972, and other threats of terrorism that had occurred in Europe: partly coming from the Middle East and partly from activities of national-based terrorist groups. Even if the latest case seems to be a national problem, a tendency for cooperation among terrorist groups from different Western countries (France, Germany, Italy, Spain, the Netherlands, the United Kingdom) in sharing information, preparing attacks, procurement of arms and even training had been observed.[25]

At the European Council of Rome on December 1–2, 1975, at the proposal of the United Kingdom, it was agreed that "Community ministers for the Interior (or Ministers with similar responsibilities) should meet to discuss matters coming within their competence, in particular with regard to

23 Article 3(2) of the United Nations Convention against Transnational Organised Crime provides with the comprehensive definition of transnational crime.

24 See PÉREZ MARÍN, María Ángeles, *La lucha contra la criminalidad en la Unión Europea*, Barcelona: Atelier, 2013, p. 204.

25 See MITSILEGAS, Valsamis; MONAR, Jörg and REES, Wyn, *The European Union and Internal Security..*, op. cit., p. 22.

law and order."[26] This informal cooperation forum was named TREVI Group which is an acronym (in French) for terrorism, radicalism, extremism and international violence.

In parallel, the President of France, Giscard d'Estaing, proposed the creation of an area of judicial cooperation in criminal matters, based on simplified extradition procedure, transmission of penal procedures, recognition of judicial decisions and common rules for transmission of detainees between the Member States. Since 1984 Ministers of Justice and Home Affairs have met twice a year to deal with matters of police, judicial and customs cooperation and free movement of persons.[27]

At the same time, Europe faced a problem of increased consumption of heroin, LSD and cocaine as a result of drug trafficking. This situation *per se* carried a cross-border element and needed a coordinated international response both within and outside the European Community.[28]

More than two decades later, other terrorist attacks (September 11, 2001 in the United States, March 11, 2004 in Madrid and July 7, 2005 in London) had created social and security shocks to both society and security organisations, and impelled a more active EU approach to the speeding up of judicial and police cooperation and information exchange.

The same has happened with the intensification of terrorist attacks during recent years, which have incremented the level of "transnationality". This is due to the links between terrorist cells and the nationalities of victims; for example, in the attacks in Barcelona and Cambrils, on August 17, 2017 there were victims of 38 nationalities.

2.1.2 Global factors facilitating criminal activities

Rapid development of financial markets became a great opportunity for many enterprises and entrepreneurs. But fast movement of big amounts of money around the world also meant great opportunities for rapid and well-masked money laundering with an estimation of 1 billion every day.[29]

26 Summary of the Conclusions of the Meeting of the European Council held in Rome on 1 and 2 December, 1975, accessed September 20, 2017, http://aei.pitt.edu/1407/.

27 See VIADA, Natacha. *Derecho penal y globalización. Cooperación penal internacional*, Madrid: Marcial Pons, 2009, p. 118–119; MORENO CATENA, Víctor and CASTILLEJO MANZANARES, Raquel, *La persecución de los delitos en el Convenio de Schengen*, Valencia: Tirant lo Blanch, 1999, p. 13.

28 On international level cooperation in combatting drug trafficking began with the establishment of International Opium Commission in 1909. See more. MADSEN Frank G., *Transnational Organised Crime*, op. cit., p. 27–28.

29 VLASSIS, Dimitri, "The Global situation of transnational organized crime, the decision of the international community to develop an international convention and the negotiation process", in *Resource Material Series*, 2002, no. 59, p. 476.

Financial Action Task Force, founded in 1989 by G-7 estimated that in the late nineties, in the USA and Europe alone, laundered money accounted for around 2 per cent of global GDP (US$ 0.34 trillion).

Almost 10 years later, the International Monetary Fund calculated that money laundering accounted for between 2 and 5 per cent of global GDP and had resulted in the following money equivalents: in 1996 between US$ 0.6 and 1.5 trillion; in 2005, between US$ 0.9 and 2.3 trillion and in 2009, between US$ 1.2 and 2.9 trillion.[30]

On the other hand, new technologies of transportation and political commitment to free or facilitated trade enabled organised crime to carry out its usual activity of smuggling much more effectively and in more sophisticated ways; as Felsen and Kalaitzidis stated, "it heightened cross-border linkages and made national frontiers seem more permeable than ever."[31]

Taking advantage of this situation at the beginning of the 1990s, organised crime changed significantly and became much more transnational in nature. As pointed out by Reinares and Resa, "This type of organised crime has three basic differences with respect to previous manifestations of the phenomenon: it tends to operate at a regional or global level, mobilising extensive cross-border connections and, above all, has the ability to challenge both national and international authorities."[32]

Geopolitical changes caused by the end of the Cold War and the start of the Balkan War also had a significant influence on the augmentation of organised crime. These circumstances gave raise to new criminal organisations involved in illegal migration, the trafficking of human beings, illegal sales of arms, as well as integration of criminal elements into politics and economies.[33]

Positive democratisation processes in Central and Eastern Europe had also had a negative effect on the European Communities as the restructuring of heavy industry, an "engine of communist block", had left many people without work and vulnerable to criminal influence. That led to the gathering of organised groups, illegal entrance to the European Community or just tolerance of the black market. New democracies with new economic changes

30 See UNITED NATIONS OFFICE ON DRUGS AND CRIME, "Estimating Illicit Financial Flows Resulting from Drug Trafficking and Other Transnational Organized Crimes: Research Report (Vienna, October 2011)", p. 18–19, accessed September 20, 2017, www.unodc.org/documents/data-and-analysis/Studies/Illicit_ financial_flows_2011_web.pdf.

31 FELSEN, David and KALAITZIDIS, Akis, "A Historical Overview of Transnational Crime" in REICHEL, Philip, *Handbook of transnational crime and justice*, California: Sage Publications, Inc., 2005, p. 12.

32 REINARES, Fernando and RESA, Carlos, "Transnational organized crime as an increasing threat to the national security of democratic regimes: assessing political impacts and evaluating state responses", paper, 1997, p. 6, accessed February 1, 2015, http://www.nato.int/acad/fellow/97-99/reinares.pdf.

33 See FELSEN, David and KALAITZIDIS, Akis. "A Historical Overview of Transnational…", loc. cit., p. 13–15.

and imperfect laws also allowed assets of criminal activities to be laundered through the privatisation of public property and conversion into legal businesses, with the desire to set up them in more stable and safer European Communities. On the other hand, new states were also in need of foreign capital and this opportunity was widely used to legalise western criminal proceeds.

Free movement not only has its physical dimension, but its virtual dimensions as well. As already mentioned, the last decades were marked with the development and increase in the use of cyberspace for criminal purposes. In addition to commissioning such crimes as malware, phishing, data breach and network attacks, child sexual exploitation online, payment fraud, attacks on critical infrastructure, the internet is used "as a communication tool, information source, marketplace, recruiting ground and financial service."[34] It facilitates authors of crimes to remain more anonymous, to conceal criminal deeds, to eliminate traces or evidence and to reduce the investigative capacities of competent authorities.[35]

2.1.3 *Side effects of the internal policies*

Crime rates in the EU between 1990 and 2001 in the same number of Member States rose by 20.9 per cent from 20,734,870 crimes to 25,061,214. Of course, part of this can be due to the changes of national penal codes and the criminalisation of some acts, but not to this extent.[36] Thus there are other factors influencing such a criminality rate.

Globally spread factors related to free trade and open financial markets had an even stronger influence in the European Communities due to the creation of the internal market and the introduction of the single currency. In this respect, Occhipinti states that "As European leaders hastened their preparations for 'E-Day', so too did organised-crime groups, especially potential money launderers, armoured-car and safe robbers, and counterfeiters."[37]

34 EUROPOL, "OCTA 2011: EU Organised Crime Threat Assessment", p. 45, accessed September 26, 2017, https://www.europol.europa.eu/content/publication/octa-2011-eu-organised-crime-threat-assesment-1465.

35 See exceptionally comprehensive information on this topic in VALLÉS CAUSADA, Luís Manuel, *La Policía judicial en la obtención de inteligencia sobre comunicaciones electrónicas para el proceso penal.* (PhD diss., National Distance Education University, 2012), p. 32–35, accessed March 20, 2017, http://e-spacio.uned.es/fez/eserv/tesisuned:Derecho-Lmvalles/Documento.pdf.

36 See SERRANO GÓMEZ, Alfonso and Vázquez GONZÁLEZ, Carlos, *Tendencias de la criminalidad y percepción social de la inseguridad ciudadana en España y la Unión Europea*, Madrid: Edisofer S.L, 2007, p. 126.
Although Austria, Finland and Sweden joined the European Communities in 1995, the figures from 1990 include crime rates from these countries as well.

37 OCCHIPINTI, John D., *The Politics of EU Police cooperation. Towards a European FBI?* Colorado, Lynne Rienner Publishers, Inc., 2003, p. 120.

The single currency eliminated the need to exchange funds received from criminal activities for their circulation in other Member States of the Eurozone. Furthermore, the 500-euro note had become one of the highest-value internationally circulating notes and it facilitated cash laundering and, as indicated by OCTA 2011, "Due to overwhelming evidence that the 500 euro note is almost exclusively the preserve of criminals, banknote wholesalers have stopped supplying the note in the UK: however, it remains legal tender."[38] At the beginning of 2016 EU finance ministers and the European Central Bank considered possible restrictions of the circulation of the 500 euro banknote and their production was discontinued.

Abolishment of internal border controls and free movement of people and goods also meant the abolishment of obstacles and risks to moving criminal activities to other Member States, as well as allowing the free circulation of criminals, either to commit crime or to hide from law enforcement and justice authorities of other Member States where crime had been committed. As defines Storbeck, the EU has become "fertilising territory for criminality".[39] In this way, in the nineties a big "migration" of Italian organised crime was noticed in Germany and Austria. At the same time in Belgium, it was found that almost half of organised groups had contacts with organised crime in neighbouring countries.

In addition to the internationalisation of organised crime, in the last decade appeared another phenomenon called "mobile criminality" that consists in the committing of crimes (usually against property) in some Member State for quite a short period of time before moving to another one. Even if it made an impression of being less dangerous than organised crime understood in more "traditional" way (with drug trafficking, huge money laundering and so on), mobile criminality directly affects the everyday life of European citizens and "there is an inverse correlation between the seriousness and the incidence of victimisation."[40]

All these factors contributed to the establishment of international cooperation and of common measures within the Member States of the European Community (and later, the EU) against terrorism and crime.

2.2 The current situation

Just as time and evolution do not stand still, crime phenomena are also changing and transforming into more sophisticated forms and new threats.

38 EUROPOL, "OCTA 2011: EU Organised Crime…", loc. cit., p. 42.

39 STORBECK, Jürgen, "La cooperación policial europea", in MONTERO, Julián, ROMERO, Francisco and VALIENTE, Elena, *¿Hacia una Policía Europea?*, Madrid: Fundación Policía Española, 2002, p. 156.

40 BENYON, John, "Policing the European Union: The Changing Basis of Cooperation on Law Enforcement" in *International Affairs (Royal Institute of International Affairs 1944-)*, July 1994, vol. 70, no. 3, p. 500.

They are analysed and evaluated by competent authorities: at international level, the United Nations Office on Drugs and Crime and in, the EU – Europol.

As revealed by Transnational Organised Crime Threat Assessment from 2010, trafficking in human beings annually amounts to 70,000 victims and a profit of US$ 3 billion, in smuggling migrants – US$ 6.75 billion, drug trafficking – US$ 105 billion, trafficking in natural resources – over US$ 3.5 billion, trafficking in arms – US$ 53 million, product counterfeiting – US$ 9.6 billion, maritime piracy – US$ 100 million, and cybercrime – US$ 1.25 billion.[41]

As these criminal activities generate such high profits, they are under constant development: changes in *modus operandi*, use of new technologies and other opportunities. This means that they will not disappear, but become more elaborate.[42]

SOCTA 2013 reveals increasing internationality of organised crime and that "Criminals act undeterred by geographic boundaries and can no longer be easily associated with specific regions or centres of gravity."[43] From an estimated 3,600 organised groups, 70 per cent are multinational, and 30 per cent are involved in multiple crime areas.[44]

SOCTA 2017 indicates approximately 5,000 international organised crime groups under investigation in the EU, with the involvement of more than 180 nationalities (although 60 per cent of suspects are EU nationals). Of these groups, 45 per cent are poly-criminal.[45]

Among crime-relevant factors, SOCTA 2013 and SOCTA 2017 distinguished:

- The economic crisis (that does not increase crime rates, but transforms them into other types, such as counterfeiting of daily consumer goods).
- Social tolerance to some crimes, such as consumption of psychoactive substances, purchase of counterfeited goods.
- Transportation and logistical hotspots that facilitate any type of transportation both within and outside the EU.

41 See UNITED NATIONS OFFICE ON DRUGS AND CRIME, "The Globalization of Crime. A Transnational Organized Crime Threat Assesment. 2010", p. 16–17, accessed September 27, 2017, https://www.unodc.org/documents/data-and-analysis/tocta/TOCTA_Report_2010_low_ res.pdf.

42 Ibid, p. 1.

43 EUROPOL, "EU Serious Organised Crime Threat Assessment (SOCTA 2013)", p. 45, accessed September 9, 2017, available at: https://www.europol.europa.eu/content/eu-serious-and-organised-crime-threat-assessment-socta.

44 Ibid, p. 33.

45 See EUROPOL, "European Union Serious Organised Crime Threat Assessment. Crime in the age of technology (SOCTA 2017)", p. 14, accessed September 9, 2017, available at: https://www.europol.europa.eu/activities-services/main-reports/european-union-serious-and-organised-crime-threat-assessment-2017

- The use of diaspora communities across the EU to facilitate irregular migration, property crime as well as entrance into countries' markets and legal business.
- Corruption with attempts to infiltrate organised crime into public and private sectors, to obtain information and to make beneficiary manipulations.
- Internet and e-commerce as places for the circulation of illicit commodities. Data has become a key commodity.
- The innovation in technology that allows greater anonymity in the commissioning of crime without the necessity of physical presence.
- The geopolitical situation both within and outside Europe that results in illegal migration flows.
- Exploitation of legal business structures and professional experts.[46]

With respect to terrorism, during recent years, the threat fostered by Al Qaeda became even stronger with the appearance of Daesh; as the threat is both outside and inside Western Countries, and as Jenkins reveals, "The current cohort of jihadist volunteers may differ from previous cohorts in the level of their commitment to jihadist ideology and their attraction to unlimited violence as a motive for volunteering, as well as in the level of military skills they may acquire."[47]

According to TE-SAT 2014 elaborated by Europol, "AQ [Al Qaeda] and IS [Islamic State] retained their capability to recruit jihadists from Europe, intensifying the threat posed to the EU. In 2014, Member States also reported an increase in women and children travelling to the region. This phenomenon may eventually lead to the emergence of a new generation of jihadist terrorists in Europe. The number of fighters that have returned to the EU has increased."[48]

The same tendency of women and children travelling is pointed out in TE-SAT 2017.[49]

In 2016, 142 victims died in terrorist attacks, 135 of them in attacks carried out by jihadists.[50] It has been noted that "violent jihadists target individuals,

46 See EUROPOL, "EU Serious Organised Crime…", loc. cit., p. 11–19; "European Union Serious …", loc. cit., p. 24, 30.

47 JENKINS, Brian Michael, "When Jihadis Come Marching Home. The Terrorist Threat Posed by Westerners Returning from Syria and Iraq" (Perspective, RADN Corporation, 2014), p. 2, accessed August 3, 2017, http://www.rand.org/pubs/perspectives/PE130-1.html.

48 EUROPOL, "EU Terrorism Situation and Trend Report 2015", p. 6, accessed August 10, 2017, available at https://www.europol.europa.eu/content/european-union-terrorism-situation-and-trend-report-2015.

49 See EUROPOL, "European Union Terrorism Situation and Trend Report 2017", p. 14, accessed August 11, 2017, available at: https://www.europol.europa.eu/activities-services/main-reports/eu-terrorism-situation-and-trend-report-te-sat-2017

50 See Ibid, p. 17, 23.

as well as small groups of people who represent values considered by them to be non-Islamic, and large unsuspecting crowds. Individuals or small groups targeted by terrorists can be both hard targets (police, the military) or soft targets (a church, synagogue, mosque)" and "attacks can be both carefully prepared and carried out spontaneously. Terrorists acting in the name of IS have proven to be able to plan relatively complex attacks – including those on multiple targets – quickly and effectively."[51]

An IOCTA carried out at the end of September 2015 by the European Cybercrime Center revealed that "Cybercrime is becoming more aggressive and confrontational. Various forms of extortion requiring little technical skills suggest changes in the profile of cybercrime offenders, and increase the psychological impact on victims."[52] In 2016 it was pointed out that cybercrime has increased in volume, scope and financial damage and "in some EU countries cybercrime may have surpassed traditional crime in terms of reporting."[53]

3 The legal framework of police cooperation within the EU

Since its origin in 1975, police and judicial cooperation had been out of the formal framework of the European Communities for around 20 years.

For the first time, the notion of public security was mentioned in the Community legislation in the Solemn Declaration on the European Union,[54] signed on June 19, 1983, including as one of its objectives (but still in the form of intergovernmental cooperation) "A common analysis and concerted action to deal with international problems of law and order, serious acts of violence, organised international crime and international lawlessness generally."[55]

Judicial and police cooperation has obtained greater relevance since the Single European Act, signed on February 17, 1986,[56] when it received the role of compensatory measure for the establishment of the internal market of the Community.

As pointed out by Moreno Catena, the Treaty of Maastricht signed on February 7, 1992 had gone beyond the pure economic idea of the old European Economic Community, making the EU something more than a common market and including the Second and the Third Pillars (common

51 Ibid, p. 5, 6.
52 EUROPOL, "The Internet Organised Crime Threat Assessment (IOCTA) 2015", p. 45, accessed October 9, 2017, https://www.europol.europa.eu/activities-services/main-reports/internet-organised-crime-threat-assessment-iocta-2016
53 EUROPOL, "IOCTA 2016. Internet Organised Crime Threat Assessment", p. 7, accessed August 11, 2017, available at: https://www.europol.europa.eu/activities-services/main-reports/internet-organised-crime-threat-assessment-iocta-2016
54 Bulletin of the European Communities, no. 6/1983, p. 24–29.
55 Ibid, p. 25.
56 OJ L 169, 29.6.1987, p. 1–19.

security as well as police and judicial cooperation).[57] Contrasting with the First Pillar (supranational nature of common market), the Second and the Third Pillars were driven by the principle of intergovernmental cooperation, meaning different legislation, supervision and implementation procedures.

Thus according to Article K.3 (2), of the Treaty of Maastricht, Member States were enabled to propose joint positions or joint action and conventions to prevent and combat terrorism, unlawful drug trafficking and other serious forms of international crime. To ensure that none of the Member States can be overruled by the rest, a unanimous decision for all mentioned legal acts was required and in the case of conventions – also ratification by each Member State. The only exceptions to this rule were measures that implement conventions as they required only qualified majority of Member States (unless otherwise provided in the convention that is subject to implementation).

At that time, the role of the European Parliament in the Third Pillar was limited to consultation on the principal aspects of activities and taking its opinion "into consideration" by the Council of the EU.[58]

The Treaty of Maastricht foresaw the minimum regulation of the Third Pillar and was quite insufficient in its proper development.

The Treaty of Amsterdam, signed on October 2, 1997, introduced significant modifications to the Third Pillar that allowed progress in this area. As noticed Fazekas "A great leap forward has been taken in the area of cooperation. Perhaps not the legislative aspect is the most important outcome here, but the fact that a common way of thinking and acting became accepted at a Union level regarding issues of internal security."[59]

First of all, its scope in justice and home affairs was changed into a "broader project of establishing an area of Freedom, Security and Justice (AFSJ) throughout the EU"[60] meaning the establishment of balance between security, justice and fundamental rights and freedoms.

Secondly, the former Third Pillar's areas of asylum, internal borders, migration and cooperation in civil matters were all moved to the First Pillar (i.e. under supranational regulation), remaining under the intergovernmental cooperation of the Third Pillar only areas of police and judicial cooperation in criminal matters.

57 See MORENO CATENA, Víctor, "El cambio de paradigma del principio de reconocimiento mutuo y sus implicaciones. Perspectivas del Tratado de Lisboa" in CARMONA RUANO, Miguel; GONZÁLEZ VEGA, Ignacio U. and MORENO CATENA, Víctor, *Cooperación Judicial Penal…*, op. cit., p. 43–44.
58 Article K.6 of the Treaty of Maastricht.
59 FAZEKAS, Judit, "Development of Justice and Home Affairs Cooperation between 2004 and 2009 in the European Union" in *European Integration Studies*, 2009, vol. 7, no 1, p. 8.
60 LONGO, Francesca, "Justice and Home Affairs as a New Dimension of the European Security Concept" in *European Foreign Affairs Review*, 2013, vol. 18, no. 1, p. 39.

Thirdly, the legislative procedure of the Third Pillar underwent important modifications.

As had been foreseen in Article K.6 of the Treaty of Amsterdam, acting unanimously on the initiative of any Member State or of the Commission, the Council could adopt common positions, framework decisions,[61] decisions[62] and conventions. New regulation laid down that every draft framework decision, decision and convention should undergo consultation with the European Parliament, although in practice its opinion has been taken into account only a few times. The Commission was given the right to take the initiative in developing policy in this Pillar.

Nevertheless, the remaining Council's unanimity resulted in a loss of ambitious content of many legislative initiatives due to the different interests of Member States. In many cases, the initial legal drafts with comprehensive regulation for the European police and judicial cooperation at the end of consensus, were converted into "light" cooperation instruments, in order not to modify national legislations or to make minimum of them.

The Third Pillar in general was without effective control of the European Commission and CJEU, i.e., the European Commission did not have the competence to start infringement procedures for non-implementation or erroneous implementation of Communities' instruments by the Member States; additionally, the CJEU had very limited jurisdiction in this area. Article K.3 (2)c of the Treaty of Maastricht foresaw the competence of the CJEU only to interpret provisions of conventions adopted within the EU, and to rule on any disputes regarding their application, but only if expressly foreseen in them. Article K.7 of the Treaty of Amsterdam also prevised the "peculiar ad hoc system whereby the member states had to opt in to judicial control by the ECJ"[63] meaning that any Member State could make a declaration to accept the jurisdiction of the CJEU in order to give preliminary rulings on the validity and interpretation of framework decisions.[64] Nevertheless, the question of what effect decisions of validity would have on other Member States which had not made such a declaration still stood. Could they apply a framework decision recognised as invalid and not applied in other Member State?

61 In order to approximate laws and regulations of Member States.

62 For any purpose consistent with judicial and police cooperation, excluding approximation of laws and regulations that shall take the form of framework decisions.

63 GUILD, Elspeth and GEYER, Florian, "Introduction: The Search for EU Criminal Law – Where is it Headed?" in GUILD, Elspeht and GEYER, Florian (eds.) *Security versus Justice? Police and Judicial Cooperation in the European Union*, Hampshire: Ashgate Publishing Limited, 2008, p. 6.

64 See VILABOY LOIS, Lotario, "El sistema jurisdiccional comunitario" in MARIÑO, Fernando M.; MORENO CATENA, Víctor and MOREIRO, Carlos, *Derecho procesal comunitario*, Valencia: Tirant lo Blanch, 2001, p. 39–42.

By the Treaty of Amsterdam, on the initiative of Member States (but not the Commission, as in other areas), the CJEU has been endowed to review the legality[65] of framework decisions and decisions in general, in order to solve disputes between Member States on the interpretation or the application of common positions, framework decisions, decisions and conventions as well as between Member States and the Commission in cases of application of conventions.

Regarding information exchange, Article K.2(9) of the Treaty of Maastricht had only envisaged the creation of the Union wide information exchange system Europol. The Treaty of Amsterdam was more comprehensive, stating in Article K.2 that common actions within police cooperation should include "the collection, storage, processing, analysis and exchange of relevant information, including information held by law enforcement services on reports on suspicious financial transactions, in particular through Europol, subject to appropriate provisions on the protection of personal data."[66]

Thus the Treaty of Amsterdam had foreseen close cooperation with Europol in general, information exchange in particular and establishment within 5 years:

- Measures allowing the use of Europol's coordination and support capacity in specific investigative activities (such as joint investigation teams),
- Europol's right to ask Member States to conduct and coordinate their investigations when the case, the same organised group or other aspect involves investigations or operational activities of more than one Member State.
- Development of Europol's specific expertise to assist Member States in investigating cases of organised crime.

By the Protocol on the location of the seats of the institutions and of certain bodies and departments of the European Communities and of Europol[67] of the latter Treaty, political steps were taken by establishing Europol's seat in The Hague.

Articles K.15-K.17 of the Treaty of Amsterdam also envisaged a close cooperation procedure (the possibility of using a cooperation tool among some Member States if unanimous agreement on it has not been reached), that was later modified and developed by the Treaty of Nice[68] (signed on February 26, 2001) as enhanced cooperation.

65 As a result of a lack of competence, infringement of an essential procedural requirement, infringement of this Treaty or of any rule of law relating to its application, or misuse of powers.

66 OJ C 340, 10.11.1997, p. 17.

67 OJ C 340, 10.11.1997, p. 112.

68 Articles 40–44 of the TEU.

Article 43a of the Treaty of Nice foresaw that "Enhanced cooperation may be undertaken only as a last resort, when it has been established within the Council that the objectives of such cooperation cannot be attained within a reasonable period by applying the relevant provisions of the Treaties."[69]

In such cases, a Member State could address a request to the Commission asking to submit a proposal of enhanced cooperation measure to the Council. If the Commission refused it, the proposal could be submitted to the Council by at least eight Member States. The Council, acting by a qualified majority and after consulting the European Parliament, could grant authorisation of enhanced cooperation.[70]

The Treaty of Nice did not include any more novelties regarding police cooperation and information exchange, as its provisions were focused on ensuring smooth procedural and institutional functioning of the European Union after its significant enlargement by ten new Member States in 2004.

Thus for the creation of the area of Freedom, Security and Justice, not only legal, but also institutional resources were put in place[71] and as very well defined by Fijnaut, "The hard core of Member State sovereignty was [...] gradually surrounded by the soft shell of the Community institutions."[72]

The Treaty of Lisbon was signed on December 13, 2007, raising the area of Freedom, Security and Justice to the level of supranational cooperation. It meant that the former Third Pillar reached its legal consolidation and became a part of the shared competence between the EU and Member States where Member States can only exercise the competence that is not assigned to the EU, or the latter has decided to cease it execution.[73] As a consequence, the system of decision-making and implementation control was changing "making them subject to proper parliamentary and judicial control, in order to improve the balance between security and the judicial protection of citizens."[74]

69 OJ C 80, 10.3.2001, p. 12.

70 Since the Treaty of Lisbon, there is a requirement for at least nine Member States (instead of eight) for enhanced cooperation. It also modified a procedure of the authorisation of enhanced cooperation that foresees a need for the consent of the European Parliament instead of its pure consultation. See Article 329 of the TFEU. The example of the promotion of such cooperation is notification made by 16 Member States on their intention to establish a European Public Prosecutor's Office.

71 See ARNÁIZ SERRANO, Amaya, *Evolución de la Cooperación Judicial...*, op. cit., p. 25.

72 FIJNAUT, Cyrille, "Police Co-operation and the Area of Freedom, Security and Justice" in WALKER, Neil, *Europe's Area of Freedom...*, op. cit., p. 244.

73 See LLORENTE SÁNCHEZ-ARJONA, Mercedes, "La cooperación judicial penal en el Tratado de Lisboa" in DE LOS SANTOS MARTÍN OSTOS, José *El Derecho Procesal en el espacio judicial Europeo: estudios dedicados al catedrático Faustino Gutiérrez-Alviz y Conradi*, Barcelona: Atelier Libros S.A., 2013, p. 325.

74 PIRIS, Jean-Claude, *The Lisbon Treaty. A Legal and Political Analysis*, New York: Cambridge University Press, 2010, p. 178.

By means of the Treaty of Lisbon, the procedure of consultation in almost all areas was substituted by the ordinary procedure (also known as co-decision procedure) called by Peers "two chamber legislation",[75] i.e. approval of decisions, directives or regulations by the European Parliament and a qualified majority of votes in the Council.

Articles 69 F and 69 H of the Treaty of Lisbon (Articles 87 and 89 of the consolidated version of the TFEU) maintains the procedure of consultation (renamed into special legislative procedure) for the measures concerning operational cooperation as well as for the establishment of the conditions and limitations under which the law enforcement authorities of the Member States may operate in the territory of another Member State. Article 69 B (article 83 of the consolidated version of the TFEU) foresees that acting unanimously, and after obtaining the consent of the European Parliament, the Council may establish minimum rules on the definition of criminal offences and sanctions in other areas of crime than those foreseen in the Article 69 B (1) part 2.[76]

Regarding the control system, Article 10 of the Protocol on Transitional Provisions of the Treaty of Lisbon[77] foresaw that not later than 5 years after the date of its entry into force, the Commission and the CJEU should apply their full competence to the field of police cooperation and judicial cooperation in criminal matters, i.e. infringement procedure and relative sanctions in cases of non-transposition, incorrect transposition or non-application of the EU legal provisions.[78] Thus since December 1, 2014, full EU control mechanism is applied to the transposition and implementation of the EU legal instruments related to police and judicial cooperation.

Nevertheless, as with previous Treaties, Article 240b[79] of the Treaty of Lisbon reiterates that "the Court of Justice of the European Union shall have no jurisdiction to review the validity or proportionality of operations carried out by the police or other law-enforcement services of a Member State, or the exercise of the responsibilities incumbent upon Member States with regard to the maintenance of law and order and the safeguarding of internal security."[80]

Article 69 G[81] of the Treaty of Lisbon regulates Europol very comprehensively, i.e. by establishing its mission, excluding the application of coercive measures from its competence, foreseeing that its structure, operation, field of

75 See PEERS, Steve, "Guide to EU decision-making and justice and home affairs after the Treaty of Lisbon" (Statewatch publication, December 2010), p. 3, accessed September 14, 2017, http://www.statewatch.org/analyses/no-115-lisbon-treaty-decision-making.pdf.

76 See Ibid, p. 3.

77 Protocol 36 of the consolidated version of the TFEU. OJ C 83, 30.3.2010, p. 322–326.

78 See PIRIS, Jean-Claude, *The Lisbon Treaty. A Legal and Political..*, op. cit., p. 188–189.

79 Article 276 of the consolidated version of the TFEU.

80 OJ C 306, 17.12.2007, p. 110–111.

81 Article 85 of the consolidated version of the TFEU.

action, tasks, scrutiny of its activities shall be established within a new legal basis, adopted in accordance with ordinary legislative procedure.[82]

As evaluation of modifications introduced by the Treaty of Lisbon in relation to police and judicial cooperation, the following observations can be made:

- Changes in the Council's voting system can allow the approval of more ambitious cooperation instruments, even if not all Member States are in favour of them;
- The European Parliament's full participation in decision-making introduces more transparency;
- Application of control measures by the Commission and the CJEU of the EU ensures better implementation of EU instruments at national level.[83]

Summing up the trajectory of legal development of the area of Freedom, Security and Justice and its growing importance, it can be said that it is no less an important issue than the introduction of Economic and Monetary Union and a Common Foreign and Security Policy.[84]

Nevertheless, some Member States still retain strong defence of sovereignty[85] and try to protect it with different means. For example:

- Protocols 21 and 22 of the Lisbon Treaty[86] entail that Denmark, Ireland and the United Kingdom will not take part in the adoption of measures within the area of Freedom, Security and Justice and will not be bound by them. Ireland and the United Kingdom maintain the possibility of "opting-in" by notification addressed to the President of the Council, informing him/her of their wish to participate in the adoption of proposed measures within the area of Freedom, Security and Justice. Such a declaration has to be submitted within three months of the presentation of the relevant proposal.
- Protocol 30[87] foresees that no court has competence to analyse whether Polish or British legal and administrative provisions are in accordance with the provisions of the of the Charter of Fundamental Rights of the European Union.[88]

82 More about the modifications introduced by the Treaty of Lisbon See MARISCAL, Nicolás, *Más allá de Lisboa: Horizontes europeos* (Técnos: Madrid, 2010), p. 174–177.
83 About unequal implementation read more in Section 2.4 of Chapter 5 and "Swedish Initiative" and Section 2 of Chapter 6.
84 See MITSILEGAS, Valsamis; MONAR, Jörg and REES, Wyn, *The European Union and Internal Security..*, op. cit., p. 6.
85 See VON BOGDANY, Armin; CRUZ VILLALÓN, Pedro and M. HUBER, Peter, *El Derecho Constitucional en el espacio jurídico europeo*, Valencia: Tirant lo Blanch, 2013, p. 93.
86 OJ, C 83, 30.3.2010, p. 295–303.
87 OJ C 83, 30.3.2010, p. 313–314.
88 OJ C 364, 18.12.2000, p. 1–22.

4 Principle of availability – the cornerstone of information exchange

In addition to the provisions of the primary EU law, establishing the main principles and aspects of EU politics, since 1999 the area of Freedom, Security and Justice has been developed by following the political guidelines of multiannual strategic programmes and their implementation plans.

After the entrance into force of the Treaty of Amsterdam, on October 16, 1999, the Presidency Conclusions "Towards a Union of Freedom, Security and Justice: Tampere Milestones" (hereinafter – Tampere Conclusions) were adopted and became the first multiannual programme. Their "jewel in the crown" was the establishment of the principle of mutual recognition of judicial decisions and judgments as well as pre-trial orders. Besides, they also expanded the institutional background of the police and judicial cooperation foreseeing creation of:

- Eurojust – a unit with the mission to facilitate the coordination of national prosecuting authorities and to support criminal investigations of organised crime.
- CEPOL – a unit for the training of senior law enforcement officials.[89]

With regards to information exchange, it did not include any general guidelines, only stressing the need for its exchange between existing financial intelligence units and sending operational data from the Member States to Europol.

The importance of effective cross-border information exchange had been raised on the EU political level after the terrorist attack of September 11, 2001 in the United States and intensified after the attack of March 11, 2004 in Madrid.[90] As Guile states, "These events have allowed many initiatives, which had previously encountered many difficulties in their development

89 Nowadays converted into a training unit for all law enforcement officials, not only senior ones.

90 See GALÁN MUÑOZ, Alfonso, "La protección de datos de carácter personal en los tratamientos destinados a la prevención, investigación y represión de delitos: hacia una nueva orientación de la política criminal de la Unión Europea" in COLOMER HERNÁNDEZ, Ignacio and OUBIÑA BARBOLLA, Sabela. *La transmisión de datos personales en el seno de la cooperación judicial penal y policial en la Unión Europea*, Navarra: Aranzadi, 2015, p. 45; LEINIUS, Katharina, *An Imbalance between Security and Liberty? An Analysis of Cross-Border Information Exchange and Data Protection in the Context of the EU's Third Pillar since 9/11*, (PhD diss, University of Twente, 2009), p. 9–10, accessed May 20, 2017, http://essay.utwente.nl/60243/1/BSc_K_Leinius.pdf; GUILLE, Laure, "Policing in Europe: An Ethnographic Approach to Understanding the Nature of Cooperation and the Gap between Policy and Practice" in *Journal of Contemporary European Research*, vol. 6, no. 2, 2010 p. 257, accessed January 30, 2017, http://www.jcer.net/index.php/jcer/article/view/192.

because of legal challenges, to see the light and be implemented in practice."[91]

Thus terrorism had been an accelerator for the constitution of the TREVI group in the 1970s and after almost 30 years, gave a commencement to a new era of cooperation and became "The 'trigger' for formalising the 'exchange' of information between law enforcement".[92]

In less than one month after the attack of March 11 in Madrid, the European Council adopted a Declaration on combatting terrorism, emphasising among other measures:

- The simplification of the information and intelligence exchange between the law enforcement authorities of the Member States in as extensive manner as possible;
- Reinforcement of Europol;
- A focus on proactive intelligence;
- Bringing proposals on the retention of communication traffic data, on the exchange of DNA profiles and dactyloscopic data;
- The establishment of a European criminal records database.

In May–June of the same year, the Commission presented two communications: "Enhancing police and customs cooperation in the European Union"[93] and "Towards enhancing access to information by law enforcement agencies"[94] and proposed establishing EU Information Policy for law enforcement based on the improvement of information exchange and to introduce the concept of intelligence-led law enforcement at EU level. In order to improve information exchange, a principle of equivalent access has been introduced as a right of "Access to data and databases within other EU Member States on comparable conditions as law enforcement authorities in that Member State. The corollary to that right is the obligation to provide

91 GUILLE, Laure, "Policing in Europe: An Ethnographic Approach…", loc. cit., p. 257.

92 BUNYAN, Tony, "The principle of availability", Statewatch, December 2006, p. 2, accessed January 26, 2017, http://www.statewatch.org/analyses/no-59-p-of-a-art.pdf.

93 EUROPEAN COMMISSION, "Communication from the Commission to the European Parliament and the Council – Enhancing police and customs cooperation in the European Union – I. Report on achievements since the entry into force of the Treaty of Amsterdam – II. Proposals for improvements", COM (2004) 376 final, accessed, September 15, 2017, http://eur-lex.europa.eu/legal-content/GA/TXT/?uri=celex:52004DC0376.

94 EUROPEAN COMMISSION, "Communication from the Commission to the Council and the European Parliament – Towards enhancing access to information by law enforcement agencies (EU information policy)", COM(2004) 429 final, accessed 15 September, 2017, http://eur-lex.europa.eu/legal-content/EN/TXT/?uri=celex:52004DC0429.

access to law enforcement officials of other Member States under the same conditions as national law enforcement officials."[95]

Although in the introductory part of the second communication, the Commission referred to the Council's Declaration on Combatting Terrorism, but the proposed scope of the principle of equivalent access to information went beyond the fight against terrorists and includes serious and organised crime.[96] It can be explained by two reasons:

a The high probability of links between terrorism and organised crime;
b Reference of Article K.2 of the Treaty of Amsterdam to information exchange is not limited to fighting against terrorism, but to common actions on the collection, storage, processing, analysis and exchange of relevant information for law enforcement purposes.

The principle proposed by the Commission "saw daylight" and obtained political support in the second multiannual strategic programme – The Hague Programme strengthening Freedom, Security and Justice in the European Union[97] (hereinafter – The Hague Programme) that established the principle of information availability, with the deadline to be fully applicable from 2008 onwards.

Equally to the principle of equivalent access, the principle of availability has converted the voluntary nature of transmitting of information into "Obligation to fulfil the information requests of other Member States."[98]

Although, as Cabezudo Bajo points out, following the idea of the Commission, the principle of availability means direct online access to the information,[99] The Hague Programme does not mention it explicitly, leaving a question of access form open for further discussion.

The principle of availability is led by the list of conditions based on rational and necessary striking the balance between security and privacy:

95 Ibid, p. 7.
96 And even more than that, the Commission has envisaged that "it should be borne in mind that often criminal activity that would not appear to come within the category of 'serious or organised' can well lead or be connected to it", EUROPEAN COMMISSION, "Communication from the Commission to the European Parliament and the Council – Enhancing police and customs..." loc. cit., p. 4.
97 OJ C 53, 3.3.2005, p. 1–14.
98 ACED FÉLEZA, Emilio, "Principio de Disponibilidad y protección de datos en el ámbito policial" in *Noticias Jurídicas*, April 1, 2010, accessed September 25, 2017, http://noticias.juridicas.com/conocimiento/articulos-doctrinales/4537-principio-de-disponibilidad-y-proteccion-de-datos-en-el-ambito-policial-/
99 CABEZUDO BAJO, María José, "La protección de datos personales tratados en el marco de la cooperación policial y judicial en materia penal". In DE LA OLIVA SANTOS, Andrés (dir.), AGUILERA MORALES, Marien and CUBILLO LÓPEZ, Ignacio (coord.), *La Justicia y la Carta de Derechos Fundamentales de la Unión Europea* (Madrid: COLEX, 2008), p. 328.

- Information is exchanged only in order to perform legal tasks of law enforcement;
- The warranty of the integrity of the exchanged data shall be applied;
- Protection of information sources and confidentiality of data at all stages of data processing shall be ensured;
- Common technical and access standards shall be introduced;
- Data protection shall be controlled;
- Protection of individuals from abuse of data shall be provided;
- The right to seek correction of incorrect data shall be assured.[100]

The principle of availability became a cornerstone for police cooperation[101] in a similar manner to the principle of mutual recognition, established by the Tampere Conclusions, for judicial cooperation[102] and "The general political and practical guideline for the exchange of law enforcement information in the European Union."[103]

Some scholars, for example Ruggeri, say that availability derives from mutual recognition as free movement of data and information is a variation of the principle of mutual recognition.[104] In this respect, it can be said that both the principle of mutual recognition and the principle of availability have a common denominator – the free movement across state borders that during long periods of time, were considered as reflections of national sovereignty. Nevertheless, the nature of the recognition of judicial decisions in other Member States, and access to information, is different as in the first case, Member States are asked to recognise the results of foreign judicial processes and to execute them, and in the second case they are asked to "open" their deposits of information for foreign use.

For its implementation, the Commission has adopted an action plan "The Hague Programme: Ten priorities for the next 5 years. The Partnership for European renewal in the field of Freedom, Security and Justice"[105]

100 See OJ C 53, 3.3.2005, p. 8.

101 See INTERNATIONAL CENTRE FOR MIGRATION POLICY DEVELOPMENT AND EUROPEAN PUBLIC LAW ORGANIZATION, "Study on the status of information...", loc. cit., p. 35.

102 Ibid.

103 COUNCIL OF THE EUROPEAN UNION; 2012; "Draft Council Conclusions on further enhancing efficient cross-border exchange of law enforcement information"; 10333/12. Available at: http://data.consilium.europa.eu/doc/document/ST-10333-2012-INIT/en/pdf (accesses 17 September 2017).

104 RUGGERI, Stefano, "La transmisión de datos personales en cooperación judicial penal y policial en la UE. La perspectiva italiana" in COLOMER HERNÁNDEZ, Ignacio and OUBIÑA BARBOLLA, Sabela, *La transmisión de datos personales...*, op. cit., p. 280.

105 EUROPEAN COMMISSION, "Communication from the Commission to the Council and the European Parliament – The Hague Programme: Ten priorities for the next 5 years The Partnership for European renewal in the field of Freedom, Security and Justice", COM(2005) 184 final, accessed 16 September, 2017,

foreseeing 14 measures for the improvement of information exchange, in particular: a general legal basis to implement the principle of availability, relevant data protection framework, mechanism on the use of passengers' data for law enforcement purposes (both at EU level as well as with the third countries, such as the United States of America, Canada, and so on), instruments on mutual consultation of DNA and fingerprint databases.

Despite the political boost for information exchange, 2 years later Bruggeman noticed that, "A lack of confidence [...] still blocks the exchange of information and raises questions concerning the protection of privacy in the use of the many electronic databases with personal data. Transnational crime often moves easily across internal borders, while police and justice still hardly provide an effective and common approach."[106]

Five years later, the deadline of implementation of the principle of availability was not met because of the slow decision making process, information protectionism by some Member States and their sensitivity to some issues.

Thus the principle of availability had not lost its relevance and was reiterated in later strategic documents:

- The Stockholm Programme of 2009 pointed out that the principle of availability will continue to give important impetus to the flow of information and acknowledged "the need for coherence and consolidation in developing information management and exchange."[107]
- The European Council Conclusions of June 26–27, 2014 (approved instead of new multiannual strategic programme)[108] reiterated that reinforced exchanges of information between the authorities of the Member States is required and that "intensifying operational cooperation while using the potential of Information and Communication Technologies'

http://eur-lex.europa.eu/legal-content/EN/TXT/HTML/?uri=CELEX:52005DC0184&from=es.

106 BRUGGEMAN, Willy, "A Vision of Future Police Cooperation with Special Focus on Europol", in W. DE ZWAAN, Jaap and A.N.J. GOUDAPPEL, Flora, *Freedom, Security and Justice in the European Union: Implementation of The Hague Programme*, Asser Press: The Hague, 2006, p. 207.

107 OJ C 115, 4.5.2010, p.18.

108 After the Treaty of Lisbon, Article 68 of the TFEU establishes that the European Council shall define the strategic guidelines for legislative and operational planning within the area of Freedom, Security and Justice. Notwithstanding, it does not foresee either term for which such guidelines shall be established nor obligation to approve them in the form of a programme. Thus in 2014, the European Council went back to the origins of strategic planning in the area of Freedom, Security and Justice and approved the strategic guidelines in the form of European Council Conclusions. In the area of security, it makes much more sense than a general programme, because almost in every area (for instance, drug trafficking, cybercrime, trafficking in human beings) there are individual multiannual programmes. And in case of the Stockholm Programme there was some overlapping and sometimes even contradiction to each other.

> innovations, enhancing the role of the different EU agencies and ensuring the strategic use of EU funds will be key."[109]

According to the Stockholm Programme and Action Plan on its implementation,[110] the Commission had been tasked to evaluate the need of the European Information Exchange Model, and in 2012 came out with the conclusion that there was no need to propose any new instrument of initiative as "cross-border information exchange generally works well" and "a strong effort is still needed to ensure relevant information is shared at Europol so as to create an EU-wide picture of cross-border criminality."[111]

In its Conclusions of June 2013,[112] the Council agreed that there is no need for new legal instruments in this area, but better use of existing ones.

After attacks in France and Belgium, the information exchange came "back on track" again. In April 2016 the Communication "Stronger and Smarter Information Systems for Borders and Security" the Commission has pointed out fragmentation of the information exchange system among various institutions, existence of different legal and policy contexts and underlined the necessity of systems' interoperability, single interface for search in different databases and common repository of data.[113] For this purpose "the Commission will set up an Expert Group on Information Systems and Interoperability at senior level with EU agencies, national experts and relevant institutional stakeholders."[114]

Following this Communication, in June 2016 the Council of Ministers of Home Affairs discussed a "Roadmap to enhance information exchange and

109 COUNCIL OF THE EUROPEAN UNION, "Extract from the 26–27 June 2014 European Council Conclusions concerning the area of Freedom, Security and Justice and some related horizontal issues", OJ C 240, 24.7.2014, p. 13.

110 EUROPEAN COMMISSION, "Communication from the Commission to the European Parliament, the Council, the Economic and Social Committee and the Committee of the Regions – A Comprehensive Approach On Personal Data Protection In The European Union", COM(2010) 171 final, accessed 17 September 2017, http://ec.europa.eu/justice/news/consulting_public/0006/com_2010_609_en.pdf.

111 Ibid, p. 14.

112 COUNCIL OF THE EUROPEAN UNION, "Draft Council Conclusions following the Commission Communication on the European Information Exchange Model (EIXM)", 7226/2/13, p. 2, accessed 17 September 2017, http://data.consilium.europa.eu/doc/document/ST-7226-2013-REV-2/en/pdf.

113 See EUROPEAN COMMISSION, "Communication from the Commission to the European Parliament and the Council – Stronger and Smarter Information Systems for Borders and Security", COM(2016) 205 final, p. 3., accessed 17 September 2017, https://ec.europa.eu/home-affairs/sites/homeaffairs/files/what-we-do/policies/securing-eu-borders/legal-documents/docs/20160406/communication_on_stronger_and_smart_borders_20160406_en.pdf.

114 Ibid, p. 15.

information management including interoperability solutions"[115] presented by the Dutch Presidency. The document stresses he need of "political commitment to feed and use the information systems to the maximum extent, as a *conditio sine qua non* for achieving an efficient sharing of information"[116] and foresees measures to solve questions of interoperability, single interface and common repository of data. Some of those measures will be analysed in the following chapters.

Besides multiannual strategies in the whole area of Freedom, Security and Justice, specialised strategies, such as "Information Management Strategy for EU Internal Security"[117] (hereinafter – Information Management Strategy) and "Internal Security Strategy for the European Union. Towards a European security model" (hereinafter – Internal Security Strategy), also deserve a special mention.[118]

Thus in parallel with the development of the Stockholm Programme, in November 2009 the Council adopted the Information Management Strategy that "aims to support, streamline and facilitate the management of information necessary for the competent authorities to ensure EU internal security, but excluding the responsibilities of Member States in safeguarding their national security."[119]

To this end, the strategy has foreseen eight steps in the planning and development of any new information exchange mechanisms:

a To evaluate business needs and requirements, to analyse how existing solutions could be used for this purpose.
b To follow already agreed law enforcement workflows and criminal intelligence models in new developments.
c To ensure the balance between data protection requirements and business operational needs.
d To ensure interoperability and coordination, both of business processes and technical solutions.

115 COUNCIL OF THE EUROPEAN UNION, "Roadmap to enhance information exchange and information management including interoperability solutions in the Justice and Home Affairs area", 9368/1/16, accessed 19 September 2017, http://data.consilium.europa.eu/doc/document/ST-9368-2016-REV-1/en/pdf.
116 Ibid, p. 6.
117 COUNCIL OF THE EUROPEAN UNION, "Draft Council Conclusions on an Information Management Strategy for EU internal security", 16637/09, accessed 17 September 2017, http://register.consilium.europa.eu/doc/srv?l=ES&f=ST%2016637%202009%20INIT.
118 COUNCIL OF THE EUROPEAN UNION. "Internal Security Strategy for the European Union. Towards a European security model", accessed September 2014, https://www. consilium.europa.eu/uedocs/cms_data/librairie/PDF/QC3010313ENC.pdf.
119 COUNCIL OF THE EUROPEAN UNION, "Draft Council Conclusions on an Information Management Strategy...", loc. cit., p. 6.

e To share and re-utilise sustainable solutions whenever possible.
f To involve Member States from the very beginning of the process.
g To establish clear responsibility for each part of the process.
h To ensure multidisciplinary coordination within the Justice and Home Affairs area.

The Information Management Strategy included a clause on its revision in 2014, and in November 2014 the Council re-affirmed the strategy and its implementation, introducing only minor wording changes and giving one new task to the Commission, "To examine the possibility of consolidating and increasing the efficiency of the existing legislation on law enforcement information exchange."[120]

In March 2010, Internal Security Strategy, foreseen in the Stockholm Programme, was approved with the aim of using a more integrated approach in tackling common threats and risks. With regard to information exchange, this strategy has reiterated the Stockholm Programme: the need to strengthen mutual trust between competent law enforcement authorities, and use of the Information Management Strategy for the development of the European Information Exchange Model.

As a continuation of Internal Security Strategy, in April 2015 the Commission approved "The European Agenda on Security"[121] which foresees better use of existing information exchange tools, such as the SIS, Prüm Decisions and Europol, as well as finding a political compromise on the European PNR system.

Summing up the evolution of information exchange, we can refer to the reflexion of Leinius that "Security activity usually is characterised by a clandestine and insular thinking that makes cooperation even between different security actors of the same member state difficult; the principle of availability therefore is no less than revolutionary in its intention."[122]

It gave a political acceleration to development in this area, and served as a basis for numerous initiatives, some of which will be analysed in the following chapters. Nevertheless, its full and proper implementation took much longer than was forecast at the beginning and it is still in the process.

120 COUNCIL OF THE EUROPEAN UNION, "Draft Council Conclusions on an updated Information Management Strategy (IMS) for EU internal security", 15701/1/14, p. 9, accessed 19 September 2017, http://data.consilium.europa.eu/doc/document/ST-15701-2014-REV-1/en/pdf.

121 EUROPEAN COMMISSION, "Communication from the Commission to the European Parliament, the Council, the European Economic and Social Committee and the Committee of the Regions – The European Agenda On Security", COM(2015) 185 final, accessed 16 September 2017, http://eur-lex.europa.eu/legal-content/EN/TXT/?uri=COM:2015:0185:FIN.

122 LEINIUS, Katharina, *An Imbalance between Security and Liberty?...*, op. cit., p. 15.

5 Information, intelligence and personal data

Legal acts regulating police cooperation refers to different terms: "information", "intelligence" and "personal data" or "intelligence". For example, legislation related to Europol includes all three terms and applies different regulations, the Swedish Initiative talks about information and intelligence, all mechanisms differentiate between information in general, and personal data. Thus a conclusion can be made that the principle of availability covers all three categories.

EU legislation on police and judicial cooperation does not foresee a definition of information with the exception of the Council Framework Decision 2006/960/JHA of December 18, 2006, on simplifying the exchange of information and intelligence between the law enforcement authorities of the Member States of the European Union (Swedish Initiative).[123] Nevertheless, its Article 2.d gives a single definition to "information and/or intelligence", and describes it as "(i) any type of information or data which is held by law enforcement authorities; (ii) any type of information or data which is held by public authorities or by private entities and which is available to law enforcement authorities without the taking of coercive measures, in accordance with Article 1(5)." Such a definition is erroneous as to determine the term "information" its definition also includes the term "information".

In these circumstances, there is a need to establish the meaning of information within the context of police investigation, and it should be understood as a piece of data that allows the re-establishment of a wide picture of a crime, and all the related circumstances, and when necessary, to follow pre-established requirements to obtain consideration of evidence.

Unlike poor discussions on the term "information" within police investigation, much more attention is paid to the term "intelligence".

But before defining criminal intelligence, two things should be pointed out. First of all, a difference should be made between "intelligence" as an element of the work of the national security services and "intelligence" in the meaning of police investigation. As points out Bruggeman, "The term intelligence can be limited to authentic intelligence services or be understand broader and include all law enforcement authorities. CIA presents it in a very simple way: intelligence is knowledge and previous knowledge of the world that is surrounding us."[124] In cases of performing functions of national security services, it will be the analysis of "information related to capacities, intentions or activities of foreign governments as well as of organisations and persons that acts against national interests."[125] Secondly, it should be taken into account that the terms "information" and "intelligence" in broad meaning

123 OJ L 386, 29.12.2006, p. 89–100.

124 BRUGGEMAN, Willy, "Los procesos de construcción de una inteligencia europea" in MONTERO, Julián; ROMERO, Francisco and VALIENTE, Elena *¿Hacia una Policía Europea?*, op. cit., p. 215.

125 DÍAZ MATEY, Gustavo, "Hacia una definición de Inteligencia" in *Revista Inteligencia y Seguridad*, no. 4 (July – November 2008), p. 71.

are mostly used in common law countries, and in Eastern Europe, intelligence is very often still understood in a narrow way in association with national security services and criminal intelligence is referred to simply as the result of the analytical work of the criminal police.

In the process of making intelligence is evaluated whether information has "material value or potential material value"[126] for the police or not. Therefore it is considered that intelligence is qualitatively different from information.[127]As pointed out by O'Neill, "It should lead to 'informed decision making', allowing for the 'targeting of offenders' as the 'best way to use our scarce police resources'."[128]

Notwithstanding, it does not mean that intelligence is necessarily more important than information. Sometimes there is no need of intelligence, but just information; for example, when there is a need to know a person's location at a certain moment or whether his or her mobile phone was switched on, or who is the owner of vehicle that was used to commit a crime, and so on.

The last example of information about the owner of the vehicle includes two types of information: information about the vehicle and information about the person. Information about the colour of the vehicle, its technical characteristics, or traces of accidents for example, will be general or depersonalised information and that about the owner, his or her driving license or address – will be personal data.

Unlike information and intelligence, personal data is defined by the European legislator in many legal acts; for example beginning with the Council Framework Decision 2008/977/JHA of November 27, 2008, on the protection of personal data processed in the framework of police and judicial cooperation in criminal matters,[129] the Council Decision 2009/936/JHA of November 30, 2009 adopting the implementing rules for Europol analysis work files,[130] the Council Decision 2009/934/JHA of November 30, 2009 adopting the implementing rules governing Europol's relations with partners, including the exchange of personal data and classified information,[131] Council Decision 2007/533/JHA of June 12, 2007 on the establishment,

126 INTERNATIONAL CENTRE FOR MIGRATION POLICY DEVELOPMENT AND EUROPEAN PUBLIC LAW ORGANIZATION, "Study on the status of information…", loc. cit., p. 16.

127 See DÍAZ-PINTADO MORALEDA, Pedro, "El modelo de inteligencia en la organización…", loc. cit., p. 231.

128 O'NEILL, Maria, "The Issue of Data Protection and Data Security in the (Pre-Lisbon) EU Third Pillar", in *Journal of Contemporary European Research*, vol. 6, issue 2, 2010, p. 229, accessed July 15, 2014, http://www.jcer.net/ojs/index.php/jcer/article/view/264/206.

129 OJ L 350, 30.12.2008, p. 60–71. Also applied to Iceland, Ireland, Norway, Switzerland, Liechtenstein and United Kingdom.

130 OJ L 325, 11.12.2009, p. 14–22.

131 OJ L 325, 11.12.2009, p. 6–11.

operation and use of the second generations Schengen Information System (SIS II)[132] and recently adopted Directive (EU) 2016/680 of the European Parliament and of the Council of April 27, 2016 on the protection of natural persons with regard to the processing of personal data by competent authorities for the purposes of the prevention, investigation, detection or prosecution of criminal offences or the execution of criminal penalties, and on the free movement of such data, and repealing Council Framework Decision 2008/977/JHA,[133] Regulation (EU) 2016/794 of the European Parliament and of the Council of May 11, 2016 on the European Union Agency for Law Enforcement Cooperation (Europol) and replacing and repealing Council Decisions 2009/371/JHA, 2009/934/JHA, 2009/935/JHA, 2009/936/JHA and 2009/968/JHA.[134]

All of the above mentioned legal acts coincide in defining personal data as "any information relating to an identified or identifiable natural person ('data subject'); an identifiable person is one who can be identified, directly or indirectly".[135]

As it was mentioned, not all legal acts on information exchange that will be analysed regulate all three categories; but definitely in all of them, the difference between the processing of depersonalised and personal data is highlighted. The last one is always subject to stricter regulation as it is directly related with the fundamental right to data protection, but the level of restriction varies depending on the information exchange mechanism.

Bibliography

ACED FÉLEZA, E., 2010, "Principio de disponibilidad y protección de datos en el ámbito policial", *Noticias Jurídicas*, accessed September 25, 2017, http://noticias.juridicas.com:8080/articulos/15-Derecho-Administrativo/322-principio-de-disponibilidad-y-proteccin-de-datos-en-el-mbito-policial-.html.

ALMAGRO NOSETE, J.; CÓRTEZ DOMÍNGUEZ, V.; GIMENO SENDRA, V. et al., 1989, *Derecho Procesal: Parte general proceso civil (1)*; Valencia: Tirant lo Blanch.

AMBOS, K., 2006, *Temas de Derecho Penal Internacional y Europeo*; Madrid: Marcial Pons.

ARNÁIZ SERRANO, A., 2013, "Evolución de la Cooperación Judicial Penal Internacional: en especial, la Cooperación Judicial Penal en Europa"; in CARMONA RUANO, Miguel, GONZÁLEZ VEGA, Ignacio U, and MORENO CATENA, Víctor, *Cooperación Judicial Penal en Europa*, Madrid: Dykinson, p. 1–40.

BASSIOUNI, C., 2003, *Introduction to International Criminal Law*, Ardsley, New York; Transnational Publisher.

132 OJ L 205, 7.8.2007, p. 63–84.

133 OJ L 119, 4.5.2016, p. 89–131.

134 OJ L 2135, 4.5.2016, p. 53–114.

135 Article 2 of the Framework Decision 2008/977/JHA, Article 1 of Decision 2009/936/JHA, Article 1 of Decision 2009/934/JHA, Article 3 of the Decision 2007/533/JHA.

BENYON, J., 1994, "Policing the European Union: The Changing Basis of Cooperation on Law Enforcement" in *International Affairs (Royal Institute of International Affairs 1944–)*, vol. 70, no. 3, 499–517.

CASSESE, A., 2008, *International Criminal Law*, 2nd ed.; New York: Oxford University Press.

BRUGGEMAN, W., 2006, "A Vision of Future Police Cooperation with Special Focus on Europol", in ZWAAN, J. and GOUDAPPEL, F., *Freedom, Security and Justice in the European Union: Implementation of The Hague Programme*, The Hague: Asser Press, p. 203–220.

BUNYAN, T., 2006, "The principle of availability", Statewatch. Available at: http://www.statewatch.org/analyses/no-59-p-of-a-art.pdf (accessed January 26, 2017).

CABEZUDO BAJO, M. J., 2008, "La protección de datos personales tratados en el marco de la cooperación policial y judicial en materia penal" in DE LA OLIVA SANTOS, A. (dir.), AGUILERA MORALES, M. and CUBILLO LÓPEZ, I. (coord.); *La Justicia y la Carta de Derechos Fundamentales de la Unión Europea*, Madrid: COLEX; p. 327–342.

COMPUTER SCIENCE and TELECOMMUNICATIONS BOARD, 1991, "Computers at Risk: Safe Computing in the Information Age", The National Academies Press. Available at: http://www.nap.edu/openbook.php?record_id=1581 (accessed January 21, 2017).

COUNCIL OF EUROPE, 2005, *Organised Crime in Europe: The Threat of Cybercrime*, Strasbourg: Council of Europe Publishing.

COUNCIL OF THE EUROPEAN UNION, 2009, "Draft Council Conclusions on an Information Management Strategy for EU internal security", 16637/09. Available at: http://register.consilium.europa.eu/doc/srv?l=ES&f=ST%2016637%202009%20INIT (accessed September 17, 2017).

COUNCIL OF THE EUROPEAN UNION, 2010, "Draft Internal Security Strategy for the European Union: Towards a European Security Model", 7120/10. Available at: http://data.consilium.europa.eu/doc/document/ST-7120-2010-INIT/en/pdf (accessed September 19, 2017).

COUNCIL OF THE EUROPEAN UNION, 2012, "Draft Council Conclusions on further enhancing efficient cross-border exchange of law enforcement information", 10333/12. Available at: http://data.consilium.europa.eu/doc/document/ST-10333-2012-INIT/en/pdf (accesses September 17, 2017).

COUNCIL OF THE EUROPEAN UNION, 2013, "Draft Council Conclusions following the Commission Communication on the European Information Exchange Model (EIXM)", 7226/2/13. Available at: http://data.consilium.europa.eu/doc/document/ST-7226-2013-REV-2/en/pdf (accessed 17 September 2017).

COUNCIL OF THE EUROPEAN UNION, 2014, "Draft Council Conclusions on an updated Information Management Strategy (IMS) for EU Internal Security", 15701/1/14. Available at: http://data.consilium.europa.eu/doc/document/ST-15701-2014-REV-1/en/pdf (accessed 19 September 2017).

COUNCIL OF THE EUROPEAN UNION, 2014, "Extract from the 26–27 June 2014 European Council Conclusions concerning the area of Freedom, Security and Justice and some related horizontal issues", OJ C 240.

COUNCIL OF THE EUROPEAN UNION, 2016, "Roadmap to enhance information exchange and information management including interoperability solutions in the Justice and Home Affairs area", 9368/1/16. Available at: http://data.consilium.europa.eu/doc/document/ST-9368-2016-REV-1/en/pdf (accessed 19 September 2017).

DE HERT, P., 2004, "Division of Competencies between National and European Levels with regards to Justice and Home Affairs" in APAP, J.; *Justice and Home Affairs in the EU: Liberty and Security Issues after Enlargement*, Cheltenham; Edward Elgar; p. 55–99.

DE LA OLIVA SANTOS, A. and DÍEZ-PICAZO GIMÉNEZ, I., 2004, *Derecho Procesal. Introducción*, 3rd ed., Madrid: Ramón Areces.

DÍAZ MATEY, G., 2008, "Hacia una definición de Inteligencia" in *Revista Inteligencia y Seguridad*, no. 4; p. 59–84.

DÍAZ-PINTADO MORALEDA, P., 2002, "El modelo de inteligencia en la organización policial"; in MONTERO, J., ROMERO, F. and VALIENTE, E.; *¿Hacía una Policía Europea?*Madrid: Fundación Policía Española, p. 227–239.

EUROPEAN COMMISSION, 2004, "Communication from the Commission to the European Parliament and the Council – Enhancing police and customs co-operation in the European Union – I. Report on achievements since the entry into force of the Treaty of Amsterdam – II. Proposals for improvements", Available at: http://eur-lex.europa.eu/legal-content/GA/TXT/?uri=celex:52004DC0376 (accessed, September 15, 2017).

EUROPEAN COMMISSION, 2004, "Communication from the Commission to the Council and the European Parliament – Towards enhancing access to information by law enforcement agencies (EU information policy)", Available at: http://eur-lex.europa.eu/legal-content/EN/TXT/?uri=celex:52004DC0429 (accessed 15 September, 2017).

EUROPEAN COMMISSION, 2005, "Communication from the Commission to the Council and the European Parliament – The Hague Programme: Ten priorities for the next five years The Partnership for European renewal in the field of Freedom, Security and Justice", Available at: http://eur-lex.europa.eu/legal-content/EN/TXT/HTML/?uri=CELEX:52005DC0184&from=es (accessed 16 September, 2017).

EUROPEAN COMMISSION, 2010, "Communication from the Commission to the European Parliament, the Council, the Economic and Social Committee and the Committee of the Regions – A Comprehensive Approach On Personal Data Protection In The European Union", Available at: http://ec.europa.eu/justice/news/consulting_public/0006/com_2010_609_en.pdf (accessed 17 September 2017).

EUROPEAN COMMISSION, 2015, "Communication from the Commission to the European Parliament, the Council, the European Economic and Social Committee and the Committee of the Regions – The European Agenda On Security", Available at: http://eur-lex.europa.eu/legal-content/EN/TXT/?uri=COM:2015:0185:FIN (accessed 16 September 2017).

EUROPEAN COMMISSION, 2016, "Communication from the Commission to the European Parliament and the Council – Stronger and Smarter Information Systems for Borders and Security"; COM(2016) 205 final. Available at: https://ec.europa.eu/home-affairs/sites/homeaffairs/files/what-we-do/policies/securing-eu-borders/legal-documents/docs/20160406/communication_on_stronger_and_smart_borders_20160406_en.pdf (accessed 17 September 2017).

EUROPOL, 2011, "OCTA 2011: EU Organised Crime Threat Assessment" report. Available at: https://www.europol.europa.eu/content/publication/octa-2011-eu-organised-crime-threat-assesment-1465 (accessed September 26, 2017).

EUROPOL, 2013, "EU Serious Organised Crime Threat Assessment (SOCTA 2013)" report. Available at: https://www.europol.europa.eu/content/eu-serious-and-organised-crime-threat-assessment-socta (accessed September 9, 2017).

EUROPOL, 2015, "EU Terrorism Situation and Trend Report 2015" report. Available at https://www.europol.europa.eu/content/european-union-terrorism-situation-and-trend-report-2015 (accessed August 10, 2015).

EUROPOL, 2015, "The Internet Organised Crime Threat Assessment (IOCTA) 2015" report. Available at: https://www.europol.europa.eu/activities-services/main-reports/internet-organised-crime-threat-assessment-iocta-2016 (accessed October 9, 2017).

EUROPOL, 2016, "IOCTA 2016. Internet Organised Crime Threat Assesment" report. Available at: https://www.europol.europa.eu/activities-services/main-reports/internet-organised-crime-threat-assessment-iocta-2016 (accessed August 11, 2017).

EUROPOL, 2017, "European Union Terrorism Situation and Trend Report 2017" report. Available at: https://www.europol.europa.eu/activities-services/main-reports/eu-terrorism-situation-and-trend-report-te-sat-2017 (accessed August 11, 2017).

EUROPOL, 2017, "European Union Serious Organised Crime Threat Assessment. Crime in the age of technology (SOCTA 2017)" report. Available at: https://www.europol.europa.eu/activities-services/main-reports/european-union-serious-and-organised-crime-threat-assessment-2017 (accessed September 9, 2017).

FAZEKAS, J., 2009, "Development of Justice and Home Affairs Cooperation between 2004 and 2009 in the European Union"; in *European Integration Studies*, vol. 7, no 1, p. 3–28.

FELSEN, D. and KALAITZIDIS, A., 2005, "A Historical Overview of Transnational Crime"; in REICHEL, P.; *Handbook of Transnational Crime and Justice*, California, Sage Publications, Inc., p. 3–19.

FIJNAUT, C., 2004, "Police Co-operation and the Area of Freedom, Security and Justice" in WALKER, N.; *Europe's Area of Freedom, security and Justice*, Oxford: Oxford University Press, p. 201–282.

GALÁN MUÑOZ, A., 2015, "La protección de datos de carácter personal en los tratamientos destinados a la prevención, investigación y represión de delitos: hacia una nueva orientación de la política criminal de la Unión Europea", in COLOMER HERNÁNDEZ, I. and OUBIÑA BARBOLLA, S., *La transmisión de datos personales en el seno de la cooperación judicial penal y policial en la Unión Europea*, Navarra: Aranzadi, p. 37–70.

GARCÍA BORREGO, J. A. and FERNÁNDEZ VILLAZALA, T., 2007, *Introducción al Derecho Procesal Penal*, Madrid: Dykinson, S.L.

GIMENO SENDRA, V., 2008, *Manual de Derecho Procesal, Penal*, Madrid: Colex.

GUILD, E. and GEYER, F., 2008, "Introduction: The Search for EU Criminal Law – Where is it Headed?"; in GUILD, E. and GEYER, F. (eds.); *Security versus Justice? Police and Judicial Cooperation in the European Union*, Hampshire: Ashgate Publishing Limited; p. 1–16.

GUILLE, L., 2010, "Policing in Europe: An Ethnographic Approach to Understanding the Nature of Cooperation and the Gap between Policy and Practice", *Journal of Contemporary European Research*, vol. 6, no. 2. Available at: http://www.jcer.net/index.php/jcer/article/view/192 (accessed January 30, 2013).

INTERNATIONAL CENTRE FOR MIGRATION POLICY DEVELOPMENT and EUROPEAN PUBLIC LAW ORGANIZATION, 2010, "Study on the status of information exchange amongst law enforcement authorities in the context of existing EU instruments", European Commission, Available at: http://ec.europa.eu/dgs/home-affairs/doc_centre/police/docs/icmpd_study_lea_infoex.pdf (accessed August 20, 2017).

JENKINS, B.M., 2014, "When Jihadis Come Marching Home. The Terrorist Threat Posed by Westerners Returning from Syria and Iraq", Santa Monica, CA: RAND Corporation. Available at: https://www.rand.org/pubs/perspectives/PE130-1.html (accessed September 15, 2017).

LEINIUS, K., 2009, *An Imbalance between Security and Liberty? An Analysis of Cross-Border Information Exchange and Data Protection in the Context of the EU's Third Pillar since 9/11*, PhD diss., University of Twente. Available at: http://essay.utwente.nl/60243/1/BSc_K_Leinius.pdf (accessed May 20, 2017).

LONGO, F., 2013, "Justice and Home Affairs as a New Dimension of the European Security Concept"; in *European Foreign Affairs Review*, vol. 18, no. 1, p. 29–46.

LLORENTE SÁNCHEZ-ARJONA, M., 2014, *Las garantías procesales en el espacio europeo de justicia penal*, Valencia: Tirant lo Blanch.

LLORENTE SÁNCHEZ-ARJONA, M., 2013, "La cooperación judicial penal en el Tratado de Lisboa"; in DE LOS SANTOS MARTÍN OSTOS, J., *El Derecho Procesal en el espacio judicial Europeo: estudios dedicados al catedrático Faustino Gutiérrez-Alviz y Conradi*, Barcelona: Atelier Libros S.A., p. 323–343.

MADSEN, F. G., 2009, *Transnational Organised Crime*, New York: Routledge.

MITSILEGAS, V., MONAR, J. and REES, W., 2003, *The European Union and Internal Security: Guardian of the People?*Hampshire: Palgrave Macmillan.

MITSILEGAS, V., BANTEKASI. and NASHS., 2003, *International Criminal Law*, 2nd ed., Coogee: Cavendish Publishing Limited.

MONTERO AROCA, J., GÓMEZ COLOMER, J. L. and BARONA VILAR, S., 2012, *Derecho Jurisdiccional I. Parte general*, 20th ed., Valencia: Tirant lo Blanch.

MONTERO AROCA, J., 1979, *Introducción al Derecho Procesal. Jurisdicción, acción y proceso*, Madrid: Tecnos.

MORENO CATENA, V. and CASTILLEJO MANZANARES, R., 1999, *La persecución de los delitos en el Convenio de Schengen*, Valencia: Tirant lo Blanch.

MORENO CATENA, V., 2013, "El cambio de paradigma del principio de reconocimiento mutuo y sus implicaciones. Perspectivas del Tratado de Lisboa"; in CARMONA RUANO, Miguel; GONZÁLEZ VEGA, Ignacio U., and MORENO CATENA, Víctor, *Cooperación Judicial Penal en Europa*, Madrid: Dykinson, p. 41–78.

O'NEILL, M., 2010, "The Issue of Data Protection and Data Security in the (Pre-Lisbon) EU Third Pillar"; in *Journal of Contemporary European Research*, vol. 6, no. 2; p. 211–235. Available at: http://www.jcer.net/index.php/jcer/issue/view/17/showToc (accessed July 15, 2017).

OCCHIPINTI, J. D., 2003, *The Politics of EU Police cooperation. Towards a European FBI?*Colorado: Lynne Rienner Publishers, Inc.

PAULUSSEN, C., 2012, "Impunity for international terrorists? Key legal questions and practical considerations" paper; International Centre for Counter-Terrorism. Avialable at: http://www.icct.nl/download/file/ICCT-Paulussen-Impunity-April-2012.pdf (accessed January 21, 2017).

PEERS, S., 2010, "Guide to EU decision-making and justice and home affairs after the Treaty of Lisbon"; Statewatch. Available at: http://www.statewatch.org/analyses/no-115-lisbon-treaty-decision-making.pdf (accessed September 14, 2017).

PÉREZ MARÍN, M. Á., 2013, *La lucha contra la criminalidad en la Unión Europea*, Barcelona: Atelier.

PIRIS, J.-C., 2013, *The Lisbon Treaty. A Legal and Political Analysis*, New York: Cambridge University Press.

REBOLLO DELGADO, L., 2008, *Vida privada y protección de datos en la Unión Europea*, Madrid: Dykinson S.L.

REINARES, F. and RESA, C., 1997, "Transnational organized crime as an increasing threat to the national security of democratic regimes: assessing political impacts and evaluating state responses". Available at: http://www.nato.int/acad/fellow/97-99/reinares.pdf (accessed February 1, 2017).

RUGGERI, S., 2015, "La transmisión de datos personales en cooperación judicial penal y policial en la UE. La perspectiva italiana"; in COLOMER HERNÁNDEZ, I. and OUBIÑA BARBOLLA, S., *La transmisión de datos personales en el seno de la cooperación judicial penal y policial en la Unión Europea*, Navarra: Aranzadi, p. 277–300.

SANDOZ, Y., 2002, "Lutte contre le terrorisme et droit international: risques et opportunités"; in *Revue suisse de droit internationale et de droit européen*; No. 2; p. 319–354.

SERRANO GÓMEZ, A. and Vázquez GONZÁLEZ, C., 2007, *Tendencias de la criminalidad y percepción social de la inseguridad ciudadana en España y la Unión Europea*, Madrid: Edisofer S.L.

STORBECK, J., 2002, "La cooperación policial europea" in MONTERO, J., ROMERO, F., and VALIENTE, E., *¿Hacia una Policía Europea?*Madrid: Fundación Policía Española, p. 155–169.

UNITED NATIONS OFFICE ON DRUGS and CRIME, 2011, "Estimating Illicit Financial Flows Resulting from Drug Trafficking and Other Transnational Organized Crimes: Research Report (Vienna, October 2011)" research report. Available at: https://www.unodc.org/documents/data-and-analysis/Studies/Illicit_financial_flows_2011_web.pdf (accessed September 20, 2017).

UNITED NATIONS OFFICE ON DRUGS and CRIME, 2010, "The Globalization of Crime. A Transnational Organized Crime Threat Assesment. 2010" report. Available at: https://www.unodc.org/documents/data-and-analysis/tocta/TOCTA_Report_2010_low_ res.pdf (accessed September 27, 2017).

VACAS FERNÁNDEZ, F., 2011, *El terrorismo como crimen internacional. Definición, naturaleza y consecuencias jurídicas internacionales para las* personas, Valencia: Tirant lo Blanch.

VALLÉS CAUSADA, L. M., 2012, *La Policía judicial en la obtención de inteligencia sobre comunicaciones electrónicas para el proceso penal*. PhD diss., National Distance Education University. Available at: http://e-spacio.uned.es/fez/eserv/tesisuned:Derecho-Lmvalles/Documento.pdf (accessed March 20, 2017).

VIADA, N. G., 2009, *Derecho penal y globalización. Cooperación penal internacional*, Madrid: Marcial Pons.

VILABOY LOIS, L., 2001, "El sistema jurisdiccional comunitario"; in MARIÑO, F. M., MORENO CATENA, V. and MOREIRO, C.; *Derecho procesal comunitario*, Valencia: Tirant lo Blanch.

VLASSIS, D., 2002, "The Global situation of transnational organized crime, the decision of the international community to develop an international convention and the negotiation process", in *Resource Material Series*, no. 59, p. 475–494.

VON BOGDANY, A., CRUZ VILLALÓN, P. and HUBER, P. M., 2012, *El Derecho Constitucional en el espacio jurídico europeo*, Valencia: Tirant lo Blanch.

3 Fundamental rights and freedoms under consideration

The European Agenda on Security states that "Security and respect for fundamental rights are not conflicting aims, but consistent and complementary policy objectives."[1]

The most important aim of security is to ensure full and free enjoyment of fundamental rights without fear that something like a terrorist attack or crime can impede it and deprive, for example, from the right to live, the right to physical or moral integrity. On the other hand, ensuring security legislators endows some authorities, including the judiciary and the police, with administrative power that comprises coercive or other measures over citizens that leads to the limitation of some fundamental rights. Notwithstanding, such limitation of fundamental rights should be balanced and always subject to legitimacy, proportionality and some additional conditions.

Nevertheless, Barona Vilar asserts that with the terrorist attack of September 11, the "honeymoon" between the world and fundamental rights came to an end.[2]

Therefore, this chapter sets out to analyse existing interrelations and balance between security and fundamental rights, and freedoms in general, and to look in depth at rights directly related to information exchange in police investigation, i.e. privacy and data protection.[3]

1 EUROPEAN COMMISSION, "Communication from the Commission to the European Parliament, the Council, the European Economic and Social Committee and the Committee of the Regions – The European Agenda on Security", COM(2015) 185 final, accessed September 22, 2017, http://eur-lex.europa.eu/legal-content/EN/TXT/?uri=COM:2015:0185:FIN.

2 See BARONA VILAR, Silvia, *Seguridad, celeridad y justicia penal*, Valencia: Tirant lo Blanch, 2004, p. 75.

3 Of course, depending on information type, other fundamental rights can be under consideration, for example, in processing of DNA data rights to non-self-incrimination, non-incrimination of descendants or relatives, the right of children to personal development. See more: SOLETO MUÑOZ, Helena and FIODOROVA, Anna, "DNA and Law Enforcement in the European Union: Tools and Human Rights Protection" in *Ultrecht Law Review*, January 2014, vol. 10, issue 1, p. 154–158; SOLETO MUÑOZ, Helena, "DNA data in criminal

It should be taken into consideration that limitation of privacy occurs at the moment data is obtained in one Member State or another, and is always subject to national regulation. Thus, the question of the legality of limitation of privacy at this stage will be solved according to the legislation of that Member State and in cases of violation, the state will be responsible for its infringement. However, responsibility for data protection lies with every Member State or agency involved in its further processing, whether the data is transferred and processed within one Member State, or is "crossing the border".

In contrast to the other chapters, where only the EU legal framework is analysed, this one will also include legislation and case law of the Council of Europe as:

- Article 6(3) of the TFUE foresees that the Fundamental rights foreseen in the ECHR are treated as general principles of the EU.
- Article 52(3) of the Charter envisages that when it and the ECHR establish the same rights, their meaning and scope shall be equal to the Convention, except where the Charter provides.
- Case law of the ECtHR shall be taken into account when interpreting the Charter.[4]

It has to be mentioned that Article 6(2) of the TEU (modified by the Treaty of Lisbon) establishes that "the Union shall accede to the European Convention for the Protection of Human Rights and Fundamental Freedoms. Such accession shall not affect the Union's competences as defined in the Treaties." Nevertheless, the CJEU in its opinion 2/13 came to the conclusion that the current project of the "agreement on the accession of the European Union to the European Convention for the Protection of Human Rights and Fundamental Freedoms is not compatible with Article 6(2) TEU or with Protocol (No 8), relating to Article 6(2) of the Treaty on European Union on the accession of the Union to the European Convention on the Protection of Human Rights and Fundamental Freedoms."[5] This conclusion was made due to the consideration that it

procedure in the European fundamental rights context" in *Recent Advances in DNA and Gene Sequences*, 2014, 8(2), p. 91–97; SOLETO MUÑOZ, Helena, *Garantías y errores en la investigación penal. Ciencia versus memoria*, Valencia: Tirant lo Blanch, 2015, p. 157.

4 EUROPEAN COMMISSION, "Report from the Commission to the European Parliament, the Council, the European Economic and Social Committee and the Committee of the Regions – 2014 Report on the Application of the EU Charter of Fundamental Rights", COM(2015) 191, accessed September 22, 2017, http://eur-lex.europa.eu/legal-content/en/TXT/?uri=CELEX:52015DC0191.

5 COURT OF JUSTICE OF THE EUROPEAN UNION, "Opinion 2/13 of the Court (Full Court) 18 December 2014", ECLI:EU:C:2014:2475.

will affect the specific characteristics of EU law and its autonomy, as well as the division of the power established in Article 344 of the TFEU. For example, there would be an overlap of the competence between the ECtHR and the CJEU, in the case of the interpretation of human rights established in the ECHR and the EU Charter.[6]

1 Security deficit vs. democracy deficit

As revealed by a Eurobarometer survey carried out in 2015 "Europeans' attitude towards security", 79 per cent of the Europeans think that the EU is a safe place to live. But asked about the main challenges to security, people mostly mentioned terrorism, secondly, the economic and financial crisis and thirdly organised crime, corruption and poverty. Besides, both terrorism and organised crime are seen as increasing threats in the future.[7] Given this scenario a reflexion made by Vallés Causada seems very accurate, "What fundamental rights would remain to people if the criminal tumour exceeded State's surgical capacities?"[8]

And in these circumstances, the question stands: what prevails? Where should we be able to find the limit or balance between the state's role as guardian of rights and arbiter in security?

From first sight, it seems that there is no doubt about the priority of fundamental rights as they are a primary necessity.[9] But what happens in case of a collision between fundamental right? A person's right to life (in the case of a victim), or the right to privacy of communication (in the case of a suspect)? The right of hostages to live, or the right of the physical integrity of a kidnapper?

The answer to these questions will not be the same, not even when making comparisons among democratic states which strongly apply the Rule of Law. For example, in the case of Sweden or Norway, greater consideration would be given to rights of a suspect or kidnapper than in France, the United States of America or the United Kingdom where, in the light of new

6 See ETXEBERRÍA GURIDI, José Francisco, "Los derechos fundamentales en el espacio de libertad, seguridad y justicia penal", in *Revista Vasca de Administración Pública*, 2008, no. 82, 2, p. 160–163.

7 EUROPEAN COMMISSION, "Special Eurobarometer 432. 'Europeans' attitude towards security', April 2015, p. 4, 6, 9, accessed July 10, 2017, http://ec.europa.eu/public_opinion/archives/ebs/ebs_432_sum_en.pdf.

8 VALLÉS CAUSADA, Luís Manuel, *La Policía judicial en la obtención de inteligencia sobre comunicaciones electrónicas para el proceso penal* (PhD diss., National Distance Education University, 2012), p. 84, accessed March 20, 2017, http://e-spacio.uned.es/fez/eserv/tesisuned:Derecho-Lmvalles/Documento.pdf.

9 See BARONA VILAR, Silvia, *Seguridad, celeridad y justicial…*, op. cit., p. 78.

circumstances (basically the threat of terrorism), and the state's duty to protect residents (and first of all their right to live), the process of re-prioritisation of human rights takes place.[10] For example, after September 11 2001, on November 19, the Parliament of the United Kingdom adopted the Antiterrorism, Crime and Security Act that foresaw a petition to the House of Commons to derogate Article 5 of the ECHR (the right to liberty and security), to establish the possibility of indefinite detention of foreign suspects of terrorism who could not be expelled, and for broader possibilities on intervention of communications or financial data, for limited possibilities of a lawyer to receive information about all evidences.[11] The Act was in force until 2004 and was then substituted by a more flexible one, but that still allowed the limitation of fundamental procedural rights.

After terrorist attacks in 2015, France declared a state of emergency, strengthened antiterrorism measures (that may restrict some fundamental rights) and informed the Secretary General of the Council of Europe about application of Art. 15 of the ECHR; this allows that in case of war and public emergency, measures derogating from the obligation to guarantee all fundamental rights can be taken. Such derogation is not applied to the right to life, to the prohibition of torture, inhumane treatment or punishment, slavery and punishment without law.[12]

On the other hand, in Norway, even after the massacre of Breivik on July 22, 2011, legislative changes giving more powers to law enforcement authorities were not made; furthermore, "Terrorism legislation remains the same and there have been no special provisions made for the trial of suspected terrorists."[13]

The position of Norway is almost unique as many countries, even not directly affected by the terrorist attacks, have strengthened security

10 See MCGHEE, Derek, *Security, Citizenship and Human Rights. Shared Values in Uncertain Times*, Hampshire: Palgrave McMillan, 2010, p. 60–61.

11 See JIMÉNEZ FORTEA, Francisco Javier, "La respuesta procesal penal al terrorismo en el marco de la Unión Europea: un ejemplo de cooperación judicial penal y policial" in CALDERÓN CUADRADO, Mº Pía and IGLESIAS BUHIGUES, José Luís, *El Espacio Europeo de Libertad, Seguridad y Justicia: Avances y Derechos Fundamentales en Materia Procesal*, Navarra: Aranzadi, 2009, p. 81; JIMÉNEZ FORTEA, Francisco Javier, "De la restricción de derechos a un 'derecho procesal del enemigo'", in MASFERRER, Aniceto, *Estado de Derecho y derechos fundamentales en la lucha contra el terrorismo*, Navarra: Aranzadi, 2011, p. 616–617.

12 See COUNCIL OF EUROPE, Reservations and Declarations for Treaty No. 005 – Convention for the Protection of Human Rights and Fundamental Freedoms, accessed September 22, 2017 http://www.coe.int/en/web/conventions/full-list/-/conventions/treaty/005/declarations?p_auth=s257bdf0

13 GALPIN, Richard, "Norway prepares for killings anniversary", *BBC*, July 20 2012, accessed July 22, 2012, http://www.bbc.com/news/world-europe-18791448.

measures that have resulted in bigger or broader restrictions of some fundamental rights.

With respect to human rights, the British Government's position in general deserves special attention. It underlines a deficit of public security and considers approval of a Modern Bill of Rights to define core values. As a consequence, the United Kingdom could stand back from the ECHR and the obligation to obey ECtHR judgments, as some of them have been found by the British authorities to misinterpret the ECHR, especially those on banning "sending home foreign criminals".[14]

One of the judgments that urged the taking of such a decision was the case *Chahal v United Kingdom* in 1996. In this case the Government of the United Kingdom took a decision to deport Mr Chahal (who was a leader of the Sikh community, a separatist movement for independence in one of the regions of India – Khalistan) to India, as it had considered his behaviour "unconducive to the public good for reasons of national security, and other reasons of a political nature, namely the international fight against terrorism."[15]

The ECtHR, found that the right to not be subjected to torture or inhuman treatment (established in Article 3 of the ECHR) is absolute and therefore, the Government's decision on deportation to India was contrary to this Article, as there was a high probability that in India, Mr Chahal, being a separatist, would be subject to torture or inhuman treatment and "in these circumstances, the activities of the individual in question, however undesirable or dangerous, cannot be a material consideration."[16]

Even recognising the correctness of such ECtHR judgments, there is still a pending question: What should competent authorities do with respect to similar persons, bearing in mind their potential threat to the security and the rights of other residents?

The British Conservatives also questioned ECtHR carrying out interpretations of the ECHR, making it a "live instrument" and considered this to be going far beyond the meaning that had been given to some rights. For

14 See MCGHEE, Derek, *Security, Citizenship and Human Rights...*, op. cit., p. 97, 99; "David Cameron: British bill of rights will 'safeguard legacy' of Magna Carta", *Guardian*, June 15 2015, accessed September 8 2015, http://www.theguardian.com/law/2015/jun/15/david-cameron-british-bill-of-rights-safeguard-legacy-magna-carta; "David Cameron Won't Rule Out Ditching European Convention On Human Rights", *The Huffington Post*, June 3 2015, accessed September 8 2017, http://www.huffingtonpost.co.uk/2015/06/03/prime-ministers-questions-human-rights-bill-of-rights-refuse-rule-out_n_7501460.html.

15 ECtHR, *Chahal v the United Kingdom* [1996], paragraph 25.

16 Ibid, paragraph 80.

example, with respect to prisoners' right to vote, the Conservatives declared "the issue of the franchise in elections was deliberately excluded from the text of the Convention. The Strasbourg Court has, however, now decided that it falls within the Convention's ambit."[17]

They also stated that "another clear example of 'mission creep' came in a 2007 ruling by the Court that required the UK Government to allow many more prisoners the right to go through artificial insemination with their partners, in order to uphold their rights under Article 8. This is not what the originators of the Convention had in mind when they framed that article."[18]

After the re-election of the Conservatives in spring 2015, the question of a new British Bill of Rights has been raised again.

In other Member States there are also signs of gradual expansion of purposes of limitation, categories of persons to whom they are applied and facilitation of the procedure in general. For example, in France categories of crimes for which DNA profiles can be stored in a national database have been expanded from sexual offences to serious crimes and then less serious offences. Originally only DNA profiles of convicted persons were processed, but later legislation has permitted the processing of those of suspects. In Germany categories of data crimes have also been expanded and previous obligation of judicial authorisation has been made more flexible.[19] The key issue of limitations has to be respect to principle of proportionality that will be discussed later. For example, in the case of *B.B. v. France*, the ECtHR recognised that processing the data of a convicted sex offender interferes with the right to data protection, but with adequate data safeguarding, limited storage and access, the public interest in that data can be ensured.[20] Many European countries directly apply principles of proportionality, establishing that the limitation of fundamental rights can take place depending on the type of crime or punishment.[21]

With respect to EU policies, the security deficit felt after the terrorist attacks of 2001, 2004 and 2005 prevailed over the democracy deficit for some time and resulted in the adoption of different measures to combat terrorism and crime that intervene in fundamental rights, reducing their

17 UK Conservatives, "Protecting Human Rights in the UK. The Conservatives' proposal for changing Britain's Human Rights Laws", 2014, p. 3, accessed August 13, 2017, https://www.conservatives.com/~/media/files/downloadable%20Files/human_rights.pdf.

18 Ibid.

19 See ETXEBERRÍA GURIDI, José Francisco, "La identificación de personas mediante pruebas genéticas y bancos de perfiles de ADN: evolución normativa en el contexto europeo" in *Revista de Derecho y Genoma Humano*, 2014, extra ordinary issue, p. 140–142, 145, 150.

20 EUROPEAN COURT OF HUMAN RIGHTS, "Affaire B.B. v France", 2009, paragraphs 61, 62, 70, ECLI:CE:ECHR:2009:1217JUD000533506.

21 MORENO CATENA, Víctor, "La garantía de los derechos fundamentales durante la investigación penal" in *Cuadernos Penales José María LIDÓN*, 2010, ed. 7, p. 18.

protection to secondary importance.[22] An attempt to re-establish the balance was made in the Internal Security Strategy by envisaging that freedom, justice and security policies would have to be developed, "Respecting fundamental rights, international protection, the rule of law and privacy."[23] Nevertheless, initiative of 2016 of interoperability of all databases, adoption of the Directive (EU) 2016/681 of the European Parliament and of the Councils of April 27 2016 on the use of passenger name record (PNR) data for the prevention, detection, investigation and prosecution of terrorist offences and serious crime[24] brings us back to the question about the real possibility of achieving security without serious impact on fundamental rights.

2 Privacy

While gathering and further processing of information, among all fundamental rights, the right to privacy has the biggest risk of violation.

This right is established in all international charters and declarations on fundamental rights, dating from the Universal Declaration of Human Rights of 1948[25] to the more recent Charter of 2000, which, along with the entrance into force of the Treaty of Lisbon in 2009, was granted the same legal value as TUE and TFUE.[26]

2.1 Content of right to privacy

According to international conventions, privacy is understood as the respect for private and family life, home and correspondence, respect for dignity, personal integrity or reputation. It derives from an understanding, that everyone has a right to share or not information about his/her private life, habits, acts, and relationships with others, freedom from intrusion and privacy of information, and the right to know about and dispose of his/her personal data.[27]

22 GALÁN MUÑOZ, Alfonso, "La protección de datos de carácter personal en los tratamientos destinados a la prevención, investigación y represión de delitos: hacia una nueva orientación de la política criminal de la Unión Europea" in COLOMER HERNÁNDEZ, Ignacio and OUBIÑA BARBOLLA, Sabela, *La transmisión de datos personales en el seno de la cooperación judicial penal y policial en la Unión Europea*", Navarra: Aranzadi, 2015, p. 48.
23 COUNCIL OF THE EUROPEAN UNION. "Internal Security Strategy for the European Union. Towards a European security model", 2010, p. 19, accessed September 2014, https://www. consilium.europa.eu/uedocs/cms_data/librairie/PDF/QC3010313ENC.pdf.
24 OJ L 119, 4.5.2016, p. 132–149.
25 The same year, a right to privacy was established in the American Declaration of the Rights and Duties of Man.
26 Article 6 of the TEU.
27 GUTIÉRREZ ZARZA, Ángeles, "Conceptos básicos. Marco legal europeo sobre protección de datos en materia penal" in GUTIÉRREZ ZARZA, Ángeles,

Due to technological developments, the right to privacy acquires new characteristics. If previously it was more understood as a person's right to decide to share or not to share information, and he or she could control it, with automated processing of information this control is lost, and privacy needs other measures of protection that prohibit the use of facilitated information.[28] This right derived from privacy is also known as the right to informative self-determination.

Together with scientific developments, the right to privacy has given rise to the right to genetic privacy that has developed with the greater use of DNA, and the need to give a data subject the right to determine conditions to access his or her genetic information.[29]

Ultimately, it is also interpreted as the right to be alone[30] and even the "right to be forgotten" that has a tendency to develop into a separate right.[31] The last point has witnessed an interesting development in case law of the CJEU. In its judgment in case C-131/12, where Google Spain SL and Google Inc. were recognised as data controllers and as such responsible for data processing, although they are search engines and not databases. The Court's reasoning was the following: "The operator of a search engine 'collects' such data which it subsequently 'retrieves', 'records' and 'organises' within the framework of its indexing programmes, 'stores' on its servers and, as the case may be, 'discloses' and 'makes available' to its users in the form of lists of search results. As those operations are referred to expressly and unconditionally in Article 2(b) of Directive 95/46, they must be classified as 'processing' within the meaning of that provision, regardless of the fact that the operator of the search engine also carries out the same operations in respect of other types of information, and does not distinguish between the latter and the personal data."[32] And, "it is the search engine operator which determines the purposes and means of that activity and thus of the

Nuevas tecnologías, protección de datos personales y proceso penal, Madrid: La Ley, 2012, p. 81.

28 LÓPEZ ORTEGA, Juan José, "La tutela de la intimidad genética en la investigación penal. A propósito de la STC 199/2013 y de la SAP Sevilla 650/2013" in CASADO, María and GUILLÉN, Margarita, *ADN forence: problemas éticos y jurídicos*, Barcelona: Universitat de Barcelona, 2014, p. 100–101.

29 See ETXEBERRIA GURIDI, José Francisco, *Los análisis de ADN y su aplicación al proceso penal*, Granada: Comares, 2000, p. 61, 190; ETXEBERRÍA GURIDI, José Francisco, "La protección de los datos de ADN en la Unión Europea y en España", in CABEZUDO BAJO, María José. *Las bases de datos policiales de ADN ¿Son una herramienta realmente eficaz en la lucha contra la criminalidad grave nacional y transfornteriza?* Madrid: Dykinson, S.L., 2013, p. 100.

30 See LÓPEZ ORTEGA, Juan José. "La tutela de la intimidad genética…", loc. cit., p. 100–101.

31 See ÁLVAREZ CARO, María, *Derecho al olvido en Internet: el Nuevo paradigm de la privacidad en la era digital*, Madrid: Universidad San Pablo, 2015, p. 72.

32 Judgment of the CJUE in *Google Spain SL, Google Inc. v Agencia Española de Protección de datos (AEPD), Mario Costeja González*, C-131/12, ECLI:EU:C:2014:317, paragraph 28.

processing of personal data that it itself carries out within the framework of that activity and which must, consequently, be regarded as the 'controller' in respect of that processing pursuant to Article 2(d)."[33]

At European level, the right to privacy is established in the ECHR (that was opened to signature on November 4, 1950 and has been in force since September 3, 1953) and since the Treaty of Lisbon also in the TEU, the TFEU and the EU Charter.

The ECHR in Article 8 envisages that "everyone has the right to respect for his private and family life, his home and his correspondence."

Even if the right to privacy is not directly written down, it derives from this provision, in particular from the "private life", which, according to the ECtHR, "must not be interpreted restrictively". In particular, respect for private life comprises the right to establish and develop relationships with other human beings; furthermore, there is no reason of principle to justify excluding activities of a professional or business nature from the notion of "private life".[34]

In the case of *Niemietz v Germany*, it also included the concept of labour environment[35] into the right to private life, and in the case *Perry v the United Kingdom*, the ECtHR declared that the use of cameras in public places for any purpose other than monitoring, is interference in privacy as well, and in this precise case, "There is no indication that the applicant had any expectation that footage was being taken of him within the police station, for use in a video identification procedure and, potentially, as evidence prejudicial to his defence at trial. This ploy adopted by the police went beyond the normal or expected use of this type of camera."[36]

2.2 Limitation of right to privacy

Right to privacy is not an absolute right and Article 8(2) of the ECHR foresees the possibility of its restriction that according to Soleto Muñoz is quite wide and flexible.[37] It allows some level of national assessment to the fundamental right and legal establishment of its limitation according to national reality.[38]

33 Ibid, paragraph 33.
34 EUROPEAN COURT OF HUMAN RIGHTS, "Case of Amann v Switzerland" 2000, paragraph 65, ECLI:CE:ECHR:2000:0216JUD002779895; "Case of Rotaru v Romania", 2000, paragraph 43, ECLI:CE:ECHR:2000:0504JUD002834195.
35 EUROPEAN COURT OF HUMAN RIGHTS, "Case of Niemetz v Germany", 1992, paragraph 29, ECLI:CE:ECHR:1992:1216JUD001371088.
36 EUROPEAN COURT OF HUMAN RIGHTS, "Case of Perry v the United Kingdom", 2003, paragraph 41, ECLI:CE:ECHR:2003:0717JUD006373700.
37 See SOLETO MUÑOZ, Helena, "Parámetros europeos de limitación de Derechos Fundamentales en el uso de datos de ADN en el proceso penal", in *Revista general de Derecho penal*, 2016, no. 28, p. 7.
38 See SANTOLAYA, Pablo, "Limitación de la aplicación de las restricciones de derechos. Art. 18 CEDH", in GARCÍA ROCA, Javier and SANTOLAYA,

In any case, according to Article 8(2) of the ECHR, restriction is possible only in cases where all three conditions listed below are fulfilled:

a Restriction is established by law which is accessible to society, foreseeable and "formulated with sufficient precision to enable the citizen to regulate his conduct: he must be able – if need be with appropriate advice – to foresee, to a degree that is reasonable in the circumstances, the consequences which a given action may entail."[39]
b It is established for the purpose of: national security, public safety, economic well-being of the country, prevention of disorder or crime, protection of health or morals, protection of the rights and freedoms of others.[40]
c It is necessary for democratic society. Such necessity is measured by the principle of proportionality that includes: necessity of restrictive measure in order to obtain the aim established by the law, adequacy, "cost-benefit" balance, i.e. the proportionality of the measure to the aim.[41]

In relation to limitation by law, it must be very precise, for example the ECtHR recognised violation of Article 8 in the case of the French authorities which bugged a private flat because it had been out of the scope of the Criminal Procedure Code that only regulates the interception of telephone lines.[42]

In the case *S and Marper v. The United Kingdom*, the ECtHR reiterated its previous judgments stating that the law shall have "clear, detailed rules governing the scope and application of measures, as well as minimum safeguards concerning, inter alia, duration, storage, usage, access of third parties, procedures for preserving the integrity and confidentiality of data and procedures for its destruction, thus providing sufficient guarantees against the risk of abuse and arbitrariness."[43]

Article 18 of the ECHR also entails that limitations can be applied only for the purpose that they have been established and their use for any other purpose will be treated as a violation.

Article 7 of the EU Charter establishes the privacy of private and family life, home and communications without going into any details about its

Pablo, *La Europa de los Derechos. El Convenio Europeo de Derechos Humanos*, Madrid: Centro de Estudios Políticos y Constitucionales, 2014, 3rd ed., p. 658.

39 EUROPEAN COURT OF HUMAN RIGHTS, "Case of the Sunday Times v United Kingdom", 1979, ECLI:CE:ECHR:1979:0426JUD000653874, paragraph 49.

40 ECHR, Article 8(2).

41 See ARENAS RAMIRO, Mónica, *El Derecho Fundamental a la protección de datos personales en Europa* (Valencia: Tirant lo Blanch, 2000), p. 121.

42 See EUROPEAN COURT OF HUMAN RIGHTS, "Affaire Vetter v. France", 2005, paragraphs 23, 24, ECLI:CE:ECHR:2005:0531JUD005984200.

43 EUROPEAN COURT OF HUMAN RIGHTS, "Case of S and Marper v. the United Kingdom", 2008, paragraph 99, ECLI:CE:ECHR:2008:1204JUD00 3056204.

possible limitation, as Article 52(1) envisages possible restrictions on all rights that are not indicated in the Charter as absolute ones. The limitation is permitted if it is foreseen by law, maintains respect to the essence of the rights under consideration, is proportional and protects general interest or rights of others.[44]

2.3 *Privacy and electronic communications*

Protection of privacy was directly established by the Directive 2002/58/EC of the European Parliament and of the Council of July 12, 2002 concerning the processing of personal data and the protection of privacy in the electronic communications sector[45] (hereinafter – Directive 2002/58/EC). On the one hand, Article 1 excludes from its scope activities related to public security and criminal law, but on the other hand, Article 15 allows the limitation of rights and obligations established by this Directive for the same purposes. The European Court of Justice in Case C-275/06 explained that it neither eliminates the possibility nor obliges the disclose of such data in civil processes,[46] but foresees that while transposing Directive 2002/58/EC, "Member States take care to rely on an interpretation [...] which allows a fair balance to be struck between the various fundamental rights protected by the Community legal order."[47]

The Directive 2002/58/EC was amended by the Directive 2006/24/EC of the European Parliament and of the Council of 15th March 2006, on the retention of data generated or processed in connection with the provision of publicly available electronic communication services, or of public communication networks and amending Directive 2002/58/EC (hereinafter – Directive 2006/24/EC).

New legislation foresaw an obligation on the part of providers of communication networks and services to retain some categories of data, and to make it available for detection, investigation and prosecution of serious crimes. That meant storing data of every user despite its potential relationship or not with serious crime. The data retained[48] is data related to communication that allows identifying a person with whom communication took place, its time and location, but not its content or the information consulted.

44 The same was reiterated by the CJUE. See COURT OF JUSTICE OF THE EUROPEAN UNION, "Judgment of the Court (Grand Chamber) of November 9 2010 in Joined Cases C-92/09 and C-93/09", paragraph 50, ECLI:EU:C:2010:662.

45 OJ L 201, 31.07.2002, p. 37–47.

46 This precise case was about the infringement of rights to intellectual property.

47 COURT OF JUSTICE OF THE EUROPEAN UNION, "Judgment of the Court (Grand Chamber) of 29 January 2008 in Case C-275/06", paragraphs 54, 55 and ruling, ECLI:EU:C:2008:54.

48 Data categories listed in Article 5 include: data necessary to trace and identify the source of a communication and its destination, to identify the date, time, duration and type of a communication, to identify users' communication

As stated by the CJEU, this data "taken as a whole, may allow very precise conclusions to be drawn concerning the private lives of the persons whose data has been retained, such as the habits of everyday life, permanent or temporary places of residence, daily or other movements, the activities carried out, the social relationships of those persons and the social environments frequented by them."[49]

Interpreting Article 52(1) of the EU Charter (possible limitation of fundamental rights), the Court came to the conclusion that as the content of the communications is not revealed, the essence of the right to privacy is not affected,[50] and as it is for the purpose of combatting serious crime, the interference is for general interest.[51]

In respect to proportionality (understood as not exceeding the limits of appropriate and necessary interference), data retention was found to be a "valuable tool for crime investigation" and therefore an appropriate tool, but the question of necessity was raised as "Article 7 of Directive 2006/24 does not lay down rules which are specific and adapted to (i) the vast quantity of data whose retention is required by that directive, (ii) the sensitive nature of that data and (iii) the risk of unlawful access to that data, rules which would serve, in particular, to govern the protection and security of the data in question in a clear and strict manner in order to ensure their full integrity and confidentiality. Furthermore, a specific obligation on Member States to establish such rules has also not been laid down."[52]

On this basis, the Directive 2006/24/EC was recognised as a disproportionate measure and invalid as a whole. It was declared invalid without any temporary continuation of its application.

As every directive, Directive 2006/24/EC had to be transposed into national law and the term for that came to an end on September 15, 2007. That meant that between September 2007 and April 2012, according to Article 258 of the TFEU, the Commission was able to start infringement procedure for Member States that had not obeyed the obligation of the transposition. In effect such procedure had been started against Germany, but withdrawn due to the recognition of the Directive as void. But in case of Sweden, the consequences were more serious as in 2010, the CJEU had recognised Sweden's failure to carry out the

equipment, and to identify the location of mobile communication equipment, data which consist, inter alia, of the name and address of the subscriber or registered user, the calling telephone number, the number called and an IP address for Internet services. See COURT OF JUSTICE OF THE EUROPEAN UNION, "Judgement of the Court (Grand Chamber) of 8 April 2014 in Joined Cases C-293/12 and C-594/12", paragraphs 26, ECLI:EU:C:2014:238.

49 Ibid, paragraph 27.

50 Ibid, paragraph 39.

51 Ibid, paragraph 41, 44.

52 Ibid, paragraph 66.

transposition,[53] and in 2013 ordered a lump sum payment of 3 million euros to be made.[54] After the judgment declaring the Directive void, this fine was returned to Sweden.

The High Courts of Bulgaria, Cyprus, the Czech Republic, Germany and Romania have recognised the transposition laws of Directive 2006/24/EC in total (Romania[55]), or partially void (Bulgaria, Cyprus, Czech Republic, Germany).[56] They did not mention anything about the validity of the Directive, as they do not have jurisdiction to pronounce over EU law. But being in the same position, the courts of Ireland and Austria asked the European Court of Justice for a preliminary ruling in this respect.[57]

As a result of the judgment of the CJEU, Constitutional Courts of Austria, Slovenia and Romania[58] declared national transposing laws void.

From these examples a few conclusions should be made:

- In the case of the infringement started against Sweden, the CJEU took a technical decision, revising only the question of transposition of the Directive 2006/24/EC, but not the content of the Directive.
- The courts of only two of the 27 Member States addressed this issue to the CJEU, questioning the content and compatibility of the directive with human rights. The rest of the countries in the worst-case scenario transposed it automatically, and in the best-case scenario their high courts recognised transposing provisions as void. Thus majority of Member States swear by the legality of European legislation.

Despite negative experience, electronic communication is so complex and overwhelming that it has to be compensated by appropriate procedural regulation to have benefits for investigation.[59]

53 See COURT OF JUSTICE OF THE EUROPEAN UNION, "Judgment of the Court (Sixth Chamber) of 4 February 2010 – European Commission v Kingdom of Sweden (Case C-185/09)", ECLI:EU:C:2010:59.

54 COURT OF JUSTICE OF THE EUROPEAN UNION, "Judgment of the Court (Fourth Chamber) of 30 May 2013 – European Commission v Kingdom of Sweden (Case C-270/11)", ECLI:EU:C:2013:339.

55 See BOEHM, Franziska and COLE, Mark D., "Data Retention after the Judgement of the Court of Justice of the European Union" (study, Greens/EFA Group in the European Parliament, 2014), p. 16, accessed September 17, 2017, http://www.janalbrecht.eu/fileadmin/material/Dokumente/Boehm_Cole_-_Data_Retention_Study_-_June_2014.pdf.

56 Ibid, p. 15–18.

57 In the case of Austria, actions before national courts were brought by more than 11 000 applicants. See judgment of the CJUE in *Digital Rights Ireland Ltd...*, loc. cit., paragraph 19.

58 After declaring the law void in 2009, a new one was adopted in 2012 and in 2014 also declared void.

59 See VALLÉS CAUSADA, Luís Manuel, "Usos delictivos no comunicativos de la telefonía móvil: una excepción a la protección del artículo 18.3 CE?" in

Council of Ministers of Justice of December 3, 2015 raised up the question of the data retention and the necessity to avoid legal fragmentation and invited the Commission to present a new draft on data retention.

Luxembourg Presidency of the Council together with Eurojust on December 10, 2015 organised a workshop "Data Retention in the Fight Against Serious Crime: the Way Forward" which outcomes were discussed on December 11, 2015 at the 10th meeting of the Consultative Forum of Prosecutors General and Directors of Public Prosecutions of the Member States of the EU where it was also pointed out fragmentation, limitation of sources of investigation and evidences. It was also stressed that "Cooperation is affected both within and outside the EU, whereby some countries are in the position to share more data than EU countries. Likewise, different retention periods seriously affect the execution of MLA requests."[60]

3 Data protection

3.1 Relation between right to privacy and right to data protection

It would be hard to find a better explanation of the interrelation between privacy and data protection than one provided by the European Data Protection Supervisor, "'Data protection' is broader than 'privacy protection' because it also concerns other fundamental rights and freedoms, and all kinds of data regardless of their relationship with privacy, and at the same time, more limited because it merely concerns the processing of personal information, with other aspects of privacy protection being disregarded."[61]

Thus the right to privacy protects persons against disclosure of personal information, and establishes some exceptions when they are allowed. Data

PÉREZ GIL, Julio, *El proceso penal en la sociedad de la información: las nuevas tecnologías para investigar y probar el delito*, Madrid: La Ley, 2012, p. 228.

60 COUNCIL OF THE EUROPEAN UNION, "Meeting of the Consultative Forum of Prosecutors General and Directors of Public Prosecutions of the Member States of the European Union and Workshop on Data Retention in the Fight Against Serious Crime: The Way Forward. Eurojust, The Hague, 10–11 December 2015. Conclusions", 5930/16, p. 3, accessed November 14, 2017, http://data.consilium.europa.eu/doc/document/ST-5930-2016-INIT/en/pdf.

61 HUSTINX, Peter, "EU Data Protection Law: The Review of Directive 95/46/EC and the Proposed General Data Protection Regulation" (article based on the course given at the European University Institute's Academy of European Law in July 2013), p. 5, accessed January 20, 2017, https://secure.edps.europa.eu/EDPSWEB/webdav/site/mySite/shared/Documents/EDPS/Publications/Speeches/2014/14-09-15_Article_EUI_EN.pdf. Similar explanation is given by KOKOTT Juliane and SOBOTTA Christoph, "The distinction between Privacy and Data Protection in the Jurisprudence of the CJEU and the ECtHR", in *International Data Privacy Law*, 2013, vol. 3, no 4, p. 225, http://idpl.oxfordjournals.org/content/3/4/222.full.pdf+html as well as by GARRIGA DOMÍNGUEZ. Also see GARRIGA DOMÍNGUEZ, Ana, *Tratamiento de datos personales y Derechos Fundamentales*, Madrid: Dykinson, 2009, 2nd ed., p. 24.

protection establishes rules for the use of all types of data, including the one already disclosed under the exception of privacy, or with the consent of the data subject.

Looking at the content of the right to a private life and the right to data protection, the last one is not the only right to be defended, but also the right to demand certain action from others.[62] It includes not only the right not to disclose personal data, but also the right to be informed about its use, the right to access to such data and the right to correct or delete it.

At the beginning, the right to data protection was understood as an element of the protection of private life.[63] It was developed as a separate concept in the mid-1960s in the United States as a consequence of the development of information processing technology.

The first laws on data protection were developed in the early 1970s with the first law adopted by the German State of Hessen in 1971 and followed by the first state-wide law, adopted by the Swedish Parliament in 1972.

3.2 Origins and development of right to data protection

As already mentioned, data protection (also called *habeas data* or informative self-determination)[64] as an independent right started to develop in the United States in the 1960s and in Europe, in the 1970s. This is the reason why it is not included as a separate right in the ECHR, but it was developed by the ECtHR as a result of the interpretation of the ECHR in a progressive, evolutionary and teleological way, considering it as a "living instrument" that must be analysed according to the actual conditions."[65] For the first time, data protection was recognised as a part of the right to private life in 1987 in the Judgment *Leander v Sweden.*[66]

Seeking to establish data protection rights as individual rights, the Committee of Ministers did not choose the possibility of signing additional protocol to the ECHR, but opted for an individual convention.

Thus with the technical developments and increased processing of personal data, the Committee of Ministers recognised the necessity of its

62 See ARENAS RAMIRO, Mónica, *El Derecho Fundamental a la protección...*, op. cit., p. 96.

63 See REBOLLO DELGADO, Lucrecio, *Vida privada y protección de datos en la Unión Europea*, Madrid: Dykinson S.L., 2008, p. 55–56, 223.

64 See DEL CASTILLO VÁZQUEZ, Isabel-Cecilia, *Protección de datos: cuestiones constitucionales y administrativas (el derecho a saber y la obligación de callar)*, Madrid: Civitas, 2007, p. 75.

65 THE LISBON NETWORK, "The Right to a Fair Trial: Analysis of the Condemnations of the Portuguese State due to the Violation of Article 6 of the European Convention on Human Rights", Council of Europe, 2008, accessed October 30, 2014, http://www.coe.int/t/dghl/cooperation/lisbonnetwork/Themis/ECHR/Paper4_en.asp.

66 EUROPEAN COURT OF HUMAN RIGHTS, "Case of Leander v Sweden", 1987, ECLI:CE:ECHR:1987:0326JUD000924881.

regulation and on January 28, 1981, the Convention for the Protection of Individuals with regard to Automatic Processing of Personal Data (hereinafter – Data Protection Convention) was opened for signature and came into force on October 1, 1985.

Though the Data Protection Convention does not explicitly exclude the processing of data by the police, in 1983 the Committee of Ministers established a working party to elaborate specific recommendations for the police on use of personal data. The Committee of Ministers finally adopted them on September 17, 1987 as Recommendation No. R (87) 15 of the Committee of Ministers to Member States, regulating the use of personal data in the police sector (hereinafter – Recommendation R (87)15).[67]

Within the European Communities, the process of regulation of data protection can be defined as bottom-up, because firstly, it was regulated by the secondary law and in primary law it was just mentioned.

With the enter into force of Lisbon Treaty, a new Article 16 of the TFEU directly establishes the individual right to personal data protection and specifies that relevant EU level rules must be approved and applied by the EU institutions and entities as well as by the Member States, while transferring such data and performing activities within the scope of EU law. It also includes institutional provision, establishing that the accomplishment of this regulation must be controlled by independent authorities.

Article 8 of the EU Charter envisages that personal data can be processed only with the consent of the subject of the data or on the basis specifically established by the law, and in any case it is possible only for specific purposes. The consent must be explicit or tacit, reasonably concrete, given by a person with legal capacity, without pressure and with information relating to the consequences.[68] Equally, as in the case of privacy, some legal limitations of the right to data protection are possible according to Article 52(1). That was also confirmed by the CJEU in case C-291/12, where it was said that both the right to privacy and the right to data protection "are not absolute rights, but must be considered in relation to their function in society".[69]

67 "Data protection", Compilation of Council of Europe texts, accessed October 30, 2014, http://www.coe.int/t/dghl/standardsetting/dataprotection/dataprotcompil_en.pdf.

68 See EUROPEAN UNION AGENCY FOR FUNDAMENTAL RIGHTS, COUNCIL OF EUROPE, *Handbook on European Data Protection Law*, 2014, p. 56, accessed October 30, 2017, http://fra.europa.eu/en/publication/2014/handbook-european-data-protection-law

69 COURT OF JUSTICE OF THE EUROPEAN UNION, "Judgement of the Court (Fourth Chamber) of 17 October 2013 in Case C-291/12", paragraph 33, ECLI:EU:C:2013:670. In the same judgment it was stated that taking both face images and fingerprints for the issuing of identity documents is proportional to the objective of preventing the falsification of passports, and does not mean bigger interference in the right to privacy and to data protection.

Establishment of the fundamental right to data protection at EU level means an obligation to assess it (as any other fundamental right) before adopting any European legislation. For this purpose the Commission has elaborated "Operational Guidance on taking account of Fundamental Rights in Commission Impact Assessments."[70]

The following subsections are dedicated to European legal instruments applicable to data processed by the police.

3.3 *Data Protection Convention (CETS 108)*

The Data Protection Convention was the first obligatory instrument on this issue, establishing its basic principles, but on the other hand, it is criticised for being a legal basis with indirect application that needs further development at national level.[71]

Article 2 entails the scope of the Data Protection Convention as "Automated personal data files and the automatic processing of personal data in the public and private sectors."[72] Implementing it at national level, the States have the possibility:

- To limit this scope;
- To expand it to groups of persons, companies, etc. (despite the fact whether they have a status of legal person or not);
- To apply it to non-automated data processing.

Article 5 foresees the main principles – the conditions for automated data processing:

- Accuracy – a controller must have reasonable certainty about data quality and reliability. For example, in the case *Khelili v Switzerland* the ECtHR recognised that inclusion of the definition of "prostitute", only on the basis of deduction from information on a calling card,[73] is not a sufficient background for its maintenance in the database and "could damage Ms Khelili's reputation and make her day-to-day life more

70 EUROPEAN COMMISSION, "Commission Staff Working Paper Operational Guidance on taking account of Fundamental Rights in Commission Impact Assessments", SEC(2011) 567 final, accessed November 14, 2017, http://ec.europa.eu/justice/fundamental-rights/files/operational-guidance_en.pdf.

71 GUASCH PORTAS, Vicente, *Las transferencias internacionales de datos en la normativa española y comunitaria*, Madrid: Boletín Oficial del Estado y Agencia Española de Protección de Datos, 2014, p. 25.

72 "Details of Treaty No. 108", Council of Europe, accessed November 3, 2014, http://conventions.coe.int/Treaty/en/Treaties/Html/108.htm.

73 "Nice, pretty woman, late thirties, would like to meet a man to have a drink together or go out from time to time. Tel. no. ..."

problematic, given that the data contained in the police records might be transferred to the authorities."[74]

- Lawfulness – law has to envisage data processing in a clear and comprehensive manner.[75]
- Specified and legitimate purposes – as explained in the Handbook on European Data Protection Law, "Every new purpose for processing data must have its own particular legal basis and cannot rely on the fact that the data were initially acquired or processed for another legitimate purpose."[76] It must be subject to necessity.[77]
- Relevancy – amount of data and their categories have to be proportionate to their purposes, without including unnecessary data.
- Limited storage – only for the time that is necessary and proportional to the purpose for which it was collected and in any case there shall be time limit.[78]
- Fair processing – society, in reasonable terms, shall be provided with information about lawful and transparent data processing and with a copy of the file concerned.[79]
- Depersonalisation – when it is no longer required for the purposes that it was stored, and for proper data control.

Great importance has Article 6, which permits the processing of special data categories (racial origin, political opinions or religious or other beliefs, as well as personal data concerning health or sex life and criminal convictions), but only with safeguards established in national law.

Comparing the possibilities of derogations from provisions of the Data Protection Convention established in its Articles 5, 6 and 8 (a person's access to his or her data) and the limitation of the right to privacy, envisaged in Article 8(2) of the ECHR, some of the bases coincide and some are different.

As a result of this comparison, it can be said that the scope of limitations of data protection is more narrow than that of limitations of privacy; as in the case of data protection only monetary interests figure instead of the broad concept of economic well-being; and instead of the prevention of disorder or crime only the suppression of criminal offences.

74 EUROPEAN COURT OF HUMAN RIGHTS, "Affaire Khelili v Suisse", 2011, paragraph 63–64, ECLI:CE:ECHR:2011:1018JUD001618807.

75 ECtHR in case *Rotaru v. Romania* concluded that the law shall define the type of information, categories of peoples and circumstances that allows limitation.

76 EUROPEAN UNION AGENCY FOR FUNDAMENTAL RIGHTS, COUNCIL OF EUROPE, *Handbook on European Data…*, op. cit., p. 68.

77 In case *Leander v. Sweden* the ECtHR recognised proportionate secret check of persons to be employed in posts related to national security.

78 See ETXEBERRÍA GURIDI, José Francisco, "La protección de los datos de ADN…", loc. cit., p. 114.

79 See EUROPEAN COURT OF HUMAN RIGHTS, "Case of K.H. and Others v. Slovakia", 2009, paragraph 47, ECLI:CE:ECHR:2009:0428JUD003288104.

Table 3.1 Limitations of the right to privacy (under the ECHR) and the right to data protection under the Data Protection Convention

Limitations of the right to privacy of the ECHR	*Limitations of the right to data protection of the Data Protection Convention*
National security	
Public safety	
Protection of the rights and freedoms of others	
Economic well-being of the country	Monetary interests of the state
Prevention of disorder or crime	Suppression of criminal offences
Protection of health or morals	Protecting the data subject

Article 12 also has great relevance in relation to the topic of this analysis. It establishes, as a general rule, no limitation of cross-border information transmission between parties to the Data Protection Convention and only two exceptions from this right are foreseen:

- When some categories of data are subject to specific protection by national law;
- In the case of onward transmission from a receiving party to a third state.

Article 2 of the Additional Protocol to the Convention for the Protection of Individuals with regard to Automatic Processing of Personal Data regarding supervisory authorities and trans-border data flows,[80] establishes the possibility of data transfer to a third state (not Party of the Data Protection Convention) only if it ensures satisfactory data protection level. The exceptions of this rule are the following: the interests of the subject of the data or public ones; special arrangements between the data controller and the receiving authority on application of adequate data protection.

Article 3 of the Data Protection Convention does not directly envisage that it is applied to data automatically processed by police and judicial authorities, but on the other hand, it foresees its application both for private and public authorities. As no exception is established in respect to application for police and judicial authorities, it can be presumed that without a special declaration of derogation from the State Party, the Data Protection Convention will be applied to those authorities.[81]

80 Opened for signature on November 8, 2001 and came into force on July 1, 2004. Not signed by Azerbaijan, Malta, San Marino and Slovenia. Not ratified yet by Belgium, Greece, Iceland, Italy, Norway, Russia, Turkey, the United Kingdom. See "Details of Treaty No. 108", loc. cit.

81 Similar conclusion is made in the Explanatory Memorandum to Recommendation No. R (87) 15 of the Committee of Ministers to member states regulating the use of personal data in the police sector, Council of Europe, accessed

3.4 Recommendation R (87)15

A working group consisting of experts from Belgium, France, Italy, the Netherlands, Portugal, Sweden, Switzerland and the United Kingdom elaborated the recommendations adopted on September 17, 1987 at the 410th meeting of the Ministers' Deputies as Recommendation R (87)15.

It established that, "The expression 'for police purposes' covers all the tasks which the police authorities must perform for the prevention and suppression of criminal offences and the maintenance of public order." Thus it also covers information processing and exchange.

Equally, as Data Protection Convention, Recommendation R (87)15 foresees the possibility of extending the application of the Recommendation to non-automated data processing as well as to groups of persons, associations, and so on, despite having legal personality or not.

Recommendation R (87)15 established 8 principles of data protection:

- The Independent supervisory authority must control data processing. It must be consulted before introducing new automatic processing methods and notified about permanent automated databases.
- Data can be collected only in order to prevent real danger or to suppress specific criminal offences and, as an exception, for other purposes foreseen by national law. Data collection on the basis of specific data is prohibited, except when it is indispensable for specific inquiry.
- Only accurate and necessary data must be stored. While storing data, it must be categorised by degree of reliability.
- It can be used exclusively for police purposes.
- Data can be transmitted to other police institutions only on the basis of a legitimate interest. Its transmission to other public bodies and private parties is subject to special conditions. International transmission is permitted only to police bodies and on the basis of national or international legal provisions or for the prevention of imminent danger or suppression of serious crime, and having reasoned request. Interconnection of databases is allowed under provisions of national legislation in general, or permission of the supervisory body for a particular case.
- Public information about the existence of databases and the right to access, rectification and appeal must be provided.
- The storage period cannot be longer than it is necessary for the purpose for which the data was stored.
- Proper secure measures of access, storage, communication and other processing shall be applied.

October 13, 2017, https://wcd.coe.int/ViewDoc.jsp?Ref=ExpRec(87)15&Language=lanEnglish&Ver=original&Site=CM&BackColorInternet=C3C3C3&BackColorIntranet=EDB021&BackColorLogged=F5D383

It reiterates some principles of the Data Protection Convention (such as definition of personal data, principle of data quality, use of special categories of data, data subject right to access, etc.) as it was thought that those members of the Council of Europe that had not ratified the Convention could be interested in joining and implementing this Recommendation.[82] Currently, all Members of the Council of Europe have ratified it, but at the moment of the adoption of Recommendations, the Data Protection Convention was only in force in France, Germany, Norway, Spain and Sweden, and very close to entering into force in the United Kingdom.[83]

On the other hand, being *soft law*,[84] Recommendation R(87)15 established a more ambitious data protection system, going beyond the European Convention on Data Protection and already in 1987 foreseeing supervising authorities that was only introduced to the Convention with the Additional protocol in 2001.

Although, as mentioned, Recommendation R(87)15 is *soft law*, the ECtHR gives it *ratio decidendi* in the case *S. and Marper v the United Kingdom* and states that principles foreseen in the European Convention on Data Protection and Recommendation R(87)15 are "core" and have to be "Consistently applied by the Contracting States in the police sector."[85]

3.5 EU regulation in force until 2018

Although police and judicial cooperation, including information exchange in the EU, can be counted for a few decades, common data protection rules in this area were approved only in 2008, as Framework Decision 2008/977/JHA. But due to new provisions on data protection brought about by the Lisbon Treaty, of May 27, 2016, Directive (EU) 2016/680 of the European Parliament and of the Council on the protection of natural persons with regard to the processing of personal data by competent authorities for the purpose of the prevention, investigation, detection or prosecution of criminal offences or the execution of criminal penalties, and on the free movement of such data, and repealing Council Framework Decision 2008/977/JHA (hereinafter – Directive 2016/680) was adopted. Its Article 59 foresees that Framework Decision 2008/977/JHA "is repealed with effect from 6th May 2018".

82 See GUTIÉRREZ ZARZA, Ángeles, "Conceptos básicos. Marco...", loc. cit., p. 78.

83 See "Details of Treaty No. 108", loc. cit.

84 LÓPEZ GUERRA describes "soft law" as international instruments that multilaterally are not binding, but in which parties express wishes or proposals how to regulate certain issues in the future. See LÓPEZ GUERRA, Luis, "*Soft law* y sus efectos en el ámbito del Derecho Europeo de los Derechos Humanos", in *Teoría y derecho. Revista de pensamiento jurídico*, 2012, 11, p. 151.

85 EUROPEAN COURT OF HUMAN RIGHTS, "Case of S and Marper v. the United Kingdom", 2008, paragraph 107, *loc. cit.* See LÓPEZ GUERRA, Luis, "*Soft law* y sus efectos...", loc. cit., p. 157–158.

Despite many deficiencies and grey areas of the Framework Decision, the importance of this legislative act is great, because until 2008, no other EU wide rules were limiting the powers of law enforcement authorities related to the access, processing or exchange of police information.[86]

3.5.1 Scope of application

Framework Decision 2008/977/JHA has received a lot of criticism due to being very watered down, with a limited application and leaving a patch system because at the very beginning of the text, in its recital 39, it is recognised that it shall not affect data protection provisions of the Europol, Eurojust, the SIS, Customs Information System and information exchange under Council Decision 2008/615/JHA of June 23, 2008 on the stepping up of cross-border cooperation, particularly in combating terrorism and cross-border crime and some other instruments. It is declared that the above-mentioned instruments have "a coherent set of rules" on data protection.

At the same time, data protection rules for other cooperation mechanisms are considered as not exhausted and can be applied only when they establish more restrictive rules than the Framework Decision 2008/977/JHA.[87]

One more exception is found in Article 1(4) where it is stated that it does not interfere in cases related to national security.

Besides, the Council of the European Union has decided that it will be applied only to cross-border information exchange (between the Member States, Member States and EU authorities or information systems), but not to internal information exchange within one Member State. On the one hand, it allows application within Member States a higher level of data protection (where it exists), but does not require raising it where the safeguards are lower.

As pointed out by Oubiña Barbolla, it gives double vision on the same data depending on its national or cross-border processing, and complicates the work of law enforcement officers who have to be always aware of which data protection rules have to be applied and makes protection weaker.[88]

3.5.2 Principles applied to data protection

Article 3(1) of the Framework Decision 2008/977/JHA establishes principles of lawfulness, proportionality and purpose saying that, "Personal data may

86 GUTIÉRREZ ZARZA, Ángeles, *Exchange of Information and Data Protection in Cross-Border Criminal Proceedings in Europe*, Berlin: Springer, 2015, p. 158.

87 See recital 40 of the Framework Decision 2008/977/JHA.

88 See OUBIÑA BARBOLLA, Sabela, "Cambio de enfoque en la cooperación judicial penal y policial en la UE en relación con la transmisión de datos personales: las nuevas propuestas normativas y la STJUE de 8 de abril de 2014", in COLOMER HERNÁNDEZ, Ignacio, OUBIÑA BARBOLLA, Sabela, *La transmisión de datos personales…*, op. cit. p. 83.

be collected by the competent authorities only for specified, explicit and legitimate purposes in the framework of their tasks and may be processed only for the same purpose for which data were collected."[89]

On the one hand, it envisages a strong relationship between data collection and purpose, but on the other hand, Article 3(2) foresees very flexible deviation from this general rule by permitting data processing for any purpose that is not incompatible with the original one if it is proportional and competent authority is authorised by law.[90]

Article 3(1) referring only to data collection principles enters, to some extent, into contradiction with Article 1 that foresees that the Framework Decision regulates entire processing of personal data. Principles established in Article 3(1) are applied for information that is collected for transmission to other Member States. But what if it has been collected for national use and then, just by coincidence, another Member States asks for it? In this case, primary purpose is not its transmission, so it seems that there is no obligation to apply Article 3(1) as collection of information for internal purposes falls out of the scope of the Framework Decision 2008/977/JHA.

Article 11 specifies three circumstances of further processing[91] of data, and foresees the fourth one as open to any other purposes, but with the requirement of the prior consent of the transmitting party or the subject of the data. Thus exceptions that seem to be very limited finally convert into almost infinite possibilities of data transmission and, as noticed by Oubiña Barbolla, totally disrespect the principle of purpose.[92]

Article 12 establishes the obligation of the receiving Member State to follow restrictions on data processing that are established in the national law of the transmitting Member State, and about which it has previously been informed. On the other hand, the transmitting Member State cannot ask for restrictions that would not be applied to its national competent institutions.

3.5.3 Regulation of data storage

Framework Decision 2008/977/EU foresees very diluted regulation of data storage. In its Article 5, a general rule of "appropriate time limits" is

89 OJ L 350, 30.12.2008, p. 65.

90 Data can be also used for historical, statistical and scientific purposes once it is depersonalised (made anonymous).

91 "1. The prevention, investigation, detection or prosecution of criminal offences or the execution of criminal penalties other than those for which they were transmitted or made available;

2. Other judicial and administrative proceedings directly related to the prevention, investigation, detection or prosecution of criminal offences or the execution of criminal penalties;

3. The prevention of an immediate and serious threat to public security."

OJ L 350, 30.12.2008, p. 67.

92 See OUBIÑA BARBOLLA, Sabela. "Cambio de enfoque en la cooperación ...", loc. cit., p. 87–88.

established; this indeed does not provide any clarity or safeguard. In Article 9 few details can be found:

- The transmitting authority can indicate storage time, which can be extended by the receiving Member State if it is still needed for on-going investigation, prosecution or enforcement of criminal penalties.
- If the transmitting authority does not give any indication, data can be stored according to the national provisions of the receiving Member State.

With the last provision, European legislators seem to accept possible refutable approach of the transmitting Member State, allowing that it does not indicate rules on personal data storage that could be treated as allowing of some negligence in data transmission. The transmitting Member State should be obliged to indicate storage and processing conditions and applicable restrictions for the receiving Member State. If obligation to provide such indications with every data transmission would be a disproportionate burden, a handbook with relevant data in relation to all Member States could be drafted.

3.5.4 Special categories of data

Another watered-down provision of Framework Decision 2008/977/JHA is the related to processing of special categories of data[93] that, according to Article 6, is allowed when it is strictly necessary and with adequate safeguards of national law. It would be understandable, to some extent, if Framework Decision 2008/977/JHA would be applicable to Europol instead of its own data protection regulation and the legislator would like to maintain already applicable provision on the possibility of including sensitive data into AWFs. But as it was mentioned, Framework Decision 2008/977/JHA is not applicable to Europol. In these circumstances, such a provision in *lex generalis* of data protection raises a lot of doubts. Besides, both expressions "strictly necessary" and "adequate safeguards" ideally need to be more precise and descriptive as data concerned can be the background for violation of the fundamental right of non-discrimination, and effectively mean the breach of the principle of legality.[94]

93 Racial or ethnic origin, political opinions, religious or philosophical beliefs or trade union membership and the processing of data concerning health or sex life.

94 See EUROPEAN ASSOCIATION FOR THE DEFENSE OF HUMAN RIGHTS AND EUROPEAN DIGITAL RIGHTS, "Report on Privacy and Personal Data Protection in the European Union", December 2009, p. 10, accessed October 13, 2017, http://www.ldh-france.org/IMG/pdf/legislation_Europeenne.pdf.

3.5.5 Personal data transfer to third countries, international organisation

Council Framework Decision 2008/977/JHA also allows controversially treated onwards data transfer to third states, or to international bodies and to private parties. On the one hand, the fact that this issue is not left without regulation can be valued positively; but then the question about necessity of onward transmission arises. As will be explained later, onward data transmission is permitted within the framework of Europol, i.e. Europol can transmit information received from Member State onward to third parties. Transmission is restricted only to third parties with whom Europol has an operation agreement (in the future there will be an agreement between the EU and third countries, or a decision by the European Commission on data protection adequacy) that allows personal data exchange and establishes at least basic data protection warranties.[95] Thus the question stands whether it is really indispensable to allow broader data transmission outside the EU as it is foreseen in the Framework Decision 2008/977/JHA. Of course, it makes sense in other areas to which Directive 95/46/EC of the European Parliament and of the Council of October 24, 1995 on the protection of individuals with regard to the processing of personal data and on the free movement of such data[96] is applied.[97] Leaving aside this question, Article 13 of the Council Framework Decision 2008/977/JHA establishes 4 conditions for onward data transmission:

a Purpose limitations – equal to general purpose of this legislative act, i.e. "prevention, investigation, detection or prosecution of criminal offences or the execution of criminal penalties";
b Such a purpose is a function of the receiving authority;
c Consent of Member State of data origin according to its law[98];
d Adequate level of data protection in the third party.

The notion of adequacy was undefined for a long, but the Advocate General Yves Bot, in Case C-362/14 considered that, "Although the English word 'adequate' may be understood, from a linguistic viewpoint, as

95 See Subsection 2.2 of Chapter IV.
96 OJ L 281, 23.11.1995, p. 31–50.
97 In this case, information can be transmitted to the State when a relevant decision on adequate data protection level is approved by the Commission. For the time being, the Commission has recognised the following states as having such an adequate data protection level: Andorra, Argentina, Canada, Faroe Islands, Guernsey, Isle of Man, Israel, Jersey, New Zealand, United States of America, Uruguay and Switzerland. But it is not applied so much to the area of police and judicial cooperation as in general.
98 Article 13(2) foresees an exception to this condition in cases "Essential for the prevention of an immediate and serious threat to public security of a Member State or a third State or to essential interests of a Member State and the prior consent cannot be obtained in good time".

designating a level of protection that is just satisfactory or sufficient, and thus as having a different semantic scope from the French word 'adéquat' ('appropriate'), the only criterion that must guide the interpretation of that word is the objective of attaining a high level of protection of fundamental rights, as required by Directive 95/46. Examination of the level of protection afforded by a third country must focus on two fundamental elements, namely the content of the applicable rules and the means of ensuring compliance with those rules."[99]

Article 14 of the Framework Decision 2008/977/JHA foresees onward transmission to private parties, but does not specify whether they can be only within the transmitting Member State or outside as well.

Article 14(1)c(ii)-(iv) entails transmission of data to private bodies when necessary for crime prevention, investigation, prosecution or execution of criminal penalty, protection of public security from imminent threat or individual rights from serious damage. Data transmission in such situations is justifiable. But it is not clear why data obtained by the competent authorities for crime prevention, investigation or prosecution purposes can be forwarded to private entities for broader purposes, including performing of their lawfully assigned tasks as established in Article 14(1)c(i).

3.5.6 *Other particularities*

Framework Decision 2008/977/JHA does not mention any difference in treatment and processing of data of different categories of persons, such as convicted persons, suspects, witnesses, victims and others. The processing of data of different categories of persons should be subject to different rules, especially in such questions as its storage or onward transmission to third or private parties.[100]

In respect of the control of data protection, application of relevant national provisions has to be supervised by the independent supervisory authorities of each country. Such authorities shall have powers to investigate, intervene and participate in legal proceedings. In this regard, O'Neill makes a very precise observation that supervisory authorities shall have security clearances as data exchanged that is subject to control, can be classified or belong to special categories.[101]

99 COURT OF JUSTICE OF THE EUROPEAN UNION, "Opinion of Advocate General Bot delivered on 23 September 2015 in Case C-362/14", paragraphs 142, 143, ECLI:EU:C:2015:627.

100 For critics of the Council Decision 2008/977/JHA also see GUASCH PORTAS, Vicente, *Las transferencias internacionales de datos…*, op. cit., p. 290–292.

101 O'NEILL, Maria, "The Issue of Data Protection and Data Security in the (Pre-Lisbon) EU Third Pillar", in *Journal of Contemporary European Research*, vol. 6, issue 2, 2010, p. 228, accessed July 15, 2014, http://www.jcer.net/ojs/index.php/jcer/article/view/264/206.

Summing up weak points of the Framework Decision 2008/977/JHA, it is the example of the result of legislative procedure under the Third Pillar, where the unanimity of all Member States was required, and when the final result seems to be more of a "wish list" of exceptions and flexible provisions than aspiration to proper and comprehensive data protection.

As pointed out, in the Third opinion of the European Data Protection Supervisor of the Proposal on the draft of this Framework Decision, "The decision-making procedure cannot justify a lowest common denominator approach that would hinder the fundamental rights of EU citizens as well as hamper the efficiency of law enforcement"[102] and "In many aspects the revised proposal even falls below the level of protection afforded by Convention 108. It is thus both unsatisfactory and will even be incompatible with international obligations of the Member States."[103]

But even this absolutely weak data protection regime had not been implemented in every Member State by the end of 2014, when there were still nine Member States that had not notified the Commission or the Council about transposition measures.[104]

As previously mentioned, with the entrance into force of the Treaty of Lisbon, the Commission took the initiative to revise the European data protection system and in 2012, presented a package of measures that have to substitute current weak regulations; this was approved in spring 2016.

3.6 EU regulation after 2018

A need for new data protection provisions were foreseen in the previously mentioned Article 16 and Declaration 21 of the Lisbon Treaty, stating that due to the specific nature of the police and judicial cooperation, separate data protection regulation in this area may be needed.[105] The need for such

102 OJ C 139, 23.6.2007, p.3.

103 OJ C 139, 23.6.2007, p.2.

In the same opinion, a very valuable example of the patchwork system created by the Council Framework Decision 2008/977/JHA is given:

"a law enforcement body at national or EU level, when dealing with a criminal file – consisting of information originating from various national, other Member States and EU authorities – would have to apply different processing rules for different pieces of information depending on whether: personal data have been collected domestically or not; each of the transmitting bodies has given its consent for the envisaged purpose; the storage is compliant with time limits laid down by applicable laws of each of the transmitting bodies; further processing restrictions requested by each of the transmitting bodies do not prohibit the processing; in case of a request from a third country, each transmitting body has given its consent according to its own evaluation of adequacy and/or international commitments. In addition, citizens' protection and rights will vary enormously and be subject to different broad derogations depending on the Member State where processing takes place."

104 Council document 11902/15, p. 4.

105 See OJ C 83, 30.3.2010, p. 345.

separate legislation was also reiterated in 2010 by the Commission in its Communication "A comprehensive approach on personal data protection in the European Union", emphasising that application to police and judicial cooperation in the criminal matters data protection regime equal to other areas could jeopardise police and judicial work.[106]

Bearing in mind new legislative framework and evaluation of the Framework Decision 2008/977/JHA, on January 25, 2012, the Commission adopted a data protection package:

- Communication from the Commission to the European Parliament, the Council, the European Economic and Social Committee and the Committee of the Regions "Safeguarding Privacy in a Connected World a European Data Protection Framework for the 21st Century"[107];
- Proposal for a Regulation of the European Parliament and of the Council on the protection of individuals with regard to the processing of personal data and on the free movement of such data[108];
- Proposal for a Directive of the European Parliament and of the Council on the protection of individuals with regard to the processing of personal data by competent authorities, for the purposes of prevention, investigation, detection or prosecution of criminal offences, or the execution of criminal penalties, and the free movement of such data[109] (hereinafter – Draft Data Protection Directive).

The Commission with the Draft Data Protection Directive aimed "to ensure a consistent, high level of data protection to enhance mutual trust

106 See COM(2010) 609 final, p. 14; GONZÁLEZ FUSTER, Gloria, "Protección de datos y cooperación policial y judicial en material penal en la UE", in PÉREZ GIL, Julio, *El proceso penal en la sociedad…*, op. cit., p. 595.

107 EUROPEAN COMMISSION, "Communication from the Commission to the European Parliament, the Council, the European Economic and Social Committee and the Committee of the Regions – Safeguarding Privacy in a Connected World: A European Data Protection Framework for the 21st Century", COM (2012) 9 final, accessed September 21, 2017, http://eur-lex.europa.eu/LexUriServ/LexUriServ.do?uri=COM:2012:0009:FIN:EN:PDF.

108 EUROPEAN COMMISSION, "Proposal for a Regulation of the European Parliament and of the Council on the protection of individuals with regard to the processing of personal data and on the free movement of such data (General Data Protection Regulation)", COM(2012) 11 final, accessed September 21, 2017, http://ec.europa.eu/justice/data-protection/document/review2012/com_2012_11_en.pdf.

109 EUROPEAN COMMISSION, "Proposal for a Directive of the European Parliament And of the Council on the protection of individuals with regard to the processing of personal data by competent authorities for the purposes of prevention, investigation, detection or prosecution of criminal offences or the execution of criminal penalties, and the free movement of such data", COM (2012) 10 final, accessed September 21, 2017, http://eur-lex.europa.eu/LexUriServ/LexUriServ.do?uri=COM:2012:0010:FIN:EN:PDF.

between police and judicial authorities of different Member States, thus contributing further to a free flow of data, and effective cooperation between police and judicial authorities."[110]

The main horizontal criticisms from the EDPS about the proposal concern the form of the legislative act – directive. The EDPS agreed that Declaration 21 had foreseen that for data protection in the area of police and judicial cooperation, special rules can be established, but it has not foreseen their legislative form. Therefore, the EDPS was of the opinion that the form of regulation would be much more effective than directive, as it would be the act of direct application and would not depend on implementation measures.

Additionally, it underlined that "whilst the law enforcement area requires some specific rules, every departure from the general data protection rules should be duly justified based on a proper balance between the public interest in law enforcement and citizens' fundamental rights."[111] The FRA acknowledged such a position and among other comments proposed explicit prohibition of the transmission of data to third states, where, on the basis of human rights records, it can be concluded that transferred data could be used to interfere in human rights.[112]

Bearing in mind that data protection is a fundamental right, it would be more reasonable to approve a directly applicable regulation, especially taking into account that the legislative procedure would be similar.

Directive 2016/680 was adopted on April 27, 2016 and according to its Article 63 the deadline for its transposition is foreseen May 6, 2018. On the same day was approved Regulation (EU) 2016/679 of the European Parliament and of the Council on the protection of natural persons with regard to the processing of personal data and on the free movement of such data, and repealing Directive 95/46/EC (General Data Protection Regulation) (hereinafter – Regulation 2016/679) that repeals Directive 95/46/EC from May 25, 2018.

The expression "free movement of data" in the title deserves special attention. On the one hand it reflects the principle of availability and on the other, it gives a sensation that data exchange becomes new liberty within the EU, as free movement of persons, goods, services and capitals.

110 EUROPEAN COMMISSION, "Communication from the Commission to the European Parliament, the Council, the European Economic and Social Committee and the Committee of the Regions – Safeguarding Privacy in a Connected…" *loc. cit.*, p. 10.

111 EUROPEAN DATA PROTECTION SUPERVISOR, "Executive summary EDPS Opinion of 7 March 2012 on the data protection reform package", OJ, C 192, 30.6.2012, p. 8

112 EUROPEAN UNION AGENCY FOR FUNDAMENTAL RIGHTS, "Opinion of the European Union Agency for Fundamental Rights on the proposed data protection reform package", 2012, p. 11, accessed September 22, 2017, http://fra.europa.eu/en/opinion/2012/fra-opinion-proposed-eu-data-protection-reform-package.

The title of Article 20 of the Directive 2016/680 "Data protection by design and by default" has become a catchphrase and means a development of technical and organisational tools (design) to ensure the application of the principles of data protection, and processing only such data that is absolutely necessary (protection by default with the exception of necessity).

3.6.1 *Scope of application*

Regarding territorial scope, the Directive 2016/680 is not applicable to Denmark, Ireland and the United Kingdom, but as it forms a part of a development of the Schengen acquis, it is applicable to Liechtenstein, Norway and Switzerland.

In relation to the subject matter, the European Commission had proposed applying the EU data protection rules, not only to cross-border information exchange, but also to intra-state.[113] However, some Member States[114] questioned whether this does not contradict the principle of subsidiarity. Finally, Article 1 makes reference "to the processing of the personal data by competent authorities" not specifying only cross-border information exchange.

Although the title of the Directive 2016/680 refers only to prevention, detection, investigation, prosecution of criminal offences and execution of criminal penalties, its Recital 7 and Article 1 also include the safeguards "against and the prevention of threats to public security". However, equal to the Framework Decision 2008/977/JHA, it is not applied to activities concerning national security. On the one hand, it is understandable due to particularities of national security, but on the other hand, in some Member States the same data can be treated as related to the national security and in others – as data related to crime prosecution.

The new Directive also entails its relationship with other legal acts that regulate data processing in police and judicial cooperation. Thus, Recital 94 specifies that EU acts adopted before the Directive should remain unaffected, but the Commission has to evaluate their conformity with Article 16 of the TFEU. According to Article 2, it is not applied for data processing in activities that are outside of the scope of the law of the EU, or that are carried out by the institutions and other entities of the EU.

Thus, for the moment the problem of the "patchwork" data protection system still exists, as the same data will fall under different data protection systems, depending on the channel used (Europol, direct bilateral exchange, etc.) and the authorities involved (national or EU, such as Europol, Eurojust).

The definition of personal data is slightly modified in comparison with the definition foreseen by the Framework Decision 2008/977/JHA, but only by a more explicit explanation of what has to be understood as "identifier".

113 It had been initially included in the draft of the Framework Decision as well, but rejected by the Member States.

114 Croatia, Czech Republic, Denmark, Romania, Slovenia, Sweden.

In both legal acts, the processing is understood as any operation or set of operations carried out by automatic means or not, such as collection, recording, organisation, storage, adaptation or alteration, retrieval, consultation, use, disclosure by transmission, dissemination or otherwise making available, alignment or combination, erasure or destruction. The Directive 2016/680 adds "structuring" and skips "blocking".

3.6.2 Principles applied to data processing

Chapter II of the Directive 2016/680 foresees the following principles of data protection: fair and lawful processing, collection for legitimate and specified purposes, proportionality for the purpose, accuracy, security, storage limitation, distinction between different data subjects, responsibility of controllers. Recital 26 also mentions principle of transparency towards data subject.

Although data shall be collected for specific purpose, Article 4(2) foresees the possibility of its further processing for other purposes and not only by the original controller, but also other controllers. Such other purposes shall be legitimated by the EU or national law and the controller shall be authorised to process the data for such purposes.

Unlike the Framework Decision 2008/977/JHA, the Directive 2016/680 establishes the principle of distinction between different data subjects, such as suspects, convicted, victims, witnesses, contacts and associates. Nevertheless, it cannot be treated fully as a principle because such division shall be made "where applicable and as far as possible". This brings us to unequal treatment of the same data subject across the EU, because in one Member State, the personal data of a victim and of a witness can be held separately and processed differently from the data of a convicted person or suspect, whereas in another Member State, there is no unconditional prohibition to keep and process data of different categories of data subjects in the same way.

The principle of data accuracy is broadened and includes the obligation to make distinctions between personal data based on facts and that based on personal assessments.

3.6.3 Special categories of data

The proposal of the Directive presented by the Commission envisaged, as a general rule, the prohibition of processing of the categories of data "revealing race or ethnic origin, political opinions, religion or beliefs, trade-union membership, of genetic data or of data concerning health or sex life", leaving three exceptions: when it is authorised by the law, in case of necessity to protect the vital interests of natural person, when the data has been made public by the data subject.

Nevertheless, the adopted Directive 2016/680 does not explicitly refer to the prohibition to process special categories of data, but establish the same cases of its processing as in the aforementioned Commission's proposal.

On the other hand, the list of special categories of personal data in Article 10 of the Directive 2016/680 is broader than in the Framework Decision 2008/977/JHA and includes "racial or ethnic origin, political opinions, religious or philosophical beliefs, or trade union membership, and the processing of genetic data, biometric data for the purpose of uniquely identifying a natural person, data concerning health or data concerning a natural person's sex life or sexual orientation". Thus, in comparison with the Framework Decision 2008/977/JHA, the new data protection instrument includes genetic and biometric data and data about sexual orientation. In any case, Article 11(2) of the new legislation foresees that decisions of competent authority adverse to the data subject, cannot be taken only on the basis of special categories of data.

3.6.4 Personal data transfer to third countries, international organisation or onwards transmission

When it comes to data transfer to third states, international organisation, Article 35 of the Directive 2016/680 entails four requirements and three of them are similar to those established by Article 13 of the Framework Decision 2008/977/JHA:

a Transmission for the purposes established by the Directive (prevention, detection, investigation, prosecution of criminal offences, execution of criminal penalties, including the safeguards against and the prevention of threats to public security).
b Transmission to authorities that are controllers and carry out functions related to the above mentioned purposes (in exceptional cases and by fulfilling special conditions established in the Article 39(1) data can be transmitted to competent authority that is not controller).
c In case of onward transmission – prior authorisation by the Member State of origin (in both cases with the exception of situations of necessity to prevent "an immediate and serious threat to public security of a Member State or a third country or to essential interests of a Member State and the prior authorisation cannot be obtained in good time". In these cases the Member State of origin (its competent authority) has to be informed without delays.)

The fourth requirement, although in its nature it is also similar, differs in its content. Framework Decision 2008/977/JHA establishes that the third state or international organisation has to ensure an adequate protection level for data processing or there is a basis of derogation as established in Article 13(3). Directive 2016/680 refers to one of three alternatives:

- The existence of the Commission's decision on adequacy of data protection in a third country or international organisation. Such a decision can be issued in respect to a third country, a territory or one or more specified sectors within third country. As it is explained in the recital 67, the Commission has to "take into account how a particular third country respects the rule of law, access to justice as well as international human rights norms and standards and its general and sectoral law, including legislation concerning public security, defence and national security, as well as public order and criminal law. The adoption of an adequacy decision with regard to a territory or a specified sector in a third country should take into account clear and objective criteria, such as specific processing activities and the scope of applicable legal standards and legislation in force in the third country. The third country should offer guarantees ensuring an adequate level of protection essentially equivalent to that ensured within the Union."

- Existence of appropriate safeguards in the third country. In this case a Member State that transfers data to third state or international organisation has to be sure that safeguards of data protection are established in binding legislation or to assess that such safeguards exist. In the latter case, as there is no reference to binding legislation, the controller that transfers personal data to a third country or international organisation has to inform its supervisory authority and to document a transfer. According to the Framework Decision 2008/977/JHA, this situation is treated as derogation, something exceptional and additionally, the legislation of the Member State that makes an evaluation has to comprehend such safeguards as adequate.
- The situation of transfer of data falls under one of the situations of derogations from previous alternatives. Article 38 establishes five derogations: four general ones (protection of vital interests of person (data subject or not), immediate and serious threat to public security, in individual cases for the purposes of this Directive or for processing of legal claims for the same purposes) and one that depends on its establishment in national legislation (safeguarding of legitimate interests of data subject) and is equal to one foreseen in the Framework Decision 2008/977/JHA.

In all cases of derogation the proportionality between public interests and protection of fundamental rights has to be evaluated. Equally, as in the previous alternative, such a transfer has to be documented.

In respect to onward data transmission, Directive 2016/680 is not very clear. The only reference to it is made in Article 35(1)e that establishes an obligation to get authorisation of the Member State that has made the "original transfer" in case of onward transmission "to another third country or international organisation". The term of "Member State of original transfer" is not very clear. For example, if Italy shares the data with Spain, Spain with Morocco and Morocco with Tunisia, who is the Member State of original transfer? Italy or Spain? If it is Spain (original transfer from the EU to third country), Italy loses the control of its data. If it is Italy (the first Member

State that has made the transfer in general), there has to be a mechanism that ensures that the third country or international organisation that will make onward transmission knows that the Member State of origin is not Spain, but Italy. This process can be more complicated if data has gone through three or more Member States before being transmitted to a third country or international organisation.

3.6.5 *Other particularities*

Section 3 of Chapter IV of the Directive 2016/680 establishes an obligation of each controller to designate a data protection officer with the exception for courts, but only if national legislation provides a possibility for such exclusion.

Regarding supervision authorities, it is essential to endow them with powers to investigate, correct and advise. Besides, supervisory authorities have to be consulted before processing the creation of new filing systems when it carries high risk to fundamental rights.

4. Brief summary and evaluation

As stated by the European Parliament, after the terrorist attacks of September 11, two tendencies in information processing and exchange can be distinguished, "Data processing in EU internal security policies is increasingly moving towards mass processing [...] Automated processing and datamining with the aim of profiling categories of person."[115]

It has shaken the sensitive balance between security and fundamental rights, moving towards the overweighting of security. Some fundamental rights can be indirectly affected by this tendency, but on the right to data protection it can have a direct effect.

In these circumstances effective data protection systems have even greater importance, including at least common minimum standards applied in all states under consideration as well as independent and effective supervision systems.

Both have been attempted within the frameworks of the Council of Europe and of the EU. Bearing in mind the wide membership of the Council of Europe, regulation does not reach much farther than the establishment of general principles. On the other hand, the EU has intended to carry this out with more precise obligations. The first attempt as Framework Decision 2008/977/JHA was quite perfunctory due to the need of unanimity of all Member States.

115 EUROPEAN PARLIAMENT, Directorate General for Internal Policies, "Developing an EU Internal Security Strategy, fighting terrorism and organized crime" (study, 2011), p. 102, accessed August 13, 2017, http://www.europarl.europa.eu/document/activities/cont/201206/20120627ATT47777/20120627ATT47777EN.pdf.

Nevertheless in 2011 the JHA Council stated that "privacy and security are possible and that there is no need to choose between being free and being safe and that the necessary and appropriate processing of personal data is vital in keeping the public safe."[116] and the EU institutions opted for comprehensive approach on data protection that resulted into Regulation 2016/679 and Directive 2016/680.

The elimination of different data protection regimes for national and cross-border data processing, the obligation to establish data protection officers within each data controller, the detailed regulation of supervisory authorities and reference to different categories of data subjects should be mentioned as very positive novelties.

Among disadvantages, first of all the scope of application of the Directive that excludes earlier adopted information exchange tools and EU agencies, and keeps a "patchwork" or "kaleidoscope" system of data protection should be pointed out.[117] Despite mentioning a need to distinguish between data of different data subjects, it sounds like a recommendation and not an unconditional obligation. Lack of regulation of data storage terms and revision as well as ambiguous and scarce regulation of onward data transmission are also very serious defects.

Bibliography

ÁLVAREZ CARO, M., 2015, *Derecho al olvido en Internet: el Nuevo paradigm de la privacidad en la era digital*, Madrid: Universidad San Pablo.

ARENAS RAMIRO, M., 2000, *El Derecho Fundamental a la protección de datos personales en Europa*, Valencia: Tirant lo Blanch.

BARONA VILAR, S., 2004, *Seguridad, celeridad y justicia penal*, Valencia: Tirant lo Blanch.

BOEHM, F. and COLE, M. D., 2014, "Data Retention after the Judgement of the Court of Justice of the European Union" Available at: https://www.janalbrecht.eu/fileadmin/material/Dokumente/Boehm_Cole_-_Data_Retention_Study - June 2014.pdf (accessed September 14, 2017).

COUNCIL OF THE EUROPEAN UNION, 2010, "Internal Security Strategy for the European Union. Towards a European security model", p. 19. Available at: https://www. consilium.europa.eu/uedocs/cms_data/librairie/PDF/QC3010313ENC.pdf (accessed September 2014).

COUNCIL OF THE EUROPEAN UNION, 2016, "Meeting of the Consultative Forum of Prosecutors General and Directors of Public Prosecutions of the

116 Council conclusions on the Communication from the Commission to the European Parliament and the Council – a comprehensive approach on personal data protection in the European Union 3071st JUSTICE and HOME AFFAIRS Council meeting Brussels, 24 and 25 February 2011.

117 PEYROU, Sylvie, "Algunas reflexiones sobre la protección de datos en el ELSJ o la crónica de una esperanza frustrada" in GOIZUETA VÉRTIZ, Juana; GONZÁLEZ MURUA, Ana Rosa and PARIENTE DE PRADA, Iñaki, *El Espacio de Libertad, Seguridad…*, op. cit., p. 148–149.

Member States of the European Union and Workshop on Data Retention in the Fight Against Serious Crime: The Way Forward". Eurojust, The Hague, 10–11 December 2015. Conclusions"; 5930/16. Available at: http://data.consilium.europa.eu/doc/document/ST-5930-2016-INIT/en/pdf (accessed November 14, 2017).

COURT OF JUSTICE OF THE EUROPEAN UNION, 2008, "Judgment of the Court (Grand Chamber) of 29 January 2008 in Case C-275/06", ECLI:EU:C:2008:54.

COURT OF JUSTICE OF THE EUROPEAN UNION, 2010, "Judgment of the Court (Sixth Chamber) of 4 February 2010 – European Commission v Kingdom of Sweden (Case C-185/09)", ECLI:EU:C:2010:59.

COURT OF JUSTICE OF THE EUROPEAN UNION, 2010, "Judgment of the Court (Grand Chamber) of November 9 2010 in Joined Cases C-92/09 and C-93/09", ECLI:EU:C:2010:662.

COURT OF JUSTICE OF THE EUROPEAN UNION, 2013, "Judgment of the Court (Fourth Chamber) of 30 May 2013 – European Commission v Kingdom of Sweden (Case C-270/11)", ECLI:EU:C:2013:339.

COURT OF JUSTICE OF THE EUROPEAN UNION, 2013, "Judgement of the Court (Fourth Chamber) of 17 October 2013 in Case C-291/12", ECLI:EU:C:2013:670.

COURT OF JUSTICE OF THE EUROPEAN UNION, 2014, "Judgement of the Court (Grand Chamber) of 8 April 2014 in Joined Cases C-293/12 and C-594/12", ECLI:EU:C:2014:238.

COURT OF JUSTICE OF THE EUROPEAN UNION, 2014, "Opinion 2/13 of the Court (Full Court) 18 December 2014", ECLI:EU:C:2014:2475.

COURT OF JUSTICE OF THE EUROPEAN UNION, 2015, "Opinion of Advocate General Bot delivered on 23 September 2015 in Case C-362/14", ECLI:EU:C:2015:627.

DEL CASTILLO VÁZQUEZ, I. C., 2007, *Protección de datos: cuestiones constitucionales y administrativas (el derecho a saber y la obligación de callar)*, Madrid: Civitas.

EUROPEAN ASSOCIATION FOR THE DEFENSE OF HUMAN RIGHTS and EUROPEAN DIGITAL RIGHTS, 2009, "Report on Privacy and Personal Data Protection in the European Union". Available at: http://www.ldh-france.org/IMG/pdf /legislation_Europeenne.pdf (accessed October 13, 2017).

EUROPEAN UNION AGENCY FOR FUNDAMENTAL RIGHTS, 2012, "Opinion of the European Union Agency for Fundamental Rights on the proposed data protection reform package". Available at: http://fra.europa.eu/en/opinion/2012/fra-opinion-proposed-eu-data-protection-reform-package (accessed September 22, 2017).

EUROPEAN UNION AGENCY FOR FUNDAMENTAL RIGHTS, COUNCIL OF EUROPE, 2014, *Handbook on European Data Protection Law*. Available at: http://fra.europa.eu/en/publication/2014/handbook-european-data-protection-law (accessed October 30, 2017).

ETXEBERRÍA GURIDI, J. F., 2000, *Los análisis de ADN y su aplicación al proceso penal*, Granada: Comares.

ETXEBERRÍA GURIDI, J. F., 2008, "Los derechos fundamentales en el espacio de libertad, seguridad y justicia penal", in *Revista Vasca de Administración Pública*, vol. 82, no. 2; p. 103–164.

ETXEBERRÍA GURIDI, J. F., 2013, "La protección de los datos de ADN en la Unión Europea y en España", in CABEZUDO BAJO, M. J.; *Las bases de datos* *policiales de ADN ¿Son una herramienta realmente eficaz en la lucha contra la criminalidad grave nacional y transfornteriza?*Madrid: Dykinson, S.L., p. 95–119.

ETXEBERRÍA GURIDI, J. F., 2014, "La identificación de personas mediante pruebas genéticas y bancos de perfiles de ADN: evolución normativa en el contexto europeo" in *Revista de Derecho y Genoma Humano*, p. 135–156.

EUROPEAN COMMISSION, 2011, "Commission Staff Working Paper Operational Guidance on taking account of Fundamental Rights in Commission Impact Assessments", SEC(2011) 567 final. Available at: http://ec.europa.eu/justice/fundamental-rights/files/operational-guidance_en.pdf (accessed November 14, 2017).

EUROPEAN COMMISSION, 2012, "Communication from the Commission to the European Parliament, the Council, the European Economic and Social Committee and the Committee of the Regions – Safeguarding Privacy in a Connected World A European Data Protection Framework for the 21st Century", COM(2012) 9 final. Available at: http://eur-lex.europa.eu/LexUriServ/LexUriServ.do?uri=COM:2012:0009:FIN:EN:PDF (accessed September 21, 2017).

EUROPEAN COMMISSION, 2012, "Proposal for a Directive of the European Parliament And of the Council on the protection of individuals with regard to the processing of personal data by competent authorities for the purposes of prevention, investigation, detection or prosecution of criminal offences or the execution of criminal penalties, and the free movement of such data", COM(2012) 10 final. Available at: http://eur-lex.europa.eu/LexUriServ/LexUriServ.do?uri=COM:2012:0010:FIN:EN:PDF (accessed September 21, 2017).

EUROPEAN COMMISSION, 2012, "Proposal for a Regulation of the European Parliament and of the Council on the protection of individuals with regard to the processing of personal data and on the free movement of such data (General Data Protection Regulation)", COM(2012) 11 final. Available at: http://ec.europa.eu/justice/data-protection/document/review2012/com_2012_11_en.pdf (accessed September 21, 2017).

EUROPEAN COMMISSION, 2015, "Communication from the Commission to the European Parliament, the Council, the European Economic and Social Committee and the Committee of the Regions – The European Agenda on Security", COM (2015) 185 final. Available at: http://eur-lex.europa.eu/legal-content/EN/TXT/?uri=COM:2015:0185:FIN (accessed September 22, 2017).

EUROPEAN COMMISSION, 2015, "Report from the Commission to the European Parliament, the Council, the European Economic and Social Committee and the Committee of the Regions – 2014 Report on the Application of the EU Charter of Fundamental Rights", COM(2015) 191. Available at: http://eur-lex.europa.eu/legal-content/en/TXT/?uri=CELEX:52015DC0191 (accessed September 22, 2017).

EUROPEAN COMMISSION, 2015, "Special Eurobarometer 432. "Europeans' attitude towards security". Available at: http://ec.europa.eu/public_opinion /archives/ebs/ebs_432_sum_en.pdf (accessed July 10, 2017).

EUROPEAN COURT OF HUMAN RIGHTS, 1979, "Case of the Sunday Times v United Kingdom", ECLI:CE:ECHR:1979:0426JUD000653874.

EUROPEAN COURT OF HUMAN RIGHTS, 1987, "Case of Leander v Sweden", ECLI:CE:ECHR:1987:0326JUD000924881.

EUROPEAN COURT OF HUMAN RIGHTS, 1992, "Case of Niemetz v Germany", ECLI:CE:ECHR:1992:1216JUD001371088.

EUROPEAN COURT OF HUMAN RIGHTS, 2000, "Case of Amann v Switzerland", ECLI:CE:ECHR:2000:0216JUD002779895.

EUROPEAN COURT OF HUMAN RIGHTS, 2000, "Case of Rotaru v Romania", ECLI:CE:ECHR:2000:0504JUD002834195.

EUROPEAN COURT OF HUMAN RIGHTS, 2003, "Case of Perry v the United Kingdom", ECLI:CE:ECHR:2003:0717JUD006373700.

EUROPEAN COURT OF HUMAN RIGHTS, 2005, "Affaire Vetter v. France", ECLI:CE:ECHR:2005:0531JUD005984200.

EUROPEAN COURT OF HUMAN RIGHTS, 2008, "Case of S and Marper v. the United Kingdom", ECLI:CE:ECHR:2008:1204JUD003056204.

EUROPEAN COURT OF HUMAN RIGHTS, 2009, "Affaire B.B. v France", ECLI: CE:ECHR:2009:1217JUD000533506.

EUROPEAN COURT OF HUMAN RIGHTS, 2009, "Case of K.H. and Others v. Slovakia", ECLI:CE:ECHR:2009:0428JUD003288104.

EUROPEAN COURT OF HUMAN RIGHTS, 2011, "Affaire Khelili v Suisse", ECLI:CE:ECHR:2011:1018JUD001618807.

EUROPEAN PARLIAMENT, DIRECTORATE GENERAL FOR INTERNAL POLICIES, 2011, "Developing an EU Internal Security Strategy, fighting terrorism and organized crime", p. 102, Available at: http://www.europarl.europa.eu/document/activities/cont/201206/20120627ATT47777/20120627ATT47777EN.pdf (accessed August 13, 2017).

GALÁN MUÑOZ, A., 2015, "La protección de datos de carácter personal en los tratamientos destinados a la prevención, investigación y represión de delitos: hacia una nueva orientación de la política criminal de la Unión Europea", in COLOMER HERNÁNDEZ, I. and OUBIÑA BARBOLLA, S., *La transmisión de datos personales en el seno de la cooperación judicial penal y policial en la Unión Europea*", Navarra: Aranzadi, p. 37–70.

GALPIN, R., 2012, "Norway prepares for killings anniversary", BBC, July 20. Available at: http://www.bbc.com/news/world-europe-18791448 (accessed July 22, 2017).

GARRIGA DOMÍNGUEZ, A., 2009, *Tratamiento de datos personales y Derechos Fundamentales*, 2nd ed., Madrid: Dykinson.

GONZÁLEZ FUSTER,G., 2012, "Protección de datos y cooperación policial y judicial en material penal en la UE"; in PÉREZ GIL, J., *El proceso penal en la sociedad de la información*, Madrid: La Ley, p. 587–604.

GUARDIAN, 2015, "David Cameron: British bill of rights will 'safeguard legacy' of Magna Carta". Available at: http://www.theguardian.com/law/2015/jun/15/david-cameron-british-bill-of-rights-safeguard-legacy-magna-carta (accessed September 8, 2017).

GUASCH PORTAS, V., 2014, *Las transferencias internacionales de datos en la normativa española y comunitaria*, Madrid:Estado y Agencia Española de Protección de Datos.

GUTIÉRREZ ZARZA, Á., 2012, "Conceptos básicos. Marco legal europeo sobre protección de datos en materia penal"; in GUTIÉRREZ ZARZA, Á., *Nuevas tecnologías, protección de datos personales y proceso penal*, Madrid: La Ley.

GUTIÉRREZ ZARZA, Á., 2015, *Exchange of Information and Data Protection in Cross-Border Criminal Proceedings in Europe*, Berlin: Springer.

HUFFINGTON POST, 2015, "David Cameron Won't Rule Out Ditching European Convention On Human Rights". Available at: http://www.huffingtonpost.co.uk/2015/06/03/prime-ministers-questions-human-rights-bill-of-rights-refuse-rule-out_n_7501460.html (accessed September 8, 2015)

HUSTINX, P., 2015, "EU Data Protection Law: The Review of Directive 95/46/EC and the Proposed General Data Protection Regulation". Available at: https://

secure.edps.europa.eu/EDPSWEB/webdav/site/mySite/shared/Documents/EDPS/Publications/Speeches/2014/14-09-15_Article_EUI_EN.pdf (accessed January 20, 2017).

JIMÉNEZ FORTEA, F. J., 2009, "La respuesta procesal penal al terrorismo en el marco de la Unión Europea: un ejemplo de cooperación judicial penal y policial"; in CALDERÓN CUADRADO, M.P. and IGLESIAS BUHIGUES, J. L., *El Espacio Europeo de Libertad, Seguridad y Justicia: Avances y Derechos Fundamentales en Materia Procesal*, Navarra: Aranzadi.

JIMÉNEZ FORTEA, F. J., 2011, "De la restricción de derechos a un "derecho procesal del enemigo", in MASFERRER, A., *Estado de Derecho y derechos fundamentales en la lucha contra el terrorismo*, Navarra: Aranzadi, p. 611–644.

KOKOTT, J. and SOBOTTA, C., 2013, "The distinction between Privacy and Data Protection in the Jurisprudence of the CJEU and the ECtHR", *International Data Privacy Law*, vol. 3, no 4, p. 222–228. Available at: http://idpl.oxfordjournals.org/content/3/4/222.full.pdf+html (accessed August 20, 2017).

LÓPEZ GUERRA, L., 2012, "Soft law y sus efectos en el ámbito del Derecho Europeo de los Derechos Humanos"; in *Teoría y derecho. Revista de pensamiento jurídico*; vol. 11; p. 151–167.

LÓPEZ ORTEGA, J. J., 2014, "La tutela de la intimidad genética en la investigación penal. A propósito de la STC 199/2013 y de la SAP Sevilla 650/2013", in CASADO, M. and GUILLÉN, M., *ADN forence: problemas éticos y jurídicos*, Barcelona: Universitat de Barcelona, p. 99–118.

MCGHEE, D., 2010, *Security, Citizenship and Human Rights. Shared Values in Uncertain Times*, Hampshire: Palgrave McMilan.

MORENO CATENA, V., 2010, "La garantía de los derechos fundamentales durante la investigación penal" in *Cuadernos Penales José María LIDÓN*, p. 13–54.

O'NEILL, M., 2010, "The Issue of Data Protection and Data Security in the (Pre-Lisbon) EU Third Pillar", in *Journal of Contemporary European Research*, vol. 6, issue 2, p. 228. Available at: http://www.jcer.net/ojs/index.php/jcer/article/view/264/206 (accessed July 15, 2014).

OUBIÑA BARBOLLA, S., 2015, "Cambio de enfoque en la cooperación judicial penal y policial en la UE en relación con la transmisión de datos personales: las nuevas propuestas normativas y la STJUE de 8 de abril de 2014", in COLOMER HERNÁNDEZ, I. and OUBIÑA BARBOLLA, S., *La transmisión de datos personales en el seno de la cooperación judicial penal y policial en la Unión Europea*", Navarra: Aranzadi, p. 71–123.

PEYROU, S., 2013, "Algunas reflexiones sobre la protección de datos en el ELSJ o la crónica de una esperanza frustrada", GOIZUETA VÉRTIZ, J., GONZÁLEZ MURUA, A. R. and PARIENTE DE PRADA, I.; *El Espacio de Libertad, Seguridad y Justicia: Schengen y Protección de Datos*, Pamplona: Aranzadi S.A.

REBOLLO DELGADO, L., 2008, *Vida privada y protección de datos en la Unión Europea*; Madrid: Dykinson S.L.

SANTOLAYA, P., 2014, "Limitación de la aplicación de las restricciones de derechos. Art. 18 CEDH", in GARCÍA ROCA, J. and SANTOYALA, P., *La Europa de los Derechos. EL Convenio Europeo de Derechos Humanos*, 3rd ed., Madrid: Centro de Estudios Políticos y Constitucionales, p. 657–667.

SOLETO MUÑOZ, H., 2014, "DNA data in criminal procedure in the European fundamental rights context", in *Recent Advances in DNA and Gene Sequences*, vol. 8, issue 2, p. 91–97.

SOLETO MUÑOZ, H., 2015, *Garantías y errores en la investigación penal. Ciencia versus memoria*, Valencia: Tirant lo Blanch.

SOLETO MUÑOZ, H., 2016, "Parámetros europeos de limitación de Derechos Fundamentales en el uso de datos de ADN en el proceso penal", *Revista general de Derecho procesal*, no. 38; p. 1–27.

SOLETO MUÑOZ, H. and FIODOROVA, A., 2014, "DNA and Law Enforcement in the European Union: Tools and Human Rights Protection", in *Ultrecht Law Review*, vol. 10, issue 1; p. 154–158.

LISBON NETWORK, 2014, "The Right to a Fair Trial: Analysis of the Condemnations of the Portuguese State due to the Violation of Article 6 of the European Convention on Human Rights". Available at: https://www.coe.int/t/dghl/cooperation/lisbonnetwork/Themis/ECHR/Paper4_en.asp (accessed October 30, 2017).

UK Conservatives, 2014, "Protecting Human Rights in the UK. The Conservatives' proposal for changing Britain's Human Rights Laws". Available at: https://www.conservatives.com/~/media/files/downloadable%20Files/human_rights.pdf (accessed August 13, 2017).

VALLÉS CAUSADA, L. M., 2012, "Usos delictivos no comunicativos de la telefonía móvil: una excepción a la protección del artículo 18.3 CE?"; in PÉREZ GIL, J. *El proceso penal en la sociedad de la información: las nuevas tecnologías para investigar y probar el delito*, Madrid: La Ley, p. 219–240.

VALLÉS CAUSADA, L.M., 2012, "La Policía judicial en la obtención de inteligencia sobre comunicaciones electrónicas para el proceso penal" (PhD diss., National Distance Education University, 2012). Available at: http://e-spacio.uned.es/fez/eserv/tesisuned:Derecho-Lmvalles/Documento.pdf (accessed March 20, 2017)

4 Information exchange under Schengen acquis

Despite the general EEC commitment to create the area of free movement, some Member States had not been able to agree on the abolition of checks on common borders for more than 25 years and it impelled intergovernmental initiatives out of the EEC framework. On July 13, 1984, France and Germany signed the Experimental Convention of Saarbrücken.[1] As the Benelux countries (Belgium, Luxemburg and the Netherlands) had created a Customs Union and had abolished checks at their borders in 1962, on December 12, 1984, the Governments of the Benelux Economic Union signed a Memorandum expressing interest in the Experimental Convention of Saarbrücken. Thus, it was rewritten and resulted in the Agreement between the Governments of the States of the Benelux Economic Union, the Federal Republic of Germany and the French Republic on the gradual abolition of checks at their common borders (hereinafter – the Schengen Agreement), signed on June 14, 1985 in Schengen – a Luxembourg border town with France and Germany.

The Schengen Agreement was largely negotiated by the ministers of transport and foreign affairs. However, an envoy from the German Ministry of Interior raised the question of compensatory measures for security in the case of abolition of the control of internal borders that was part of the security mechanism. Therefore, Article 9 of the Schengen Agreement established that in the short term, the exchange of information shall be improved, but still on the basis of national law. Its Article 18 foresaw that for long-term measures "parties shall open discussions, in particular on the following

1 See CALESINI, Giovanni, *European Police Law Handbook*, Roma: Laurus Robuffo, 2007, p. 20–21; SCHATTENBERG, Bernd, "Schengen Information System: Privacy and Legal Protection" in SCHERMERS, Henry G., FLINTERMAN, Cees, KELLERMANN, Alfred E. et al. *Free Movement of Persons in Europe*, Dordrecht: Martinus Nijhoff, 1993, p. 43; DONAIRE VILLA, Francisco Javier, *La Constitución y el Acervo de Schengen*, Valencia: Tirant lo Blanch, 2002, p. 44.

matters, account being taken of the results of the short-term measures: (a) drawing up arrangements for police cooperation on crime prevention and investigation; (b) examining any difficulties that may arise in applying agreements on international judicial assistance and extradition, in order to determine the most appropriate solutions for improving cooperation between the Parties in those fields; (c) seeking means to combat crime jointly, inter alia, by studying the possibility of introducing a right of hot pursuit for police officers, taking into account existing means of communication and international judicial assistance."

Long-term measures were supposed to be in force and applied by January 1, 1990,[2] but due to the merging of the Federal Republic of Germany and the German Democratic Republic, and the opening of their inner borders on November 9, 1989, the signing of the CISA had been postponed[3] and eventually took place after the foreseen deadline on June 19, 1990. On June 25, 1991, Portugal and Spain also joined the Schengen Agreement and the CISA.

Implementing the CISA, checks at common borders was finally abolished on March 26, 1995.

In parallel, the signing of the Schengen Agreement was immediately echoed at the Fountainebleau European Council on June 25–26, 1985, asking the Council and the Member States to study the measures for the abolition of "all police and customs formalities for people crossing intra-Community frontiers".[4]

Further steps towards the abolition of checks on internal borders of EEC were made with the Single European Act[5] signed on February 17[6] and 28,[7] 1986. It supplemented the TEEC by the new Article 8A, foreseeing that the area without internal frontiers had to be established over a period expiring on December 31, 1992. The Justice and Home Affairs policy introduced by the Maastricht Treaty meant that real free movement would be reached with the accompanying measures in this area.[8]

But it was not enough, and finally a Protocol of the Amsterdam Treaty, signed on October 2 1997, incorporated the Schengen acquis[9] into the EU

2 See DONAIRE VIILA, Francisco Javier, *La Constitución y el Acervo de Schengen*, op. cit., p. 46.
3 See SCHATTENBERG, Bernd, "Schengen Information System...", loc. cit., p. 44.
4 Conclusions of the European Council 22/84, Fontainebleau, June, 28, 1984.
5 OJ L 169, 29.6.1987, p. 1–19.
6 Signed by Belgium, Germany, France, Ireland, Luxembourg, Netherlands, Portugal, Spain and United Kingdom.
7 Signed by Denmark, Greece and Italy.
8 See ALVARGONZÁLES SAN MARTÍN, Fernando, "Hacia un nuevo escenario de cooperación en asuntos de justicia e interior". In MINISTERIO DEL INTERIOR, *El espacio europeo de libertad, seguridad y justicia*, Madrid: Secretaría General Técnica, 2000, p. 15.
9 According to the Annex of the Protocol integrating the Schengen acquis into the framework of the European Union of the Amsterdam Treaty, Schengen acquis consists of:

legal system. That meant the application of the existing regulation of the Schengen area to all EEC and putting all future measures related to the Schengen area under EU decision-making procedures.[10] The Schengen acquis[11] became a part of EU law on May 1, 1999 with the coming into force of the Treaty of Amsterdam.

Notwithstanding, membership of the EU did not mean automatic membership of the Schengen area. According to Article 2(2) of the Protocol integrating the Schengen acquis into the framework of the EU, EU Member States not signatories to the Schengen Agreement and the CISA could become members of the Schengen area only after a unanimous decision of the Council. Such a decision was (and still is) based on evaluations of the conditions that every country must meet before joining the Schengen area: application of common visa issuing policy; common asylum granting policy; operational readiness of N-SIS and its interoperability with C-SIS; police cooperation; protection of external land, sea and air borders and data protection.

At the end of 2017 the Schengen area consisted of 26 countries: 22 EU Member States and 4 non-Member States and with the special partial Schengen acquis application to Ireland and access of Bulgaria, Romania and the United Kingdom to SIS II.

In the same way as Ireland, according to Article 4 of the Protocol integrating the Schengen acquis into the framework of the European Union of the Amsterdam Treaty, the United Kingdom was not bound by the Schengen acquis, but had a right at any time to request partial or entire participation in it.

- "the Schengen Agreement,
- the CISA,
- Agreements on Accession,
- Decisions and declarations of Executive Committee, acts adopted for the implementation of the Convention by the organs upon which the Executive Committee has conferred decision-making powers."

10 At the time of the adoption of Schengen acquis (due to the existence of the three pillars system abolished by the Lisbon Treaty) different EU / ECEC decision-making processes were applied. The Schengen acquis provisions on free movement of persons fell under the Community decision-making (former First Pillar) and supposed to be regulated by the TEEC and the police and judicial cooperation fell under intergovernmental cooperation (former Third Pillar) and supposed to be regulated by the TEU. Precise EU / EEC legal basis for the different provisions of the Schengen acquis was determined by the Council Decision 1999/436/EC determining, in conformity with the relevant provisions of the Treaty establishing the European Community and the Treaty on European Union, the legal basis for each of the provisions or decisions which constitute the Schengen acquis, OJ L 176, 10.7.1999, p. 17–29.

11 The Schengen acquis as referred to in Article 1(2) of Council Decision 1999/435/EC of May 20, 1999, OJ L 239, 22.9.2000, p. 1–473.

Table 4.1 Belonging to EU and Schengen area

EU Member State and member of Schengen area	*EU Member State, but not member of Schengen area*	*Member of Schengen area, but not member of EU*
Austria, Belgium, Czech Republic, Denmark, Estonia, Finland, France, Germany, Greece, Hungary, Italy, Latvia, Lithuania, Luxembourg, Malta, Netherlands, Poland, Portugal, Slovakia, Slovenia, Spain, Sweden.	Bulgaria,[12] Croatia,[13] Cyprus, Ireland,[14] Romania,[15] United Kingdom.	Iceland,[16] Liechtenstein,[17] Norway, Switzerland.[18]

12 But already using SIS II.

13 But already using SIS II.

14 According to Article 4 of the *Protocol integrating the Schengen acquis into the framework of the European Union of the Amsterdam Treaty*, Ireland is not bound by the Schengen acquis, but has a right at any time to request partial or entire participation in it. Such participation has to be approved by the unanimity of the Council (OJ C 340, 10.11.1997, p. 95). According to the requests of the Government of Ireland, of June 16, 2000 and November 1, 2001, to participate in certain provisions of the Schengen acquis and the *Council Decision 2002/192/EC concerning Ireland's request to take part in some of the provisions* of the Schengen acquis it is participating in the police and judicial cooperation established by the Schengen acquis, except cross-border hot pursuit and surveillance (OJ L 64, 7.3.2002, p. 20–24). Nevertheless, those provisions of the CISA are still not applicable in Ireland and it is currently in the process of preparatory activities to connect to the SIS II.

15 But already using SIS II.

16 On July 12, 1957 Iceland, Norway, Sweden, Finland and Denmark signed Convention on the Abolition of Passport Controls at Intra-Nordic borders and created Nordic Union of Passports. As Sweden, Finland and Denmark joined the EU and the Schengen area, in order to assure further functioning of the Nordic Union of Passport, on December 19, 1996, the Agreement between the 13 Member States of the European Union, signatories to the Schengen Agreements and the Republic of Iceland and the Kingdom of Norway was signed. Therefore, Article 6 of the Protocol integrating the Schengen acquis into the framework of the European Union of the Amsterdam Treaty established that Iceland and Norway shall be associated with the implementation of the Schengen acquis and its further development. It was reflected in the Council Decision 1999/437/EC of 17 May 1999 on certain arrangements for the application of the Agreement concluded by the Council of the European Union and the Republic of Iceland and the Kingdom of Norway concerning the association of those two States with the implementation, application and development of the Schengen acquis (OJ L 176, 10.07.1999, p. 1–16).

17 On 28 February 2008 a Protocol between the European Union, the European Community, the Swiss Confederation and the Principality of Liechtenstein on the accession of the Principality of Liechtenstein to the Agreement between the European Union, the European Community and the Swiss Confederation on the Swiss Confederation's association with the implementation, application and development of the Schengen acquis was signed (OJ L 160, 18.6.2011, p. 21–36).

18 On 26 October 2004 Agreement between the European Union, the European Community and the Swiss Confederation on the Swiss Confederation's association with the implementation, application and development of the Schengen acquis was signed (OJ L 53, 27.2.2008, p. 52–79).

According to the request of May 22, 1999 (and its further modifications on July 9 and October 6) and to the Council Decision 2000/365/EC concerning the request of the United Kingdom of Great Britain and Northern Ireland to take part in some of the provisions of the Schengen acquis, the United Kingdom participates in police and judicial cooperation, except cross-border hot pursuit.[19] On December 22, 2004, the Council Decision 2004/926/EC on putting into effect of parts of the Schengen acquis by the United Kingdom of Great Britain and Northern Ireland was adopted.[20] Partial participation in the application of the CISA also entailed the United Kingdom in the participation of the SIS, with regard to criminal law and policing information; but due to the difficulties with N.SIS, it was decided to wait until the second generation of the SIS is created and to join that.[21] The United Kingdom became operational in April 2015 and was granted access to SIS II, but as it does not apply Schengen acquis with respect to free movement, it has not abolished its border controls.

Going back to compensatory measures, the CISA foresaw a long list of security measures applied together with the abolishment of common borders, most of them in the Title III "Police and Security":

- Information exchange and / or police assistance (Articles 39, 46);
- Cross-border surveillance (Article 40);
- Cross-border pursuit (Article 41);
- Liaison officers (Articles 7, 47);
- Supplement to the existing acts on mutual assistance (Articles 48–53, 59–66);
- Transfer of the enforcement of criminal judgments (Articles 67–69);
- Cooperation in combating drug trafficking (Articles 70–76);
- Cooperation in control of firearms and ammunition (Articles 77–91).

But due to the quick development of cooperation in the area of justice in the last 15 years, the CISA's provisions related to mutual assistance, enforcement of criminal judgements, combating drug trafficking and controlling firearms and ammunition were derogated by more comprehensive and modern EU legislation.[22]

19 OJ L 131, 1.6.2000, p. 43–47. See FERNÁNDEZ-PITA Y GONZÁLEZ, Rafael, "El Tratado de Ámsterdam y el Acervo de Schengen" in MINISTERIO DEL INTERIOR. *El espacio Europeo de libertad, seguridad y justicia*, Madrid: Secretaría General Técnica, 2000, p. 93.

20 OJ L 395, 31.12.2004, p. 70–80.

21 See HOUSE OF LORDS, EUROPEAN UNION COMMITTEE "Schengen Information System II (SIS II)", Report with Evidence, 2007, p. 12–14, accessed October 18, 2017, http://www.publications.parliament.uk/pa/ld200607/ldselect/ldeucom/49/49.pdf.

22 Articles 59 to 66 of the CISA were replaced by the Council Framework Decision 2002/584/JHA of the European arrest warrant and the surrender procedures between Member States (hereinafter – Framework Decision 2002/584/JHA), OJ

Another and more important compensatory measure, the SIS, was established by Title VI of the CISA. It was described as a system of obligatory use on external borders and a direct tool for the law enforcement authorities and for criminal investigation.

1 Schengen Information System

Before abolishment of the control of common borders, each country was responsible only for its own security and chose who it was going to send information about real or potential threats.[23] But within the obligation to contribute to the security of all the Schengen area, as noticed by Hreblay, the privileged partner does not exist anymore as all of them have be equally aware of all threats and receive the same information.[24]

With the abolishment of common borders, more thorough control of persons and goods and additional measures were moved to the external border. The tool that is obligatory in the protection of external borders (land, air and maritime) and issuing visas for the Schengen area is SIS. It can also be used in internal checks performed by the law enforcement agencies when a person or an object raises suspicions.

SIS is one of very few centralised systems of the EU and the biggest in terms of content. It allows the sharing of information about persons that can be a threat to internal security or need special attention and the objects of crime or investigation.

The core element of the SIS is alert – a set of data on a person or object that requires special attention from the authorities performing the check. An alert sent by one country is automatically seen by the rest of the partners.

1.1 From SIS to SIS II

The SIS is based on interaction of the central system C.SIS[25] and national systems N.SIS of every Schengen state.

L 190, 18.7.2002, p. 1–18. Articles 77 to 81 and Articles 83 to 90 of the implementing Convention have been superseded by the Council Directive 91/447/EEC on control of the acquisition and possession of weapons, OJ L 256, 13.9.1991, p. 51–58, with the following amendments (OJ L 179 of 8.7.2008, p. 5–11). Its Articles 49(a), 52, 53 and 73 have been substituted by the Convention established by the Council in accordance with Article 34 of the Treaty on European Union, on Mutual Assistance in Criminal Matters between the Member States of the European Union, OJ L 197, 12.7.2000, p. 3–23.

23 See HREBLAY, Vendelin, *Les accords de Schengen: Origine, Fonctionnement, Avenir*, Brussels: Bruylant, 1998, p. 149–150.

24 Ibid.

25 It is located in Strasbourg (France) with the back-up system in Sankt Johann im Pongau near Salzburg (Austria).

Competent authorities of the countries insert alerts on persons or goods into their N.SIS from where they are transmitted to C.SIS which has a mirror image of all existing alerts of the states. Other countries, performing checks, directly consult the C.SIS (and not the N.SIS of other countries) and see all alerts issued in the Schengen area. When a performed check of a person or object results in a match with the alert (a so called "hit"), the system automatically informs the issuing country and national SIRENE[26] offices of the searching and issuing states. SIRENE offices continue with the exchange of all necessary information (confirmation of alert, sending of additional information that could help to identify the person or object).

Information exchange through the SIS started in 1995 between seven countries: Belgium, France, Germany, Luxembourg, the Netherlands, Portugal and Spain.

Since then, the SIS has technically been extended to SIS I+ in order to cope with the connection of 18 states. Fifteen countries[27] were connected in 2000, with the perspective to connect United Kingdom, Ireland and keeping one extra connection. The accession of ten new countries to the EU in 2004 also meant the future extension of the Schengen area and a need for a technical solution for the connection of new countries to the SIS.[28]

On September 28, 2001, the Commission decided to take responsibility both for the funding of SIS II and for the development work.[29]

Council Decision 2001/886/JHA of December 6, 2001 on the development of the second generation Schengen Information System (SIS II)[30] foresaw a deadline for its development – December 2006. Besides the technological development of the central system and the need to adjust or to create new N.SIS, there was a need to adopt new legislation under the EU decision-making process in order to replace Articles 92–119 of the CISA.

The legislative basis for the operation of the SIS II was adopted in 2006–2007: Regulation (EC) No 1987/2006 of the European Parliament and of the Council on the establishment, operation and use of the second generation Schengen Information System (SIS II)[31] (hereinafter – Regulation 1987/2006) and Council Decision 2007/533/JHA of June 12, 2007 on the establishment,

26 SIRENE – Supplementary Information Request at the National Entries, Supplément d'Information Requis a l'Entrée Nationale.

27 Austria, Belgium, Denmark, Finland, France, Germany, Greece, Iceland, Italy, Luxembourg, The Netherlands, Norway, Portugal, Spain and Sweden.

28 The idea of the SIS II was already raised in 1997 in the Decision of the Executive Committee of 7 October 1997 on the development of the SIS (SCH/Com-ex (97) 24) (OJ L 239, 22.9.2000, p. 442).

29 EUROPEAN COMMISSION, "Communication from the Commission to the Council and the European Parliament – Development of the Schengen Information System II", COM(2001)720 final, p. 4, accessed November 16, 2017, http://eur-lex.europa.eu/legal-content/EN/ALL/?uri=CELEX:52001DC0720.

30 OJ L 328, 13.12.2001, p. 1–3.

31 OJ L 381, 28.12.2006, p. 4–23.

operation and use of the second generation Schengen Information System (SIS II)[32] (hereinafter – Decision 2007/533/JHA).

Art. 1 of the above mentioned legal instruments establishes that the purpose of the SIS II is "to ensure a high level of security within the area of freedom, security and justice of the European Union including the maintenance of public security and public policy and the safeguarding of security in the territories of the Member States [...]."

Although SIS II legal bases were adopted with only a slight delay, the technical development of the SIS II faced much bigger problems and setbacks. As noticed by the European Court of Audits, "The delay and overspending resulted partly from the challenging governance context which limited the Commission's ability to address operational issues and partly from weaknesses in the Commission's management."[33]

This delay meant keeping EU "newcomers" outside the Schengen area and the creation of a two speed EU. Nevertheless, the Presidency Conclusions of the European Council held on June 15 and 16, 2006 expressed a political commitment to enlarge the Schengen area in April 2007.[34]

In mid-2006, Portuguese Presidency of the Council of the European Union came up with the proposal of an interim solution to use a clone of the Portuguese system to connect new countries to SIS and then make the transition of all to SIS II.

On December 5, 2006 the Council adopted the Conclusions on the SIS II, the SIS 1+ and the enlargement of the Schengen area.[35] It was agreed to apply the intermediate solution proposed by Portuguese experts, "A clone of the Portuguese national system developed by experts from Portugal's Border and Foreign Service of the Ministry of Internal Affairs, relied upon extending the current version of the SIS to enable access by the new member states"[36] named "SISone4all". It allowed nine of ten newcomers to the EU

32 OJ L 205, 7.8.2007, p. 85–106.

33 EUROPEAN COURT OF AUDITS, "Lessons from the European Commission's development of the second generation Schengen Information System (SIS II)" (Special Report, 2013), p. 6, accessed October 16, 2017, http://www.eca.europa.eu/Lists/ECADocuments/SR14_03/SR14_03_EN.pdf.

34 COUNCIL OF THE EUROPEAN UNION, "Brussels European Council 15/16 June 2006. Presidency Conclusions", 10633/1/06, p. 2, accessed November 18, 2017, http://data.consilium.europa.eu/doc/document/ST-10633-2006-REV-1/en/pdf.

35 COUNCIL OF THE EUROPEAN UNION, "SIS II, SIS I + and the enlargement of the Schengen area – Council Conclusions", 16391/1/06, accessed November 18, 2017, http://data.consilium.europa.eu/doc/document/ST-16391-2006-REV-1/en/pdf.

36 PARKIN, Joanna, "Difficult Road to the Schengen Information System II: the legacy of 'laboratories' and the cost for fundamental rights and the rule of law" Report, Centre for European Policy Studies, June 17, 2011, p. 3, accessed September 9, 2017, http://www.ceps.eu/book/schengen-information-system-and-eu-rule-law, p. 6.

(Czech Republic, Estonia, Hungary, Latvia, Lithuania, Malta, Poland, Slovakia and Slovenia) to lift checks on their internal borders.[37]

As pointed out by Bertozzi, "Thanks to the Portuguese idea, mutual distrust and anger did not degenerate into outspoken hostility to Schengen enlargement, which would have created an irreparable rift between the old Schengen member states and 'Schengen candidates'."[38]

On December 6, 2007, the Council Decision 2007/801/EC on the full application of the provisions of the Schengen acquis in the Czech Republic, the Republic of Estonia, the Republic of Latvia, the Republic of Lithuania, the Republic of Hungary, the Republic of Malta, the Republic of Poland, the Republic of Slovenia and the Slovak Republic[39] was adopted. It allowed their internal land and sea borders' control to be abolished on December 21, 2007 and internal air borders control on March 30, 2008.

SIS II finally became operational on April 9, 2013[40] with a 6-year delay and exceeding the primary budget eight times.[41]

1.2 Content and functionalities of SIS II

Regulation 1987/2006 and Decision 2007/533/JHA (equally as the CISA) foresee six categories of alerts that can be inserted and consulted in the system:

- Alerts on persons wanted for arrest and extradition / surrender;
- Alerts on refusing the entry of third country nationals;
- Alerts on missing persons, including those that need special protection;
- Alerts on persons sought to assist with a judicial procedure;
- Alerts on persons and objects for discreet or specific checks;
- Alerts on objects for seizure or use as evidence in criminal proceedings.

37 The only "newcomer", Cyprus, declared that its national N.SIS would not be ready for 2007, and it would join SIS II directly.

38 BERTOZZI, Stefano, "Schengen: Achievements and Challenges in Managing and Area Encompassing 3.6 million km^2", Working document no. 284, Centre for European Policy Study, 2008, p. 16–22, accessed October 12, 2017, http://papers.ssrn.com/sol3/papers. cfm?abstract_id=1337624.

39 OJ L 323, 8.12.2007, p. 34–35.

40 It was established in the Council Decision 2013/157/EU fixing the date of application of Decision 2007/533/JHA on the establishment, operation and use of the second generation Schengen Information System (SIS II) (OJ L 87, 23.3.2013, p. 8–9), and Council Decision 2012/158/EU fixing the date of application of Regulation (EC) No 1987/2006 of the European Parliament and of the Council on the establishment, operation and use of the second generation Schengen Information System (SIS II) (OJ L 87, 23.3.2013, p. 10–11).

41 Final budget was around 500 million euro for the whole project, including 189 million euro for the new C.SIS II instead of initially estimated 23 million euro. See EUROPEAN COURT OF AUDITS, "Lessons from the European Commission's...", loc. cit., p. 33–49.

Based on the experience from SIS, new legislation foresees some improvements:

- Direct insertion of the European Arrest Warrant;
- Possibility to include biometric data (photographs and fingerprints);
- Extension of the list of objects that can be subject to alert (aircrafts, boats, industrial equipment, and so on);
- Possibility to make a link between different alerts;
- Access of Eurojust and vehicle registration service providers.

1.2.1 *Alerts: content and issuing rules*

As mentioned before, SIS contains alerts on persons and objects that are somehow linked to the alternation of internal security. That shows erroneous judgement in the common understanding that SIS contains information about everyone. It is true that everybody can be subject to alert, despite his or her citizenship, but a person has to be linked to some police investigation or judicial procedure, violation of rules allowing entrance into the Schengen area or in need of special attention due to his/her age or physical or mental state. At the end of 2016, SIS II contained 70,827,959 alerts, but only 1,17 per cent of them (830,002) were alerts on persons.[42]

The first type of alerts in SIS II is on persons wanted for arrest for extradition or surrender purposes. The difference between regulation of the CISA and the Decision 2007/533/JHA is that in the CISA, only extradition procedure was mentioned and in the Decision 2007/533/JHA both extradition and surrender under the European Arrest Warrant are foreseen. Despite this change, the factual content of this category of alerts remains the same.

During the drafting and approval of the CISA, the process known as extradition procedure was based on the principle of mutual assistance between involved states and meant the application of more complicated national procedure to surround a person wanted by another country[43] (involving judicial authorities and authorities of the executive power[44]). The evolution of judicial cooperation in the EU resulted in moving from the principle of mutual assistance to mutual recognition[45]; that means

42 EU LISA, "SIS II – 2016 statistics", February, 2017, p. 9–10, accessed October 17, 2017, http://www.eulisa.europa.eu/Publications/Reports/SIS%20II%20-%20Statistics%202016.pdf.

43 As extradition very often is accompanied by the detention of a wanted person, it is always based on a judicial decision.

44 Such as Ministries of Justice or even Ministries of Foreign Affairs or governmental committees or councils.

45 As mentioned before, for the first time mutual recognition was established by the Tampere Conclusions of the Tampere European Council October 15–16, 1999 that were adopted in order to implement measures of the judicial and police cooperation established by the Amsterdam Treaty:

recognition of the judicial decision of other EU Member States without complicated internal procedure.[46] The first instrument of practical implementation of the mutual recognition was the Council Framework Decision 2002/584/JHA of June 13, 2002 on the European arrest warrant and the surrender procedures between Member States (hereinafter – Decision 2002/584/JHA),[47] applied instead of the extradition procedure among EU Member States since January 1, 2004.[48] Due to that Chapter V of the Council Decision 2007/533/JHA refers to the persons wanted for arrest for surrender (among the EU Member States members of Schengen area) or extradition purposes (when one of the parties (issuing or requested) is a member of the Schengen zone, but not one applying the Framework Decision 2002/584/JHA).

In both cases, the basis for the alert is a decision of the judicial authority. The novelty is that according to Article 27 of the Decision 2007/533/JHA, in the case of surrender on the basis of the EAO, an alert issuing Member State is also obliged to enter in the SIS II a copy of such EAO.

For example, border guards or police authorities perform checks in the airport and detect that a person is subject to alert on surrender or extradition. A copy of the EAO permits immediate access to both information on crime committed, and the judicial authority that has issued the EAO. The issuing country will receive a notification that its alert resulted in a hit in another country and SIRENE offices of both countries will exchange all necessary information for the decision on further actions. If the issuing state confirms its need for a person's surrender or extradition, then execution of the European Arrest Order or extradition request, according to the national law of the requested state, will take place.

"Enhanced mutual recognition of judicial decisions and judgements and the necessary approximation of legislation would facilitate co-operation between authorities and the judicial protection of individual rights. The European Council therefore endorses the principle of mutual recognition which, in its view, should become the cornerstone of judicial co-operation in both civil and criminal matters within the Union. The principle should apply both to judgements and to other decisions of judicial authorities. [...] the formal extradition procedure should be abolished among the Member States as far as persons are concerned who are fleeing from justice after having been finally sentenced, and replaced by a simple transfer of such persons [...]".

46 Although it is not an automatic recognition of a foreign judicial decision, but it does mean the application of simplified checking procedure by the national judicial authority (only judicial, without involving of the Executive Power) if a foreign judicial decision is not opposed to national judicial system and legislation.

47 OJ L 190, 18.7.2002, p. 1–18.

48 Further modified by the Council Framework Decision 2009/299/JHA of February 26, 2009 amending Framework Decisions 2002/584/JHA, 2005/214/JHA, 2006/783/JHA, 2008/909/JHA and 2008/947/JHA, thereby enhancing the procedural rights of persons and fostering the application of the principle of mutual recognition to decisions rendered in the absence of the person concerned at the trial. OJ L 81, 27.3.2009, p. 24–36.

In the case of alerts on surrender, it is very important to take into consideration the principle *non bis in idem*. As a general rule, Member States assess the existence of *non bis in idem* only at the stage of the authorisation of surrender procedure to the requesting Member State, i.e. when a person is detected and possibly detained on the basis of alert. Nevertheless, this assessment should take place at the moment of appearance of the alert in the system, i.e. Member States receiving a new alert through SIS II should check whether a person was already convicted or acquitted for the same act on their territory. This would allow many inconveniences and violations of the fundamental rights of the person concerned to be avoided, including first of all his or her arrest.

The second category of alerts covers refusing the entrance of third-country nationals to the Schengen area based on the decision of the competent administrative or judicial authority of one of the members of the Schengen area. This is the only category of alerts regulated by the Regulation 1987/2006 as they are directly related to the free movement of persons (former First Pillar of the EU) and not to compensatory measures and police cooperation.

Only third-country nationals can be subject to this category of alert, i.e. according to Article 3(d) of the Regulation 1987/2006, "Any individual who is neither citizen of the European Union within the meaning of Article 17(1) of the Treaty nor a national of a third country who, under agreements between the Community and its Member States on the one hand, and these countries, on the other, enjoys rights of free movement equivalent to those of citizens of the European Union."

According to its Article 27, besides police, customs and judicial authorities, "The right to search data under this category of alert may be exercised by the authorities responsible for issuing visas, the central authorities responsible for examining visa applications and the authorities responsible for issuing residence permits and for the administration of legislation relating to third country nationals in the context of the application of the Community acquis relating to the movement of persons."

The third category of alerts is on missing persons, including those that need special protection (as minors or persons who have to be interned).

In case of this category of alert, regulation foreseen in the CISA and the Decision 2007/533/JHA is slightly different in terms but not in content. Article 97 of the CISA entailed that the basis for alert is a decision of the competent authority or competent judicial authority, while Article 32(1) of the Decision 2007/533/JHA refers to the request of the competent national authority without emphasising judicial ones. Alerts on missing persons can be issued despite their nationality, and special attention is paid to missing minors.

Article 33 deserves special observation as it foresees that information found on an adult missing person (if he/she is not a minor and does not need special protection), can be transmitted to others (e.g. his/her family), apart from competent authorities, only with his/her consent. Competent authorities are permitted to communicate to the person who reported the disappearance the fact that the alert has been erased due to the missing person's appearance, but without revealing his/her place of stay.

The fourth category of alerts is on persons sought in order to assist with a judicial procedure. According to the Article 34 of the Decision 2007/533/JHA those are:

- Witnesses;
- Persons ordered or summoned to appear before the judicial authorities for acts for which they are prosecuted;
- Persons to be served with the sentence or other procedural document of the process in which they are prosecuted or summoned to carry out the penalty.

Article 98 of the CISA foresaw that such an alert can be issued on the request of the judicial authority, but Article 34 of the Decision 2007/533/JHA broadens the concept of the requesting authorities from judicial to competent ones. A new regulation also foresees that the alert could be issued not only to serve a summons in relation to the penalty applied, but also criminal judgment or other procedural documents related to the prosecution of the person in question. From first sight, this widening of the reasons to issue an alert could seem unnecessary and widening the list of people "under alert", but from another perspective, it allows a prosecuted person to be informed about the process against him / her and to ensure his / her procedural warranties, including better defence.

The fifth category of alerts is for discreet checks (surveillance), or specific checks on persons and objects and has experienced the biggest modification in the new legislation.

First, it is related to the terms used. The CISA had foreseen "discreet surveillance" and "specific check" and the Decision 2007/533/JHA modified "surveillance" into "check", establishing in this way alerts for "discreet checks" and "specific checks". But legal provisions on the performance of "discreet surveillance" / "discreet checks" did not undergo any changes: it still remains a collection of information when border, other police and customs controls are carried out.[49] That means that this discreet action is performed only at the moment of the border, police or customs check and is not continued afterwards, i.e. after this check the person or object is allowed to continue the journey and is no longer observed. Therefore, the modification of "discreet surveillance" into "discreet check" is reasonable, as "surveillance" is an action more coherent with the process of movement after the followed subject and lasting in time. The change into "discreet check" also helps to avoid mixing up the category of alert in SIS II with the police

49 See Article 99(4) of the CISA and Article 37(1) of the Decision 2007/533/JHA.

cooperation instrument "Cross-border surveillance", foreseen in Article 40 of the CISA. In later cases "surveillance is a continuous process with the involvement of the competent authority of different Member State and can last hours, days or months, depending on the need."[50]

The following modification is more significant as Decision 2007/533/JHA extends the categories of the object that could be under discreet or specific checks and includes not only vehicles, but also boats, aircraft and containers.

The general purpose of checks remains the same: prosecuting criminal offences and prevention of threats to public security, internal or external national security. Table 4.2 presents in detail the differences between previous and current regulation.

The first modification (from "clear evidence" to "concrete indication") can raise contradictory discussions. From the perspective of fundamental rights, "clear evidence" is a more accurate background for the restriction of the right to private and family life than is made by the discreet or specific check and the term "concrete indication" is much broader and could lead to the violation of the above mentioned right.

From the procedural perspective, evidence is a term more related to the judicial trial than to the phase when discreet or specific checks are ordered, i.e. the phase of investigation or operational activity. There could be concrete intelligence information or indication about the preparation to commit a crime, or about the object being related to a serious crime, but no evidence as yet. For example, one of the countries is gathering intelligence on the group of people that, according to police sources (agents, undercover officers, etc.) are related to the trafficking of drugs, but competent authorities are missing information about the modus operandi used and the organisers. As trafficking is usually a cross-border crime, the competent authorities have the need to issue an alert for discreet checks, in order to find out missing information, e.g. the movement of suspects, their contacts and people who they mix with. This can help to reveal drug trafficking schemes and also possible relationships with organised crime groups acting in other Schengen area countries.

The second modification (from "extremely serious criminal offence" to "serious criminal offence such as offences referred to in Article 2(2) of the Framework Decision 2002/584/JHA") brings legal certainty, because there is no definition of "extremely serious criminal offence", but Art. 2(2) of the Framework Decision 2002/584/JHA foresees the exhaustive list of criminal

50 Misuse of the term "surveillance" is also pointed out by the Association of Chief Police Officers of England, Wales & Northern Ireland who states that, "There is no intrusive, directed surveillance in this alert". See ASSOCIATION OF CHIEF POLICE OFFICERS OF ENGLAND, WALES & NORTHERN IRELAND, "Guidelines for the use of the Schengen Information System II to locate people for judicial purposes", version 7, 2010, p. 5, accessed October 16, 2017, http://www.acpo.police.uk/documents/criminaljustice/2008/200810CJUSIS01.pdf.

Table 4.2 Difference between regulation of alerts on discreet and specific checks in SIS and SIS II

CISA – Art. 99	*Decision 2007/533/JHA – Art. 36*
Such an alert may be issued for the purposes of prosecuting criminal offences and for the prevention of threats to public security:	Such an alert may be issued for the purposes of prosecuting criminal offences and for the prevention of threats to public security:
(a) where there is clear evidence that the person concerned intends to commit or is committing numerous and extremely serious criminal offences; or	(a) where there is clear indication that a person intends to commit or is committing a serious criminal offence, such as the offences referred to in Article 2(2) of the Framework Decision 2002/584/JHA; or
(b) where an overall assessment of the person concerned, in particular on the basis of past criminal offences, gives reason to suppose that that person will also commit extremely serious criminal offences in the future.	(b) where an overall assessment of a person, in particular on the basis of past criminal offences, gives reason to suppose that that person will also commit serious criminal offences in the future, such as the offences referred to in Article 2(2) of Framework Decision 2002/584/JHA.
3. In addition, the alert may be issued in accordance with national law, at the request of the authorities responsible for national security, where there is clear evidence that the information referred to in paragraph 4 is necessary in order to prevent a serious threat by the person concerned or serious threats to internal or external national security. [...]	3. In addition, an alert may be issued in accordance with national law, at the request of the authorities responsible for national security, where there is concrete indication that the information referred to in Article 37(1) is necessary in order to prevent a serious threat by the person concerned or serious threats to internal or external national security. [...]

acts that are the background for the surrender procedure and are classified as serious crimes.[51]

51 According to Article 2(2) of the Framework Decision 2002/584/JHA, there are two conditions for treating a crime as serious:

1. It has to be one of the following crimes: "participation in a criminal organisation, terrorism, trafficking in human beings, sexual exploitation of children and child pornography, illicit trafficking in narcotic drugs and psychotropic substances, illicit trafficking in weapons, munitions and explosives, corruption, fraud, including that affecting the financial interests of the European Communities within the meaning of the Convention of July 26, 1995 on the protection of the European Communities' financial interests, laundering of the proceeds of crime, counterfeiting currency, including of the euro, computer-related crime, environmental crime, including illicit trafficking in endangered animal species and in endangered plant species and varieties, facilitation of unauthorised entry and residence, murder, grievous bodily injury, illicit trade in human organs and tissues, kidnapping, illegal restraint and hostage-taking, racism and xenophobia,

The last category of alerts in SIS II is related to objects for seizure or use as evidence in criminal proceedings. Article 38(2) of the Decision 2007/533/JHA has widened some of the existing types of objects and added new ones. For the sake of clarity, changes are shown in Table 4.3.

Table 4.3 Differences between regulation of alerts on object for seizure or use as evidence in SIS and SIS II

CISA – Art. 100(3)	*Decision 2007/533/JHA – Art. 38(2)*
Stolen, misappropriated or lost motor vehicles (capacity over 50 cc)	Motor vehicles (capacity over 50 cc)
Stolen, misappropriated or lost trailers and caravans over 750 kg	Trailers over 750 kg, caravans
	Stolen, misappropriated, lost or invalidated vehicle registration certificates and license plates
	Boats and aircraft
	Industrial equipment, outboard engines and containers
Stolen, misappropriated or lost firearms	Firearms
Stolen, misappropriated or lost blank official documents	Stolen, misappropriated or lost blank official documents
Stolen, misappropriated or lost identity documents	Stolen, misappropriated, lost or invalidated identity and travel documents
Banknotes	Banknotes
	Securities and means of payment

organised or armed robbery, illicit trafficking in cultural goods, including antiques and works of art, swindling, racketeering and extortion, counterfeiting and piracy of products, forgery of administrative documents and trafficking rein, forgery of means of payment, illicit trafficking in hormonal substances and other growth promoters, illicit trafficking in nuclear or radioactive materials, trafficking in stolen vehicles, rape, arson, crimes within the jurisdiction of the International Criminal Court, unlawful seizure of aircraft/ships, sabotage."

2. It shall be punishable in the alert issuing Member State by a custodial sentence or a detention order for a maximum period of at least 3 years (without verification of the double criminality of the act).

As correctly noticed by Oubiña Barbolla, in theory it sounds perfect, but in practice, one or other crime will face inexistence in some Member State, or the application of a lesser punishment than the maximum of 3 years; the regulation of the requesting (issuing) authority also has to be taken into account. See OUBIÑA BARBOLLA, Sabela "The European Arrest Warrant in Law and Practice" in RUGGERI, Stefano, *Liberty and Security in Europe. A comparative analysis of pre-trial precautionary measures in criminal proceedings* (Göttingen: V&R Unipress GmbH, 2012), p. 53–54.

Changes brought by the Decision 2007/533/JHA have not only broadened the list of the objects that can be subject to the alert, but has also relinquished conditions on issuing alerts for vehicles, trailers, caravans and firearms.

According to Art. 100 of the CISA alerts on vehicles, trailers, caravans and firearms for seizure or use as evidence, could only be issued if those objects were "stolen, misappropriated or lost". Disclaiming these conditions should be regarded as a positive change, because in the criminal process a need to seize, or to use as evidence, an object used for the commission of a crime appears (e.g. a car or a gun used for the robbery, container or caravan used for trafficking), but not necessarily stolen, misappropriated or lost.

The category of identity documents is broadened by the inclusion of invalidated documents (in addition to previous categories of those stolen, misappropriated or lost) and the addition of new travel documents. This extension makes sense as a document could be invalid or out of legal use, not only due to it having been lost, misappropriated or stolen, but also due to the decision of the competent authority. Inclusion of travel documents is justified by the wide circulation of visas that are not identity documents but very relevant in order to enter the Schengen area.

The inclusion of new objects (boats, aircrafts, travel documents, vehicle registration certificates, vehicle license plates and payment methods) was influenced by changes in crime trends (use of objects to commit a crime or objects of a crime) and developments in society (different modalities of payment methods). In the first half of the year of using the SIS II, the "champion" among the new types of object was payment measures, 99.8 per cent of which were entered by Italy.[52]

From the analysis above, the differences in authorities that are allowed to request the issuing of the alert can be noticed, as summarised in Table 4.4.

The diversity of authorities is justified by the actions that have to be taken in relation to an alert. The most precise requirement (or limitation) is established for the alert with respect to a person wanted for extradition or surrender. Only judicial authority is permitted to make this request as the consequence of an alert could be deprivation of liberty. In other cases, the term "competent authorities of the Member State" is used and can include both judicial and law enforcement authorities, depending on the national legislation.

For alerts on objects for seizure, or use as evidence in criminal procedure, no authority is specified, but it could also be interpreted as a "competent authority", because national rules on SIS II have to indicate the authorities allowed to come out with an alert request.

52 Information provided by KLEIN Dominique, representative of the Unit C3 (Transeuropean Networks for Freedom and Security and Relations with eu-LISA) of the Directorate General HOME of the European Commission on the Heads of SIRENE Offices Conference in Vilnius on 30 October, 2013.

Table 4.4 Authorities authorised to request different types of alerts

Category of the alert	*Background*
Alert with respect to a person wanted for extradition or surrender	Request of judicial authority
Alert on a missing person	Request of competent authority of the Member State
Alert on persons sought to assist with a judicial procedure	Request of competent authority of the Member State
Alerts on persons and objects for discreet checks or specific checks	Request of authorities foreseen in national law and authorities responsible for national security
Alerts on objects for seizure or use as evidence in criminal procedure	Not specified

Every alert contains a certain amount of data on subjects or objects, including personal ones. For the sake of personal data protection, Article 94 of the CISA, Article 20 of the Council Decision 2007/533/JHA and Article 20 of the Regulation 1987/2006 establish limitations on data contained in the system. All three legal acts foresee the following categories of data on a person subject to an alert that can be stored:

- Surname and forenames, any aliases possibly entered separately;
- Any specific objective physical characteristics, not subject to change;
- First letter of second forename;
- Date and place of birth;
- Sex;
- Nationality;
- Whether the persons concerned are armed;
- Whether the persons concerned are violent;
- Reason for the alert;
- Action to be taken.

Article 20 of Decision 2007/533/JHA and Article 20 of the Regulation 1987/2006 increase the scope of the data included in SISI II by introducing new categories:

- Photographs;
- Fingerprints;
- Authority issuing the alert;
- A reference to the decision giving rise to the alert;
- Links to other alerts in SIS II;
- The type of offence.

New categories of data directly related to the person (subject to alert) are photographs and fingerprints. Article 22(1b) of Decision 2007/533, and

Article 22(1b) of Regulation 1987/2006 state that these new categories can be used only to confirm the identity of a person that has been detected on the basis of the alphanumeric data in SIS II. Introducing photos and fingerprints into SIS II allows verification with greater accuracy, whether the person subject to an alert and the one that is checked are the same. There are numerous cases when the offender commits a crime using stolen documents and his/her real identity is not known to the law enforcement and judicial authorities, and therefore, an alert is issued in the name of the misused identity. In this case, a photo and the fingerprints of the offender are the crucial criteria to verify whether a person checked is a wanted person, or the legal owner of stolen documents. Previously to this modification of SIS II, an officer having a hit of alphanumeric data in some cases had to arrest a person and wait to receive the photo or fingerprints as supplementary information.

Special emphasis should be given to the introduction of information on foreign fighters. Thus in 2015, the countries of the Schengen area agreed that introducing information about whether a person is a foreign fighter or a terrorist suspect could be mentioned in the alert.[53] It is especially applicable to alerts on specific and discreet checks. In the case of an alert hit that includes such information (irrespective of the category of the alert), the authority that carries out searches has an obligation to immediately inform the SIRENE bureau of the state which issued an alert.

Just two days after the terrorist attack at the Christmas Market in Berlin on December 19, 2016, the European Commission presented a package of improvement of SIS II by introducing new categories of alerts and data.[54] It is proposed to create alerts on:

53 EUROPEAN COMMISSION, "Communication from the Commission to the European Parliament, the Council, the European Economic and Social Committee and the Committee of the Regions – The European Agenda on Security", COM(2015) 185 final, p. 5, accessed November 16, 2017, http://eur-lex.europa.eu/legal-content/EN/TXT/HTML/?uri=CELEX:52015DC0185&from=ES.

54 See EUROPEAN COMMISSION, "Proposal for a Regulation of the European Parliament and of The Council on the use of the Schengen Information System for the return of illegally staying third-country nationals", COM(2016) 881 final, accessed November 16, 2017, http://eur-lex.europa.eu/legal-content/EN/TXT/HTML/?uri=CELEX:52016PC0881&rid=1; "Proposal for a Regulation of the European Parliament and of the Council on the establishment, operation and use of the Schengen Information System (SIS) in the field of border checks, amending Regulation (EU) No 515/2014 and repealing Regulation (EC) No 1987/2006", COM(2016) 882 final, accessed November 16, 2017,http://eur-lex.europa.eu/legal-content/EN/TXT/?uri=COM:2016:0882:FIN; "Proposal for a Regulation of the European Parliament and of the Council on the establishment, operation and use of the Schengen Information System (SIS) in the field of police cooperation and judicial cooperation in criminal matters, amending Regulation (EU) No 515/2014 and repealing Regulation (EC) No 1986/2006, Council Decision 2007/533/JHA and Commission Decision 2010/261/EU", COM(2016) 883 final, accessed November 16, 2017, http://eur-lex.europa.eu/legal-content/EN/TXT/?uri=COM:2016:0883:FIN.

- Return decisions and entry bans in case of alerts on refusing the entrance of third-country nationals.
- Unknown wanted persons that would be based on fingerprints data found at crime scene.
- Children at risk of parental abduction.

It also includes proposals to implement biometric identification on the basis of facial images and to introduce DNA profiles of missing persons and persons that need special protection.

1.2.2 Relationships between multiple alerts: compatibility, links and priorities

By entering an alert into SIS, a Member State can face a situation of the existence of another alert on the same person or subject. It could be an alert of the same or another category entered by the other institution of the same or other Member State. For example:

- SIS contains an alert on a person sought to assist with a judicial procedure and then, in relation to another (or the same case) judicial authority of the same or another Member State, issues EAO and orders the issue of an alert for arrest for surrender procedure.
- A car is subject to a specific check in the investigation of drug trafficking, but in another case, run by another authority, this car figures as a mean to commit a robbery and an alert for seizure has to be issued.

For such cases, SIRENE Manual and other implementing measures for SIS II[55] approved by the Commission Implementing Decision (EU) 2015/219 (hereinafter – SIRENE Manual), foresee the protocol to be followed and establish compatibility of alerts and priorities in cases of multiple alerts.

Every country can intruduce only one alert per person or object, i.e. if one institution is looking for a person as a witness to a crime, and another institution of the same country has issued an EAO, only one of these issues can be announced as an alert in the SIS II. The remaining one is kept at national level and can be introduced only when the prevailing alert is deleted from SIS II. The Member State has to decide the priority in which its alerts would be entered into the SIS II by itself, but the reference rules of the SIRENE manual on priority between alerts of different Member States can be applied.

Different Member States can have alerts on the same person if they are compatible among themselves according to the rules established by the SIRENE Manual as is presented in Table 4.6.

Thus alert for arrest is compatible with all categories of alerts except alerts for specific or discreet checks. Alerts for specific or discreet checks are

55 OJ L 44, 18.2.2015, p. 75–116.

Table 4.5 Priority in case of multiple alerts[56]

On persons	*On objects*
– Arrest with a view to surrender or extradition – Refusing entry or stay in the Schengen territory – Placing under protection – Specific checks with immediate action – Specific checks – Discreet checks with immediate action – Discreet checks – Communicating whereabouts	– Use as evidence – Seizure of document invalidated for travel purposes – Seizure – Specific checks with immediate action – Specific checks – Discreet checks with immediate action – Discreet checks

Table 4.6 Compatibility of alerts on persons[57]

	Arrest	*Refusal of entry*	*Missing person (protection)*	*Specific check (immediate action)*	*Specific check*	*Discreet check (immediate action)*	*Discreet check*	*Missing person (whereabouts)*	*Judicial procedure*
Arrest	+	+	+	-	-	-	-	+	+
Refusal of entry	+	+	-	-	-	-	-	-	-
Missing person (protection)	+	-	+	-	-	-	-	+	+
Specific check (immediate action)	-	-	-	+	+	-	-	-	-
Specific check	-	-	-	+	+	-	-	-	-
Discreet check (immediate action)	-	-	-	-	-	+	+	-	-
Discreet check	-	-	-	-	-	+	+	-	-
Missing person (whereabouts)	+	-	+	-	-	-	-	+	+
Judicial procedure	+	-	+	-	-	-	-	+	+

neither compatible with any other category of checks nor among themselves (alert on discreet check with alert on specific check) an only few alerts of the same category (e.g. discreet check) are compatible.

In the case of multiple alerts for arrest, decision about the order of execution has to be taken by the executing judicial authority in the country where the arrest has occurred on the basis of the Article 16 of the Framework Decision 2002/584/JHA.

If alerts are incompatible, SIRENE bureaux of the countries involved have to consult each other and decide, which alert remains in the SIS II. If an

56 OJ L 44, 18.2.2015, p. 92.
57 OJ L 44, 18.2.2015, p. 91.

Table 4.7 Compatibility of alerts on objects[58]

	For use as evidence	*Invalidated doc. for travel*	*For seizure*	*Specific check (immediate action)*	*Specific check*	*Discreet check (immediate action)*	*Discreet check*
For use as evidence	+	+	+	-	-	-	-
Invalidated doc. for travel	+	+	+	-	-	-	-
For seizure	+	+	+	-	-	-	-
Specific check (immediate action)	-	-	-	+	+	-	-
Specific check	-	-	-	+	+	-	-
Discreet check (immediate action)	-	-	-	-	-	+	+
Discreet check	-	-	-	-	-	+	+

agreement cannot be reached on the basis of the above mentioned list of priorities, the oldest alert is kept in the system.

In the case of alerts on objects, the rules of compatibility are as presented in Table 4.7.

In the case of the example with the car, the Member State has to issue an alert for seizure and the existing alert to check has to be deleted. If the Member States involved cannot reach an agreement, the older alert will be kept in the SIS II, i.e. alert for check.

Article 52 of the Decision 2007/533/JHA and Article 37 of the Regulation 1987/2006 bring a novelty that has not been possible in the SIS – links between alerts. In cases of operational need, it allows a relationship between two or more alerts on different persons or objects to be established. The link can be made only if the same Member State enters those alerts. For example, if one Member State investigates an organised group that steals cars, it can make a link between alerts on stolen cars, persons (members of the organised group) to be subject to discreet checks, other persons involved and already wanted for arrest.[59]

58 OJ L 44, 18.2.2015, p. 92.

59 SIS and SIRENE experts foresaw a non-exhaustive list of possible links:
- gang members + family members wanted for surrender or extradition;
- EU national offender wanted for surrender or extradition + convicted companion to be refuse entry;
- kidnapper + missing person;
- (sexual) offender + his child-victim or child-witness to crime;
- husband wanted terrorist or convicted to be refused entry + specific or discreet check of wife suspected accomplice;
- wanted person + specific or discreet check of his yacht or car;

1.3 SIRENE bureaux

As already mentioned, SIRENE stands for "Supplementary Information Request at the National Entries". The need of the SIRENE bureaux (as a unit for the proper and quick exchange of supplementary information on the alerts and other information) was pointed out in the feasibility study on the CISA. Nevertheless, SIRENE bureaux were officially mentioned only in 2005 by the modification of the Article 92 of the CISA by the Article 1 of the Council Decision 2005/211/JHA and Article 1 of the Council Regulation 871/2004 of 29 April 2004 concerning the introduction of some new functions for the Schengen Information System, including in the fight against terrorism.[60] Currently SIRENE activities are regulated by the Article 7 of the Decision 2007/533/JHA and the Article 7 of the Regulation 1987/2006.

The SIRENE bureau is the unique contact point working on a 24/7 basis, in order to provide supplementary information not stored in the C.SIS, but related to alerts, and is the "human interface" of SIS.[61] As highlighted by Hayes, "There is no effective limit on the data that can be exchanged through the SIRENE bureaux",[62] but there is a restriction on its use, as, according to Article 8 of Decision 2007/533/JHA and of Regulation 1987/2006, it can be used only for the purpose for which it was transmitted.

The importance of the SIRENE Bureau within the functioning of the SIS is highlighted by the CJEU in the case *Commission v Spain* (case C-503/03) where it is stated that the SIRENE bureau has to be consulted before taking any further decision on action with a person that is subject to the alert.[63]

According to SIRENE Manual, the supplementary information shall be exchanged:

- wanted person + stolen object;
- parent to be refused entry + missing child (third country national);
- person to be refused entry + stolen identity document;
- two or more missing siblings;
- missing person + person wanted for questioning on that missing person;
- missing child + car used for abduction, etc.

See COUNCIL OF THE EUROPEAN UNION, "SIS II functions / Open Issues", 12573/3/04, p. 3, accessed November 18, 2017, http://data.consilium.europa.eu/doc/document/ST-12573-2004-REV-3/en/pdf.

60 OJ L 162, 30.4.2004, p. 30.

61 See GARCÍA VÁZQUEZ, Sonia, "La cooperación policial y judicial como ejes de consolidación del espacio de Libertad, Seguridad y Justicia e instrumentos de protección de los derechos fundamentales en la Unión Europea" in GOIZUETA VÉRTIZ, Juana and CIENFUEGOS MATEO, Juan, *La eficacia de los Derechos Fundamentales de la UE* (Navarra: Aranzadi, 2014), p. 436.

62 HAYES, Ben, "From the Schengen Information System to SIS and the Visa Information (VIS): proposals explained" (Statewatch analysis, February 2004), p. 14, accessed October 20, 2017, http://www.statewatch.org/news/2005/may/analysis-sisII.pdf.

63 See Judgment of the Court of Justice in *Commission of the European Communities v Kingdom of Spain*, C 503/03, ECLI:EU:C:2006:74.

- For consultation with other countries whilst entering an alert;
- To inform about hit;
- To inform that actions required cannot be performed;
- For ensuring the quality of the SIS II data;
- To deal with the exercise of the right to access;
- To deal with the compatibility and priority of the alerts.

Thus the SIRENE bureaux can be defined as a dynamic part of the SIS II as it helps to solve any question and problem related to the static alert of the C.SIS: to clarify uncertainties of alert, to find out whether it is still in force, to assure that the person or object detected is the one searched for under the alert, to agree on further actions, and so on.

2 Information exchange under Articles 39 and 46 of the CISA

Article 39 of the CISA establishes the legal basis for the assistance between national police authorities. Its content is not explained, but according to Moreno Catena and Castillejo Manzanares it can be understood in a broad sense and includes any measures, procedures or actions that constitute the competence of the requested authority.[64] Nevertheless, using a systematic analysis of the CISA, some form of assistance must be excluded, for example, hot pursuit, cross-border surveillance and controlled delivery, as they have separate specific regulation.

Even if in the first paragraph of Article 39, the broad term "assistance" is used, the following paragraphs mainly focus on information exchange for the purpose of preventing and detecting criminal offences.

Article 46 of the CISA foresees almost the same rules for spontaneous information exchange, i.e. providing information without previous request, if it is considered useful to combat future crime and prevent offences and threats to public security.

In the nineties, these provisions were of the utmost importance as they provided an opportunity for any kind of multinational police assistance, except one demanding coercive measures. But the millennium came along with a wide range of specific instruments, channels and agencies for police cooperation and the above mentioned articles of the CISA lost their significance.

Moreover, their application has been significantly limited by Framework Decision 2006/960/JHA of 18 December 2006 on simplifying the exchange of information and intelligence between law enforcement authorities of the Member

64 See MORENO CATENA, Víctor and CASTILLEJO MANZANARES, Raquel, *La persecución de los delitos en el Convenio de Schengen*, Valencia: Tirant lo Blanch, 1999, p. 65.

States of the European Union[65] (hereinafter – Framework 2006/960/JHA, Swedish Initiative) which develops the provisions of the Schengen acquis.[66]

Article 12 of the Framework Decision 2006/960/JHA establishes that the provisions of Article 39(1), (2) and (3) and Article 46 of the CISA are replaced as far as information and intelligence exchange for the purpose of conducting criminal investigations or criminal intelligence operations are concerned.

Table 4.8 Interrelationship between Article 39 of the CISA and Framework Decision 2006/960/JHA

	Art. 39 of the CISA	*Framework Decision 2006/960/JHA*
Action	Assistance	Exchange
Object	Not specified	Information and intelligence
Purpose for the exchange	Preventing and detecting criminal offences	- Art. 1: Conducting criminal investigations[67] or criminal intelligence operations.[68] - Art. 5: Detection, prevention or investigation of an offence.
Competent authorities	Police authorities	National police, customs or other authorities that are authorised by national law to detect, prevent and investigate offences or criminal activities and to exercise authority and take coercive measures in the context of such activities.
Limitations	- Not applied in the case of a need for judicial cooperation. - Not applied in the case of a request whose execution demands a measure of constraint. - Provided information cannot be used as evidence without the consent of the competent judicial authority of the requested Contracting Party.	- Request does not impose any obligation to obtain information or intelligence by means of coercive measures. - Provided information cannot be used as evidence before a judicial authority without the consent or providing Member State. Such consent can be given at the time of transmittal of the information or intelligence.

65 OJ L 386, 29.12.2006, p. 89–100.

66 SEC(2011) 593 final, p. 3.

67 A definition is provided in Article 2(b) of the Decision 2006/960/JHA "A procedural stage within which measures are taken by competent law enforcement or judicial authorities, including public prosecutors, with a view to establishing and identifying facts, suspects and circumstances regarding one or several identified concrete criminal acts".

68 A definition is provided in the Article 2(c) of the Decision 2006/960/JHA "A procedural stage, not yet having reached the stage of a criminal investigation, within which a competent law enforcement authority is entitled by national law to collect, process and analyse information about crime or criminal activities with a view to establishing where concrete criminal acts have been committed or may be committed in the future."

This formulation means that Articles 39 and 46 of the CISA are not replaced totally, and to some extent still stay in force. To find out the scope of current Article 39 of the CISA, Table 4.8 presents a comparison of its content with the relevant provisions of the Framework Decision 2006/960/JHA.

Thus the purpose of the information exchange under the Framework Decision 2006/960/JHA is established in two articles using different wording which, from the perspective of legal technique is not the best option. It seems problematic to put an "equal" sign between "conducting criminal investigations or criminal intelligence operations" and "detection, prevention or investigation of an offence", especially when talking about crime prevention. A criminal intelligence operation is not yet an investigation, but already has its own procedural form and rules to be followed and mostly sticks to the gathering of intelligence that leads to investigation and prosecution. Prevention by nature is much broader and seeks to preclude factors that provoke crime.

Articles 4(1) and 4(3) of the Framework Decision 2006/960/JHA mention exchange of information and intelligence in relation to the offences listed in Article 2(2) of the Council Framework Decision 2002/584/JHA; this could lead to understanding that information exchange does not go beyond these limits. Notwithstanding, systematic analysis of Articles 1 (Objective and scope), 3 (Provision of information and intelligence), 4 (Time limits for provision of information and intelligence), 5 (Request for information and intelligence) and 7 (Spontaneous exchange of information and intelligence) leads to the conclusion that the Member State is free to make any request for information and intelligence when its purpose is conducting criminal investigations or criminal intelligence operations, but deadlines for urgent response[69] are applied only when the request is related with the offence mentioned in Art. 2(2) of Framework Decision 2002/584/JHA.

Taking all that into account, the conclusion can be made that the Framework Decision 2006/960/JHA creates a "grey area" in which information exchange for crime prevention hangs without certainty, whether it falls within its scope or remains under Article 39 of the CISA.

On the basis of the analysis presented above, a very cautious conclusion can be made about the actual scope of Article 39 of the CISA. It has to be applied to:

a Police cooperation assistance, other than providing information and intelligence in the prevention and detection of criminal offences;
b Information exchange on crime prevention when it does not take place under the procedure of the criminal intelligence operation.

69 At the most, 8 hours in case of urgent requests and 1 week in non-urgent cases when the information requested is directly accessible by the requested authority. In other cases – 14 days.

The Catalogue of Recommendations for the correct application of the Schengen acquis and Best practices on Police cooperation,[70] updated in 2011 (more than 2 years after the deadline to implement the Framework Decision 2006/960/JHA) does not help too much in establishing the line between the application of the Article 39 and the Framework Decision 2006/960/JHA because:

- Recommendation 6 says that "In the field of public order and public security, the central authorities should hold a list of requests for which direct assistance can be given in urgent situations"[71] and as the best practice, the reference to Articles 3 and 4 of the Framework Decision 2006/960/JHA is given. It means that the "equal" sign between "assistance" and "exchange" (of information) is made.
- Recommendation 28 establishes that all police personnel should have basic knowledge of Article 39 of the CISA and Article 12 of the Framework Decision 2006/960/JHA. This introduces even more confusion, because it focuses on the article from the CISA dedicated to assistance (including information exchange) and on the article from the Framework Decision dedicated only to the spontaneous information exchange (without previous request), leaving articles on the information exchange on request on the margin.
- Recommendation 36, 37 and 39 on the information exchange on request totally refers to the Framework Decision 2006/960/JHA.

Even more inconsistency shows recommendations 40–46 on the spontaneous information exchange, as they do not make any reference to the Framework Decision 2006/960/JHA and its Article 12, which was mentioned in recommendation 28. It seems that Member States are urged to provide knowledge on Article 12, but are not urged to use it.

The latest recommendations lead to the analysis of spontaneous information exchange under Article 46 of the CISA, and relevant provisions of the Framework Decision 2006/960/JHA. For the sake of coherence with the analysis carried out on Article 39 of the CISA, Table 4.9 provides a comparison of the content of both mechanisms on spontaneous information exchange.

In this case, the object covered by the regulation of the Framework Decision 2006/960/JHA is even broader (information and intelligence) than the one from Article 46 of the CISA (information), but from another perspective, it is not clear, whether the provision of the information or intelligence

70 COUNCIL OF THE EUROPEAN UNION, "Updated Catalogue of Recommendations for the correct application of the Schengen Acquis and Best practices: Police cooperation", 15785/2/10, accessed November 18, 2017, http://data.consilium.europa.eu/doc/document/ST-15785-2010-REV-3/en/pdf.

71 Council document 15785/2/10.

Table 4.9 Interrelationship between Article 46 of the CISA and Framework Decision 2006/960/JHA

	Art. 46 of the CISA	*Council Framework Decision 2006/960/JHA*
Action	Exchange	Exchange
Object	Information	Information and intelligence
Purpose for the exchange	Not identified precisely, but the Contracting Party has to consider it useful to combat future crime and prevention of offences against, or threats to public policy and public security.	- Article 1: Conducting criminal investigations or criminal intelligence operations. - Article 7: There have to be factual reasons to believe that information and/or intelligence could assist in the detention, prevention or investigation of offences referred to in Art. 2(2) of the Framework Decision 2002/584/JHA.
Competent authorities	Not specified	National police, customs or other authorities that are authorised by national law to detect, prevent and investigate offences or criminal activities and to exercise authority and take coercive measures in the context of such activities.
Limitations	Not specified	Information and intelligence shall be limited to what is deemed relevant and necessary for the successful detection, prevention or investigation of the crime or criminal activity in question.

without previous request can take place for the sake of any criminal investigations or criminal intelligence operation, or is limited only to the detention, prevention or investigation of offences referred to in Art. 2(2) of the Framework Decision 2002/584/JHA?

In the first case, the application of Article 46 of the CISA would be redundant; in the second case, it could be applied to combat future crime and prevention of offences against or threats to public policy and public security when they do not fall under Article 2(2) of the Framework Decision 2002/584/JHA.

The European Commission, in its Communication of 2010, "Overview of information management in the area of freedom, security and justice"[72] did

72 EUROPEAN COMMISSION, "Communication from the Commission to the European Parliament and the Council – Overview of information management in the area of freedom, security and justice", COM(2010) 385 final, accessed November 16, 2017, http://eur-lex.europa.eu/LexUriServ/LexUriServ.do?uri=COM:2010:0385:FIN:EN:PDF.

not make any reference at all to Articles 39 and 46 of the CISA; it only mentions the SIS.

On the contrary, the International Centre for Migration Policy Development, in its Study on the status of information exchange amongst law enforcement authorities in the context of existing EU instruments, has stated that "The SIS might be used as legal basis more often than it gets credit, as reference might still be made to Arts 39 and 46 of the Schengen Convention while Art. 12 of the Swedish Framework Decision largely supersedes these two Articles."[73]

The current SIRENE Manual[74] makes a step backwards and foresees that, "Additional tasks may be entrusted to the Sirene Bureaux, in particular, by the national law implementing Framework Decision 2006/960/JHA, Articles 39 and 46 of the Schengen Convention, in as far as they are not replaced by Framework Decision 2006/960/JHA".

Without legal clarity at European level, Member States make different use of these Articles. For example, Italy presumes that Article 39 can be applied to provide the information following the match (hit) in the SIS. Hungary applies them in cooperation between law enforcement authorities of border regions, Poland uses it only in cases of offences that do not fall under Art. 2(2) of the Framework Decision 2002/584/JHA.

3 Police and Customs Cooperation Centres

Articles 39(4) and 39(5) of the CISA allow cooperation measures by bilateral (or trilateral) arrangements and agreements that give rise to the possibility of establishing other cooperation arrangements as compensatory measures, among which PCCC deserves special attention.

PCCC is a centre operative in border areas, usually in the premises of the former border checkpoint of one of the contracting parties (or in common premises if contracting parties have had common checkpoints), or in the immediate vicinity. Located in positions of strategic importance for observing cross-border crime, PCCCs play a key intelligence role for the operational services. As stated by Moral Torres, it is a mechanism that has contributed to security improvements in border areas where the border control had been abolished but law enforcement services maintained exclusively national competence.[75]

73 INTERNATIONAL CENTRE FOR MIGRATION POLICY DEVELOPMENT AND EUROPEAN PUBLIC LAW ORGANIZATION, "Study on the status of information exchange amongst law enforcement authorities in the context of existing EU instruments", European Commission, 2010, p. 40, accessed October 20, 2017, https://ec.europa.eu/home-affairs/sites/homeaffairs/files/doc_centre/police/docs/icmpd_study_lea_infoex.pdf.

74 OJ L 44, 18.2.2015, p. 75–116.

75 DEL MORAL TORRES, Anselmo, *Cooperación policial en la Unión Europea: la necesidad de un modelo de inteligencia criminal eficiente*, Madrid: Dykinson, S.L., 2011, p. 184.

According to its nature, PCCC consists of representatives responsible for police, border and customs tasks in the border area. Representatives of the relevant services must be granted with the access to their national police and customs databases that are used for prevention and detection of crimes. Working in common premises, they can rapidly exchange information on suspicious persons or vehicles in the border area (both by request and spontaneously), provide assistance in the case of continuation of hot pursuit or urgent surveillance[76] on the territory of neighbouring countries, and any other assistance that can be needed. As a rule, PCCCs should be open 24/7, but for the sake of the rational use of human resources, it is common to have only one duty officer 24/7.

It should be noted that PCCC is an effective cooperation tool in the border areas with a high density of towns and population, or even towns divided between countries and these PCCCs are mainly open 24/7. In less

76 Cross-border hot pursuit and cross-border surveillance are compensatory measures for the abolishment of border control, foreseen in Articles 40 and 41 of the CISA.

Article 40 previses a possibility to continue the surveillance started in one country of the Schengen area on the territory of its neighbouring country of the Schengen area, and Article 41 establishes the same possibility for hot pursuit. Their main feature is the performance of law enforcement functions on the territory of the other country, with the general possibility (if it is not agreed to the contrary) to use official cars weapons and uniforms.

In the case of surveillance, two modalities are possible:

- Pre-planned surveillance: in which a permission of its continuation and/or takeover is agreed in advance.

- Urgent surveillance: that happens unexpectedly (person or object of a surveillance were not expected to move towards the border) and the permission is asked "on the spot" of the operation. In this case, according to Article 40(2), surveillance shall be ceased when neighbouring country which territory was entered requests so or, where authorisation has not been obtained in the 5 hours after crossing the border.

In the case of hot pursuit, it is always unexpected and the permission to continue the pursuit is requested before the crossing of the border, or at the same moment. Hot pursuit is possible only over land borders and shall cease when the neighbouring country, whose territory was entered, so requests.

Surveillance and hot pursuit are allowed in prosecution of any extraditable offence, evasion after an accident that has resulted in death or serious injury, escape from provisional custody or while serving a sentence involving deprivation of liberty.

In both cases, it is forbidden to enter into private homes and places not accessible to the public, and to use weapons in situations other than legitimate self-defence.

Surveillance and hot pursuit rules established in the CISA can be extended by bilateral agreement and in any case, it is up to bilateral agreements to establish the area (distance) or time for the surveillance and hot pursuit on the territory of the neighbouring country.

Thus the allowed distance of pursuit between France and Spain is 10 km, between Portugal and Spain – 50 km or 2 hours, between Lithuania and Poland – 1 hour or 100 km, between Latvia and Lithuania – 1 hour.

populated border regions there are part-time PCCCs (called by Hufnagel[77] "multijurisdictional police facilities"), or other compensatory measures, like in the case of the Lithuanian and Latvian border, where, in 2009, a bilateral decision to substitute PCCCs with Border Region Cooperation Model was taken (the same applies to the Lithuanian–Polish border).[78]

PCCC existed before the CISA, as in 1965, Spain and France signed the first agreement on National Offices of Joint Controls. In 1969, Belgium, Germany and the Netherlands established Euroregional Police Information and Coordination Centres. Within the CISA, the first model of PCCC and its agreement was concluded on French–German PCCC (Stasbourg–Kehl).

Depending on geographical situation, there are bilateral and multilateral centres. The biggest centre in terms of the number of countries and institutions involved is the Belgian–French–German–Luxembourgish Centre, established in Luxembourg. Trilateral centres also see Austria, Hungary and Slovenia (Dolga Vas), Austria, Italy and Slovenia (Thörl-Maglern), Austria, Italy and Romania (Oradea), Belgium, the Netherlands and Germany (Heerlen).

PCCCs are also created with the countries of the Schengen area that are not EU Member States, e.g. the PCCCs of France, Germany and Switzerland (Basel), Italy and Switzerland (Chiasso), France and Switzerland (Geneva), Austria, Lichtenstein and Switzerland (Schaanwald).

Due to its nature in combatting cross-border crime, PCCCs can be also established with the third neighbouring countries. Such centres exist between

77 HUFNAGEL, Saskia, *Policing cooperation across borders: comparative perspectives on law enforcement within the EU and Australia*, Hampshire: Ashgate Publishing Limited, 2013, p. 189.

78 After a joint Lithuanian–Latvian study visited the French–German PCCC in Kehl, it was bilaterally decided for the time being to not establish a PCCC, but to apply the Border Region Cooperation Model. A decision was taken in 2009 and was reasoned by lack of essential problems in cross-border cooperation, increasing the number of cross-border crimes or of insufficiency of existing cooperation means, as well as difficulties with financial and human resources caused by the global economic crisis. The Border Region Cooperation Model foresees that the main PCCC functions are performed by border area police forces. As a compensation for PCCC, the following are applied:

- Creation of bilingual forms for information exchange that in urgent cases, can be sent directly between competent authorities in border areas (informing about that the central authorities);
- Enhanced use of joint patrolling;
- Establishment of protocols that must be followed in the case of cross border surveillance and hot pursuit;
- Exchange of radio communication means and frequencies, and facilitation of other communication means;
- Periodical meetings of different police units' representative in order to share information about crime situation in the border area and to prepare annual analysis;
- Annual organisation of joint training.

Bulgaria and Serbia, Bulgaria and Macedonia, Moldova and Romania, Romania and Ukraine.

Although every bilateral or trilateral agreement can foresee different PCCC tasks, European Best Practice Guidelines for Police and Customs Cooperation Centres foresee three main functions:

- Information collection and exchange;
- Assisting operations in border area;
- Perform analysis of cross-border crime.

Direct cooperation through PCCC can be very helpful in effective and rapid resolution of "local" cases, especially when bilateral or multilateral agreement allows the use of all legal measures and all communication forms which are allowed by national law in order to achieve PCCC's goals,[79] as foreseen in Article 7 of the Agreement of November 19, 2005, between The Kingdom of Spain and The Portuguese Republic on cross-border cooperation in police and customs matters.

Due to the prompt process of information exchange, the most discussed question related to information exchange through PCCCs are the so-called "chain requests" between different PCCCs that take place in practice, but are not formally regulated. Let's imagine that Spain needs urgent information from Poland, and instead of sending a request to its central authority, a request is sent through the chain of PCCCs: Spanish–French PCCC, French–German PCCC and the latter German–Polish PCCC.

For this reason, during the fourth PCCC conference in October 2013, it was proposed to foresee the possibility of "chain requests" in urgent cases, but only if allowed by bilateral/multilateral agreements and the national central authorities of the countries are involved.[80]

From first sight, the process does not seem difficult, but if we take the already mentioned example of Spain–Poland, the possibility of a chain request shall be established in bilateral agreements between Spain and France, France and Germany, and Germany and Poland. Also, it is not clear which National central authorities should be informed: Only those of Spain and Poland or also those of France and Germany? The last option does not make too much sense, because it means the overloading of information (including personal data) for states that are used only as a chain (channel) for the information, but do not have any interest in its content.

79 See MARTÍN DIZ, Fernando, "Aspectos recientes de la cooperación judicial y policial hispano-portuguesa; especial consideración del Acuerdo de Évora" in *Revista de Estudios Europeos*, 2010, no. 56, p. 103.

80 See COUNCIL OF THE EUROPEAN UNION, "Outcome of the 4th Conference on Police and Customs Cooperation Centres (PCCCs) on 21 and 22 October 2013, Brussels, Belgium", 16249/13, p. 2, accessed November 18, 2017, http://data.consilium.europa.eu/doc/document/ST-16249-2013-INIT/en/pdf.

As Guille points out, "Although central authorities were not pleased with this increasingly important networking system of information exchange through CPCCs,[81] the high volume of exchanges demonstrated that this network of CPCCs responded to real needs, and therefore the central level informally allowed this information exchange to take place to a certain extent".[82]

It could be concluded that due to their typical functions, PCCCs contribute to common and agreed responses to crime in countries that share borders. All this is possible due to the face-to-face work of police, border and customs authorities which allows, on a daily basis, familiarisation with the legal system of neighbouring countries and so to find out the best possible solution to common security challenges.

4 Liaison officers: within the Schengen Agreement and beyond

In general, "liaison officer" is defined as a person who liaises between groups or units. In the case of international police cooperation, a liaison officer is an officer or servant delegated to another country, region, international or regional organisation, to keep close contact with its law enforcement and judicial authorities in order to facilitate cooperation between sending and hosting countries.

Liaison officers were used for the first time at the turn of the nineteenth and twentieth centuries, during the Anarchist era, in order to share information and to counter cross-border political concerns; later, they started to be used to combat drug trafficking.[83]

Within the Schengen acquis, Article 47 of the CISA foresees a possibility to conclude agreements for the secondment of liaison officers to another state of the Schengen area, as well as to the third countries. Although this article mentions secondment "to the police authorities of another Contracting Party", it has to be interpreted more broadly than just the police, and to be understood as law enforcement authorities that have the function of combatting crime and ensuring internal security within the Schengen area.

In parallel with the CISA, the interior ministers of the Member States of the EEC had started discussions on liaison officers within the TREVI group and:

81 It must be noted that in some research, "Police and Customs Cooperation Centres" are called "Centres for Police and Custom Cooperation", although the official name used by the European Union is "PCCC".

82 GUILLE, Laure, "Policing in Europe: An Ethnographic Approach to Understanding the Nature of Cooperation and the Gap between Policy and Practice", in *Journal of Contemporary European Research*, vol. 6, no. 2, 2010 p. 267, accessed October 20, 2017, http://www.jcer.net/index.php/jcer/article/view/192.

83 See YON, Hasan, "Police liaisons as builders of transnational security cooperation" in AYDINLI Ersel, *Emerging Transnational (In)Security Governance: A Statist-transnationalist approach*, New York: Routledge, 2010, p. 137.

- In 1987, Agreement on the development of a network of drugs liaison officers was adopted, to the benefit of European Community Member States.
- In 1996, the Council adopted Joint action 96/602/JHA of October 14, 1996, on the basis of Article K.3 of the Treaty on the European Union providing for a common framework for the initiatives of the Member States concerning liaison officers (hereinafter – Joint action 96/602/JHA).[84]

While Joint action 96/602/JHA talks about both intra-community liaison officers and those seconded to third states, the Council Decision 2003/170/JHA of February 27, 2003 on the common use of liaison officers posted abroad by the law enforcement agencies of the Member States[85] (hereinafter – Decision 2003/170/JHA) that repeal it, envisages only posting and common use of liaison officers in third countries and international organisations. Thus it seems that the political signal is to use this cooperation tool with the third countries, leaving the cooperation within the EU under the auspices of other cooperation instruments.

Decision 2003/170/JHA concentrates on the most efficient, common use of the liaison officers seconded to the third countries, and in Article 5 foresees the possibility for law enforcement institutions of the Member State that does not have them in the third country, to request liaison officers from another Member State, with a view to the exchange of relevant information. It also establishes meetings between all Member States' liaison officers posted in third countries or international organisations; and with the amendment of the Decision 2003/170/JHA made by the Council Decision 2006/560/JHA on July 24, 2006, amending Decision 2003/170/JHA on the common use of liaison officers posted abroad by the law enforcement agencies of the Member States[86] (hereinafter – Decision 2006/560/JHA), previses that such meetings are organised by the Member State holding the Presidency of the Council or the European Union or on the initiative of Member States with liaison officers posted there or, as a novelty, by the Member State to which responsibility for coordination (leading) of the EU cooperation in a particular country or region has been given. The outcomes of meetings are discussed in the preparatory bodies of the Council of the European Union, and serve as indispensable input for the policy in judicial and home affairs cooperation with third countries.

Decision 2006/560/JHA also foresees information exchange between Member States' liaison officers in the third countries and Europol, as well as between Member States' law enforcement institutions and Europol's liaison officers posted in third countries.

84 OJ L 268, 19.10.1996, p. 2–4.
85 OJ L 67, 12.3.2003, p. 27–30.
86 OJ L 219, 10.8.2006, p. 31–32.

Going back to the CISA, its Article 47 does not entail any special scope of action by liaison officers, establishing that the purpose is to combat crime by means of both prevention and law enforcement. In the case of Decision 2003/170/JHA, its recital 15 establishes the aim to regulate questions relating to the fight against serious cross-border crime.

Even if liaison officers cannot perform operational activities in the hosting state, their role is much more significant and comprehensive than just information exchange.[87] As pointed out by Block, "Requests for information, usually referred to as 'cases', are likely to be routed through liaison officers instead of through the other available channels whenever a case requires more active support than a simple information-exchange because of its complexity, sensitivity or urgency."[88]

The biggest advantage of the liaison officer in information exchange is his/her familiarity with the system and personal contacts with the law enforcement authorities of the hosting country. Also, knowledge of the language and cultural particularities play an important role in "breaking the ice" and smoothing contacts with representatives of the hosting country, region or organisation. Depending on the situation and needs, liaison officers have the possibility to manoeuvre between using personal informal contacts, or more official ones within the authorities of the hosting country.

5 Data protection rules applied to SIS II

As already mentioned in Chapter 3, the general data protection framework established in the Council Framework Decision 2008/977/JHA of November 27, 2008 on the protection of personal data, processed in the framework of police and judicial cooperation in criminal matters[89] (hereinafter – Decision 2008/977/JHA), had not been applied to the Schengen Information System, neither to SIS or to SIS II. With respect to other information exchange options under Schengen acquis, such as PCCCs, liaison officers, the Decision 2008/977/JHA was applied as *lex generalis*, foreseeing that *lex especialis* can be included in bilateral or multilateral agreements that regulate PCCC and or liaison officers as well as the national law of the Member States involved.

Recital 25 of Directive (EU) 2016/680 of the European Parliament and of the Council of April 27, 2016 on the protection of natural persons with regard to the processing of personal data by competent authorities for the purposes of the prevention, investigation, detection or prosecution of

87 See INTERNATIONAL CENTRE FOR MIGRATION POLICY DEVELOPMENT AND EUROPEAN PUBLIC LAW ORGANIZATION, "Study on the status of information…", loc. cit., p. 60.

88 BLOCK, Ludo, "Bilateral Police Liaison Officers: Practices and European Policy" in *Journal of Contemporary European Research*, 2010. vol. 6, issue 2, p. 196, accessed October 20, 2017, http://www.jcer.net/ojs/index.php/jcer/article/view/266/205.

89 OJ L 350, 30.12.2008, p. 60–71.

criminal offences or the execution of criminal penalties, and on the free movement of such data, and repealing Council Framework Decision 2008/977/JHA[90] (hereinafter – Directive 2016/680) has not changed the situation radically, foreseeing that "This Directive should be without prejudice to the specific rules laid down in (…) Council Decision 2007/533/JHA".

However, Article 64 of the proposal for a Regulation of the European Parliament and of the Council on the establishment, operation and use of the Schengen Information System (SIS) in the field of police cooperation and judicial cooperation in criminal matters, amending Regulation (EU) No 515/2014 and repealing Regulation (EC) No 1986/2006, Council Decision 2007/533/JHA and Commission Decision 2010/261/EU foresees that "Regulation (EU) 2016/679 shall apply to the processing of personal data provided that national provisions transposing Directive (EU) 2016/680 do not apply. For processing of data by competent national authorities for the purposes of the prevention, investigation, detection, or prosecution of criminal offences of the execution of criminal penalties including the safeguarding against the prevention of threat to public security national provisions transposing Directive (EU) 2016/680 shall apply." Thus it could be that in the future the system will be more unified and coherent.

5.1 *Persons included*

Each category of alerts held in SIS directly indicates persons or objects to which it is applied. Thus SIS consists of the following alerts on persons:

- Wanted for surrender, i.e. prosecuted or convicted;
- Missing or in need of special protection due their physical or mental condition;
- Sought for assistance in judicial procedure;
- Needed to be checked;
- Not allowed to enter one of the members of the Schengen zone.

In addition to predetermined types of alerts, Article 51 of the Decision 2007/533/JHA and Article 36 of Regulation 1987/2006 allow the inclusion of data on persons whose identity was misused. But unlike other categories of persons, for such data inclusion the consent of the data subject is needed, and there is a complete list of data that can be entered to the SIS II. Therefore, only the following data on a person whose identity was misused can be processed: names and surnames, data and place of birth, sex, nationality, photographs, fingerprints, any specific and permanent characteristics and number of identity documents.

According to Articles 44(1) and 45(1) of Decision 2007/533/JHA, alerts are stored for the period that is necessary to achieve their purpose. But in any

90 OJ L 119, 4.5.2016, p. 89–131.

case, the state that has issued an alert shall make a revision on such a need and inform C.SIS if it is necessary to store it longer. If the state does not communicate such a need, an alert is automatically deleted after:

- 1 year if it concerns discreet or specific check of person;
- 3 years – other alerts on persons;
- 5 years – discreet or specific check of object;
- 10 years – other alerts on objects.

The SIRENE office shall delete data exchanged in relation to an alert as soon as the purpose of its transfer has been achieved, and in any case, not later than 1 year after the deletion of the alert. This provision can be criticised because of the meaninglessness and purposelessness of keeping data when an alert to which it is related has been deleted. Besides, from a practical point of view, it is much easier to delete data related to an alert once it is withdrawn from the system, than to remember it within 1 year.

5.2 Access

According to the general rule, established in Article 40 of the Decision 2007/533/JHA and Article 27 of the Regulation 1987/2006/EC, access to SIS II data and the right to search is granted to the authorities responsible for border controls, other police and customs checks. Nevertheless, according to Art. 40(2), giving access to the national judicial authorities is allowed, including those responsible for the initiation of public prosecutions in criminal proceedings and for judicial inquiries prior to charge within the limits that are needed for their duties.

With respect to the purpose, information from alerts can be used for purposes other than for which they were issued, only in order to prevent serious threats to public policy or security, to national security or to prevent serious crimes. In such cases, consent from the Member State that has issued the alert has to be obtained.

Decision 2007/533/JHA does not provide a definition of serious crime. But as in Article 36, a reference to the list of Article 2(2) of the Framework Decision 2002/584/JHA is made, serious crime should be understood as one of the offences mentioned.

According to Articles 41 and 42 of the Decision 2007/533/JHA, Europol and Eurojust are also allowed to access some categories of alerts as it is presented in Table 4.10.

Apart from the limitation in relation to the content of the SIS II, Europol's and Eurojust's right to access is different from the one granted to the states (and their national authorities), from a technical point of view as well. Europol and Eurojust are not able to access either N.SIS or C.SIS, but only special SIS II database copies with the relevant categories of alerts for which they have an authorisation. These copies are updated by the C.SIS.

Table 4.10 Categories of alerts that can be accessed by Europol and Eurojust

Europol	*Eurojust*
– On wanted persons – On persons and objects for discreet or specific checks – On objects for seizure or use as evidence	– On wanted persons – On missing persons – On persons sought to assist with a judicial procedure – On objects for seizure or use as an evidence

The European Data Protection Supervisor in its Opinion on the legislative proposals concerning the Second Generation Schengen Information System (SIS II) has highlighted that Europol and Eurojust, unlike competent institutions of states, are not authorised to take specific actions on alerts (arrest a person, perform specific or discreet check, etc.) and therefore these agencies will not use the SIS II as a compensatory measure for the abolition of the borders. They will use SIS II for their own institutional purposes and moreover, the legislation does not provide any specification of the purposes to access and allows "fishing expeditions".[91]

According to Article 41(3) of the Decision 2007/533/JHA, Europol can use the information obtained from a search in the SIS II with the consent of the Member State that has issued the alert, but it is clear that this use does not derive directly from the purpose of the SIS II.

In the case of Eurojust, Article 42(6) permits access to the SIS II only to the national members of Eurojust and their assistants and excludes Eurojust staff. According to the Article 2(1) of the Council Decision 2002/187/JHA of February 28, 2002 setting up Eurojust with a view to reinforcing the fight against serious crime,[92] national members are prosecutors, judges or police officers of equivalent competence. And it does not contradict the general right of access to the SIS II established in the aforementioned Article 40(2) of Decision 533/2007/JHA.

The package of modifications proposals by the European Commission on December 21, 2016 includes broadening the right of access of Europol to all categories of alerts and granting it to other EU agency – European Border and Coast Guard Agency.[93]

Regulation (EC) 1986/2006 of the European Parliament and of the Council, regarding access to the Second Generation Schengen Information System

91 COUNCIL OF THE EUROPEAN UNION, Opinion of the European Data Protection Supervisor on the legislative proposals concerning the Second Generation Schengen Information System (SIS II), 14091/05, p. 12, accessed November 18, 2017, http://data.consilium.europa.eu/doc/document/ST-14091-2005-INIT/en/pdf.

92 OJ L 63, 6.3.2002, p. 2.

93 See EUROPEAN COMMISSION, "Proposal for a Regulation of the European Parliament and of The Council on the use of the Schengen Information System…", *loc. cit.*, p. 57, 59.

(SIS II), by the services of the Member States responsible for issuing vehicle registration certificates,[94] foresees access of the aforementioned services to alerts for seizure or use as evidence in criminal proceedings of the following objects: motor vehicles, trailers, in order to check whether the vehicles presented to them are stolen, misappropriated or lost, or are sought as evidence in criminal procedure.

Talking about persons having access to the SIS II data, each of them shall fulfil national rules of confidentiality. At SIRENE level, usually this would be equivalent to having security clearance and at other levels – the duty to maintain professional secrecy. Breach of secrecy, depending on its severity, can result in disciplinary or criminal responsibility.

According to Articles 12, 18, and 41(4) of Decision 2007/533/JHA, all access to and exchanges of personal data shall be recorded and shall include "the history of the alerts, the date and time of the data transmission, the data used to perform a search, a reference to the data transmitted and the name of both the competent authority and the person responsible for processing the data."

Its Article 16 establishes Management Authority (since May 2013 is eu-LISA) that controls access (including facilities and persons) and processing (including input, communication and storage) of the data.

5.3 *Third parties*

As a general rule established in Article 54 of the Decision 2007/533/JHA, data from SIS II cannot be transferred to third parties, meaning neither countries nor organisations. The only permitted exception is data submission to the Interpol database on stolen or missing travel documents (Article 55). Such transfers include only data on the type of stolen, lost, invalid or misappropriated document, its number and issuing country, and can be performed only with the following conditions:

a Interpol and the European Union sign relevant agreement;
b Issuing Member States gives a consent for such transfer;
c Data shall be accessible only to those Interpol members (third countries) that provide with the relevant data protection level.

Such provision is useful for those countries that do not have a system that allows submitting the same information to a different database. Those who have such a system do not need an application of the Article 55 as introducing information into its own system, a competent authority from the same interface chooses in which data bases it wants to announce an alert: national, SIS, Interpol, and so on.

94 OJ L 381, 28.12.2006, p. 1–3.

For the time being, this provision is not applicable as the relevant agreement between Interpol and the European Union has not been signed.

5.4 Data subject's rights

Article 49 of Decision 2007/977/JHA establishes Member State's responsibility for the accuracy of entered data and its correction.

Its Article 58 entails data subject's right of access, deletion and correction, but more specific regulation on implementation of this right is left to the national legislation of each Member State. The European legislator foresees only two restrictions:

- Access shall be denied if it necessary to the performance of tasks related to an alert, or in order to protect the rights of third parties.
- If a request is related to data submitted to SIS II by another Member State, it has to be consulted before an answer being given to the data subject.

Replies shall be provided within the deadlines foreseen by the national law of the requested Member State, but not later than within 60 days in cases of implementation of the right to access, and within 3 months in cases of implementation of the right to deletion or correction. This is a novelty of the SIS II legal basis in comparison with the previous one that did not envisage any deadlines for replies.[95]

As all N.SIS are identical reflections of C.SIS, the data subject can file a request in any Member State.[96]

The majority of Member States (e.g. Austria, Bulgaria, Czech Republic, Denmark, Estonia, Finland, Germany, Greece, Iceland, Italy, Latvia, Liechtenstein, Lithuania, Malta, the Netherlands, Norway, Poland, Romania, Slovakia, Slovenia, Spain, Sweden, Switzerland and United Kingdom) provide direct access, meaning that the data subject can address his or her request directly to the competent authority that handles the data. Very few Member States (e.g. Belgium, Luxembourg and Portugal) apply indirect access, meaning that

95 See BROUWER, Evelien, "The Other Side of Moon: The Schengen Information System and Human Rights: A Task for National Courts", Working Document No. 288, Centre for European Policy Studies, April 2008, p. 4, accessed October 20, 2017, http://www.ceps.eu/publications/other-side-moons-schengen-information-system-and-human-rights-task-national-courts.

96 RECUERO, Paz, "La protección de datos y Schengen: Una visión desde la experiencia española" in GOIZUETA VéRTIZ, Juana; GONZÁLEZ MURUA, Ana Rosa and PARIENTE DE PRADA, Iñaki. *El Espacio de Libertad, Seguridad y Justicia: Schengen y Protección de Datos*, Pamplona: Aranzadi, SA., 2013, p. 213.

the data subject has to address the request to the national supervisory authority (independent data protection institution).[97]

France and Hungary apply a mixed access system based on different principles. In the case of France, access depends on the category of alert, i.e. direct access is granted in relation to alerts on persons being searched for in relation to family reasons, minors and those that are referred to in alerts on stolen vehicles. In the case of the remaining alerts, indirect access is used. In Hungary, a request can be addressed both to competent and supervisory authorities, but finally the national SIRENE office deals with all of them.[98] The system applied by France seems a little bit confusing as it can be applied only when a person knows what kind of alert is issued in relation to him or herself. And without such knowledge, the person will need to use both mechanisms.

5.5 *Supervising authorities*

To ensure the application of data protection, as with any fundamental right, there is a need for a control mechanism. As SIS II consists of central and national systems, its supervision is divided between national and European authorities.

The European Data Protection Supervisor performs supervision at EU level. Controls can be performed in respect to some category of alert, data, specific basis or complaint, but in any case, at least once every 4 years, a comprehensive audit of eu-LISA's data processing activities is performed.

To control data processing within N.SIS and SIRENE, each Member State has to nominate a national, independent, supervising authority. National supervisory authorities also perform comprehensive national auditing at least every 4 years and on an ad hoc basis when necessary.

To ensure smooth and equal data protection, the European Data Protection Supervisor and national authorities have to cooperate and meet at least twice a year.

6 Brief summary and evaluation

Although the direct objective of the multilateral Schengen agreement, the CISA and its incorporation into the EU legal system as Schengen acquis, is the free movement of persons and goods within the Schengen area, it is also the pioneer tool of the police and judicial cooperation; it is the first, and for the moment the last, so comprehensive legal framework that regulates

97 See SIS SUPERVISION COORDINATION GROUP, "The Schengen Information System. A Guide for Exercising the Right of Access", October 2014 (updated October 2015), p. 11–29, 33–38, 41–89, accessed November 3, 2015, https://edps.europa.eu/sites/edp/files/publication/16-11-07_sis_ii_guide_of_access_en.pdf

98 Ibid., p. 30, 39.

the centralised data base, its supporting offices and data protection, information exchange and other non-data base assistance; the setting up a network of cooperation officers and units, as well as cross-border actions.

Despite criticisms of being a "Big Brother" tool, regulation of the SIS followed by SIS II is one of the most comprehensive regulations which has ever existed at international level, with precise foreseeing of data categories that can be exchanged, and the prohibition of exchange sensitive data.

With respect to rights to privacy and data protection, the Schengen agreement, the CISA, incorporation of the Schengen acquis through the primary law of the EU (Treaty of Amsterdam), later joining the Schengen area by third countries, required ratification by the national parliament of each country, and therefore can be treated more as a fulfilment of the legality criteria for restriction of the above mentioned fundamental rights. Current participation of the European Parliament in ordinary legislative procedure and possible pronunciation of national parliaments within 3 months after issuing of the legislative proposal also ensure legality.

Its purpose also seems to be justified as the abolition of control on internal borders has meant increased danger to public safety, and compensatory measures used on external borders and within the area of free movement were, and still are, needed.

With respect to proportionality criteria, SIS II includes alerts on limited categories of persons and objects. The inclusion of persons wanted for extradition or surrender is totally justifiable and proportional to public safety and combatting crime. Missing persons, or those needing special protection due their physical or mental conditions, generally do not present a direct threat to public safety. But public authorities are responsible for their safety (especially in the case of minors) and abolition of the control of internal borders makes this responsibility difficult to exercise and therefore requires some additional measures. The introduction of persons sought for assistance in judicial procedure can also be justified as their detection allows the performance of justice and in some cases, the prevention of malicious avoidance of it and in further cases, making a person aware of his or her inclusion in it.

More problematic are alerts on persons that have to be checked, as it is not established to what extent information should be gathered and processed, and it could, therefore, mean interference into personal and family life. This situation could be avoided by indicating in the alert, which precise information is needed, for example only the itinerary of his or her journey, means of transport used, and so on.

Although SIS II is equipped with its *lex especialis*, in relation to data protection that is quite comprehensive, taking into account the existence of other centralised data bases and the creation of *lex generalis* for all data exchange within the area of police and judicial cooperation, it would be more coherent to apply it to SIS II as well, and to ensure the application of the same standards to all databases.

Bibliography

ALVARGONZÁLES SAN MARTÍN, F., 2000, "Hacia un nuevo escenario de cooperación en asuntos de justicia e interior", in MINISTERIO DEL INTERIOR; *El espacio europeo de libertad, seguridad y justicia*, Madrid: Secretaría General Técnica, p. 15–25.

ASSOCIATION OF CHIEF POLICE OFFICERS OF ENGLAND, WALES & NORTHERN IRELAND, 2010, "Guidelines for the use of the Schengen Information System II to locate people for judicial purposes", version 7. Available at: http://www.acpo.police.uk/documents/criminaljustice/2008/200810CJUSIS01.pdf (accessed October 16, 2017).

BERTOZZI, S., 2008, "Schengen: Achievements and Challenges in Managing and Area Encompassing 3.6 million km^2", working document no. 284, Centre for European Policy Study. Available at: http://papers.ssrn.com/sol3/papers.cfm?abstract_id=1337624 (accessed October 12, 2017).

BLOCK, L., 2013, "Bilateral Police Liaison Officers: Practices and European Policy"; in *Journal of Contemporary European Research*, vol. 6, issue 2, p. 194–210. Available at: http://www.jcer.net/ojs/index.php/jcer/article/view/266/205 (accessed October 20, 2017).

BROUWER, E., 2008, "The Other Side of Moon: The Schengen Information System and Human Rights: A Task for National Courts", working Document No. 288, Centre for European Policy Studies. Available at: http://www.ceps.eu/publications/other-side-moons-schengen-information-system-and-human-rights-task-national-courts (accessed October 20, 2017).

CALESINI, G., 2007, *European Police Law Handbook*, Roma: Laurus Robuffo.

COUNCIL OF THE EUROPEAN UNION, 2004, "SIS II functions/Open Issues", 12573/3/04. Available at: http://data.consilium.europa.eu/doc/document/ST-12573-2004-REV-3/en/pdf (accessed November 18, 2017).

COUNCIL OF THE EUROPEAN UNION, 2004, "Opinion of the European Data Protection Supervisor on the legislative proposals concerning the Second Generation Schengen Information System (SIS II)", 14091/05. Available at: http://data.consilium.europa.eu/doc/document/ST-14091-2005-INIT/en/pdf (accessed November 18, 2017).

COUNCIL OF THE EUROPEAN UNION, 2006, "Brussels European Council 15/16 June 2006. Presidency Conclusions", 10633/1/06. Available at: http://data.consilium.europa.eu/doc/document/ST-10633-2006-REV-1/en/pdf (accessed November 18, 2017).

COUNCIL OF THE EUROPEAN UNION, 2006, "SIS II, SIS I + and the enlargement of the Schengen area – Council Conclusions", 16391/1/06. Available at: http://data.consilium.europa.eu/doc/document/ST-16391-2006-REV-1/en/pdf (accessed November 18, 2017).

COUNCIL OF THE EUROPEAN UNION, 2010, "Updated Catalogue of Recommendations for the correct application of the Schengen Acquis and Best practices: Police cooperation", 15785/2/10. Available at: http://data.consilium.europa.eu/doc/document/ST-15785-2010-REV-3/en/pdf (accessed November 18, 2017).

COUNCIL OF THE EUROPEAN UNION, 2013, "Outcome of the 4th Conference on Police and Customs Cooperation Centres (PCCCs) on 21 and 22 October 2013, Brussels, Belgium"; 16249/13. Available at: http://data.consilium.europa.eu/doc/document/ST-16249-2013-INIT/en/pdf (accessed November 18, 2017).

DONAIRE VILLA, F.J., 2002, *La Constitución y el Acervo de Schengen*, Valencia: Tirant lo Blanch.

DEL MORAL TORRES, A., 2011, *Cooperación policial en la Unión Europea: la necesidad de un modelo de inteligencia criminal eficiente*, Madrid: Dykinson, S.L.

EU LISA, 2017, "SIS II – 2016 statistics". Available at: http://www.eulisa.europa.eu/Publications/Reports/SIS%20II%20-%20Statistics%202016.pdf (accessed October 17, 2017).

EUROPEAN COMMISSION, 2001, "Communication from the Commission to the Council and the European Parliament – Development of the Schengen Information System II", COM(2001)720 final. Available at: http://eur-lex.europa.eu/legal-content/EN/ALL/?uri=CELEX:52001DC0720 (accessed November 16, 2017).

EUROPEAN COMMISSION, 2010, "Communication from the Commission to the European Parliament and the Council – Overview of information management in the area of freedom, security and justice", COM(2010) 385 final. Available at: http://eur-lex.europa.eu/LexUriServ/LexUriServ.do?uri=COM:2010:0385:FIN:EN:PDF (accessed November 16, 2017).

EUROPEAN COMMISSION, 2015, "Communication from the Commission to the European Parliament, the Council, the European Economic and Social Committee and the Committee of the Regions – The European Agenda on Security", COM (2015) 185 final. Available at: http://eur-lex.europa.eu/legal-content/EN/TXT/HTML/?uri=CELEX:52015DC0185&from=ES (accessed November 16, 2017).

EUROPEAN COMMISSION, 2016, "Proposal for a Regulation of the European Parliament and of The Council on the use of the Schengen Information System for the return of illegally staying third- country nationals", COM(2016) 881 final. Available at: http://eur-lex.europa.eu/legal-content/EN/TXT/HTML/?uri=CELEX:52016PC0881&rid=1 (accessed November 16, 2017).

EUROPEAN COMMISSION, 2016, "Proposal for a Regulation of the European Parliament and of the Council on the establishment, operation and use of the Schengen Information System (SIS) in the field of border checks, amending Regulation (EU) No 515/2014 and repealing Regulation (EC) No 1987/2006", COM (2016) 882 final. Available at: http://eur-lex.europa.eu/legal-content/EN/TXT/?uri=COM:2016:0882:FIN (accessed November 16, 2017).

EUROPEAN COMMISSION, 2016, "Proposal for a Regulation of the European Parliament and of the Council on the establishment, operation and use of the Schengen Information System (SIS) in the field of police cooperation and judicial cooperation in criminal matters, amending Regulation (EU) No 515/2014 and repealing Regulation (EC) No 1986/2006, Council Decision 2007/533/JHA and Commission Decision 2010/261/EU", COM(2016) 883 final. Available at: http://eur-lex.europa.eu/legal-content/EN/TXT/?uri=COM:2016:0883:FIN (accessed November 16, 2017).

EUROPEAN COURT OF AUDITS, 2013, "Lessons from the European Commission's development of the second generation Schengen Information System (SIS II)". Available at: http://www.eca.europa.eu/Lists/ECADocuments/SR14_03/SR14_03_EN.pdf (accessed October 16, 2017).

FERNÁNDEZ-PITA Y GONZÁLEZ, R., 2000, "El Tratado de Ámsterdam y el Acervo de Schengen" in MINISTERIO DEL INTERIOR, *El espacio Europeo de libertad, seguridad y justicia*, Madrid: Secretaría General Técnica, p. 83–95.

GARCÍA VÁZQUEZ, S., 2014, "La cooperación policial y judicial como ejes de consolidación del espacio de Libertad, Seguridad y Justicia e instrumentos de protección de los derechos fundamentales en la Unión Europea" in GOIZUETA

VÉRTIZ, J. and CIENFUEGOS MATEO, J., *La eficacia de los Derechos Fundamentales de la UE*, Navarra: Aranzadi, p. 417–472.

GUILLE, L., 2010, "Policing in Europe: An Ethnographic Approach to Understanding the Nature of Cooperation and the Gap between Policy and Practice", in *Journal of Contemporary European Research*, vol. 6, no. 2, p. 257–271. Available at: http://www.jcer.net/index.php/jcer/article/view/192 (accessed October 20, 2017).

HAYES, B., 2004, "From the Schengen Information System to SIS and the Visa Information (VIS): proposals explained", p.00A0;10. Available at: http://www.statewatch.org/news/2005/may/analysis-sisII.pdf (accessed October 20, 2017).

HOUSE OF LORDS, EUROPEAN UNION COMMITTEE, 2007, "Report with Evidence: Schengen Information System II (SIS II)". Available at: http://www.publications.parliament.uk/pa/ld200607/ldselect/ldeucom/49/49.pdf (accessed October 18, 2017).

HREBLAY, V., 1998, *Les accords de Schengen: Origine, Fonctionnement, Avenir*, Brussels: Bruylant.

HUFNAGEL, S., 2013, *Policing cooperation across borders: comparative perspectives on law enforcement within the EU and Australia*, Hampshire: Ashgate Publishing Limited.

INTERNATIONAL CENTRE FOR MIGRATION POLICY DEVELOPMENT and EUROPEAN PUBLIC LAW ORGANIZATION, 2010, "Study on the status of information exchange amongst law enforcement authorities in the context of existing EU instruments". Available at: https://ec.europa.eu/home-affairs/sites/homeaffairs/files/doc_centre/police/docs/icmpd_study_lea_infoex.pdf (accessed October 20, 2017).

MARTÍN DIZ, F., 2010, "Aspectos recientes de la cooperación judicial y policial hispano-portuguesa; especial consideración del Acuerdo de Évora" in *Revista de Estudios Europeos*, no. 56, p. 95–107.

MORENO CATENA, V. and CASTILLEJO MANZANARES, R., 1999, *La persecución de los delitos en el Convenio de Schengen*, Valencia: Tirant lo Blanch.

OUBIÑA BARBOLLA, S., 2012, "The European Arrest Warrant in Law and Practice" in RUGGERI, S.; *Liberty and Security in Europe. A comparative analysis of pre-trial precautionary measures in criminal proceedings*, Göttingen: V&R Unipress GmbH, p. 47–66.

PARKIN, J., 2011, "Difficult Road to the Schengen Information System II: the legacy of 'laboratories' and the cost for fundamental rights and the rule of law", Report, Centre for European Policy Studies. Available at: http://www.ceps.eu/book/schengen-information-system-and-eu-rule-law (accessed September 9, 2017).

RECUERO, P., 2013, "La protección de datos y Schengen: Una visión desde la experiencia española" in GOIZUETA VéRTIZ, J.; GONZÁLEZ MURUA, A.R. and PARIENTE DE PRADA, I., *El Espacio de Libertad, Seguridad y Justicia: Schengen y Protección de Datos*, Pamplona: Aranzadi, SA; p. 197–216.

SCHATTENBERG, B., 1993, "Schengen Information System: Privacy and Legal Protection" in SCHERMERS, H.G.; FLINTERMAN, C.; KELLERMANN, A.E. et al. *Free Movement of Persons in Europe*, Dordrecht: Martinus Nijhoff, p. 43–52.

SIS SUPERVISION COORDINATION GROUP, 2015, "The Schengen Information System. A Guide for Exercising the Right of Access". Available at: https://edps.europa.eu/sites/edp/files/publication/16-11-07_sis_ii_guide_of_access_en.pdf (accessed November 1, 2017).

YON, H., 2010, "Police liaisons as builders of transnational security cooperation" in AYDINLI, E.; *Emerging Transnational (In)Security Governance: A Statist-transnationalist approach*, New York: Routledge, p. 124–142.

5 Europol

The European Police Office (hereinafter – Europol), nowadays is an EU agency regulated in the Article 88(2) of the TFUE and aims "to support and strengthen action by the Member States' police authorities and other law enforcement services and their mutual cooperation in preventing and combating serious crime affecting two or more Member States, terrorism and forms of crime which affect a common interest covered by a Union policy."[1]

The establishment of Europol's predecessor dates back to the beginning of the 1990s, but due to the changes introduced by different modifications of TFUE over the decades, both to Europol's status and the area of security, liberty and justice, the legal regulation of Europol has been modified recently, as modifications brought about by the Lisbon Treaty have included an obligation to adopt the regulation that determines the Agency's structure, operation, field of action and tasks of Europol. Therefore on May 11, 2016 Regulation (EU) 2016/794 of the European Parliament and of the Council on the European Union Agency for Law Enforcement Cooperation (Europol) and Replacing and Repealing Council Decisions 2009/371/JHA, 2009/934/JHA, 2009/935/JHA, 2009/936/JHA and 2009/968/JHA[2] (hereinafter – Europol Regulation) was adopted and is applicable since May 1, 2017.

Before entering into an analysis of Europol's role in information exchange, there is a need for a clear definition of its competence.

Although one can encounter that Europol is called European FBI, federal police, or is ascribed with executive powers, its main objectives are information exchange, threat analysis and assistance to national law enforcement institutions.

As pointed out by Bures, Europol "Is not an executive police force with autonomous supranational authority to conduct its own investigations, undertake searches, or arrest suspects."[3]

1 Article 88.1 of the TFEU.

2 OJ L 135, 24.5.2016, p. 53–114.

3 BURES, Oldrich, "Europol's Fledging Counterterrorism Role" in *Terrorism and Political Violence*, 2008, vol. 20, no. 4, p. 501.

From the very beginning, Germany was in favour of endowing Europol with the same coercive and executive competence as the *Bundeskriminalamt*,[4] but there was little support for this idea from other Member States, and the focus was on the improvement of the information flow.

As stated by Fijnaut, "While the integration of the 1990 Schengen Convention can be described as bottom up cross-border operationalization of police co-operation in the EU, the intention to include Europol more closely – in particular through joint teams – in criminal investigations of Member States in the field of organized crime can be called a top down attempt at cross-border operationalization of the action."[5]

1 From ministerial agreement to regulation by the TFEU

The idea to create a police entity at European level dates back to the beginning of the informal, intergovernmental cooperation within the TREVI, where from time to time, informally different visions of possible common law enforcement cooperation body were raised. In the modest vision, such agency was imagined with competence limited to some categories of crime. The most political and ambitious one was based on the wish of independence from information and intelligence gathered by the Unites States.[6]

Nevertheless, it took 15 years for the proposal to create a European police entity to be presented by German Chancellor Helmut Kohl at the European Council of June 28–29, 1991, where the TREVI ministers were asked to submit a report on the possible development of a central European criminal intelligence office. After prompt reception of the report, the Summit of December 9–10, 1991 agreed on the establishment of the European Police Office, beginning with its Drug Intelligence Unit.

A few months later, Article K1(9) of the Treaty of Maastricht on European Union foresaw that one of the areas of common interest would be "Police co-operation for the purposes of preventing and combating terrorism, unlawful drug trafficking and other serious forms of international crime, including if necessary certain aspects of customs co-operation, in connection

4 This idea was strongly supported by the Germans. For example, German Chancellor Schröder proposed to transform Europol into a European police force with the same coercive and executive competence as the *Bundeskriminalamt*. See STORBECK, Jürgen, "La cooperación policial europea", in MONTERO, Julián, ROMERO, Francisco and VALIENTE, Elena, *¿Hacia una Policía Europea?* Madrid: Fundación Policía Española, 2002, p. 500.

5 FIJNAUT, Cyrille, "Police Co-operation and the Area of Freedom, Security and Justice" in WALKER, Neil, *Europe's Area of Freedom, Security and Justice*, Oxford: Oxford University Press, 2004, p. 249–250.

6 See BIGO, Didier, "EU Police Cooperation: National Sovereignty Framed by European Security?" in GUILD, Elspeht and GEYER, Florian (eds.), *Security versus Justice? Police and Judicial Cooperation in the European Union*, Hampshire: Ashgate Publishing Limited, 2008, p. 94.

with the organization of a Union-wide system for exchanging information within a European Police Office (Europol)."[7]

Although the Treaty was signed on February 7, 1992, it was obvious that its ratification would take some time and that it would take even longer to agree on to ratify a Convention that would regulate Europol's mandate and activities. Therefore, first regulation of European police cooperation entity had the form of ministerial agreement.

1.1 Ministerial agreement

Ministerial Agreement on the Establishment of the Europol Drug Unit was signed on June 2, 1993 in Copenhagen.

Consequently, a non-operational team of the liaison officers of all the participating countries were sent to the EDU headquarters for the establishment of intelligence exchange and analysis. The EDU's mandate was limited to actions where the crime or organised group affected two or more Member States. Each liaison officer had to perform his or her duties according to the national regulation, including that on data protection. The agreement entailed only the following data exchange and protection rules:

- All information exchange takes place on a bilateral basis between requesting and requested states.
- If information related to the request has other than the requested state, this information can be transmitted to the requesting state only by that other state, and not by the requested one.
- It is not allowed to transmit personal data to the non-Member State, or to any international organisation.
- No personal information can be stored centrally in the EDU.
- National data protection authorities supervise the activities of their liaison officers.

Despite giving the first initiative towards a European police cooperation institution, the ministerial agreement had been far from sufficient to establish a full time functioning international office (defining its structure, competences, responsibility, accountability, maintenance, etc.) and therefore, two weeks later,[8] the Summit of Brussels determined that the Ministerial Agreement should be replaced by a Convention on Europol before October 1994.[9]

7 OJ C 191, 29.7.1992, p. 61.
8 On December 10–11, 1993.
9 See BRUGGEMAN, Willy, "Europol and the Europol Drugs Unit: Their Problems and Potential for Development" in BIEBER, Roland and MONAR, Joerg, *Justice and Home Affairs in the European Union. The Development of the Third Pillar*, Brussels: European Interuniversity Press, 1995, p. 220–221.

1.2 Europol Convention

Despite the established deadline, Europol had been in "embryonic existence"[10] for over 5 years, as ratification of the Convention signed in 1995 lasted until mid-1998, and Europol only replaced the EDU from July 1, 1999.

As had been supposed, the Convention based on Article K.3 of the Treaty on European Union, on the establishment of a European Police Office[11] (hereinafter – Europol Convention) expanded the scope of action foreseen for the EDU, envisaging as Europol's objective the prevention and combatting of terrorism, unlawful drug trafficking and other serious forms of international crime when they affect two or more Member States. It had foreseen some kind of transitional period until full functioning: Europol had to start with the prevention and combatting of crimes of trafficking in drugs, human beings, nuclear and radioactive substances and motor vehicles as well as illegal immigrant smuggling, and after 2 years of functioning to cover terrorism and also other crimes, if decided by the Council. In all cases, Europol's competence included money laundering and other criminal offences related to the above-mentioned forms of crime.

1.2.1 New information processing and exchange scheme

Compared with the EDU, Europol had the right to maintain a computerised system of collected information, and to notify Member States about information possessed which was related to them.

The information exchange scheme became the following:

- Every Member State has only one liaison body between its competent authorities and Europol – its national unit (ENU);
- Every Member State sends at least one liaison officer to Europol's headquarters in order to maintain contacts and forward information between Europol and its ENU.

The Europol Convention, equal to other instruments, did not endow Europol with the application of coercive measures. As explained by Storbeck, (the first director of Europol), Europol "is not authorised to perform either telephone tapping, or searches or detentions or other types of police measures that seldom violate citizens' fundamental rights and therefore in addition to the requirement to be performed in conformity with relevant legal provisions, they have to be subject to the supervision of a prosecutor or other democratically competent institution."[12]

10 PEERS, Steve, *EU Justice and Home Affairs Law*, 3rd edition, New York, Oxford University Press Inc., 2011, p. 931.
11 OJ C 316, 27.11.1995, p. 1–32.
12 STORBECK, Jürgen, "La cooperación policial europea...", loc. cit., p. 167.

The third Round of Mutual Evaluations[13] has shown that Member States are not in favour of granting it operation activities, but to strengthening analytical ones,[14] which by some authors such as Gómez-Jara Díez, is seen as a lack of real efficiency of Europol.[15]

In 2005 was created the EIS, containing information contributed by Member States in compliance with their national procedures as well as one received by Europol from third parties.

With respect to the content of the EIS, it was allowed to process data on:

- Persons suspected of already committed crime that is subject to Europol's competence, their accomplices;
- Persons suspected in future commission of such crime;
- Committed crimes, *modus operandi*;
- Convicted persons.

Direct access to the EIS was provided to ENUs, liaison officers and authorised Europol staff.

A possibility was also established by the agreement of two thirds of the members of the Management Board to create thematic[16] data (work) files, also called AWF. The rules of authorisation to open AWFs were modified by the Protocol drawn up on the basis of Article 43(1) of the Convention on the Establishment of a European Police Office (Europol Convention). Instead of a mandate of the authorisation to open AWFs, the Management Board was endowed with the right to close it. Thus Europol (the Director) became free to open AWFs, sending relevant information to the supervisory body and the Management Board, and to continue its development and use until objection was received from the latter.

The purpose of AWFs was (and still remains) analysis, processing or utilisation of data with the aim of helping a criminal investigation of all interested Member States.

13 Member States had agreed to organize evaluations to assess applications of different police and judicial cooperation mechanisms, and the third round was dedicated to information exchange with Europol.

14 See COUNCIL OF THE EUROPEAN UNION, "Third round of Mutual Evaluations 'Exchange of information and intelligence between Europol and the Member States and among the Member States respectively' Final Report on the evaluation visits of all 27 Member States", 13321/07, p. 35, accessed November 19, 2017, http://data.consilium.europa.eu/doc/document/ST-13321-2007-REV-3/en/pdf.

15 See GÓMEZ-JARA DÍEZ, Carlos, "¿Federalismo jurídico-penal en la Constitución Europea? Un diálogo con el profesor Silva Sánchez" in ARROYO ZAPATERO, Luis and NIETO MARTíN, Adán, *El Derecho Penal de la Unión Europea. Situación actual y perspectivas de future*, Cuenca: Universidad de Castilla-La Mancha, 2007, p. 89.

16 Focused on phenomenon, organised group or region.

Thus Europol staff, using analytical tools, would compare information transmitted by Member States to AWF in order to establish possible links between crimes, persons, *modus operandi* and then would provide information and intelligence related to the topic. For example, such an AWF was created to combat trafficking in cocaine (to investigate, dismantle laboratories, and so on) and sought "to collect intelligence associated with the activities of suspected criminal organisations and networks involved in the production, processing or trafficking of cocaine, including intelligence relating to precursor chemicals and cutting agents."[17]

Unlike the EIS, AWFs can contain not only data on convicted persons and persons suspected of commissioning crime, but also data on victims, witnesses, contacts and associates, providers of information related to offences under consideration.

AWFs can also contain data on criminal offences, modus operandi, entities responsible for the investigation, case references, even if no references to persons exist.

In addition to information processing, Europol was also endowed with the additional tasks of developing specialist knowledge, providing strategic intelligence and preparing general situation reports.

The Management Board – as already mentioned – is Europol's decisive body. As Europol was the result of intergovernmental cooperation, there was the need for a body that would ensure the participation of all Member States in approval of essential decisions on Europol's functioning (those not regulated or endowed to the Council), and so the Management Board was created as such a unit. It became responsible for the definition of rules for liaison officers (their rights and obligations), regulation of security clearance, participation with the Council in the extension of Europol's mandate, appointment of the Director, his or her Deputies and financial controller, drawing up the budget (consisting of Member States' contributions[18] and other incidental incomes).

1.2.2 Way forward

The Europol Convention was subject to modification by three protocols signed in 2000, 2002 and 2003:

17 EUROPEAN MONITORING CENTER FOR DRUGS AND DRUG ADDICTION, EUROPOL, "Cocaine: A European Union Perspective in the global context", 2010, p. 33, accessed, June 7, 2017, https://www.google.es/#q=analytical+work+file+Cola.

18 According to Article 35 of the Europol Convention, "Each Member State's financial contribution shall be determined according to the proportion of its gross national product to the sum total of the gross national products of the Member States for the year preceding the year in which the budget is drawn up." In the Ministerial Agreement the cost was borne, "within the limits of their budgetary rules and annual procedures, each Ministry's voluntary annual contribution [...] will be determined on the basis of the country's gross national product."

- Council Act of November 30, 2000 drawing up, on the basis of Article 43 (1) of the Convention on the establishment of a European Police Office (Europol Convention), of a Protocol amending Article 2 and the Annex to that Convention[19] that included money laundering into Europol's competence, as well as any other crime which predicates the crime that represents its core competence;
- Council Act of November 28, 2002 drawing up a Protocol amending the Convention on the establishment of a European Police Office (Europol Convention), and the Protocol on the privileges and immunities of Europol, the members of its organs, the deputy directors and the employees of Europol,[20] that spelled out Europol's possibility to participate in joint investigation teams and to request Member States to conduct or coordinate investigations.
- Council Act of November 27, 2003 drawing up, on the basis of Article 43(1) of the Convention on the Establishment of a European Police Office (Europol Convention), a Protocol amending that Convention[21] that established the regulation of Europol's operational agreements with third states for information exchange and their participation in AWFs.

Due to a long ratification procedure, all three protocols only came into force in 2007. It was a clear sign that with the application of conventional procedure, Europol would not be able to adapt rapidly to changing crime tendencies with relevant modifications of its competences, tasks or functions. Under these circumstances, it was decided to change the Convention by the Council Decision that would be allowed, in case of necessity, to make rapid changes without the need to wait for the ratification process of all Member States, especially taking into account that since the first decisions on Europol, their number had increased from 12 to 27. This initiative was presented by the Austrian Presidency of the Council of the European Union in 2006, and resulted in the Commission's proposal on draft Council Decision.[22]

After more than 2 years of discussions, on April 6, 2009 the Council Decision 2009/371/JHA establishing the European Police Office (Europol)[23] (hereinafter – Europol Decision) was adopted and remained in force until May 1, 2017 and substituted the Europol Regulation.

19 OJ C 358, 13.12.2000, p. 1–7.
20 OJ C 312, 16.12.2002, p. 1.
21 OJ C 2, 6.1.2004, p. 1–11.
22 See more explicitly AMICI, Victoria, "Europol et la nouvelle décision du Conseil: entre opportunités et contraintes" in *Revue du Droit de L'union Européenne*, 2010, no. 1, p. 80–81.
23 OJ L 121, 15.5.2009, p. 37–66.

2 Europol – EU agency

With entry into force of the Europol Decision, Europol became a European agency financed from the EU Budget, and subject to the same staff and other administrative requirements as other EU institutions and entities, as well as being accountable to the European Parliament. Although the title of the Europol Decision included the term "establishment", it only referred to the change of Europol's legal form, and Article 1(2) states that it "shall be regarded as the legal successor of Europol, as established by the Europol Convention."[24] The Europol Regulation declares that "Europol as established by this Regulation shall replace and succeed Europol as established by Decision 2009/371/JHA."[25]

With respect to its objective, it has changed since the entry into force of the Convention and so nowadays it covers a broader scope of criminality. According to the Europol Convention, the relationship with organised crime had been a compulsory condition in assigning crimes of terrorism, drug trafficking and other serious crime to Europol's competence. Europol Decision entailed the support and strengthening action of cooperation and referred to the prevention and combatting of organised crime, terrorism and other forms of serious crime affecting two or more Member States. That means that terrorism and other serious crimes were within the competence of Europol when they affected two or more Member States, but not necessarily related to organised crime. Europol Regulation goes further and establishes that in addition to what was foreseen by the Europol Decision, Europol supports and strengthens action and cooperation of Member States in terrorism as such and in forms of crime "which affect a common interest covered by a Union policy".[26] That means that both terrorism and these categories of crimes do not necessarily have to affect two or more Member States.

Comparing annexes with lists of crimes from Europol Decision and Europol Regulation, almost the same crimes in the first case were defined as serious crimes, and in the second case as serious crimes or crimes affecting common EU interests.[27] In addition to some legal-linguistic correction of

24 OJ L 121, 15.5.2009, p. 39.
25 OJ L 135, 24.5.2016, p. 62.
26 OJ L 135, 24.5.2016, p. 64.
27 Unlawful drug trafficking, illegal money-laundering activities, crime connected with nuclear and radioactive substances, illegal immigrant smuggling, trafficking in human beings, motor vehicle crime, murder, grievous bodily injury, illicit trade in human organs and tissue, kidnapping, illegal restraint and hostage taking, racism and xenophobia, organised robbery, illicit trafficking in cultural goods, including antiquities and works of art, swindling and fraud, racketeering and extortion, counterfeiting and product piracy, forgery of administrative documents and trafficking therein, forgery of money and means of payment, computer crime, corruption, illicit trafficking in arms, ammunition and explosives, illicit trafficking in endangered animal species, illicit trafficking in endangered plant species and varieties, environmental crime, illicit trafficking in hormonal substances and other growth promoters.

some types of crimes (e.g. instead of referring to illegal money-laundering activities using "money-laundering activities"), Europol Regulation broadened the list by including: terrorism, organised crime, aggravated theft, crime against the financial interests of the Union, insider dealing and financial market manipulation, sexual abuse and sexual exploitation, including child abuse, genocide, crimes against humanity and war crimes. The repetitive inclusion of terrorism into the list is redundant, because it is already mentioned separately in the Article 3(1) and disassociated from affectation of two or more Member States.

The same policy in relation to "related crimes"[28] remains throughout the Europol Convention (Article 2(3)), Europol Decision (Article 4(3)) and Europol Regulation (Article 3(2)).

Regarding the processing of information, changes were not great, as Member States remain responsible for making decisions relating to the scope of information that can be provided to Europol. The Europol Decision only established the legal basis allowing wider access to its databases in order to ensure better use of Europol's capacities and to enhance trust in it as a partner.[29] The same idea is followed in the Europol Regulation.

Although since its establishment, Europol had been carrying out analytical functions, only the Europol Decision established the task to elaborate threat assessments and strategic analysis. The Europol Regulation also obliges to elaborate strategic analysis and threat assessment that facilitates the Council and the Commission to establish priorities in the fight against crime, and to assist in their implementation.

The general structure and cooperation mechanism has remained the same, with the obligation of Member States to maintain single ENU and to send at least one liaison officer to Europol's Headquarters.

2.1 Information exchange tools

Since becoming an Agency, a description of Europol as an information exchange hub, a centre of expertise, can be encountered and finally it has been recorded in the Recital 12 of the Europol Regulation: "Europol should be a hub for information exchange in the Union."[30]

28 See for example Art. 3.2 of the Europol Regulation: criminal offences committed in order to procure the means for commission of criminal acts, to facilitate or perpetrate such acts or those committed in order to ensure the impunity of authors. In all cases "related criminal offences" should have relation to crime in respect of which Europol is competent.

29 See SANTOS VARA, Juan, "Las consecuencias de la integración de Europol en el Derecho de la Unión Europea (comentario a la Decisión del Consejo 2009/371/JAI, de 6 de abril de 2009)" in *Revista General de Derecho Europeo*, 2010, no. 20, p. 10.

30 OJ L 135, 24.5.2016, p. 55.

The Europol Decision, like the Europol Convention, directly established and regulated the Europol Information System and AWFs. It also foresaw that the Management Board should approve the creation of a new personal data processing system. Consequently, the Management Board agreed on the establishment of the SIENA.

Nevertheless, this legislative logic has been changed in the Europol Regulation that almost does not refer to any particular database, leaving flexibility to establish what is needed upon operational needs of Europol, but for the ended list of purposes established in the Article 18(2). It would allow Europol to adapt rapidly the needs of databases to changing reality without the necessity of waiting for the relevant modification of Regulation.

First of all, Article 18(2) talks about cross-checking of data on crimes, convicted persons and those suspected of already having committed a crime or with "factual indications or reasonable grounds to believe that they will commit criminal offences".

Secondly, it refers to the purpose of strategic, operational analysis and facilitating information exchange between competent authorities.

Already existing information processing tools fit the aforementioned purposes and the EIS is used mainly for cross-checking (and due to some extent analysis), AWF – mainly for operational analysis (but it also performs cross-checking), SIENA – for the exchange of information between competent authorities.

As the Europol Regulation replaces and repeals Europol Decision and other Council Decision related to Europol's activities, and does not enter into detailed regulation of data exchange tools, its Article 18(7) foresees that the Management Board has to adopt guidelines that specify procedures of the information processing within Europol. It has both advantages and disadvantages. On one hand, it allows more flexibility and adaptation to constantly changing needs and will be carried out by the organ that has direct knowledge of needs; on the other hand, it decreases legal certainty. For example, if AWF was previously regulated by the Council Decision 2009/936/JHA adopted at the level of ministers, and with at least some minimum consultation with the European Parliament, the Europol Regulation descends the approval to the level of Member States' and Commission's representatives in the Management Board. The positive aspect is that the Management Board shall consult EDPS.

Article 19 of the Europol Regulation establishes an obligation of the provider to determine the purpose for which information can be processed and says that information for other purposes than for which it was submitted cannot be processed without a consent of the provider. The exception from this rule is established in the Article 18(3)b and will be analyses in the part on AWF. It also permits the provider to establish any restrictions on access.

2.1.1 Europol Information System as a tool of cross-checking

The functioning of the EIS was based on Articles 7–9 of the Europol Convention and Articles 11–13 of the Europol Decision. EIS continues to be a database that stores information about offences and individuals involved, as well as other related criminal data.

Before Europol Regulation, EIS included data on persons under national law suspected of already having committed a crime, of being accomplices or of its future commission and convicted persons. New Regulation envisages that within the cross-checking of data in case of suspicions that a person can commit a crime in the future, they have to be based on "factual indications or reasonable grounds". However, it remains unclear what "reasonable grounds" means.

In addition to the data categories foreseen by the Europol Convention (surname, maiden name, given names, alias, assumed name, date and place of birth, nationality, sex and where necessary other characteristics likely to assist in identification[31]), Article 12 of the Europol Decision allowed the inclusion of the place of residence and whereabouts, profession, social security numbers, driving licences and identification documents. In the case of other characteristics, previously not specified, dactyloscopic data and DNA profiles were distinguished. Europol Regulation maintains the same categories of data.

Access to the EIS (both for input and retrieval) is granted to Europol staff empowered by the Director, liaison officers and ENUs. Article 13(6) of the Europol Decision established that Member States can decide to give EIS access to other competent authorities, but it will be limited to the possibility of verifying whether or not requested information exists (hit/no hit bases). In the case of a hit, a request for relevant information has to be sent through the ENU of that country. In the Europol Regulation the access of other competent authorities of Member States is not so clearly regulated as it refers to "access by Member States" in general.

2.1.2 Analysis Work Files as a tool for operational analysis

As already mentioned, in performing its tasks, when necessary, Europol can create AWFs to process and analyse information on some types of crime, organised groups or modus operandi.

The Europol Decision foresaw the same categories of persons that can be included in AWFs as the Europol Convention, i.e. categories of persons whose data can be processed in the EIS, and data of witnesses who can be called to testify, victims, contacts and associates of suspects as well as of informers. The Europol Regulation lists the same categories of persons as subjects whose data can be processed for the purpose of operational, strategic or thematic analysis. According to Article 18(3) for operational analysis project, its "specific purpose, categories of personal data and categories of data subjects, participants, duration of storage and conditions for access, transfer and use of the data concerned" shall be defined by the Executive

31 Article 8 of the Europol Convention.

Table 5.1 Categories of data stored in AWFs depending on category of person

Categories of person	*Categories of data collected*
All categories of persons	1. Present and former surnames (i.e. real and alias, nickname, residence, nationality, etc.) 2. Physical description (except informers) 3. Identification means (i.e. documents, ID and other official numbers)
Suspect of a crime (already committed or future), accomplice, convicted persons, contacts and associates[32]	1. Education, skills, employment (including associated legal persons) 2. Economic and financial information 3. Information on behaviour data 4. Contacts and associates 5. Communication means 6. Transport means 7. Criminal activities under the competence of Europol (including associated legal persons) 8. References to other databases 9. Other identification means (images, DNA, fingerprints)
Victims	1. Identification 2. Motives for victimisation 2. Damage suffered 3. Need to guarantee anonymity 4. Possibility to participate in a court hearing 5. Their provided information about crime Data categories mentioned in relation to suspect also can be collected if it is necessary for analysis
Witnesses	1. Need to guarantee anonymity 2. Need to guarantee protection 3. New identity 4. Possibility of participating in a court hearing 5. Their provided information about crime Data categories mentioned in relation to suspect also can be collected if it is necessary for analysis
Informers	1. Type of information provided 2. Encrypted personal data 3. Negative experiences 4. Rewards 5. Data categories applied to witnesses Data categories mentioned in relation to suspect can also be collected if it is necessary for analysis

Director. The data collected can be processed only for a pre-established purpose of such project.

Data categories that can be stored in AWFs depend on each category of person and vary considerably as shown in Table 5.1.

32 ENU or in urgent cases, competent authorities directly. See Article 3 of the Council Decision 2009/936/JHA

Among the information that can be included on victims, witnesses and informers, anonymity, use of new identity, need or application of protection measures deserve special attention. These categories can make any AWF a very powerful tool in the wrong hands and therefore, very high standards of secure communication, confidentiality and data protection shall be applied.

The right of direct input to an AWF is a responsibility of Europol's analysts designated for that file. Thus the role of Member States[33] is limited to the submission of information to Europol, where it is evaluated before being stored. Nevertheless, it is up to Member States to establish a degree of data sensitivity and the processing conditions.

Third parties directly related to AWFs can participate in them if there is a relevant agreement between the third party and Europol, and all participants of AWF agree to that.

In 2012, Europol ran 23 AFWs and from years of experience, it came to the conclusion that a vertical approach (on one region, group or phenomenon) is not always sufficient, and a generative thinking approach is needed. In these circumstances, and basing its decision on Article 18(1)a of Decision 2009/936/JHA, Europol proposed to participants of all AWFs, that they merge into two large AWFs: an AFW for serious and organised crime (AWF SOC), and an AWF for counter terrorism (AWF CT). Thus in May–July 2012, 18 AWFs related to serious and organised crime migrated to AWF SOC, and five AWFs related to counter terrorism – to AFW CT. A characteristic of the new AWFs is that within them, different analyses and actions could be carried out. A distinction was made between a Focal Point and a Target Group. The first one focuses on a certain phenomenon from the perspective of topic, regional angle or commodity, and Europol provides it mainly with analysis and support information and intelligence exchange. The second one is more operational than a Focal Point, as in addition to analysis, Europol designates its team to support an investigation or intelligence operation against a specific target.

2.1.3 Secure Information Exchange Network Application

SIENA was created in 2009 without having direct reference to either the Europol Convention or the Europol Decision. It was created on a general basis that allowed the creation of new systems processing personal data. The Europol Regulation does not directly regulate SIENA, but its recital 24 states that "Europol should also be able to act as a service provider, in particular by providing a secure network for the exchange of data, such as the secure information exchange network application (SIENA), aimed at facilitating the exchange of information between Member States, Europol, other Union bodies, third countries and international organisations".

33 ENU or in urgent cases, competent authorities directly. See Article 3 of the Council Decision 2009/936/JHA.

SIENA allows the exchange of strategic and operational information within the mandate of Europol, assuring a high level of communication, security and interoperability with other Europol systems and enabling the secure exchange of restricted and confidential information.

SIENA provides two possibilities:

- To exchange information using a web browser.
- Since 2012, to exchange information "system to system" that allows two types of connection: simple (to receive SIENA messages) and advanced (to receive and send them). The latter means the connection of a national system in such a way that it could be used both for national and international information exchange.

SIENA has multilingual user interface in all languages of the EU. Nevertheless, the text of a message is not translated and must normally be written in English, except in those cases when the parties in question agree to use another language.

SIENA can be used both for information exchange purely under Europol's mandate, and for bilateral or multilateral communication among Member States that remain outside its scope (that according to the technical report on Evaluation of the implementation of the Europol Council Decision and of Europol's activities carries out a majority of information exchange).[34] But on addressing one of Europol's cooperation partners (third party), Member States will be notified via SIENA that this exchange should only take place as far as crimes within Europol's mandate are concerned.

Depending on national arrangements, SIENA can be used not only by the ENU and liaison officers, but other competent authorities as well. Nevertheless, all the authorities of one Member State must be connected through one national system.

Before connecting to SIENA, it has to be ensured that the national system fulfils all security and data protection requirements (authentication, access control, input and output validation, logging and error handling, infrastructure controls).

2.2 Information exchange within and outside EU

Exchange of information between Member States through Europol, or its submission to Europol's databases directly derives from the Agency's

34 See DISLEY, Emma, IRVING, Barrie, HUGHES, William et al., "Technical report on Evaluation of the implementation of the Europol Council Decision and of Europol's activities", Cambrige: RAND Corporation, 2012, p. 49, accessed September 4, 2017, https://www.europol.europa.eu/content/publication/evaluation-implementation-europol-council-decision-and-europol's-activities-1655.

objective to support and strengthen the actions of competent authorities, and their cooperation. Nevertheless, in achieving this objective and acting against threats to the EU internal security information and intelligence from entities other than Member States (inside the EU as well as from third states and organisations), can be of upmost importance. For example:

- Information exchange with the European Agency for the Management of Operational Cooperation at the External Borders of the Member States of the European Union (FRONTEX) can help to identify links between organised crime, trafficking in human beings and illegal migration; information from Eurojust – to make link with ongoing investigations, and so on.
- Such crimes as drug trafficking, illegal migration and trafficking in human beings usually have their origin outside the EU, envisaging its Member States as the point of final destination. Therefore, to guarantee EU internal security, effective international cooperation with competent authorities in countries of origin and transit is indispensable. For example, as big drug flows come from West Africa, and South and Central America, a closed cooperation and effective information exchange with the competent authorities in these countries has to take place. In the case of criminal organisations of Albanian[35] or Russian[36] origin which act within the EU, information and intelligence from these countries is vital as well. Such cooperation could be based on reciprocity, which does not guarantee either rapidness or effectiveness, or on cooperation agreements. In reference to bilateral agreements, it is difficult to imagine that each Member State would have the necessary agreements with all important partners outside of the EU, because they are usually concluded in line with national priorities of cooperation with neighbouring states or specific regions, depending on their geographical position, historical links with other countries and threats to their security. In these circumstances, the optimum would be EU wide possibility of information exchange, which would serve to combat threats at EU level.[37]

Therefore, the Europol is envisaged with the possibility to exchange information with other EU bodies and third parties.

35 See STORBECK, Jürgen, "La cooperación policial europea…", loc. cit., p. 157.
36 See ESPIGARES MIRA, Jesús, "Instrumentos internacionales de cooperación" in MONTERO, Julián, ROMERO and Francisco, VALIENTE, Elena. *¿Hacía una Policía Europea?*, Madrid: Fundación Policía Española, 2002, p. 119.
37 See more in RENARD, Thomas, "Partners in crime? The EU, its strategic partners and international organised crime", Working Paper, European Strategic Partnership Observatory, May 2014, p. 15–20, accessed June 2, 2017, http://fride.org/publication/1191/partners-in-crime?-the-eu,-its-strategic-partners-and-international-organised-crime.

When it comes to exchange of strategic information and analysis, operational analysis, non-personal, personal and confidential data, different regulations are applied. In the case of personal data, a general rule of its transmission established in the Europol Decision was a purpose of prevention or combat of "criminal offences in respect of which Europol is competent".[38] The scope used in the Europol Regulation is broader as it refers to "performance of Europol's tasks".[39]

2.2.1 Information exchange with EU institutions and other entities

Article 22 of the Europol Decision permitted cooperative relations with all institutions, bodies, offices and agencies of the EU, and in particular with those directly or indirectly related to the Europol's activities. It envisaged an obligation to conclude agreements or working arrangements on operational, strategic, technical and classified information exchange with Eurojust, the European Anti-Fraud Office (OLAF), Frontex, the European Police College (CEPOL), the European Central Bank and the European Monitoring Centre for Drugs and Drug Addiction (EMCDDA).[40] With other bodies, agreements could be concluded with double authorisation of the Management Board: prior to negotiations and subsequent to closure of negotiations on the draft.

Europol's agreements with EU institutions, agencies and other entities can be:

- Strategic – permitting only the exchange of general information and strategic analysis without providing any personal data or confidential information.
- Operative – regulating in depth data protection and allowing the exchange of personal data.

On this basis Europol concluded:

- Strategic agreements (on the exchange of non-personal data) with the European Commission, European Central bank, CEPOL, EMCDDA, OLAF, the European Centre for Disease Prevention and Control, as well as the Office for Harmonisation in the Internal Market and the European Union Agency for Network and Information Security.
- Operational agreement (includes the exchange of personal data) with Eurojust and FRONTEX.

On the other hand, Article 22(3) allowed information exchange (without specific rules concerning personal data) prior to any agreement for the

38 Article 8 the Council Decision 2009/934/JHA.
39 Articles 23–25 of the Europol Regulation.
40 Strengthening of cooperation between the EU agencies is also foreseen in the European Internal Security Strategy.

necessity to perform the recipient's tasks (Europol's or of other EU institution).

As a general rule, Article 24 of the Europol Regulation established much more simplified regulation, saying that "Europol may directly transfer personal data to a Union body, insofar as such transfer is necessary for the performance of its tasks or those of the recipient Union body". Thus, the purpose has not been changed, but instead of referring to both sides' information exchange, it regulates only information transfer from Europol to Union body. In addition to the purpose limitation, such transfer shall obey rules established in Articles 19(2) and (3) and 67 of the Europol Regulation, i.e. Europol has to follow restrictions of access established by the provider of information. In cases of information obtained directly by Europol from public sources, it can also establish restrictions and shall accomplish with its own rules on sensitive and classified data.

Europol Regulation specially distinguishes cooperation with Eurojust and OLAF. Thus, Article 21 foresees indirect access Eurojust and OLAF to information processed by Europol to the extent of their mandate. Cooperation between Europol and Eurojust can go even further, as they are allowed to conclude a working arrangement on searching for, and access to, all information that has been provided for cross-checking. The exception would be data with restrictions imposed by its provider.

2.2.2 Information exchange with third states and international organisations

Article 23 of the Europol Decision foresaw the possibility of establishing and maintaining cooperative relations with third countries and organisations. Normally such cooperation, the same as in cases of the EU institutions and other entities, had to be based on strategic or operational agreements.

The list of countries and organisations with which Europol was able to conclude agreements had been established by the Council Decision 2009/935/JHA of November 30, 2009 determining the list of third states and organisations with which Europol shall conclude agreements[41] (hereinafter – Decision 2009/935/JHA) naming: Albania, Australia, Bolivia, Bosnia and Herzegovina, Canada, China, Colombia, Croatia[42], former Yugoslav Republic of Macedonia, Iceland, India, Israel, Liechtenstein, Moldova, Monaco, Montenegro, Morocco, Norway, Peru, Russia, Serbia, Switzerland, Turkey, Ukraine, United States of America, ICPO-Interpol, United Nations Office on Drugs and Crime and World Customs Organisation. It should be mentioned that it did not envisage whether strategic or operational agreement with one or another country or organisation has to be concluded. According to Articles 5 and 6 of Decision 2009/935/JHA, it depended on the data

41 OJ L 325, 11.12.2009, p. 12–13.

42 The agreement is not necessary since June 1, 2013 as Croatia became EU Member State.

protection level of the third country or organisation that is subject to evaluation prior to negotiations. After finalising negotiations, each draft agreement was submitted for the endorsement of the Management Board and approval of the Council of the European Union (in the case of operational agreement, opinion of the Joint Supervisory Body was also necessary).

For the time being, Europol has concluded:

- Strategic agreements with China, Russian Federation and Turkey.
- Operational agreements with Albania, Australia, Bosnia and Herzegovina, Canada, Colombia, Former Yugoslav Republic of Macedonia, Georgia, Iceland, Moldova, Montenegro, Norway, Republic of Serbia, Switzerland, the Principality of Liechtenstein, the Principality of Monaco, Ukraine and United States of America.

It has to be stressed that the scope of purpose of cooperation in agreements differs. Thus in agreements with Albania, Australia, Bosnia and Herzegovina, Colombia, former Yugoslav Republic of Macedonia, Georgia, Liechtenstein, Moldova and Ukraine, the scope of cooperation is all or almost all crimes that fell under Europol's mandate at the date of entry into force of agreement. In the case of Iceland, Monaco, Norway, Switzerland and United States of America, the scope is limited to a few types of crime, such as unlawful drug trafficking, trafficking in nuclear and radioactive substances, illegal immigrant smuggling, trade in human beings, motor vehicle crime, crimes committed or likely to be committed in the course of terrorist activities against life, limb, personal freedom or property, and the forgery of money and means of payment.[43]

Before Europol Regulation entered into force and in case of lacking cooperation agreement with third states, Europol was able to receive any data necessary for performing its tasks, but was limited to transmitting only non-personal and non-confidential data to the states and organisations mentioned in Decision 2009/935/JHA, and if transmitted information had been provided by a Member State – only with its consent. The only exception was established in 23(8) of the Europol Decision and reiterated in Article 14 of the Decision 2009/934/JHA as necessary in order to safeguard essential interests of the Member State (and it is within the scope of Europol's objectives) or prevent imminent danger, crime or terrorist attacks. In the case of countries and organisations not listed in Decision 2009/935/JHA, Europol was allowed to transmit only non-personal and non-confidential data in "absolutely necessary individual cases".

43 See, for example, Article 3 of the Agreement between the Kingdom of Norway and the European Police Office; Agreement between the United States of America and the European Police Office; Agreement between the Republic of Iceland and the European Police Office.

Article 25 of the Europol Regulation refers only to the "transfer of personal data" from Europol (but not to information exchange) and the rules change significantly. New legal provisions establish the possibility of transferring data from Europol in case of:

- The Commission's decision that the data protection level of the third state or a territory is adequate;
- EU agreement with a third party;
- Europol's and third parties' already existing operational agreements. Additionally, the Commission has to provide the European Parliament and the Council with the evaluation of Europol's agreements by June 14, 2021. When appropriate, it can recommend opening negotiations on agreement between the European Union and the third country or organisation.

According to Article 23(4), Europol by itself can only conclude working arrangements that exclude exchange of personal data and are not binding the EU or its Member States.

Nevertheless, the Europol Regulation widens the list of exceptions from the general rule of personal data transfer to third states or international organisations without any cooperation background with the EU and foresees the following:

- "Immediate and serious threat to public security of a Member State or a third country" instead of essential interests of Member State or imminent terrorist attack threat to it;
- "Prevention, investigation, detection or prosecution of criminal offenses or the execution of criminal sanctions" eliminating the reference to previously existing condition that crime under consideration must fall within the competence of Europol;
- "In individual cases for the establishment, exercise or defence of legal claims relating to the prevention, investigation, detection or prosecution of a specific criminal offence or the execution of a specific criminal sanction";
- "The vital interests of data subject or of another person";
- "Legitimate interests of the data subject where the law of the Member State transferring the personal data so provides".[44]

A significant novelty is the establishment of the possibility of the Management Board with the authorisation of the European Data Protection Supervisor to allow a set of transfers to the third state during 1 year (renewable) for the above mentioned five purposes. It is a significant alteration from the general requirement of the existence of the Commission's

44 Article 25(5) of the Europol Regulation.

adequacy decision, or agreement with third countries that gives an option for long lasting data transfer.

2.2.3 Information exchange with private parties

The rules of information retrieval established in Article 25 of the Europol Decision and Article 26(1–2) of the Europol Regulation are quite similar, allowing information to be obtained via ENUs, contact points of a third state or international organisations that have operational agreements with the Europol, or as specified in the Europol Regulation – is subject to an adequacy decision or a party of the respectful agreement.

As a general rule, the Europol cannot transfer personal data to private parties, but Article 26(5) of the Europol Regulation for the first time foresees exceptions that are possible if Articles 19(2) (3) and 67 are respected and if private parties are established in one of the Member States, third party subject to agreement with Europol, with the EU or to adequacy decision:

- For the benefit of interest of data subject with his or her expressed or clearly presumed consent,
- For the prevention of imminent perpetration of a crime under the Europol's mandate,
- In case of publicly available personal data in order to support Member States' actions in combating crimes facilitated, promoted or committed by using the internet and if it concerns a specific case, and public interest prevails over the fundamental rights of the data subject.

Transmission to other parties is possible only for the same purposes as its transfer to the third states without any legal background of cooperation.[45]

2.3 Obtaining trust from Member States

According to what has been already presented, since mid-1999, Member States have had an opportunity to use a new cooperation tool in combatting cross-border crime.[46] Moreover, the success of this tool depended on the good faith of cooperation of national law enforcement agencies, as Europol

45 Article 26(6) of the Europol Regulation: immediate and serious threat to public security of a Member State or a third country; prevention, investigation, detection or prosecution of criminal offenses or the execution of criminal sanctions; in individual cases for the establishment, exercise or defence of legal claims relating to the prevention, investigation, detection or prosecution of a specific criminal offence or the execution of a specific criminal sanction; the vital interests of data subject or of another person; legitimate interests of the data subject where the law of the Member State transferring the personal data so provides.

46 See AMICI, V., "Europol et la nouvelle décision...", loc. cit., p. 96.

Convention had not established obligations either to submit information or to reply to requests.[47]

In parallel with the entrance into force of the Convention on Europol and the last preparatory works, political emphasis on the promotion of the cooperation with this entity came with the Amsterdam Treaty, as well as with the statement of the Tampere Conclusions, declaring that within 5 years Europol's role "should be strengthened by means of receiving operational data from Member States and authorising it to ask Member States to initiate, conduct or coordinate investigations or to create joint investigative teams in certain areas of crime, while respecting systems of judicial control in Member States."[48]

But the process of obtaining trust in politically originated law enforcement entity was long and complicated, as not all Member States were ready to reveal their national investigations and provide Europol with the relevant information. After 2 years of functioning, in 2001, Europol's director, Storbeck, recognised this problem and tried to justify it saying that, "Even now when European interests coincide like never before, intercultural conflicts and fears of population about the establishment of federal super-state very seldom are obstacles for closer cooperation in a big variety of matters within the European Union. For some of them any small progress is a big step forwards."[49]

Six years later, in 2007, only Denmark, France, Germany and Spain had issued internal instructions to prioritise the Europol channel for information exchange. In other Member States, Interpol remained the preferred channel for day-to-day cooperation.[50] At the same time, Bruggeman noticed that, "With reference to the coordinating role [of Europol], it can be said that this is very important from a European Perspective, but that the real impact right now is still very limited, since many police officers in the field still work bilaterally (the so-called 'old boys' network)."[51]

47 See ARROYO ROMERO, Francisco Javier, *La influencia de EUROPOL en la comunitarización de la policía europea*, Madrid: Akal, 2006, p. 39.

48 Presidency Conclusions, Tampere European Council, 15–16 October 1999, http://www.consilium.europa.eu/uedocs/cms_data/docs/pressdata/en/ec/00200-r1.en9.htm.

49 STORBECK, Jürgen, "La cooperación policial europea…", loc. cit., p. 158.

50 See COUNCIL OF THE EUROPEAN UNION, "Third round of Mutual…", *loc. cit.*, p. 24, 31.

51 BRUGGEMAN, Willy, "A Vision of Future Police Cooperation with Special Focus on Europol", in DE ZWAAN, Jaap W. And GOUDAPPEL, Flora A.N. J., *Freedom, security and Justice in the European Union: Implementation of The Hague Programme*, The Hague: Asser Press, 2006, p. 209. The same observation in much broader context (any changes brought by the EU law into national system) made MITSILEGAS, MONAR, REES saying that it provokes "almost instinctive reaction against such European 'interference' with well-established national approaches, basic concepts and traditions". See MITSILEGAS, Valsamis; MONAR, Jörg and REES, Wyn, *The European Union and Internal Security: Guardian of the People?* Hampshire: Palgrave Macmillan, 2003, p. 10.

And even a technical report from 2012 on the Evaluation of the implementation of the Europol Council Decision, and of Europol's activities, reveals that there is a fear that submitted information is automatically available to all Member States. Therefore, bilateral agreements are used more as they allow better control of the provision of information and "Law enforcement officials under time pressure tend to use familiar, national-level systems, and might see entering data into Europol systems as too burdensome or time-consuming."[52]

Nevertheless, during recent years, more and more information has been published about Europol's assistance and participation in operations, beginning with on the spot support to one Member State (as in the case of operation Walker[53]) or multinational operations such as Archimedes or Blackshades. In operation Archimedes all Member States participated, along with Australia, Colombia, Norway, the United States, Serbia and Switzerland with the final result of more than 1,000 people being arrested, 339 seizures of 2.1 tonnes of drugs and more than 1 million euros in cash.[54] In operation Blackshades (coordinated by Eurojust and supported by EC3 at Europol), 16 Member States took part; it resulted in more than 80 arrests and 359 house searches in combatting Blackshades malware.[55]

3 Data protection

Until now protection of data processed in Europol has been regulated by an individual set of provisions established by the Europol Decision, and other, already mentioned, Council Decisions; on some occasions considered as comprehensive and exemplary to guarantee the right to data protection.[56] On the other hand there are opinions that, "The adequacy of the current

52 DISLEY, Emma; IRVING, Barrie; HUGHES, William et al. "Technical report on Evaluation…", loc. cit., p. 50–51.

53 Europol assisted Spanish police to target an organised group responsible for telecommunication fraud in total of at least 2 million euros and its laundering. Although the group acted from Spain, victims of their crimes were from all over the EU. See "Europol supports Spanish Police to dismantle serious cybercriminal group" (Europol Press Release, 10 July 2015), accessed July 13, 2017, https://www.europol.europa.eu/content/europol-supports-spanish-police-dismantle-serious-cybercriminal-group.

54 See EUROPOL, "Operation Archimedes infographics", September 2014, accessed July 6 2017, https://www.europol.europa.eu/content/operation-archimedes-infographics.

55 See EUROPOL, "Worldwide Operation against Cybercrime", May 2014, accessed July 6, 2017, https://www.europol.europa.eu/content/worldwide-operation-against-cybercriminals.

56 See DISLEY, Emma; IRVING, Barrie; HUGHES, William et al. "Technical report on Evaluation…", loc. cit., p. 91–92; DE HERT, Paul; PAPAKONSTANTINOU, Vagelis and RIEHLE, Cornelia, "Data protection in the third pillar: cautious pessimism", in MAIK, Martin, *Crime, rights and the EU: the future of police and judicial cooperation*, London: Justice, 2008, p. 141.

legislative framework governing Europol in terms of privacy protection, judicial control, transparency and accountability leaves much to be desired."[57]

With the Europol Regulation and Directive 2016/680 this individual regulation remains, to some extent, as the directive (as already mentioned) will not be applied for data processing in activities carried out by the EU institutions and its other entities. On the other hand, recital 40 of the Europol Regulation envisages that "the data protection rules of Europol should be autonomous while at the same time consistent with other relevant data protection instruments applicable in the area of police cooperation in the Union. Those instruments include, in particular, Directive (EU) 2016/680 of the European Parliament and of the Council, as well as the Convention for the Protection of Individuals with regard to Automatic Processing of Personal Data of the Council of Europe and its Recommendation No R(87) 15."

It should also be pointed out that under the Europol Decisions, in some cases, the national law of the country providing information also had to be accomplished, for example,

- Article 4(2) of the Council Decision 2009/936/JHA envisaged that a Member State decides on the basis of its national law about what data and to which extent can be supplied to AWF;
- Article 15(1) of the same Decision foresaw that information on the use of data from AWF shall be transmitted to the Member State of its origin when national legislation of the receiving Member State so allows;
- Article 13(5) of the Europol Decision established that transmission of information included in the EIS between ENU and competent authorities of the same Member States is regulated by its national law;
- Its Article 17 foresaw that other use of information than by the competent authorities or for other purposes is allowed only according to the national law of transmitting Member State;
- Its Article 25(3)a and 25(5) envisaged fulfillment of national law in transmitting information from private parties.

Europol Regulation also makes reference to national law, for example,

- Articles 7(6)d and 17(1)a foresee that in data supply from ENU to Europol, a national law of supplying Member State has to be followed.
- Article 8(4) establishes that information exchange through liaison officers has to be done according to the EU and national law.
- Articles 20(1) and 20(3) refer both to the national law and EU provisions as a legal basis for the regulation of access of Member States to data

57 MITSILEGAS, Valsamis, "The third wave of third pillar law: which direction for EU criminal justice?" in *European Law Review*, 2009, vol. 34, no. 4, p. 552.

possessed by Europol, for the purposes of cross-checking and strategic or thematic analysis.

- Article 26(1)a points out that ENU transmits data from private parties to the Europol in accordance with its national law.
- Article 35(3) states that national procedure will be applied when a Member State has to communicate to a data subject about the breach of his or her personal data.
- Article 42 foresees that national supervisory authority acts under its national law.
- Article 50 establishes that if a data subject requires compensation from a Member State for damage for unlawful data processing, national rules will be applied.

If the Europol Decision made a reference to the principles established in the Data Protection Convention and the Recommendation R (87)15 (accuracy, lawfulness, specified and legitimate purpose, relevancy, limited storage, fair processing and depersonalisation, independent supervisory authority, right to access, security) saying that they have to be taken into account, Articles 28, 29, 31, 35 and 41 of the Europol Regulation establish that it is obligatory to follow these principles. Additionally, Article 30 envisages principles of necessity and proportionality in processing sensitive data or any personal data on victims, witnesses, informers and minors.

3.1 Persons included

As mentioned in previous sections, in Europol's different information processing tools, the data of different categories of persons is processed. Its summary is presented in Table 5.2.

According to Article 12(1) of the Europol Decision as well as to the point A.1.a of the Annex II to the Europol Regulation, the notion of suspect and backgrounds for suspicion of future commitment of a crime are left to the definition of the national law of each Member State. Thus they depend on national procedural law and vary among themselves. For example:

- Spanish Criminal Procedure Code does not provide a definition of a suspect, and with the modifications of the Criminal Procedure Code from 2015, the terms *investigated person* and *prosecuted person* are used. The only Article that mentions "suspect" is 363 which regulates taking samples for DNA analysis.[58]

58 See more SOLETO MUÑOZ, Helena and ALCOCEBA GIL, Juan, "Protección de datos y transferencia de perfiles de ADN" in CABEZUDO BAJO, María José, *Las bases de datos policiales de ADN ¿Son una herramienta realmente eficaz en la lucha contra la criminalidad grave nacional y transfornteriza?* (Madrid: Dykinson, S.L., 2013), p. 338–339; SOLETO MUÑOZ, Helena and FIODOROVA, Anna,

Table 5.2 Categories of persons that can be included in EIS, AWFs and SIENA

Europol's information system or other information exchange through Europol	*Categories of persons whose data can be included*
EIS	– Suspects of already committed crime – Suspects of possible future commission of the crime – Convicted persons
AWF	– Suspects of already committed crime – Suspects of possible future commission of the crime – Convicted persons – Witnesses – Victims – Contacts, associates – Informers
SIENA	Not specified by the legislation. Interpreted as "crime-related information".[59] SIENA can be used both for information exchange purely under Europol's mandate and for bilateral or multilateral communication among Member States out of its mandate.

- According to Article 21 of the Lithuanian Code on Criminal Procedure, a suspect is a person detained or questioned under suspicion of committing a crime, or to whom a notification of suspicion is addressed, or if his or her place of residence is not known he or she is recognised as a suspect on the basis of the prosecutor's or pre-trial judicial authority's resolution.
- According to Article 71 of the Polish Code on Criminal Procedure, a suspect is a person towards whom a resolution on allegation of committing a crime is issued, or who is questioned as a suspect without the previously mentioned resolution.
- According to Article 27 of the Dutch Code on Criminal Procedure, a suspect is a person reasonably suspected in commission of offence.

European legislation on minimum standards in criminal procedure is applied to suspects and accused persons, but it does not include their definition, and that results in no point of reference on this issue.

Article 5 of the Decision 2009/936/JHA foresaw that in every case, the Director taking the decision to open an AWF, also has to specify the categories of personal data that can be processed, meaning that not all data categories automatically allowed by this Council decision would be processed in every AWF, but applying a principle of "need to know". In cases

"DNA and Law Enforcement in the European Union: Tools and Human Rights Protection" in *Utrecht Law Review*, January 2014, vol. 10, issue 1, p. 156.

59 See DISLEY, Emma; IRVING, Barrie; HUGHES, William et al., "Technical report on Evaluation…", loc. cit., p. 78.

of special categories of data[60] about the victims, witnesses, contacts, associates and informers, according to Article 5(2) they could be included only upon request by two or more Member States participating in the AWF.

As previously mentioned, Article 30 of the Europol Regulation adds minors to the categories of person listed in Article 5 of the Europol Decision and establishes that data on these categories of persons can be processed only following principles of necessity and proportionality.

Within the previous legal framework (Decisions), every piece of data included in an AWF had to be categorised according to its source (reliability) and information evaluation (accuracy) codes as is shown in Table 5.3.

With the Europol Regulation (Article 29) this assessment is applied not only to the data processed within AWF, but to all information possessed by the Europol.

When information comes from a Member State, the latter is responsible for its assessment. According to Article 29(6), "Information from publicly available sources shall be assessed by Europol..." and according to Article 29(5) the evaluation codes also have to be applied to data received from a EU body, third state, international organisation and private party, but it is not specified who has to make such evaluation: a subject from whom it comes to Europol or Europol itself? From the wording of Article 29 the conclusion can be reached that such an assessment has to be made by sending country or body, and Europol only has the right to point out that the evaluation code has to be corrected.

3.2 Access

Access rights to Europol's information systems differ, depending on their nature; and they are not equal. Thus access to all EIS data is granted to

Table 5.3 Evaluation codes of sources and information processed in AWFs

Source evaluation code	*Information evaluation code*
(A): trustworthy and authentic source (B): information from a reliable source (C): information from a source which has, in most instances, proved to be unreliable (X): reliability assessment is not possible	(1): no doubts about accuracy of information (2): the source knows the information personally, but not the official passing it on (3): the source does not know the information personally, but it coincides with already recorded information (4): the source does not know the information and it cannot be corroborated

60 Data revealing racial or ethnic origin, political opinions, religious or philosophical beliefs or trade-union membership and data concerning health or sex life.

empower Europol staff, liaison officers and ENUs. Access on a hit/no hit basis can be granted to national competent institutions according to national provisions. This allows broader use of Europol's stored information, making EIS a more useful tool for law enforcement institutions, and increasing its efficiency, but at the same time relevant requirements on secure connection and data protection must be applied. Third parties do not have access to the EIS. If they need information, Europol makes the search on their behalf and on the basis of existing operational cooperation agreement.

Access to AWFs is much more restricted and given on a "need to know" basis,[61] i.e. only to authorised analysts from the Europol, authorised staff of participating competent authorities, authorised liaison officers and ENU staff from participating Member States. Access to AWF Index System that allow its consultation on a hit/no hit basis is given to all liaison officers of Member States, ENUs and competent Europol staff.

Such access restriction in respect to AWF is indispensable due to the possibility of processing data of victims, witnesses and informers, as well as special categories of information.

Regarding SIENA, it can be used as an information communication tool by Europol's staff, liaison officers, ENUs, competent authorities designated on the basis of national law, as well as third parties that have cooperation agreements with Europol. In the last case, third parties with concluded operational agreements can send request messages directly to the destination (Europol or the Member State), but in the case of strategic agreement, messages pass through the Europol Operational Centre, where a decision on its acceptance and further transmission or rejection is taken.

3.3 Third parties and onward transmission

As mentioned before, Europol is allowed to exchange information, including personal data, with third countries and organisations that currently takes place on the basis of bilateral agreements between Europol and third states or international organisations; or in some exceptional cases without such agreement. Additionally, in some circumstances the "addressee" of the data has a possibility of its further transmission. The data protection regime is not equal in all these cases and therefore deserves special analysis.

3.3.1 Data protection in transmission to third parties

According to Article 10 of the Decision 2009/934/JHA, "Europol shall be responsible for the legality of the transmission of data. Europol shall keep a record of all transmissions of data under these rules and of the grounds for such transmissions. Data shall be transmitted only if the recipient gives an

61 See DISLEY, Emma; IRVING, Barrie; HUGHES, William et al., "Technical report on Evaluation...", loc. cit., p. 83.

undertaking that the data will be used only for the purposes for which they were transmitted."

As mentioned before, as a general rule personal data exchange with third countries and organisations is possible on the basis of operational agreements concluded before the enter into force of the Europol Regulation. Those agreements could not be finalised without the inclusion of relevant data protection requirements and, therefore, it was considered that Europol had become the key protagonist in exporting the European model of data protection and in achieving that, many of the third state modified their legislation in order to get access to Europol's data.[62] An example of quite rigorous data protection requirements applied in agreements is the many years of ongoing negotiation process with the Russian Federation on operational agreement, as there is insufficient proof of relevant data protection rules; even the Russian Federation ratified the Data Protection Convention in 2013 and it is in force.

Supposedly, the Commission's decisions on data protection adequacy and the EU agreements in the future will be based on thorough scrutiny of data protection rules applied by the third state and not only in police judicial cooperation, but in general.

The problem appears in cases of data transfer to third states on an exceptional basis that were mentioned in Article 23(8) of the Europol Decision, Article 14 of the Decision 2009/934/JHA and are established in Article 25(5) of the Europol Regulation. The first two legal acts foresaw that the Director has to evaluate the data protection level in the third country and the balance between the protection of data and interest under consideration. Article 25(5) of the Europol Regulation says that if the Director considers that fundamental rights have priority over necessity in individual cases, in order to prevent, detect, investigate, prosecute crime or to establish, exercise or defend legal claims in those cases, the transfer of personal data will not take place. This consideration is not applied to other exceptions (vital interests of data subject or another person, legitimate interest of data subject, serious threat to public security).

In case the of annual authorisation for a set of transfers of personal data for the purposes that are considered as exceptional in Article 25(5), protection of privacy and other fundamental rights has to be taken into account, but is not comprehensively regulated.

3.3.2 *Onwards transmission of personal data*

Regarding further transmission of received data (onwards transmission), three situations have to be taken into account:

62 See BLASI CASAGRAN, Cristina, "El papel de Europol como actor normativo de la UE en el intercambio de datos con terceros estados" in PI LLORENS, Montserrat and ZAPATER DUQUE, Esther, *La dimensión exterior de las agencias del espacio de libertad, seguridad y justicia*, Madrid: Marcial Pons, 2014, p. 111.

- Transmission by Europol of data received from Member States,
- Transmission of data by the competent authority of a third state to another authority within the same state,
- Transmission by a third state or organisation to another third state or organisation.

In the first case, prior consent of the Member State is required (Article 18 (3) of Decision 2009/934/JHA and Article 23(6) of the Europol Regulation).

In the second case, according to the Article 17(1) of the Decision 2009/934/ JHA, an onward transmission was possible only within the third state or organisation that had had an operational agreement with Europol, and only to the competent authorities mentioned therein.

As a general rule, according to Article 18 of Decision 2009/934/JHA third countries or organisations received personal data under agreement of non-further transmission. Part 2 of the same Article established two exceptions from non-onwards transmission:

- The final state or organisation has an operational agreement with Europol and onwards transmission is done with the prior consent of Europol.
- Necessity to protect the essential interests of the Member States or to prevent imminent danger of crime or terrorist offences and under authorisation by the Director.

In both cases, such exceptions are allowed if the transmitting third state also has an operational agreement with Europol. Nevertheless, different agreements establish different regulations with regard to this issue. Thus, agreements with:

- Canada, Iceland, Norway and Switzerland do not allow data transmission to third states;
- Albania, Bosnia and Herzegovina, Georgia, Liechtenstein, Moldova, Serbia and Ukraine permit it in both directions (onward by this third country or Europol) with the previous consent of the information provider;
- Australia, former Yugoslav Republic of Macedonia and Monaco permit it only from this third state to another third party and with the previous consent of Europol,
- United States of America does not regulate this question.

The chain of information transmission: Member State – Europol – Third party with operational agreement – other third party seems to be quite long in order to assure proper data protection on all levels. Finally, there is no effective mechanism to control data at the final destination and to guarantee that its further onward transmission will not occur.

Article 23(7) of the Europol Regulation has stricter wording, saying that as a general rule onwards transmitting is prohibited, unless prior and explicit authorisation from Europol is obtained. Thus, the new regulation does not foresee any more restricted exceptions other than Europol's authorisation. However, nothing is said about the authorisation of a Member State which is the original source of transferred information, and the question of the provisions of the existing operational agreements that allow such transmission.

3.4 Data subject's right to access

Article 30 of the Europol Decision and Article 36 of the Europol Regulation established the data subject's right to "obtain information on whether personal data relating to him or her are processed by Europol".

The data subject can address his or her request to the designated authority of any Member State who shall forward it to Europol. Such a system facilitates the implementation of the data subject's rights, giving possibility to apply in Member States that are more convenient to a person due to his or her interests, language, place of residence or other motives. The request has to be forwarded to Europol within a month and the latter has to provide the data subject with the answer within three months.

Europol, analysing the request, must consult the competent authorities of Member States, including the provider of the data (this is significant clarification made in the Europol Regulation as previous wording did not refer specifically to the data provider, but only to competent Member States).

Article 30(5) of the Europol Decision and Article 36(6) of the Europol Regulation foresee that in some cases information cannot be given to the data subject. Such an obligation falls to Europol when it would jeopardise: the proper fulfilment of Europol's tasks, crime prevention, security, public order, national investigation and rights and freedoms of third parties. If the provision of information is forbidden, Europol notifies the data subject that checks have been carried out. But it is done in such a manner that it would be impossible to verify whether the person's information is processed or not.

In the same way, the data subject can apply for rectification, correction or deletion/restriction of his or her personal data.

Despite the establishment of the data subject's access right, and the system of its implementation, for many years it could not be considered comprehensive due to the lack of clear judicial protection rules, as there was no judicial authority to whom Europol's decisions or those of its Joint Supervisory Body could be appealed. It was of utmost importance, especially when taking into account that Europol tends not to reveal information to the data subject, motivated by the reason that it could be requested by organised crime members and therefore jeopardise investigation. Besides, the Joint Supervisory Body overruled such a decision/reply only in a very few cases.[63] The situation has changed, but only with the entrance into force of the Treaty of Lisbon; Article 263(1) of the TFUE allows individual claims to the Court of Justice of the EU against acts of all EU institutions and entities, including those of the former Third Pillar.[64] Thus, Article 48 of the Europol Regulation expressly established such a right as well.

A significant novelty of the Europol Regulation is also the establishment of notification to EDPS and national competent authorities about any personal data breach (Article 34) and to the data subject if such a breach significantly harms his or her rights and freedoms (Article 35).

3.5 Supervising authorities

In relation to the data processed by Europol, a three step mechanism supervising data protection is established:

- An independent national supervisory body in each Member State that monitors data input, retrieval and communication to Europol, and supervises the activities of its ENU and liaison officers when they are related to data protection.
- A Data Protection Officer established at the level of Europol[65] that acts independently and supervises compliance of the data protection provisions at Europol's level, by advising its staff and unit on data protection.[66] In the case of incompliance of rules, he or she informs the Europol Director about the need to resolve it. In case of non-resolution, the Data Protection Officer has the right to address this issue to the Management Board, and if the problem is not resolved, to the EDPS.
- The third level of structure established in the Europol Regulation differs from one of the Europol Decision. The latter talked about a Joint Supervisory Body established at the level of Europol and consisted of up to two representatives of each National supervisory body, supervising data subjects' rights in relation to the data held in Europol and monitoring its transmission. Nevertheless, the highest level to which the Joint Supervisory Body could address the problem of breach of data protection rules was the Management Board. The Europol Regulation, rather than the Joint Supervisory Body talks about the supervision by the EDPS that in case of breach of data protection provision can address

63 See MARICA, Andreea, *Manual de Europol*, Navarra: Aranzadi, 2014, p. 218, 229–231.

64 See ESQUINAS VALVERDE, Patricia, *Protección de datos personales en la Policía Europea*, Valencia: Tirant lo Blanch, 2010, p. 98–101.

65 Appointed by the Management Board.

66 See DREWER, Daniel and GUTIÉRREZ ZARZA, Ángeles, "Intercambio de información y protección de datos personales en el ámbito de Eurojust, Europol y OLAF" in GUTIÉRREZ ZARZA, Ángeles, *Nuevas tecnologías, protección de datos personales y proceso penal*, Madrid: La Ley, 2012, p. 178.

it to the European Parliament, the Council, the Commission and the CJEU.

All supervisory authorities shall be provided with access to the information stored by the authorities that are subject to their control:

- National supervisory bodies: to the data input to Europol's databases and premises of its ENU and liaison officers.
- Data Protection Officer and the EDPS: to data held by Europol and its premises.

4 Brief summary and evaluation

During the 20 years of its existence (counting from the establishment of the EDU), Europol has undergone development from a top-down decision established organisation,[67] to the EU Agency, with precisely defined competence and reference in primary EU legislation, with the primordial task of "Information management together with the capacity to generate intelligence."[68]

Although EDU was created at the same time, when implementation of the CISA took place; further developments of Europol and Schengen acquis have taken different paths. In the case of Schengen acquis, it was more related to improvement of its functioning and embracing more new Members, and in the case of Europol – dynamic widening of its competence both in meaning of scope and cooperation methods and entities. A summary of what has been said in this chapter about the scope of Europol's activities is presented in Table 5.4.

With respect to the information exchange scheme, if at the beginning it took place only directly between Member States, later the scheme was changed, establishing cooperation in a chain: Europol – liaison officer – ENU and finally giving hit/no hit access to all interested law enforcement institutions. Thus Europol evolved from facilitating direct contacts between competent national authorities to the entity in possession of information and intelligence, and has become a much more active partner in combatting crime.[69]

With respect to the right to privacy and data protection in Europol's activities, the question is quite controversial.

First, referring to the establishment of restrictions by law, this requirement can be treated as fulfilled when democratically elected institutions have participated in its adoption. Thus provisions established by means of Convention or Treaties, fulfil this requirement due to their ratification by national parliaments. Europol Decision deserves a special mention. Even if it

67 BURES, Oldrich, "Europol's Fledging Counterterrorism Role" in *Terrorism and Political Violence*, 2008, vol. 20 (4), p. 501.
68 MARICA, Andreea. *Manual de Europol*, op. cit., p. 119.
69 PEERS, Steve, *EU Justice and Home Affairs..*, op. cit., p. 873.

Table 5.4 Development of Europol's competences

Legal basis (signed/into force)	*Type of crimes*	*Conditions*
Treaty of Maastricht (1992/1993)	– Terrorism – Unlawful drug trafficking – Other serious forms of international crime	
Ministerial Agreement (1993)	– Illicit drug trafficking – Criminal organisations involved – Associated money laundering	Affecting two or more Member States
Amsterdam Treaty (1997/1999)	No changes of scope	
Europol Convention (1995/1998)	– Terrorism, – Unlawful drug trafficking – Other serious forms of international crime + – Money laundering and other crimes related the above mentioned	Possibly affecting two or more Member States and Organised crime involved.
Council Decision 2009/371/JHA	– Organised crime, – Terrorism, – Other forms of serious crime + – Related offences	Affecting two or more Member States.
Lisbon Treaty (2007/2009)	– Serious crime	Affecting two or more Member States *or* Terrorism and forms of crime which affect a common interest covered by a Union policy.
Europol Regulation	– Equally as Lisbon Treaty + – Related offences	Equally as Lisbon Treaty

was approved according to existing legislative procedure, neither the European Parliament nor national parliaments directly participated. The Europol Regulation can also be considered as sufficient legal basis given that the European Parliament was directly participating in the decision-making process.

Second, data processing for the purpose of combatting transnational terrorism, organised and serious crime can be treated as protection of general interest and be justifiable reasons to restrict fundamental rights.

Third, proportionality of the processing of information to the purpose is a more complicated and versatile issue.

In the case of EIS, it contains information on very few categories of persons: suspects and convicted and besides includes limited categories of data. Such information is indispensable to combat cross-border crime and its processing is proportional to the purpose.

Nevertheless, the question stands in the case of the collection of special categories of data in AWFs, data transmission to third parties as well as onwards transmission.

Special categories of data perhaps could help to identify the risks of radicalisation or extremism, therefore, its processing shall be, if not totally forbidden, used only in counter terrorism AWFs.

With respect to information transmission to third parties, on the one hand, it is understandable that if Europol needs information from them in order to ensure the internal security of the EU, third parties will expect reciprocal actions from Europol. But such practice should be based solely on the basis of relevant agreements, with the unique exception of combatting terrorism or vital interests.

Bibliography

AMICI, V., 2010, "Europol et la nouvelle décision du Conseil: entre opportunités et contraintes"; in *Revue du Droit de L'union Européenne*; no. 1; p. 77–100.

ARROYO ROMERO, F.J., 2006, *La influencia de EUROPOL en la comunitarización de la policía europea*, Madrid: Akal.

BIGO, D., 2008, "EU Police Cooperation: National Sovereignty Framed by European Security?"; in GUILD, E. and GEYER, F., *Security versus Justice? Police and Judicial Cooperation in the European Union*, Hampshire: Ashgate Publishing Limited, p. 91–108.

BLASI CASAGRAN, C., 2014, "El papel de Europol como actor normativo de la UE en el intercambio de datos con terceros estados"; in PI LLORENS, M., ZAPATER DUQUE, E., *La dimensión exterior de las agencias del espacio de libertad, seguridad y justicia*, Madrid: Marcial Pons, p. 101–123.

BRUGGEMAN, W., 1995, "Europol and the Europol Drugs Unit: Their Problems and Potential for Development" in BIEBER, R. and MONAR, J., *Justice and Home Affairs in the European Union: The Development of the Third Pillar*, Brussels: European Interuniversity Press, p. 220–221.

BRUGGEMAN, W., 2002, "Los procesos de construcción de una inteligencia europea"; in MONTERO, J., ROMERO, F. and VALIENTE, E., *¿Hacia una Policía Europea?*, Madrid: Fundación Policía Española, p. 215–226.

BRUGGEMAN, W., 2006, "A Vision of Future Police Cooperation with Special Focus on Europol"; in DE ZWAAN, J. W. and GOUDAPPEL, F.A.N.J.; *Freedom, security and Justice in the European Union: Implementation of The Hague Programme*, The Hague: Asser Press, p. 203–220.

BURES, O., 2008, "Europol's Fledging Counterterrorism Role"; in *Terrorism and Political Violence*, vol. 20, no. 4; p. 498–517.

COUNCIL OF THE EUROPEAN UNION, 2007, "Third round of Mutual Evaluations 'Exchange of information and intelligence between Europol and the Member

States and among the Member States respectively' Final Report on the evaluation visits of all 27 Member States", 13321/07. Available at: http://data.consilium.europa.eu/doc/document/ST-13321-2007-REV-3/en/pdf (accessed November 19, 2017).

DE HERT, P., PAPAKONSTANTINOU, V. and RIEHLE, C., 2008, "Data protection in the third pillar: cautious pessimism", in MAIK, M., *Crime, rights and the EU: the future of police and judicial cooperation*, London: Justice, p. 121–194.

DISLEY, E., IRVING, B., HUGHES, W. et al., 2012, "Technical report on Evaluation of the implementation of the Europol Council Decision and of Europol's activities", Cambridge: RAND Corporation. Available at: https://www.europol.europa.eu/content/publication/evaluation-implementation-europol-council-decision-and-europol's-activities-1655 (accessed September 4, 2017).

DREWER, D. and GUTIÉRREZ ZARZA, Á., 2012, "Intercambio de información y protección de datos personales en el ámbito de Eurojust, Europol y OLAF"; in GUTIÉRREZ ZARZA, Á.; *Nuevas tecnologías, protección de datos personales y proceso penal*, Madrid: La Ley, p. 131–194.

ESPIGARES MIRA, J., 2002, "Instrumentos internacionales de cooperación", in MONTERO, J., ROMERO, F., and VALIENTE, E., 2002, *¿Hacía una Policía Europea?*, Madrid: Fundación Policía Española, p. 117–138.

ESQUINAS VALVERDE, P., 2010, *Protección de datos personales en la Policía Europea*, Valencia: Tirant lo Blanch.

EUROPEAN MONITORING CENTER FOR DRUGS and DRUG ADDICTION, EUROPOL, 2010, "Cocaine: A European Union Perspective in the global context". Available at: http://www.emcdda.europa.eu/publications/joint-publications/cocaine_en (accessed, October 5, 2017).

FIJNAUT, C., 2004, "Police Co-operation and the Area of Freedom, security and Justice"; in WALKER, N., *Europe's Area of Freedom, Security and Justice*, Oxford: Oxford University Press, p. 201–282.

GÓMEZ-JARA DÍEZ, C., 2007, "¿Federalismo jurídico-penal en la Constitución Europea? Un diálogo con el profesor Silva Sánchez"; in ARROYO ZAPATERO, L. and NIETO MARTíN, A., *El Derecho Penal de la Unión Europea. Situación actual y perspectivas de future*, Cuenca: Universidad de Castilla-La Mancha, p. 87–105.

MARICA, A., 2014, *Manual de Europol*, Navarra: Aranzadi.

MITSILEGAS, V., 2009, "The third wave of third pillar law: which direction for EU criminal justice?", in *European Law Review*, vol. 34, no. 4, p. 523–560.

MITSILEGASV., MONAR, J. and REES, W., 2003, *The European Union and Internal Security: Guardian of the People?*, Hampshire: Palgrave Macmillan.

PEERS, S., 2011, *EU Justice and Home Affairs Law*, 3rd ed., New York: Oxford University Press Inc.

RENARD, T., 2014, "Partners in crime? The EU, its strategic partners and international organised crime". Available at: http://fride.org/publication/1191/partners-in-crime?-the-eu,-its-strategic-partners-and-international-organised-crime (accessed October 2, 2017).

SANTOS VARA, J., 2010, "Las consecuencias de la integración de Europol en el Derecho de la Unión Europea (comentario a la Decision del Consejo 2009/371/JAI, de 6 de abril de 2009)"; in *Revista General de Derecho Europeo*, no. 20; p. 1–24.

SOLETO MUÑOZ, H. and ALCOCEBA GIL, J., 2013, "Protección de datos y transferencia de perfiles de ADN"; in CABEZUDO BAJO, M.J.; *Las bases de datos policiales de ADN ¿Son una herramienta realmente eficaz en la lucha contra la criminalidad grave nacional y transfronteriza?*, Madrid: Dykinson, S.L., p. 325–344.

SOLETO MUÑOZ, H. and FIODOROVA, A., 2014, "DNA and Law Enforcement in the European Union: Tools and Human Rights Protection"; in *Ultrecht Law Review*, vol. 10, issue 1, p. 149–162.

STORBECK, J., 2002, "La cooperación policial europea" in MONTERO, J., ROMERO, F., and VALIENTE, E., *¿Hacia una Policía Europea?*, Madrid: Fundación Policía Española, p. 155–169.

6 Swedish initiative

1 First attempt to implement the principle of availability: the Commission's proposal

Following the guidelines of The Hague Programme and execution of the Council and Commission Action Plan, implementing the Hague Programme on strengthening Freedom, Security and Justice in the European Union,[1] in October 2005 the Commission presented a Proposal for a Council Framework Decision on the exchange of information under the principle of availability[2] (hereinafter – the Commission's Proposal).

The proposal is worthy of appreciation as it was both comprehensive and ambitious.[3] Comprehensive because of the intention to present it in the package with a proposal for a legislative act on the protection of data exchanged for the purpose of police and judicial cooperation in penal matters. But after the terrorist attacks of July 7, 2005 in London, the Council of Ministers of the Interior called the Commission to present the proposal on the implementation of the principle of availability, as soon as possible, leaving the data protection proposal for later.

Ambitious because of the attempt to create "direct online access to the available information and to index data for information that is not accessible online"[4] or in other words, complete implementation of the principle of availability.

1 OJ C 198, 12.8.2005, p. 1–22.

2 EUROPEAN COMMISSION, "Proposal for a Council Framework Decision on the exchange of information under the principle of availability", COM(2005) 490 final, accessed November 19, 2017, http://eur-lex.europa.eu/legal-content/EN/TXT/?uri=COM:2005:0490:FIN.

3 Although, for example VERVAELE calls it very general. See VERVAELE, John A. E., "Medidas de investigación de carácter proactivo y uso de información de inteligencia en el proceso penal" in PÉREZ GIL, Julio, *El proceso penal en la sociedad de la* información, Madrid: La Ley, 2012, p. 35.

4 COM(2005) 490 final, p. 2.

It would oblige each Member State to grant direct access to its databases to competent authorities of other Member States, and to create index systems when some category of data is not available online. The Annex II of the Commission's Proposal has included exhaustive list of the categories of data that are supposed to be directly accessible among Member States: DNA profiles, fingerprints, ballistics, vehicle registration information, telephone numbers and other communications data (excluding traffic and content), and persons' identification data.

Information availability would be limited to the exchange of already collected data, without the obligation to collect new data.

According to Articles 2 and 7 of the Commission's Proposal, the information exchange would take place before the commencement of a prosecution, and for the purposes of prevention and detection as well as investigation of crimes for which information has been provided.

As already mentioned, the proposed mechanism would include on-line access to existing databases and to databases of indexes, in cases of information not being stored in automated databases. That would result in the establishment of two modalities of information availability:

- Direct availability: direct access to the information in online databases of other Member States (Article 9);
- Indirect availability: direct access to the index system of data not available online and in cases of an index match with the searched data, sending a request for full data to the competent authority of the Member State whose index system was searched (Article 10). According to the Article 11, the requested authority would be obliged to respond within 12 hours.[5]

Article 14 of the Commission's Proposal has foreseen a closed list of motives to refuse the provision of information:

- To protect the security of persons and their fundamental rights;
- To protect sources of information or confidentiality;
- Not to prejudice ongoing investigation.

The application of the aforementioned limitations would be completely possible in cases of indirect availability, as in this case, information would be forwarded by the possessing authority that at any moment can assess whether there are motives of refusal. But the question arises, how to apply these limitations in case of direct access to databases? It would be possible

5 If there is a need for authorisation to provide the information, it must be supplied within 12 hours of it being received.

only with the application of a relevant technical solution in a database: either to withdraw information temporally from the database or to block access to it. But in both cases, it would be an additional burden to the data owning authority.

Kietz and Mourer have contemplated that "this decision, if adopted, would replace the reliance on national legal provisions for the exchange of personal data with common criteria that would apply to all EU member states. In contrast to the Prüm provisions, this would overcome the diversity of national legal assistance provisions, which so far have hampered the efficient exchange of information."[6]

But despite sound support for the principle of availability, Member States have refused this ambitious draft as "the regulation of the six key areas of information (DNA; fingerprints; ballistics; vehicle registrations; telephone numbers; other telecommunications data) and minimum data for the identification of persons (identity, address) must be developed gradually, one by one."[7]

Both objective and subjective reasons for this rejection can be outlined. Among the subjective reasons, protectionism of national databases and lack of mutual trust can be pointed out as the main ones. The comprehension of the protection of internal security as a part of a state's sovereignty has been already mentioned in this work, and now we are facing one of the examples: Member States have wished to keep direct access to their national database only to themselves. But the determining reasons for refusal of Commission's proposal have been lack of trust that direct access would be used in a proper way, and only for the pre-established purposes. It would not be precise to talk about absolute mistrust, but more about differentiated treatment among Member States or different levels of mutual trust, as in 2005 seven states (Austria, Belgium, France, Germany, Luxemburg, the Netherlands and Spain) granted such access among themselves for DNA profiles, dactyloscopics and vehicle registration databases.

Regarding the objective reasons, of course implementation of such a mechanism would be very expensive and long-lasting due to the need to establish new databases or modify existing ones, and to ensure EU wide interoperability and technical capacity to deal with all searches. For example, the dactyloscopic database of one of the smaller countries would need

6 KIETZ, Daniela and MAURER, Andreas, "From Schengen to Prüm" (Comments, German Institute for International and Security Affairs, May 2006), p. 2, accessed November 1, 2017, http://www.swp-berlin.org/fileadmin/contents/products/comments/Com15_06_Ktz_Mrr_Ks.pdf.

7 FAZEKAS, Judit, "Development of Justice and Home Affairs Cooperation between 2004 and 2009 in the European Union" in *European Integration Studies*, 2009, vol. 7, no 1, p. 8.

technical capacity to provide access to the rest of the Member States and handle their requests on a daily basis.

As Mr. Jonathan Faull (at that moment the Director General of the Commission's JHA Directorate General) said, "Our proposal [...] is seen by delegations [...] as a longer-term project which will provide for a wider sharing of information between law enforcement authorities of the Member States in the future."[8]

Seen from another perspective, it was possible to reduce the number of categories of the exchanged information at the first stage, leaving, for example, ballistics and telephone numbers and other communications data for later. Especially taking into account that in the end, in a little bit more than 1 year, at the beginning of 2007, during the German Presidency of the Council, a draft on the automated access to national DNA, dactyloscopic and vehicle registration files was proposed; and approved in 2008. Essential difference of the adopted tools from the Commission's proposal was envisaging mutual evaluation of legal, technical and data protection readiness as a pre-condition to direct access.

At the same time, after experiencing terrorist attacks, Member States needed the immediate effect of the principle of availability, even if in limited scope; and that is why the Commission's Proposal was left without deeper analysis, and the Council came back to a draft proposed by Sweden in 2004. Thus instead of the ambitious and comprehensive Commission's Proposal, the Member States had chosen much more simplified and more easily implemented legislation on information exchange.

2 Swedish Initiative – compromise on information availability

Instead of the Commission's Proposal, the Council went back to the Swedish proposal from June 2004, and after multiple rounds of discussions and numerous compromises, on December 18, 2006, adopted Council Framework Decision 2006/960/JHA on simplifying the exchange of information and intelligence between law enforcement authorities of the Member States of the European Union[9] (hereinafter – Framework Decision 2006/960/JHA), also popularly called the "Swedish Initiative". As this legal act modifies some provisions of the Schengen acquis, Norway, Island, Lichtenstein and Switzerland also joined it.

The Swedish Initiative, like the Commission's Proposal, foresees broader scope of information availability than only combatting terrorism and it

8 HEMPEL, Leon; CARIUS, Michael and ILTEN, Carla, "Exchange of information and data between law enforcement agencies within the European Union" (Discussion paper Nr. 29/09, Zentrum Technik und Gesellschaft, 2009), p. 28, accessed November 1, 2017, http://www.ztg.tu-berlin.de/pdf/Nr_29_Hempel_Carius_Ilten.pdf.

9 OJ L 386, 29.12.2006, p. 89–100.

includes other crimes as well.[10] As noticed by Hempel, Carius and Ilten, "In the Framework Decision the key concern of the proposal has been made invisible: the phrase referring to terrorism in the title is deleted. Terrorism is now seen – so to say, normalised – as one serious offence among others."[11]

Article 1(4), 1(5) of Framework Decision 2006/960/JHA establishes what is not covered and what is not required by this instrument: to collect and store information for its transmission, to obtain it by coercive measures or provide it as evidence. As stated by Mitsilegas, "These provisions can be seen as an attempt to safeguard national autonomy in not requiring national authorities to be proactive in obtaining information or intelligence on behalf of their counterparts in other Member States."[12]

Differently from the Commission's Proposal, Article 3(2) of the Framework Decision 2006/960/JHA establishes:

- Information exchange on the basis of requests, i.e. indirect exchange without the possibility to access other Member States' databases;
- Spontaneous information exchange possibility (sending it to other Member State without its previous request (for prevention, detection and investigation of crimes listed in the Framework Decision 2002/584/JHA of 13 June 2002 on the European arrest warrant and the surrender procedures between Member States[13] (hereinafter – Framework Decision 2002/584/JHA).

2.1 Scope of information exchange

Although the Swedish Initiative is quite a short legal document (13 articles in total), it is not so simple as it may look at first. For example, in order to identify its scope, four articles should be taken into account:

- Articles 1 and 3(2) that establish as a purpose for information exchange, "Conducting criminal investigations or criminal intelligence operations."
- Article 5 that foresees information requests for the "Purpose of detection, prevention or investigation of offences."
- Article 7 that limits the spontaneous sending of information to assist, "In detection, prevention or investigation of offences to referred in Article 2(2) of the Framework Decision 2002/584/JHA."

This variety of definitions can lead to misunderstandings among law enforcement agencies at the time of practical information exchange, because

10 See HEMPEL, Leon; CARIUS, Michael and ILTEN, Carla, "Exchange of information and data...", loc. cit., p. 25.

11 Ibid.

12 See MITSILEGAS, Valsamis, *EU Criminal Law*, Oxford and Portland, Oregon: Hart Publishing, 2009, p. 254.

13 OJ L 190, 18.7.2002, p. 1–20.

requesting country can choose as a basis Article 5, and ask the information for crime prevention for non-serious crime, and the requested country can base its answer on Article 3.2 that obliges it to provide information only for the purpose of ongoing investigations or intelligence operations. Thus as a general rule, information will be provided only for the purposes established in the Article 1 and 3(2), but problems can arise in cases of crime prevention. The prevention purpose established in Article 7 does not coincide with Article 1 and 3(2), but limitation to crimes listed in Article 2(2) of the Framework Decision 2002/584/JHA in Article 7 can be justified, as here, the legislator refers to spontaneous submission of information, and in order to make this flow proportionally, it is allowed only in cases of more serious crimes.

2.2 Deadlines for reply

Article 4 of the Framework Decision 2006/960/JHA foresees deadlines for answer, limiting answers to:

- 8 hours in urgent cases when it is related with the crimes listed in the Art. 2(2) of the Framework Decision 2002/584/JHA, and when requested information is directly accessible by the requested law enforcement institution. This time limit can be extended to 3 days when replies would represent a disproportional burden.
- 1 week in non-urgent cases under the conditions of the previous indent.
- 14 days in any other cases, i.e. crimes not included on the list provided in the Art. 2(2) of the Framework Decision 2002/584/JHA, and with irrelevance to the request's urgency.

Unfortunately, apart from the very detailed examination of the draft Swedish Initiative in the Council's preparatory body, the notion of urgency was not determined.

To avoid totally different interpretations of this important term, the Member States tried to establish some framework of urgency in the Guidelines on the implementation of the Council Framework Decision 2006/960/JHA of December 18, 2006, on simplifying the exchange of information and intelligence between law enforcement authorities of the Member States of the European Union[14] (hereinafter – the Guidelines). They foresee that urgency must be established on a case by case basis, but taking into account whether it is related to:

14 COUNCIL OF THE EUROPEAN UNION, "Guidelines on the implementation of Council Framework Decision 2006/960/JHA of 18 December 2006 on simplifying the exchange of information and intelligence between law enforcement authorities of the Member States of the European Union", 9512/1/10, accessed November 19, 2017, Available at: http://data.consilium.europa.eu/doc/document/ST-9512-2010-REV-1/en/pdf.

- Prevention of risk of death/harm to persons or serious damage to property;
- Short-term decisions about deprivation of liberty;
- Prevention of information loss that can affect the investigation.

Let's analyse how this system of information exchange would work in the case of a person's identity check on his arrival from a third country at Adolfo Suárez Madrid–Barajas Airport.[15] Based on the pre-established criteria or unusual behaviour of a person, a border guard officer can suspect that the presented identification document belonging to another state of the Schengen area is false. A check in SIS does not give a positive result on matching with lost or stolen documents, but it does not eliminate the possibility that the document is misused as there are cases when identification documents are sold by the legal owners and of course, such documents are not declared either as lost or stolen, and will never appear in SIS. In this case, there is a need to check in the database of the country that has issued the document, whether the identity of the person registered in the database matches the identity of the person presenting the document at the airport, e.g. coincidence of names and surnames, date of birth, photo and other data.[16] The person concerned can be detained for identity misuse, or use of false documents and according to the criteria of urgency established in the Guidelines, it should be treated as urgent. But on the other hand, the use of false documents is not included in the list of Article 2(2) of the Framework Decision 2002/584/JHA (only falsification and trafficking of administrative documents, but not their incidental use) and thus the situation does not match the legal requirements for urgency, established in the Article 4(1) of the Framework Decision 2006/960/JHA. What should prevail in this case: obligatory provision of the Article 4(1) or non-obligatory Guidelines that refer to the protection of a fundamental human right – liberty?

Of course, limitation of urgency to more serious crimes can be justified by limited resources of every state to provide information on any kind of investigation or intelligence operation within 8 hours. Another consideration that has to be taken into account is the "fairness" of the state in using urgency, or, in other words, abusing the label of urgency in cases that really can wait.

15 That means that a person has crossed an external border of the Schengen area and despite whether he or she is a national of one of the countries forming Schengen area or not, an identity check must be performed.

16 In some cases, none of this information is altered, but the ID is misused and only on the basis of answers to additional questions about the person's identity (such as names, dates of birth of family members, place of issue of the ID document, etc.) is it possible to verify the misuse. The performance of this questioning is possible only by having accessible data from the Civil Registry or equivalent database.

From another point of view, this problem would not appear in cases of direct access to databases, which would be established as it was foreseen in the Commission's Proposal.

This uncertainty about urgency plays an even bigger role in information exchange, taking into account that according to the DAPIX Report from 2012, participating states use this instrument mainly for urgent information requests and for the rest of the cases, other information exchange instruments are used.[17] With respect to its compliance, the Commission's Staff Working Paper on the implementation of the Swedish Initiative indicates that "Member States do take urgent requests seriously. Twenty six per cent of Member States report that such requests have always been complied with, while 62 per cent of Member States report that they have often been complied with. On the negative side, 9 per cent of Member States see no compliance at all, while 3 per cent see compliance as a rare occurrence."[18]

2.3 *Data exchange and reasons for denial*

Article 2(d) of the Framework Decision 2006/960/JHA establishes that the object of exchange could be any type of data held directly by the law enforcement authorities, or by public or private authorities and available for law enforcement purposes. On the other hand, unlike the Commission's Proposal, no minimum categories of information that must be exchanged are envisaged; i.e. there is no assurance that at least some minimum categories of information and data will be available across the whole EU. It leads to great differences of information availability between countries, as some of them will be obliged to provide many categories of information (everything available), while others would provide very few of them as only those categories are available to law enforcement institutions. It definitely will not help to build common trust and readiness to share information, taking into account that as feedback, very few categories can be received.

In comparison with the Commission's Proposal, Swedish Initiative foresees different motives to deny information.

Half of the motives foreseen in the current legislation are related to requested Member States and reflect the tendency of protection of its interests. It can be understandable in cases of damage to national security, but it

17 See COUNCIL OF THE EUROPEAN UNION, "Council Framework Decision 2006/960/JHA on simplifying the exchange of information and intelligence between law enforcement authorities of the Member States of the European Union ('Swedish Framework Decision') – Assessment of compliance pursuant to Article 11(2) – Draft Report", 14755/1/12, p. 19–21, accessed November 19, 2017, http://data.consilium.europa.eu/doc/document/ST-14755-2012-REV-1/en/pdf.

18 EUROPEAN COMMISSION, "Commission Staff Working Paper Operation of the Council Framework Decision 2006/960/JHA of 18 December 2006 ('Swedish Initiative')", SEC(2011) 593 final, p. 9, accessed November 19, 2017, http://data.consilium.europa.eu/doc/document/ST-10316-2011-INIT/en/pdf.

Table 6.1 Obligatory and dispositive reasons to deny provision of information according to the Commission's proposal and Framework Decision 2006/960/JHA

Article 14 of the Commission's proposal	*Article 10 of Framework Decision 2006/960/JHA*
Dispositive – To protect the security of persons and their fundamental rights – To protect sources of information or confidentiality – Not to prejudice the ongoing investigation	*Obligatory* – Lack of judicial authorisation *Dispositive* – Damage of national security interests of the requested MS – Prejudicing the success of ongoing investigation or intelligence operation in requested MS – Individual's safety – Disproportion with the purpose of request – Request on offence with the imprisonment punishment of 1 year or less in requested MS

raises doubts about linking availability of information to crimes with punishment of imprisonment of more than 1 year. It makes investigation, or other actions of the requesting party, conditional to punishments foreseen by legislation of the requested Member State. And as it is a dispositive provision, again it shows disproportion between information that will be provided by different Member States. Besides, all or part of dispositive refusal reasons can be established in national law as obligatory ones. But if such rules are equally applied to information transmission at national level, it does not mean the breach of the principle of availability, as national law enforcement authorities and those of other Member States are put under the same legal requirements.[19]

In relation to denial due to an ongoing investigation, the wording of the Commission's proposal was more precise as a request can jeopardise not only investigation carried out by the requesting party, but also by another Member State, and on some occasions the requested Member State can be aware of that (for example when it already provided information to another state).

Despite quite superficial regulations in general, Framework Decision 2006/960/JHA contains two Annexes that provide the forms that must be used as requests and as denial. The form of request includes 12 comprehensive fields

19 As happened, for example, when implementing Swedish Initiative in Germany. See more. BOERGER, Björn, "The transmission of personal data as part of the police and judicial cooperation in criminal matter in the EU: German experience" in COLOMER HERNÁNDEZ, Ignacio and OUBIÑA BARBOLLA, Sabela, *La transmisión de datos personales en el seno de la cooperación judicial penal y policial en la Unión Europea*, Navarra: Aranzadi, 2015, p. 252, 266.

to be filled in. On the one hand, it allows assurance in relation to the purpose of request, but on a the other it discourages the use of this basis of cooperation, especially in non-urgent cases as it is much easier to write a free-text request.

2.4 Practical use

Despite the hurry by Member States to approve the Swedish Initiative, its implementation took much longer than had been foreseen. As an established indirect information exchange does not suppose complicated and expensive implementation measures, the reason should be long legislative process or (and) its disadvantages or lack of strong added value in comparison with the already used information exchange mechanisms.

As stated in the Council's Report from 2011, "The general standards for cross-border information exchange asked for by the Decision were often already in place. Therefore, it was stated that the process had not notably been improved. From a specific technical point of view, it must be noted that the required use of form A and B for submitting and requesting information, complicates information exchange as they are deemed to be cumbersome."[20]

On this basis, the following question can arise: does the Swedish Initiative really have added value in information exchange and implementation of the principle of availability? Or was it a measure adopted just to demonstrate European political concern about information exchange, and to somehow fulfil tasks established by The Hague Programme?

Of course any draft that needs a unanimous agreement of 25 Member States[21] can be much diluted from content and obligations, and that probably happened with the Swedish Initiative. But is it possible to regulate such broad scope of information exchange by the legal act of 13 articles in total, with 10 of them dedicated to regulate this process? What added value does a three-page form have, furthermore, one that has more similarities with EAO that with simple information exchange?

This has made the Swedish Initiative a limited used mechanism only for situations of urgency and additionally, not in all States. Five years after its approval, only Slovenia and Sweden use this instrument frequently and other Member States "do not draw on it on a regular basis."[22] But even in

20 COUNCIL OF THE EUROPEAN UNION, "Council Framework Decision 2006/960/JHA on simplifying the exchange of information and intelligence between law enforcement authorities of the Member States of the European Union ('Swedish Framework Decision') – Assessment of compliance pursuant to Art. 11(2) – Report", 15278/11, p. 6, accessed November 19, 2017, http://data.consilium.europa.eu/doc/document/ST-15278-2011-INIT/en/pdf.

21 At the moment of its adoption, Bulgaria, Romania and Croatia were not EU Member States yet.

22 EUROPEAN COMMISSION, "Commission Staff Working…", *loc. cit.*, p. 6.

this case, Swedish law enforcement authorities use the form only when it is specifically indicated by the requested Member States.[23]

As pointed out in the Study of the International Centre for Migration Policy Development, "Users prefer free text reporting, instead of filling in several pages of modular information, increasing time spent handling the requests. Even the simplified version of form B, developed during the Czech Presidency, has not brought the expected results."[24]

DAPIX group has agreed on the possibility of using a simplified request form, but these modifications were not formally introduced into the Council Framework Decision 2006/960/JHA, so the question of their legality stands. From another angle, some states (Spain, Switzerland, Lichtenstein) literally implemented the official text of the Swedish Initiative in the national legislation and have foreseen obligatory use of the request form and cannot use the simplified one.

In addition to all practical inconveniences and unlike the Commission's Proposal, the Swedish Initiative does not foresee any obligation to gather statistics on its use, and therefore there is no way to measure its effectiveness and to identify areas of improvement.

In non-automated information exchange, the collection of statistics is an additional burden for law enforcement institutions; in cases of automated information exchange (access to databases) it would be a technical solution that does not require any further efforts and could be used additionally for supervision of data protection.

Recently, the European Commission launched the project to assess the implementation of the Swedish Initiative that has to be carried out in 2018.

3 Data protection

As the Swedish Initiative by itself is a very laconic legal instrument, provisions on data protection tend to be too, and are regulated by Articles 8 and 9.

Article 8 foresees a double data protection regime:

- For information exchange as such, data protection rules applied to the channel of communication are used. Thus if information is requested through SIENA, Europol's data protection rules will be obligatory.
- Use of received information, as a general rule, is regulated by the national law of the receiving Member State that must be in conformity

23 COUNCIL OF THE EUROPEAN UNION, "Council Framework Decision 2006/960/JHA…", *loc. cit.*, p. 17.

24 INTERNATIONAL CENTRE FOR MIGRATION POLICY DEVELOPMENT AND EUROPEAN PUBLIC LAW ORGANIZATION, "Study on the status of information exchange amongst law enforcement authorities in the context of existing EU instruments", European Commission, 2010, p. 40, accessed August 20, 2017, https://ec.europa.eu/home-affairs/sites/homeaffairs/files/doc_centre/police/docs/icmpd_study_lea_infoex.pdf.

> with the European Convention on Data Protection, and should take into consideration Recommendation (87) 15.

Nevertheless, the requested Member State can foresee conditions on its use and reporting results. But such special conditions will not be applied to judicial, legislative and other institutions performing supervisory functions of law enforcement authorities. In any case, the opinions of transmitting Member State must be taken into account as far as possible.

As it was adopted in 2006, no reference to the general data protection framework of police or judicial cooperation is made. But as Swedish initiative have only two aforementioned Articles as *lex especialis*, the Directive (EU) 2016/680 of the European Parliament and of the Council of 27 April 2016 on the protection of natural persons with regard to the processing of personal data by competent authorities for the purposes of the prevention, investigation, detection or prosecution of criminal offences or the execution of criminal penalties, and on the free movement of such data, and repealing Council Framework Decision 2008/977/JHA should be used as *lex generalis* for transnational information exchange.

Transmitted information can be processed only for the purpose for which it was transferred. Its use for other purposes has to be authorised by requested Member State, and envisaged by the national law of receiving one.

With respect to confidential information and intelligence, Article 9 only entails the application of relevant national provisions. Even if the legislator does not explain whether it is applied only in order to reply or also in order to request, it should be applied to both, as request can also contain confidential information in relation to the investigation performed.

4 Brief summary and evaluation

The Framework Decision 2006/960/JHA was the first attempt to implement the principle of information availability, where Member States, after sound declaration of the need to significantly improve information exchange, have chosen quite superficial mechanism for its implementation. Regulation does not provide clarity of purpose; it includes very few provisions on data protection and establishes complicated data exchange forms.

The only advantage can be considered an obligatory timeframe to provide information for urgent requests. Notwithstanding, it also has its problems as the definition of urgency is not provided and its misuse cannot be controlled.

As a result, even after a decade the information exchange background is not widely used, and instead of being a universal law enforcement information exchange tool is treated as "an optional/supplementary legal instrument for sending requests for information."[25]

25 Ibid, p. 16.

Thus to make the principle of availability work effectively, an innovative and open-minded approach is needed[26] and it seems that it had been followed in the Commission's Proposal, but left aside by Member States at least for the moment.

Bibliography

BOERGER, B., 2015, "The transmission of personal data as part of the police and judicial cooperation in criminal matter in the EU: German experience"; in COLOMER HERNÁNDEZ, I. and OUBIÑA BARBOLLA, S., *La transmisión de datos personales en el seno de la cooperación judicial penal y policial en la Unión Europea*", Navarra: Aranzadi, p. 187–214.

EUROPEAN COMMISSION, 2005, "Proposal for a Council Framework Decision on the exchange of information under the principle of availability", COM(2005) 490 final. Available at: http://eur-lex.europa.eu/legal-content/EN/TXT/?uri=COM:2005:0490:FIN (accessed November 19, 2017).

EUROPEAN COMMISSION, 2011, "Commission Staff Working Paper Operation of the Council Framework Decision 2006/960/JHA of 18 December 2006 ("Swedish Initiative")"; SEC(2011) 593 final. Available at: http://data.consilium.europa.eu/doc/document/ST-10316-2011-INIT/en/pdf (accessed November 19, 2017).

COUNCIL OF THE EUROPEAN UNION, 2010, "Guidelines on the implementation of Council Framework Decision 2006/960/JHA of 18 December 2006 on simplifying the exchange of information and intelligence between law enforcement authorities of the Member States of the European Union", 9512/1/10. Available at: http://data.consilium.europa.eu/doc/document/ST-9512-2010-REV-1/en/pdf (accessed November 19, 2017).

COUNCIL OF THE EUROPEAN UNION, 2011, "Council Framework Decision 2006/960/JHA on simplifying the exchange of information and intelligence between law enforcement authorities of the Member States of the European Union ('Swedish Framework Decision') – Assessment of compliance pursuant to Art. 11(2) – Report" 15278/11. Available at: http://data.consilium.europa.eu/doc/document/ST-15278-2011-INIT/en/pdf (accessed November 19, 2017).

COUNCIL OF THE EUROPEAN UNION, 2012, "Council Framework Decision 2006/960/JHA on simplifying the exchange of information and intelligence between law enforcement authorities of the Member States of the European Union ('Swedish Framework Decision') – Assessment of compliance pursuant to Article 11(2) – Draft Report"; 14755/1/12. Available at: http://data.consilium.europa.eu/doc/document/ST-14755-2012-REV-1/en/pdf (accessed November 19, 2017).

FAZEKAS, J., 2009, "Development of Justice and Home Affairs Cooperation between 2004 and 2009 in the European Union"; in *European Integration Studies*; vol. 7; no 1; p. 3–28.

HEMPEL, L., CARIUS, M. and ILTEN, C., 2009, "Exchange of information and data between law enforcement agencies within the European Union" (Discussion

26 VERMEULEN, Gert; VANDER BEKEN, Tom; VAN PUYENBROECK, Laurens et al., *Availability of law enforcement information in the European Union. Between mutual recognition and equivalent right of access*, Antwerp: Maklu Publisher, 2005, p. 47.

paper Nr. 29/09, Zentrum Technik und Gesellschaft). Available at: http://www.ztg.tu-berlin.de/pdf/Nr_29_Hempel_Carius_Ilten.pdf (accessed November 1, 2017).

INTERNATIONAL CENTRE FOR MIGRATION POLICY DEVELOPMENT and EUROPEAN PUBLIC LAW ORGANIZATION, 2010, "Study on the status of information exchange amongst law enforcement authorities in the context of existing EU instruments", European Commission. Available at: http://ec.europa.eu/dgs/home-affairs/doc_centre/police/docs/icmpd_study_lea_infoex.pdf (accessed August 20, 2017).

KIETZ, D.; MAURER, A., 2006, "From Schengen to Prüm" (Comments, German Institute for International and Security Affairs). Available at: http://www.swp-berlin.org/fileadmin/contents/products/comments/Com15_06_Ktz_Mrr_Ks.pdf (accesses November 1, 2017).

MITSILEGAS, V., 2009, *EU Criminal Law*, Oxford and Portland, Oregon: Hart Publishing.

VERMEULEN, G., VANDER BEKEN, T., VAN PUYENBROECK, L. et al., 2005, *Availability of law enforcement information in the European Union. Between mutual recognition and equivalent right of access*, Antwerp: Maklu Publisher.

VERVAELE, J.A.E., 2012, "Medidas de investigación de carácter proactivo y uso de información de inteligencia en el proceso penal"; in PÉREZ GIL, J.; *El proceso penal en la sociedad de la información*, Madrid: La Ley, p. 27–85.

7 Example of networking: Financial Intelligence Units and Asset Recovery Offices

Although the word "network" can appear not to be very solemn in the context of law enforcement authorities, well defined and regulated networks are very useful tools to put specialised experts in contact; furthermore, in cases of necessity they can make contact directly and exchange information according to an agreed legal basis. As examples of such networks the European Network for the Protection of Public Figures, the European Network of National Officials to Detect and Combat New Cases of Cross-Border VAT Fraud, the European Network of Law Enforcement Specialists on Carrier-Grade Network Address Translation, and Network Against Corruption can all be mentioned.

Regarding the EU primary law, Article 85 of the TFEU expressly mentions only European Judicial Network, leaving the rest of the networks up to the necessity of cooperation.

As all tools so far presented in this research are analysed from the perspective of their use in crime investigations, the following networks have been selected:

- Network of FIUs (network of Financial Intelligence Units for the information exchange on suspicious transactions, that can be related to money laundering or terrorism financing) officially created by the Council Decision 2000/642/JHA of October 17, 2000 concerning arrangements for cooperation between the Financial Intelligence Units (FIUs) of the Member States in exchanging information[1] (hereinafter – Decision 2000/642/JHA).
- Network of AROs (network for the tracing and identification of ill-gotten gains) officially created by the Council Decision 2007/845/JHA of December 6, 2007 concerning cooperation between the Asset Recovery Offices of the Member States in the field of tracing and identification of

1 OJ L 271, 24.11.2000, p. 4–6.

proceeds from, or other property related to, crime[2] (hereinafter – Decision 2007/845/JHA).

They were selected for a few reasons. Firstly, money laundering has already been mentioned as one of the factors that gave rise to international police cooperation as it is a "global business" and "The United Nations Office on Drugs and Crime (UNODC) estimates that the sum of money laundered globally amounts to between 2 and 5 per cent of global GDP or between EUR 615 billion and EUR 1.54 trillion each year."[3]

Secondly, because the final goals of FIUs and AROs networks are the same, although they have different regulations and different information exchange rules. Thirdly, the FIU network has a new regulation that is one of the last legislative developments.

1 Network of Financial Intelligence Units (FIUs)

Although the first anti-money laundering regulation within the European Communities was adopted in 1991 as Council Directive 91/308/EEC, with the aim of establishing links between suspicious financial transactions and underlying criminal activity, in order to prevent and to combat money laundering,[4] (the so called First AML/CFT Directive), at that moment its focus was on obliging credit and financial institutions to identify suspicious financial transactions to national competent authorities without making any reference to cross-border information exchange.

Within the following decade, Member States established FIUs or endowed already existing competent authorities with this function.

At global level, in 1995 the Egmont Group, as an informal group to facilitate international cooperation in the fight against money laundering and terrorism financing was established. Currently, this group unites FIUs from 151 countries and has stable structure with division by topics and regions. Nevertheless, information exchange within its framework takes place under the principle of reciprocity, which does not always ensure effectiveness.[5]

Therefore, within the EU Decision 2000/642/JHA was adopted. It provides us with the following FIU definition: "A central, national unit which, in order to combat money laundering, is responsible for receiving (and to the extent permitted, requesting), analysing and disseminating to the competent

2 OJ L 332, 18.12.2007, p. 103–105.
3 EUROPOL, "EU Serious Organised Crime Threat Assessment (SOCTA 2013)", p. 27, accessed September 9, 2017, available at: https://www.europol.europa.eu/content/eu-serious-and-organised-crime-threat-assessment-socta.
4 OJ L 166, 28.6.1991, p. 77–82.
5 See "The Egmont group of Financial Intelligence Units", accessed October 16, 2017, https://www.egmontgroup.org/en/membership/list.

authorities, disclosures of financial information which concern suspected proceeds of crime or are required by national legislation or regulation."[6] According to its Article 3, depending on national structure, it can be an administrative, police or judicial entity, but its national status does not have to be an obstacle for effective cooperation.

Its Article 1 established possibilities to exchange information on request, or spontaneously between the FIUs of Member State. The scope for information exchange is defined very broadly foreseeing that it is, "any available information that may be relevant to the processing or analysis of information or to investigation by the FIU regarding financial transactions related to money laundering and the natural or legal persons involved."

Requests shall provide requested Member States with the facts related to the investigation or suspicions, as well as with information on how the received information will be used. For requests sent on the basis of this Decision, relevant information shall be answered without any additional requirement to send another request on the basis of bilateral or multilateral agreements. The receiving Member State has to follow the limitations of use of data, foreseen by the requested Member State.

To make this information as available as possible, Decision 2000/642/JHA establishes only three backgrounds of denial: ongoing criminal investigation in the requested Member State, disproportion between the revealing of information and the legitimate interests of person (data subject) or requested Member State; disagreement with other crucial legal principles of the requested Member State.

In the same year France, Italy, Luxembourg, the Netherlands and the United Kingdom started a FIU.NET project that became operational in 2002. Currently FIU.NET as safe communication network, is functioning under the auspice of Europol.[7]

Although it was mentioned that the First AML/CFT Directive had not regulated cross-border cooperation and FIUs, the following AML/CFT Directive[8] actually did.

The last directive in force, the Fourth AML/CFT Directive (Directive (EU) 2015/849 of the European Parliament and of the Council of May 20, 2015 on the prevention of the use of financial system for the purposes of money laundering or terrorist financing, amending Regulation (EU) No 648/2012 of the European Parliament and of the Council, and repealing Directive 2005/60/EC of the European Parliament and of the Council and Commission

6 See Article 2 of the Decision 2000/642/JHA.

7 See DEL MORAL TORRES, Anselmo, *Cooperación internacional de interés* policial, Aranjuez (Madrid): Centro Universitario de la Guardia Civil, 2016, p. 193–194.

8 See Chapters III and V of Directive 2005/60/EC of the European Parliament and of the Council of October 26, 2005 on the prevention of the use of the financial system for the purpose of money laundering and terrorist financing, OJ L 309, 25.11.2005, p. 15–36.

Directive 2006/70/EC)[9] provides very comprehensive regulation of FIUs; first of all drawing attention to their operational independence, i.e., "The FIU has the authority and capacity to carry out its functions freely, including the autonomous decision to analyse, request and disseminate specific information." It also lays down extensive regulation of cooperation between FIUs.

Thus Article 52 establishes that "Member States shall ensure that FIUs cooperate with each other to the greatest extent possible, regardless of their organisational status."

Unlike Decision 2000/642/JHA, exchanged information is not only related to money laundering, but to terrorism financing as well. Maintaining requirements to provide investigation facts, and how data will be used, it is required to mention reasons for requests being made. Nevertheless, if the type of offence implied is not yet determined, this is not a reason to deny the request.

With regard to the cooperation channel, FIU.NET is mentioned in particular; but it does not impede the use of others.

Article 53(2) includes a provision that reiterates principles of information availability by establishing that, "Member States shall ensure that the FIU to whom the request is made is required to use the whole range of its available powers which it would normally use domestically for receiving and analysing information when it replies to a request for information [...] from another FIU."

The fourth AML/CFT Directive remains only one reason for the denial of information that is "Fundamental principles of its national law." In June 2016, the European Commission proposed the Fifth AML/CFT Directive[10] that would not substitute the Fourth one, but to complement it with some new provisions. It includes such novelties as: adding virtual currency exchange platforms and custodian wallet providers to the list of entities obliged to provide information; setting lower transaction limits for some pre-paid payment instruments and the harmonization of the EU approach to high-risk third countries. It also expands the competence of the FIUs by stipulating their right to obtain and use information from any obliged entity, as well as obtaining any additional information they need.

Summing up, it can be said that the latest developments related to the FIU network comprehensively cover legal aspects of cooperation and give state-of-the-art technical background to its implementation.

9 OJ L 141, 5.6.2015, p. 73–117.

10 EUROPEAN COMMISSION, "Proposal for a Directive of the European Parliament and of the Council amending Directive (EU) 2015/849 on the prevention of the use of the financial system for the purposes of money laundering or terrorist financing and amending Directive 2009/101/EC, COM 2016(450), accessed November 19, 2017, http://eur-lex.europa.eu/legal-content/EN/TXT/?uri=COM:2016:0450:FIN.

2 Network of Asset Recovery Offices (AROs)

If FIUs are dedicated to analytical, intelligence-led work, specialising in identifying suspicious transactions that can be related to money laundering or the financing of terrorism, AROs are oriented to looking for criminal proceeds, their seizure and confiscation. Thus if the FIUs role is more proactive or warning, the AROs role is more reactive, designed to deprive criminals from benefit, and to ensure that "crime does not pay".

The origins of cooperation in tracing, freezing, seizing and confiscating criminal proceeds can be found in the Convention on Laundering, Search, Seizure and Confiscation of the Proceeds from Crime (CETS 141) of the Council of Europe.

Within the European Communities, one of the first legal acts on this topic was Joint Action 98/699/JHA of December 3, 1998 on money laundering, the identification, tracing, freezing, seizing and confiscation of instrumentalities and the proceeds from crime.[11] It entailed an obligation to establish national legal provision that would allow, upon request from other Member States, the identification and tracking of criminal proceeds, and foreseeing the necessity of approximation of laws on criminal assets seizure and confiscation.

Later, a range of political declarations strengthened the importance of this issue. For example, the Tampere Conclusions envisaged that money laundering "should be rooted out wherever it occurs", the Hague Programme pointed out, "the monitoring of suspicious financial flows and the freezing of assets".[12]

In September 2004, Austria, Belgium, Germany, Ireland, the Netherlands and the United Kingdom established CARIN – a global network for the purpose of exchange of experience and best practice in order to deprive illicit proceeds.[13] Nowadays, it associates more than 50 national authorities from Europe as well as the United States, nine international organisations and is linked with equivalent networks in Asia Pacific, Latin America and South Africa.[14] Its Secretariat is hosted within the Europol Criminal Asset Bureau.[15]

The CARIN network is not authorised in case-related data exchange, and therefore within the EU,[16] in 2007 Decision 2007/845/JHA was adopted. It

11 OJ L 333, 9.12.1998, p. 1–2.

12 OJ C 53, 3.3.2005, p. 8.

13 See EUROPOL, "Camden Asset Recovery Inter-agency Network (CARIN)", accessed October 16, 2017, https://www.europol.europa.eu/content/camden-asset-recovery-inter-agency-network-carin-leaflet.

14 Ibid.

15 See EUROPOL "Camden Asset Recovery Inter-Agency Network (CARIN): the History, Statement of Intent, Membership and Functioning of CARIN. Manual", 2012, p. 3, accessed October 16, 2017, https://www.europol.europa.eu/content/publication/camden-asset-recovery-inter-agency-network-carin-manual-1665

16 See ibid., p. 3.

has emphasised the need for effective tracing of assets, that can be reached by rapid and direct information exchange between competent authorities. From its Article 2 a conclusion can be made that, depending on peculiarities of national systems, ARO can be within an administrative, law enforcement or judicial authority. Each Member State can nominate up to two AROs. Thus, for example:

- France, first nominated the Central Department of Judicial investigation and later Agency for Administration and Recovery of Seized and Confiscated Assets as an ARO; managed by the Ministry of Justice and the Ministry of Finance;
- The United Kingdom nominated the Serious Organised Crime Agency (for England, Wales and North Ireland)[17] and Scottish Crime and Drug Enforcement Agency (for Scotland) as AROs.[18]

According to Article 3 of the Decision 2007/845/JHA, information requests to AROs of other Member States can be sent either by national ARO or another authority "charged with the facilitation of the tracing and identification of proceeds of crime". Thus the requested authority will always be an ARO, but the range of requesting authorities is wider.

Decision 2007/845/JHA makes a reference to the Council Framework Decision 2006/960/JHA of December 18, 2006 on simplifying the exchange of information and intelligence between law enforcement authorities of the Member States of the European Union[19] (hereinafter – Swedish Initiative) as to the legal basis for information requests and to the form of request established.

As reference is made to the Swedish Decision, for denial of information, backgrounds established in its Article 10 are applied, i.e. offence punished with less than 1 year of imprisonment, risk to national security, undergoing investigation or intelligence operation in the requesting Member State, jeopardising individuals' safety or disproportionality.

Decision 2007/845/JHA also allows the spontaneous provision of information between the aforementioned authorities when it is considered useful for the performance of the ARO functions of the receiving Member State.

In relation to the recuperation of crime benefits, in 2008, a Communication from the Commission to the European Parliament and the Council, "Proceeds of organised crime: Ensuring that 'crime does not pay'", was

17 Currently National Crime Agency.

18 See CORRAL ESCARIZ, Vicente, "La nueva estrategia económica contra la delincuencia organizada y la corrupción: comiso y recuperación de activos.", in *La Guardia Civil en la lucha contra la Delincuencia Económica*, Madrid, 2013, p. 105, 108, accessed October 16, 2017, http://www.interior.gob.es/documents/642317/1203227/La_Guardia_Civil_en_la_lucha_contra_delincuencia_economica_126140481.pdf/be81de27-8378-4dc4-9326-02178ce2711b.

19 OJ L 386, 29.12.2006, p. 89–100.

issued. It emphasised that "national agencies charged with tracing assets are a precondition for a successful confiscation, as well as for international cooperation."[20] It also pointed out access to relevant databases, granting of coercive and provisional freezing powers to AROs and effective coordination (with suggestion to endow it to Europol) as indispensable elements for effective asset recovery.[21]

Later, illicit proceeds were the object of the Stockholm Programme that called upon their more effective identification and seizure (but within the context of combatting terrorism)[22], and an Internal Security Strategy that foresaw the involvement of information from private sector for the tracing of assets.

Although according to Decision 2007/845/JHA, Member States had to establish their ARO until the end of 2008, in 2010 the Council Conclusions on Confiscation and Asset Recovery[23] and in the Communication on Implementation of ISS, obligation to establish fully functioning ARO was still reiterated.[24]

In 2011, ARO were still not notified by Malta, Italy, Portugal and Slovenia.[25] In the case of Italy, creation of ARO (National Agency for the Administration and Use of Seized and Confiscated from Organised Crime) was established by the Law 50/2010, but at the moment of the Commission's Report, it was not yet functioning.[26]

In October 2012, there were still two Member States without ARO, and the Council, in its Final report on the fifth round of mutual evaluations – "Financial crime and financial investigations" stated that Member States were still encouraged to promote efficient cooperation through AROs and "when possible, pro-actively and exclusively use this channel in the fight against financial crime as regards asset recovery."[27]

20 EUROPEAN COMMISSION, "Communication from the Commission to the European Parliament and the Council – Proceeds of organised crime: ensuring that 'crime does not pay'", COM(2008) 766, p. 8, accessed November 19, 2017, http://eur-lex.europa.eu/legal-content/EN/TXT/?uri=COM:2008:0766:FIN.

21 Ibid, p. 9.

22 OJ C 115, 4.5.2010, p. 23.

23 COUNCIL OF THE EUROPEAN UNION, "Council Conclusions on Confiscation and Asset Recovery", 7769/3/10, accessed November 19, 2017, http://data.consilium.europa.eu/doc/document/ST-7769-2010-REV-3/en/pdf.

24 Ibid, p. 6.

25 See EUROPEAN COMMISSION, "Report from the Commission to the European Parliament and to the Council based on Article 8 of the Council Decision 2007/845/JHA of 6 December 2007 concerning cooperation between Asset Recovery Offices of the Member States in the field of tracing and identification of proceeds from, or other property related to, crime", COM(2011) 176, p. 2, accessed November 19, 2017, http://eur-lex.europa.eu/LexUriServ/LexUriServ.do?uri=COM:2011:0176:FIN:EN:PDF.

26 See CORRAL ESCARIZ, Vicente, "La nueva estrategia económica…", loc. cit., p. 107.

27 COUNCIL OF THE EUROPEAN UNION, "Final report on the fifth round of mutual evaluations – 'Financial crime and financial investigations'", 12657/2/12,

Article 10(1) of the Directive 2014/42/EU of the European Parliament and of the Council of 3 April 2014 on the freezing and confiscation of instrumentalities and proceeds of crime in the European Union reiterates that "Member States shall take the necessary measures, for example by establishing centralised offices, a set of specialised offices or equivalent mechanisms, to ensure the adequate management of property frozen with a view to possible subsequent confiscation."[28]

On May 18, 2017 the Council of Ministers (of Interior) approved Council conclusions on setting the EU's priorities for the fight against organised and serious international crime between 2018 and 2021; one of ten priorities for coming years is the combatting of criminal finances and money laundering and facilitate asset. For this purpose a Multi Annual Strategic Plan for the Criminal Finances/Money Laundering/Asset recovery priority of the EU Policy Cycle 2018/2021 has already been adopted and serves as the background for Operation Action Plans in this subject.

3 Data protection

As both networks have different legal bases, their data protection regimes are also different. Decision 2000/642/JHA makes a reference to the European Convention on Data Protection, its Protocol and Recommendation R(87) 15 as principles that have to be followed in information exchange between FIUs. The only specific rule foreseen by Decision 2000/642/JHA prohibits access to submitted information by any other authority than FIU.

The Fourth AML/CFT Directive is less strict and foresees the possibility of access to other competent authorities, but only with the prior consent of the requested FIU that can refuse such consent only for the same reasons as applied to information denial for requests for information.

It also established that *lex generalis* applied to the cooperation of FIUs and the implementation of this directive in general is Directive 95/46/EC of the European Parliament and of the Council of October 24, 1995 on the protection of individuals with regard to the processing of personal data and on the free movement of such data[29] (hereinafter – Directive 95/46/EC), and the Regulation 45/2001 of the European Parliament and of the Council of December 18, 2000 on the protection of individuals with regard to the processing of personal data by the Community institutions and bodies and on the free movement of such data.[30] That means that the European legislator did not treat the Fourth AML/CFT Directive as one falling into the category police and judicial cooperation, because in such cases it would be

p. 27, accessed November 19, 2017, http://data.consilium.europa.eu/doc/document/ST-12657-2012-REV-2/en/pdf.

28 OJ L 127, 29.4.2014, p. 49.

29 OJ L 281, 23.11.1995, p. 31–50.

30 OJ L 8, 12.1.2001, p. 1–22.

established as *lex generalis* Council Framework Decision 2008/977/JHA of November 27, 2008 on the protection of personal data processed in the framework of police and judicial cooperation in criminal matters[31] (hereinafter – Framework Decision 2008/977/JHA). The inertia probably arose previously, as the First AML/CFT Directive formed a part of the former First Pillar, and did not even mention FIUs. But the actual scope of regulation is different, and includes issues of the former First and Third Pillars.

As Directive 95/46/EC was repealed by the Regulation 2016/679 of the European Parliament and of the Council of April 27, 2016 on the protection of natural persons with regard to the processing of personal data and on the free movement of such data, and repealing Directive 95/46/EC (General Data Protection Regulation)[32] (hereinafter – Regulation 2016/679), its provisions should be applied to data exchange among FIUs.

Article 23 of the Regulation 2016/679 (previously Article 13 of Directive 95/46/EC) allows exceptions from data subject right to be informed, to access and to publicise processing operations in cases where its processing could prevent, investigate or prosecute a crime. Thus in the case of information exchange between FIUs, these exceptions could be applied.

As noticed by the European Commission, the full application of data subject's rights "would be particularly contradictory with pursued objectives as it would oblige the FIU to inform the person concerned that a suspicious transaction report concerning them has been integrated in a data processing exercise whose objective is to combat money laundering and terrorism financing."[33]

In the case of AROs, Article 5 of the Decision 2007/845/JHA makes reference to the principles of the European Convention on Data Protection, its Protocol, Recommendation R(87)15, as well as to national data protection rules of the Member States and received data has to be protected in the same way as national data related to the same topic.

But as information exchange between AROs takes place under the Swedish Initiative, data protection provisions of the latter shall be applied as *lex specialis*. As already mentioned, information received under Swedish Initiative can be processed only for the purpose for which it was transmitted and its use for other purposes has to be authorised by the requested Member State and envisaged by the national law of the receiving one.

Additionally to *lex specialis*, the Swedish Initiative also has *lex generalis* that is Framework Decision 2008/977/JHA that in 2018 will be substituted by the Directive 2016/680 of the European Parliament and of the Council of 27 April 2016 on the protection of natural persons with regard to the

31 OJ L 350, 30.12.2008, p. 60–71.

32 OJ L 119, 4.4.2016, p. 1–88.

33 EU FINANCIAL INTELLIGENCE UNITS' PLATFORM, "Report on Confidentiality and Data Protection in the Activity of FIUs", April 2008, p. 4, accessed October 16, 2017, http://ec.europa.eu/internal_market/company/docs/financial-crime/fiu-report-confidentiality_en.pdf.

processing of personal data by competent authorities for the purposes of the prevention, investigation, detection or prosecution of criminal offences or the execution of criminal penalties, and on the free movement of such data, and repealing Council Framework Decision 2008/977/JHA.[34]

4 Brief summary and evaluation

Although functioning under different legal bases and using different information exchange tools, networks of FIUs and AROs aim to combat illicit proceeds by their elimination from legal financial markets.

The European legislator leaves it up to Member States to decide whether national FIUs and AROs are administrative, police or judicial entities. The only requirement is to ensure that the nature of the unit will not prejudice effective cooperation.

In different ways, both networks contribute to the implementation of the principle of availability: in the case of FIUs, they are directly established in the Fourth AML/CFT Directive and in the case of AROs – indirectly, through the Swedish Initiative. Nevertheless, the difference lies in time limits for response. In cases of information exchange through AROs, in urgent cases related to serious crime mentioned in Article 2(2) of Framework Decision 2002/584/JHA on the European arrest warrant and the surrender procedures between Member State,[35] the response shall be given within 8 hours. In cases of cooperation through FIUs, no deadlines are given. From one angle, this can give an impression of less importance being given by the European legislator to intelligence related to money laundering and the financing of terrorism, but looking at the scope of requests in both cases, it is obvious that requests to FIUs can be much broader than asking for any available information and not for precise criminal proceeds.

Bibliography

CORRAL ESCARIZ, V., 2013, "La nueva estrategia económica contra la delincuencia organizada y la corrupción: comiso y recuperación de activos.", in *La Guardia Civil en la lucha contra la Delincuencia Económica*, p. 95–131. Available at: http://www.interior.gob.es/documents/642317/1203227/La_Guardia_Civil_en_la_lucha_contra_delincuencia_economica_126140481.pdf/be81de27-8378-4dc4-9326-02178ce2711b (accessed October 16, 2017).

COUNCIL OF THE EUROPEAN UNION, 2010, "Council Conclusions on Confiscation and Asset Recovery"; 7769/3/10. Available at: http://data.consilium.europa.eu/doc/document/ST-7769-2010-REV-3/en/pdf (accessed November 19, 2017).

COUNCIL OF THE EUROPEAN UNION, 2012, "Final report on the fifth round of mutual evaluations – 'Financial crime and financial investigations'", 12657/2/12.

34 OJ L 119, 4.5.2016, p. 89–131.
35 OJ L 190, 18.7.2002, p. 1–20.

Available at: http://data.consilium.europa.eu/doc/document/ST-12657-2012-REV-2/en/pdf (accessed November 19, 2017).

DEL MORAL TORRES, A., 2016, *Cooperación internacional de interés policial*, Aranjuez (Madrid): Centro Universitario de la Guardia Civil.

EU FINANCIAL INTELLIGENCE UNITS' PLATFORM, 2008, "Report on Confidentiality and Data Protection in the Activity of FIUs". Available at http://ec.europa.eu/internal_market/company/docs/financial-crime/fiu-report-confidentiality_en.pdf (accessed October 16, 2017).

EUROPEAN COMMISSION, 2008, "Communication from the Commission to the European Parliament and the Council – Proceeds of organised crime: ensuring that 'crime does not pay'", COM(2008) 766. Available at: http://eur-lex.europa.eu/legal-content/EN/TXT/?uri=COM:2008:0766:FIN (accessed November 19, 2017).

EUROPEAN COMMISSION, 2011, "Report from the Commission to the European Parliament and to the Council based on Article 8 of the Council Decision 2007/845/JHA of 6 December 2007 concerning cooperation between Asset Recovery Offices of the Member States in the field of tracing and identification of proceeds from, or other property related to, crime", COM(2011) 176. Available at: http://eur-lex.europa.eu/LexUriServ/LexUriServ.do?uri=COM:2011:0176:FIN:EN:PDF (accessed November 19, 2017).

EUROPEAN COMMISSION, 2016, "Proposal for a Directive of the European Parliament and of the Council amending Directive (EU) 2015/849 on the prevention of the use of the financial system for the purposes of money laundering or terrorist financing and amending Directive 2009/101/EC", COM 2016(450). Available at: http://eur-lex.europa.eu/legal-content/EN/TXT/?uri=COM:2016:0450:FIN (accessed November 19, 2017).

EUROPOL, 2012, *Camden Asset Recovery Inter-Agency Network (CARIN): the History, Statement of Intent, Membership and Functioning of CARIN. Manual*. Available at: https://www.europol.europa.eu/content/publication/camden-asset-recovery-inter-agency-network-carin-manual-1665 (accessed October 16, 2017).

EUROPOL, 2013, "EU Serious Organised Crime Threat Assessment (SOCTA 2013)" report. Available at: https://www.europol.europa.eu/content/eu-serious-and-organised-crime-threat-assessment-socta (accessed September 9, 2017).

EUROPOL, 2015, "Camden Asset Recovery Inter-agency Network (CARIN)". Available at: https://www.europol.europa.eu/content/camden-asset-recovery-inter-agency-network-carin-leaflet (accessed October 16, 2017).

8 Information exchange under Prüm decisions

On the initiative of the German Presidency of the Council of the European Union in 2007, in a surprisingly short time, 27 EU Member States unanimously adopted Council Decision 2008/615/JHA of June 23, 2008 on the stepping up of cross-border cooperation, particularly in combating terrorism and cross-border crime (hereinafter – Decision 2008/615/JHA) and Council Decision 2008/616/JHA of June 23, 2008, on the implementation of Decision 2008/615/JHA on the stepping up of cross-border cooperation, particularly in combating terrorism and cross-border crime[1] (hereinafter – Decision 2008/616/JHA) also called Prüm Decisions.

As stated by Bellanova, Prüm Decisions "suppose to offer legal and technological instruments for fighting terrorism and international crime more efficiently, compensating potential negative spill-overs of the Schengen area."[2]

Besides updated regulation of "traditional" methods of police cooperation and information exchange (such as the spontaneous provision of information, joint operations), they have also given a legal basis for one of the newest information exchange mechanism, i.e. direct access to national DNA, dactyloscopic and vehicle registration databases among EU Member States.[3]

1 OJ L 210, 6.8.2008, p. 1–72.

2 BELLANOVA, Rocco, "The 'Prüm Process': The Way Forward for EU Police Cooperation and Data Exchange?" in GUILD, Elspeth and GEYER, Florian (eds.), *Security versus Justice? Police and Judicial Cooperation in the European Union*, Hampshire: Ashgate Publishing Limited, 2008, p. 204.

3 European criminal record exchange system (ECRIS) based on the Council Framework Decision 2009/315/JHA of April 6, 2009 on the organisation and content of the exchange of information extracted from the criminal record between Member States and Council Decision 2009/316/JHA of April 6, 2009 on the establishment of the European Criminal Records Information System (ECRIS) in application of Article 11 of Framework Decision 2009/315/JHA (OJ L 93, 7.4.2009, p. 23–348) is also a system of direct access and was launched in April 2012. It is a decentralised system based on the criminal records databases in each Member State, linked with the common software and communication

1 From multilateral convention to European instrument

Prüm Decisions take their origin in the multilateral Convention between the Kingdom of Belgium, the Federal Republic of Germany, the Kingdom of Spain, the French Republic, the Grand Duchy of Luxembourg, the Kingdom of the Netherlands and the Republic of Austria on the stepping up of cross-border cooperation, particularly in combating terrorism, cross-border crime and illegal migration signed on May 27, 2005 in the German town of Prüm (and therefore called the Prüm Treaty) and considered as, "the maximum possible level of police cooperation."[4]

The initiative came from the German Ministry of the Interior, Otto Schily, who in spring 2003 proposed it to his counterparts from France, Belgium, Luxembourg and the Netherlands (lately joined by Austria and Spain).

Factual similarities between the development of the Schengen Agreement and the Prüm Treaty can be noticed as both of them were led by Germany and all the primary parties of the Schengen Agreement (Belgium, France, Germany, Luxembourg and the Netherlands) later made up five of the seven signatures of the Prüm Treaty. Therefore, it is sometimes called "Schengen III".

1.1 Between multilateral and enhanced cooperation

But unlike the Schengen Agreement, adoption of the Prüm Treaty has raised grand discussion about the disobedience of the enhanced cooperation procedure.

As the Prüm Treaty was signed by seven Member States and almost immediately joined by seven more (Bulgaria, Estonia, Finland, Hungary, Romania, Slovenia, Slovakia), it has raised a lot of doubts about "sincerity" in the use of the intergovernmental agreement of the seven Member States, instead of more complicated enhanced cooperation procedure that should be used with the implications of eight Member States.[5]

infrastructure and accessible by judges and prosecutors of all EU Member States. In addition to data about criminal records, transmission of other personal data such as fingerprints, amongst others, is allowed which makes it possible to identify the subject, and so this is a possibility with regard to DNA profiles. This system was launched in April 2012.

4 CALESINI, Giovanni, *European Police Law Handbook*, Roma, Laurus Robuffo, 2007, p. 193.

5 See ZILLER, Jaques, "Le traité de Prüm. Une vraie-fausse cooperation renforcée dans l'Espace de sécurité de liberté et de justice", Working Paper, LAW No. 2006/32, European University Institute, 2006, p. 3, accessed October 21, 2017, http://cadmus.eui.eu/handle/1814/6401; DE HOYOS SANCHO, Montserrat, "Obtención, registro e intercambio de perfiles de ADN de sospechosos en el espacio de libertad, seguridad y justicia" in CABEZUDO BAJO, María José, *Las bases de datos policiales de ADN ¿Son una herramienta realmente eficaz en la lucha contra la criminalidad grave nacional y transfornteriza?*, Madrid: Dykinson, S.L.,

It could be justified if the content and the purpose of the agreement would be outside EU policy, but the content of the Prüm Treaty was in line with EU policies in the security area, as it:

a Corresponded to the general objective to strengthen internal security;
b Foresaw measures in line with the objective of The Hague Programme, to intensify cooperation in combatting terrorism, cross-border crime and illegal migration[6];
c Made an allusion to the general principle of The Hague Programme on information availability by establishing the goal of "better information exchange"[7] (although availability was limited only to the signatory states instead of all EU Member States).

Mr Peter Hustinx, the European Data Protection Supervisor, directly described this situation as evasion of the substantive and procedural requirements of enhanced cooperation.[8]

Other scholars called it a contribution to the "patchwork" legal system and strengthening of a two speed Europe.[9] For example, Guild and Geyer pondered that "Seven Member States free to turn their backs on eighteen others, to decide among themselves on a model of police cooperation and data exchange only to return to the originally excluded

2013, p. 67–68; CÁMARA VILLAR, Gregorio, "La garantía de los derechos fundamentales afectados por la Convención de Prüm" in *Revista de Derecho Constitucional Europeo*, Enero-Junio 2007, no 7, p. 98–100; FREIXES SANJUÁN, Teresa, "Protección de datos y globalización. La Convención de Prüm" in *Revista de Derecho Constitucional Europeo*, Enero-Junio de 2007, no 7. p. 11.

6 See OJ C 53/1, 3.3.2005, p. 7–11.

7 See MARTÍNEZ PÉREZ, Fernando and POZA CISNEROS, María, "El Principio de Disponibilidad: Antecedentes Penales y Convenio de Prüm". In CARMONA RUANO, Miguel; GONZÁLES VEGA, Ignacio U. and MORENO CATENA, Víctor, *Cooperación Judicial Penal en Europa*, Madrid: Dykinson, 2013, p. 425; KIETZ, Daniela, MAURER, Andreas, "From Schengen to Prüm", Comments, German Institute for International and Security Affairs, May 2006, p. 2, accesses November 1, 2017, http://www.swp-berlin.org/fileadmin/contents/products/comments/Com15_06_Ktz_Mrr_Ks.pdf.

8 HOUSE OF LORDS. "Prüm: an effective weapon against terrorism and crime?" (Report with Evidence, May 2007), p. 31, accessed November 1, 2017, http://www.statewatch.org/news/2007/may/eu-hol-prum-report.pdf.

9 GUILD, Elspeth, "Merging Security from Two-Level Game: Inserting the Treaty of Prüm into EU law?", (CEPS Policy Brief, March 2007, no. 124), p. 1, accessed October 16, 2017, http://ceps.be/book/merging-security-two-level-game-inserting-treaty-prüm-eu-law. BALZACQ, Thierry, BIGO, Didier, CARRERA, Sergio et al., "Security and the Two-Level Game: the Treaty of Prüm, the EU and the Management of Threats" (Working Document no. 234, Centre for European Policy Studies, January 2006), p. 3, accessed October 16, 2017, http://www.ceps.be/book/security-and-two-level-game-treaty-prüm-eu-and-management-threats.

rest to sell their product as the latest innovation in managing threats, a product that no responsible European government could nowadays afford to miss."[10]

Additionally, the institutional and political preconditions of 1985 and 2005 were totally different. The Schengen Agreement and Schengen Convention were adopted out of the framework of the European Communities due to significant delays in the creation of the free movement area by all EC, and they had never included any allusion about its imposition on the EU. It was created as a consequence of an institutional vacuum[11] and when, "the European Communities were still far from being able to agree upon the concept of an area of Freedom, Security and Justice."[12] Nevertheless, the Prüm Treaty was adopted after the tabling by the Commission a comprehensive proposal on automated information exchange, that also included DNA profiles, dactyloscopic and vehicle registration data.

1.2 Transformation into EU instrument

Although the Prüm Treaty came into force on November 23, 2006[13] and only between Austria, Germany and Spain, it was already presented at EU level at the beginning of 2007. On January 1, 2007, Germany had taken over the Presidency of the Council of the European Union, and within 1 month, in February 2007, its Minister of Interior Dr Wolfgang Schäuble presented the Prüm Treaty at an informal meeting of Justice and Home Affairs Ministers, as an instrument that was ready to be "transplanted" into EU law. He also confirmed deliberate avoidance of the enhanced cooperation procedure by saying that it was an example of avoidance of the bottlenecks of usual EU procedures. Four days later, the Council Secretariat officially published "European-wide Prüm Treaty" as the initiative of 14 Member States: Austria, Belgium, Bulgaria, Finland, France, Germany, Luxembourg, the Netherlands, Portugal, Romania, Slovakia, Slovenia, Spain and Sweden.

10 GUILD, Elspeth and GEYER, Florian, "Getting local: Schengen, Prüm and the dancing procession of Echternach. Three paces forward and two back for UE police and judicial cooperation in criminal matters" (Commentaries, Centre for European Policy Studies, 2006), p. 2, accessed October 16, 2017, http://aei.pitt.edu/11629/.

11 See BALZACQ, Thierry, "From a Prüm of 7 to a Prüm of 8+: What Are the Implications?", (Briefing Paper, DG Internal Policies, Citizens Rights and Constitutional Affairs, 2006), p. 4.

12 GUILD, Elspeth and GEYER, Florian, "Getting local: Schengen...", loc. cit., p. 4.

13 The same year, parties signed an Administrative and technical implementing Agreement to the Prüm Convention. See Council document 5473/07.

The political agreement of the ministers on the proposal was reached in less than half a year – on June 12, 2007 and the Council of the European Union adopted its final version on June 23, 2008. The European Parliament expressed its regrets that it had not had time for an appropriate review of the proposal, and drew the attention to the absence of an explanatory memorandum, the evaluation of future costs, comprehensive impact assessment and an evaluation of the multilateral agreement, as well as lack of an adequate data protection framework.[14]

By Decision 2008/615/JHA and Decision 2008/616/JHA the Prüm Treaty was not literally integrated into the framework of the EU as both experts and politicians had expressed concerns about some of its aspects.

Both the Treaty and the Decisions seek the same general aim: to step up cross-border cooperation, in particular, law enforcement information exchange. Comparing the areas of cooperation covered by the two instruments, the Prüm Treaty foresees more cooperation instruments than Prüm Decisions; this is presented in Table 8.1.

Both the multilateral convention and the EU legal instruments include provisions on their interrelationship.

- Article 47 of the Prüm Treaty foresaw that its provisions shall apply only in so far as they are compatible with the EU law.
- Article 35 of the Council Decision 2008/615/JHA established that for contracting parties of the Prüm Treaty, the relevant provisions of the Decision shall be applied instead of the corresponding provisions contained in the Prüm Treaty. But any other provisions of the latter shall remain applicable between the contracting parties.

2 Prüm Decisions: possibilities given and benefit made

The Prüm Decisions foresee the exchange of different categories of data:

a Data related to personal characteristics such as DNA and dactyloscopics;
b Vehicles registration data;

14 See EUROPEAN PARLIAMENT, "Report on the initiative by the Kingdom of Belgium, the Republic of Bulgaria, the Federal Republic of Germany, the Kingdom of Spain, the French Republic, the Grand Duchy of Luxembourg, the Kingdom of the Netherlands, the Republic of Austria, the Republic of Slovenia, the Slovak Republic, the Italian Republic, the Republic of Finland, the Portuguese Republic, Romania and the Kingdom of Sweden on the stepping up of cross-border cooperation, particularly in combating terrorism and cross-border crime (6566/2007 – C6–0079/2007–2007/0804(CNS))", p. 6, accessed October 20, 2017, http://www.europarl.europa.eu/sides/getDoc.do?type=COMPARL&mode=XML&language=EN&reference=PE386.698; O'NEILL, Maria, "The Issue of Data Protection and Data Security in the (Pre-Lisbon) EU Third Pillar", in *Journal of Contemporary European Research*, vol. 6, issue 2, 2010, p. 227, accessed October 16, 2017, http://www.jcer.net/index.php/jcer/article/view/264.

c All data important in prevention of terrorism;
d All data important in prevention of offences and threats to the security in major events with a cross-border dimension.

With regard to the first two categories, a State has DNA samples, a DNA profile, fingerprints, palm prints, a vehicle registration number or chassis, and is looking for its "owner", or wants to find out more information. Regulation on this kind of data (Articles 3, 9 and 12 of the Council Decision 2008/615/JHA) allows Member States to perform an automated search in the relevant national databases of other Member States.

Table 8.1 Cooperation areas covered by Prüm Treaty and Prüm Decisions

<table>
<tr><th>Areas covered by Prüm Treaty</th><th>Areas covered by Prüm Decisions</th></tr>
<tr><td colspan="2">Creation of national DNA, dactyloscopic databases[15]</td></tr>
<tr><td colspan="2">Automated searching in national DNA, dactyloscopic and vehicles registration databases and further information exchange</td></tr>
<tr><td colspan="2">Supply of personal and non-personal data for crime prevention, maintenance of public order and security for major events with a cross-border dimension</td></tr>
<tr><td colspan="2">Assistance in connection with major events, disasters and serious accidents</td></tr>
<tr><td>– Combatting terrorism by information supply and exchange, giving the possibility to deploy "air marshals" on the aircraft registered in the deploying country
– Cross-border police cooperation through provisional measures necessary to preclude imminent danger to the physical integrity of individuals; common patrols and other joint operations when officers from one Contracting Party should perform their duties within the territory of another
– Combatting illegal migration by secondment of document advisers, assistance in repatriation measures
– Other cooperation upon request</td><td>– Prevention of terrorist offences by information supply
– Common patrols and other joint operations when officers of one Contracting Party should perform their duties within the territory of another</td></tr>
</table>

15 At the beginning, there was an idea to create centralised DNA, dactyloscopic and vehicle registration databases, but it was declined at the ministerial meeting on November 26, 2004 opting for decentralised databases. See LUIF, Paul, "The Treaty of Prüm: A Reply of Schengen?" (deliverable of the Project within the framework EU-CONSENT "*Wider Europe, Deeper Integration? Constructing Europe Network*", May, 2007), p. 8–9, accessed, October 16, 2017, http://www.eu-consent.net/library/deliverables/D38c.pdf.

In the following two categories, the State faces a potential threat and is looking for any information that can prevent it. In this case, a non-automated information exchange takes place and the State sends a request for any information or a notice of the existing threat.

It should be noted that Prüm Decisions, as well as the Framework Decision 2006/960/JHA of 18 December 2006 on simplifying the exchange of information and intelligence between law enforcement authorities of the Member States of the European Union (hereinafter – Framework Decision 2006/960/JHA), do not oblige States to collect any information, but solely make available already existing information.[16] The only exception is Article 7 of the Council Decision 2008/615/JHA that foresees the possibility of requesting assistance on collection of cellular material and supplying DNA profiles when they are needed for on-going investigations or criminal proceedings.

In addition to the EU Member States, Iceland and Norway signed the agreement on the application of certain provisions of Prüm Decisions in November 2009.[17] Furthermore, in 2014, the United Kingdom had decided to opt-out from Prüm Decisions due to delays in its implementation, but in 2016 decided to rejoin with the declaration of readiness to apply all its provisions until 2020.[18]

2.1 Automated data search

For automated data exchange, Decision 2008/615/JHA obliges the States to establish national databases of DNA, dactyloscopic (fingerprints, palm prints or soleprints) and vehicle registration and to grant the search right (subject to some conditions explained below) to competent authorities of other States, and to perform further information exchange.

Although the general aim of the Prüm Decisions is to step up cross-border cooperation, in particularly information exchange, its provisions foresee different information access purposes, depending on the category of data that is subject to automatic search. Thus according to Article 3, national DNA databases can be accessed and reference data can be obtained only for the investigation of a criminal offence. Article 9 allows automated search and access to the reference data in fingerprint identification systems for the prevention and investigation of criminal offences. Vehicle registration data can be searched and accessed for the prevention and investigation of criminal offences, other offences under the jurisdiction of the courts, or the public

16 See AGUILERA RUIZ, Luis, "La protección de datos de ADN en la Unión Europea y en España" in CABEZUDO BAJO, María José, *Las bases de datos policiales..*, op. cit., p. 34.

17 OJ L 353, 31.12.2009, p. 1–8.

18 OJ L 132, 21.5.2016, p. 105–106.

prosecution service of the searching Member State and for the maintenance of public security. The deadline to implement these measures expired on August 26, 2011.

2.1.1 Data search and access

Three categories of automatically searched data are regulated in the same Chapter 2 of the Council Decision 2008/615/JHA. Regulation of DNA profiles and dactyloscopic data is almost the same, but access to vehicle registration data is handled in a different way.

Thus in cases of DNA profiles and dactyloscopic data, the search is directly performed in the national database of the other country and in cases of vehicle registration – access is through the centralised European Vehicle[19] and Driving Licence Information System (Eucaris)[20] which offers a multilingual web client, enabling enquiries to other countries to be sent via national web browser.

To carry out queries in relation to DNA profiles and dactyloscopics, reference data is entered. For DNA profiles it means a non-coding part of the DNA and reference number, and for dactyloscopics – the dactyloscopic data and reference number. It is disassociated from any data that can lead to direct identification of a person in a search. Both the non-coding part of DNA and fingerprints, palm prints and soleprints help to distinguish one person from another. The non-coding DNA part also indicates the gender, but does not provide any other type of genetic information, such as race, ethnic group, diseases, and so on.

While performing an automated search of DNA profile or dactyloscopic data, data stored in databases is not accessed directly. State A can only find out whether there is a DNA profile or dactyloscopic data in the relevant database of State B, corresponding to the searched data, and will only receive an automated answer on positive or negative search result. In the case of a positive result, together with an automated reply, the reference data of the stored DNA profile or dactyloscopics that resulted in the match will be sent. Providing personal data and other information will be performed on the basis of the further request of the searching State (Articles 5 and 10 of

19 It should be noted that Prüm Decisions use a term "vehicle" although officially Eucaris stands for "European *Car* and Driving Licence Information System".

20 Eucaris was established in 1994 by the initiative of five European countries (Belgium, the Netherlands, Germany, Luxembourg and the United Kingdom) in order to support data communication between vehicle registration authorities and to combat exportation of stolen cars as well as driving licence "tourism". Currently Eucaris is expanded with other forms of information exchange between countries, e.g. Prüm Treaty and Prüm Decisions and in 2012, it was appointed as the technical platform for the cross-border exchange of information under Directive 2011/82/EU of the European Parliament and of the Council of 25 October 2011 facilitating cross-border exchange of information on road safety and related traffic offences (OJ L 288, 5.11.2011, p. 1–15).

the Decision 2008/615/JHA), i.e. state A will send a request to state B, indicating reference data of the stored DNA profile or dactyloscopics received with automatic answer on coincidence and will explain the purpose for which the data is requested.

That means that:

- The DNA or dactyloscopic database searching State will not obtain data that does not match that submitted for the search;
- The establishment of separate "hit" and "post hit" (data exchange) stages allows the requested Member State absolute control of the possessed data and to evaluate whether the purpose for the search and other conditions meet the requirements to share the data.[21]

It should be mentioned that in this process, different legislation is used: a search is performed in compliance with the national law of the searching party, an automated answer on match is regulated by EU law, and the request for further data shall be in accordance with the requested State's national law.

Moreover, it should be taken into account that national rules of DNA and dactyloscopic collection, use and processing can differ among States and affect data exchange and its further use in the process. In many European countries dactyloscopic data is treated as police data[22] and its collection does not affect either the fundamental right of physical and moral integrity, or the right of privacy.[23] But talking about DNA profiles and related data, the situation is more complicated as its collection has different restrictions, due to the possible effects of fundamental rights:

- In some states, a judicial authorisation to collect DNA samples is needed (e.g. Spain) and in others, the police can do it without judicial authorisation (e. g. the United Kingdom).[24]
- National law differs in relation to categories of crimes in which collection is permitted. For example, in Finland collection is permitted only

21 See AGUILERA RUIZ, Luis, "La protección de datos ADN…", loc. cit., p. 35.

22 See MCCARTHNEY, Carole I., WILSON, Tim J. and WILLIAMS, Robin, "Transnational Exchange of Forensic DNA: Viability, Legitimacy, and Acceptability" in *European Journal on Criminal and Research*, 2011, vol.17, no. 4, p. 310.

23 See SOLETO MUÑOZ, Helena, *La identificación del imputado: Rueda, fotos, ADN…De los métodos basados en la percepción a la prueba científica*, Valencia: Tirant lo blanch, 2009, p. 83.

24 See ALCOCEBA GIL, Juan Manuel, "Tratamiento y transmisión de datos genéticos con fines de la investigación penal en la UE" in COLOMER HERNÁNDEZ, Ignacio and OUBIÑA BARBOLLA, Sabela, *La transmisión de datos personales en el seno de la cooperación judicial penal y policial en la Unión Europea*, Navarra: Aranzadi, 2015, p. 624–635; SOLETO MUÑOZ, Helena and ALCOCEBA GIL, Juan, "Protección de datos y transferencia de perfiles de ADN" in CABEZUDO BAJO, María José, *Las bases de datos policiales…*, op. cit., p. 338–340.

for crimes with a punishment of imprisonment higher than 6 months. In Netherlands – 4 years.[25]

- Regarding storage and further use of data, in Austria, Belgium, the Czech Republic, Hungary, Slovakia, Slovenia, Sweden and the Netherlands it is forbidden to store and use data without conviction.[26]

In the case of vehicle registration data, full chassis number or full registration number shall be used for automated search and of course, by itself it does not contain any personal data. In this case, there is no two stage procedure and the answer for the search already includes some personal data (vehicle and insurance information together with the respective vehicle owner and/or holder) and is returned directly in encrypted form.

This difference in procedure can be defended by the fact that the backgrounds for vehicle registration search are much broader than for "bio information", and the flow of searches is more intensive. From another angle, personal data on the vehicle's owner or operator is usually more basic (name and surname) than one included into DNA of dactyloscopic database.

2.1.2 Granting access to national databases

An automated search carried out in the database of another state means that the searching authority has previously been given access to it. It is a sensitive issue as it supposes actions on "virtual territory" of another state, and demands strong trust in the partner, its legal system and professionals. Doubts can arise at every stage, for instance: how will the searching state ensure that only authorised staff will have access? Whether data protection rules of another country will guarantee the same protection level as national ones? Are information search and use rules strict enough? Without answering these questions and the disappearance of these doubts mutual access to national databases is hardly imagined.

Therefore, Prüm Decisions establish mechanisms that allow strengthening mutual trust and making information exchange effective and free of mutual suspicions. Article 25(2) of Decision 2008/615/JHA establishes that access to another state's databases is granted when the Council decides that the country has met all the technical, legal, data protection requirements applied to every category of data exchanged (DNA, dactyloscopic and vehicle registration data).[27] The evaluation mechanism is not applied for Member States

25 WILLIAMS, Robin, "Making Forensic DNA Databases: Global Themes and Local Variations" in CABEZUDO BAJO, María José, *Las bases de datos policiales...*, op. cit., p. 366.

26 See ibid, p. 367.

27 It should be noted that this requirement is not applied to Member States that started to exchange data under the Prüm Treaty.

where the supply of personal data has already started, pursuant to the Prüm Treaty. According to Article 20 of the Council Decision 2008/616/JHA, the Council's decision is taken on the basis of an evaluation report, developed by the experts of already operational Member States, and based on information from the questionnaire answered by the evaluated state, its evaluation visit and pilot run of the relevant database.

Thus before granting access to the national database, operational Member States have the opportunity to assess the state's readiness in this regard. Although evaluation is performed and a report is drafted by a limited number of persons representing already operational countries (3–4 persons), other countries can acquaint themselves with the whole evaluation process and documentation through the different bodies of the Council of the European Union, i.e. through the DAPIX, the Committee of Permanent Representatives (COREPER 2) and Justice and Home Affairs Council.

Unlike Schengen evaluation mechanism, Prüm evaluations are performed only with regard to automated data exchange and only once, i.e. in order to grant access. It does not have any follow-up as in the case of periodical Schengen evaluations.

2.1.3 Implementation measures

As already mentioned, Prüm Decisions' implementation deadline for automated data search expired on August 26, 2011. The earliest available statistics on this issue present the figures of the state of play on December 31, 2011,[28] when:

- 14 Member States (Austria, Bulgaria, Finland, France, Germany, Latvia, Lithuania, Luxembourg, the Netherlands, Portugal, Romania, Slovakia, Slovenia, Spain) were entitled to exchange DNA related data and twelve of them were already operational;
- 10 Member States (Austria, Bulgaria, Czech Republic, France, Germany, Lithuania, Luxembourg, Slovakia, Slovenia, Spain) were operational for fingerprint related data exchange;
- 10 Member States (Austria, Belgium, Finland, France, Germany, Luxembourg, the Netherlands, Romania, Slovenia, Spain) were operational for vehicles registration data exchange.

28 See COUNCIL OF THE EUROPEAN UNION, "Council Decision 2008/615/JHA of 23 June 2008 on the stepping up of cross-border cooperation, particularly in combating terrorism and cross-border-crime, Council Decision 2008/616/JHA of 23 June 23, 2008 on the implementation of Council Decision 2008/615/JHA of 23 June 2008 on the stepping up of cross-border cooperation, particularly in combating terrorism and cross-border-crime ('Prüm Decisions') – statistics and reports on automated data exchange for 2011", 11367/12, p. 2.

Even now, some Member States are still not operational. According to the data from September 2017, 23 Member States were operational for DNA related data exchange, 22 – for exchange of dactyloscopic data and 19 – for exchange data on vehicle registration.[29]

As Home Affairs Ministers gather for the Council at least every 2–3 months, and the Council's preparatory bodies meet almost every month, decision-making processes (i.e. Council Decision on granting of access) are not the reason for delays. Problems lie in Member States who face different obstacles to establish or modify databases and to create appropriate legal and data protection regimes. As stated in the Report from the Commission to the European Parliament, and the Council on the implementation of Council Decision 2008/615/JHA of June 23, 2008, on the stepping up of cross-border cooperation, particularly in combating terrorism and cross-border crime (hereinafter – Implementation Report 2012), the main reasons for the delay are technical in nature and caused by a lack of human and financial resources in the Member States.[30]

Thus the automated data exchange mechanism is quite expensive and the question stands, whether its use and effectiveness for crime investigation compensates such expenditures. The majority of Member States have opted for a statistics model focusing on the number of hits, but not on the data of the influence of this information exchange on the final result of investigation and prosecution. Thus it is not clear what percentage of hits was really significant in finding offenders and bringing them to justice; e.g. Spain's search of DNA profile had resulted in a hit in the German DNA database and was reflected in the statistics, but there is no information on the level of its importance in comparison with other data related to the investigation or on its use as evidence in the trial.[31]

2.2 Non-automated data exchange

As mentioned, Decision 2008/615/JHA also establishes some rules on "traditional" information exchange on request or by own initiative. Its Chapters 3 and 4 regulate such information exchange for:

29 See Council document 5081/4/17, p. 2–5.

30 COM(2012) 732 final, p. 5.

31 Such data had been collected, implementing a pilot project in Denver, USA related to DNA evidence use in the investigation of burglaries. From all cases where DNA extraction was possible (about 7% of all burglaries) in 76 %, the crucial element for prosecution was DNA analysis. ASHIKMIN, Simon; BERDINE, Susan G.; MORRISSEY, Mitchel R. et al., "Effectiveness and Cost Efficiency of DNA Evidence in Volume Crime. Denver Colorado Site Summary", p. 2, accessed October 16, 2017, http://www.denverda.org/dna_documents/dnaburgrcostefficiencyreserch1.pdf.

- Terrorism prevention;
- Prevention of criminal offences and maintaining public order and security in major events with a cross-border dimension.

These provisions are not widely analysed, either by experts or by scholars as all their attention is focused on revolutionary automated data exchange.

Before getting into the analysis of these Chapters of Decision 2008/615/JHA, it is worth trying to find out if there are any other EU legal instruments that regulate exchange of the same categories of data, and to make their comparison.

2.2.1 Relation with other EU legal instruments

Decision 2008/615/JHA is surely not the first one that regulates information exchange in such important issues as combatting terrorism or events of cross-border dimensions (summits of heads of states, important international sport events, etc.).

Such information can be exchanged on the basis of Framework Decision 2006/960/JHA as general background to any information exchange, as well as on specific bases, such as Council Decision 2005/671/JHA of 20th September 2005 on the exchange of information and cooperation concerning terrorists[32](hereinafter – Decision 2005/671/JHA) or Council Decision 2002/348/JHA of 25th April 2002 concerning security in connection with football matches with an international dimension[33] (hereinafter – Council Decision 2002/348/JHA).

Framework Decision 2006/960/JHA covers information exchange related to any criminal investigation or criminal intelligence operations, including terrorism. From first sight, Council Decision 2008/615/JHA regulates information exchange for terrorism prevention and differs from the Council Framework Decision 2006/960/JHA that covers information exchange on any crime, including terrorism, in the case of criminal investigation or criminal intelligence operations. Nevertheless, as mentioned before, the scope of the Swedish Initiative differs in its articles:

- Article 2(c) defines criminal intelligence as a procedural stage in which information about a crime or criminal activities is gathered in order to establish whether concrete criminal acts have been committed or may be committed in the future. This gives reason to believe that the Swedish Initiative also covers crime prevention matters when it has the form of a criminal intelligence operation;

32 OJ, L 253, 29.9.2005, p. 22–24.

33 OJ L 121, 8.5.2002, p. 1–3. Partly amended by the Council Decision 2007/412/JHA (OJ, L 155, 15.6.2007, p. 76–77).

- Article 5(1) establishes that information and intelligence may be requested for the purpose of detection, prevention or investigation of an offence.

Furthermore, Article 7(1) which has already been mentioned, obliges spontaneous information and intelligence supply to other Member States' law enforcement authorities, where there are factual reasons to believe that the information and intelligence could assist in the detection, prevention or investigation of offences referred to in Article 2(2) of Council Framework Decision 2002/584/JHA of 13 June 2002 on the European arrest warrant and the surrender procedures between Member States which, among other crimes, also includes terrorism.

Regarding specialised regulation, Article 2(6) of Decision 2005/671/JHA foresees that "each Member State shall take the necessary measures to ensure that any relevant information included in documents, files, items of information, objects or other means of evidence, seized or confiscated in the course of criminal investigations or criminal proceedings in connection with terrorist offences can be made accessible as soon as possible, taking account of the need not to jeopardise current investigations, to the authorities of other interested Member States."

Additionally, as mentioned previously, Europol also carries AWF CT where all relevant information can be submitted.

In case of major events, Article 3 of Decision 2002/348/JHA establishes that "before, during and after a football event with an international dimension, national football information points shall engage, at the request of a national football information point concerned or on its own initiative, in mutual exchange of general information and [...] personal data."

This indicates that Decision 2008/615/JHA is partly overlapping already existing legislation. It would make more sense to expand application of Decision 2002/348/JHA to other sorts of events that establish separate overlapping regulations. In cases of major meetings, such as the European Council, it would be more appropriate to foresee information exchange amending Council Decision 2002/956/JHA of November 28, 2002 setting up a European Network for the Protection of Public Figures[34] as its Article 4 (e) as one of the objective establishes, "Favouring the exchange, in accordance with the national legislation, of operational information, either through the contact points or by means of direct contacts between the responsible services."

This being said, the provisions of Chapters 3 and 4 of Decision 2008/615/JHA seem to be redundant, and do not contribute too much added value in EU regulation regarding information exchange. It is also reflected in the Implementation Report 2012, as Chapter 3 is often used only by eight

34 OJ L 333, 10.12.2002, p. 1–2; OJ L 283, 30.10.2009, p. 62.

Member States and Chapter 4 only by five of them.[35] But given that the regulation is in place, it deserves some analysis.

2.2.2 Information supply and exchange

With respect to information exchange and supplying security at major events, Articles 13 and 14 of Decision 2008/615/JHA make a difference between the supply of personal and non-personal data; but in the case of terrorism prevention, Article 16 refers to information as such, without making a previously mentioned division.

Personal data exchange or supply for the security of major events is permitted when there is a reason to believe that, due to conviction or other circumstances, the data subject will commit criminal offences at the events or pose a threat to public order and security.

In the case of terrorism prevention, information (without specifying whether it is personal data or not) exchange and supply is conditioned to the reason to suspect that a person could commit the crime of terrorism.[36]

Article 16(2) foresees that data supplied for terrorism prevention shall comprise surname, first names, date and place of birth and a description of the circumstances giving rise to the belief that a person will commit a crime of terrorism. From the text, it is not clear whether it is minimum or maximum data that is supplied in such circumstances; i.e. whether a supplying Member State is restricted to providing only the personal data mentioned above, or facilitating other related data as well. Taking into account the information

35 See COM(2012) 732 final, p. 9–10.

36 For the unified understanding of terrorism, the European legislator makes a reference to the crimes listed in Articles 1–3 of the Council Framework Decision 2002/475/JHA on combating terrorism (O J L 164, 22.6.2002, p. 3). Those crimes are: attacks upon a person's life which may cause death; attacks upon the physical integrity of a person; kidnapping or hostage taking; causing extensive destruction to a Government or public facility, a transport system, an infrastructure facility, including an information system, a fixed platform located on the continental shelf, a public place or private property likely to endanger human life or result in major economic loss; seizure of aircraft, ships or other means of public or goods transport; manufacture, possession, acquisition, transport, supply or use of weapons, explosives or of nuclear, biological or chemical weapons, as well as research into, and development of, biological and chemical weapons; release of dangerous substances, or causing fires, floods or explosions the effect of which is to endanger human life; interfering with or disrupting the supply of water, power or any other fundamental natural resource, the effect of which is to endanger human life; threatening to commit any of above listed acts. To be recognised as crime of terrorism, the crime must have been committed with the aim of seriously intimidating a population, or unduly compelling a Government or international organisation to perform or abstain from performing any act, or seriously destabilising or destroying the fundamental political, constitutional, economic or social structures of a country or an international organisation. In addition, a crime of terrorism includes directing or participating in activities of a terrorist group.

exchange purpose, there should be the possibility to provide any other meaningful data, especially taking into account that surname, name, date and place of birth could be the result of identity fraud. Supplying photos, dactyloscopic and DNA data should be allowed in these cases as well.

When regulating information supply (without a previous request) on terrorism prevention and security at major events, in the first case the legislator uses the term "may" and in the second – "shall". This brings us to the conclusion that in the case of major events, the requested Member State or Member State possessing information is obliged to share it, and in the case of terrorism prevention has the right to do so. Such regulation seems a little bit strange, taking into consideration the seriousness of terrorism.

3 Data protection

As in case of Schengen acquis and Europol's regulation, Prüm Decisions also establish their individual data protection regime instead of applying the *lex generalis*. Recital 94 of the Directive (EU) 2016/680 of the European Parliament and of the Council of April 27, 2016 on the protection of natural persons with regard to the processing of personal data by competent authorities for the purposes of the prevention, investigation, detection or prosecution of criminal offences, or the execution of criminal penalties, and on the free movement of such data, and the repealing of Council Framework Decision 2008/977/JHA, still maintains this system.

Unlike the data exchange tools mentioned above, Prüm Decisions' data protection rules do not regulate any central data processing, but establish minimum standards that have to be applied by Member States that remain data processors and responsible at all stages.

Article 25 of Decision 2008/615/JHA establishes that national rules are applied to the processing of received data and shall ensure at least the data protection level foreseen in the European Convention on Data Protection, its Protocol and Recommendation (87)15.

As already mentioned, before granting access to databases in other states, and before data processing is started, the application of relevant data protection requirements in each state is evaluated. Thus there is a real control measure to verify the application of relevant data protection principles.

Article 26 of Decision 2008/615/JHA envisages that data processing by the requesting state shall be performed only for the purposes that it was provided. Proceeding for other purposes is subject to the authorisation of the requested Member State and is possible only if its national law permits such use of data.

Prüm Decisions also establish that data provided at the first automated information exchange stage (verification of hit/no hit), can be processed by the searching state only for establishing the existence of a match, preparation and the sending of a request for personal data related to the match, and for recording that will be used only for data control. The searched state can process data received as a result of comparison only for this purpose and delete it immediately after comparison has taken place. Exception is made only when it is necessary for the preparation of a request or recording for the control, and the data is deleted after such action.

Such detailed provisions are quite unusual, because in search and automated responses on match, no personal data is involved, but nonetheless, the European legislator has established its special treatment.[37]

Unlike Europol and Schengen acquis, Prüm Decisions do not establish any precise term for received data deletion, but envisage that it shall be carried out as soon as the data is no longer necessary for the aim that it was submitted, or when the storage term is over, according to the national law of the submitting state. There is also the possibility to block data instead of its deletion if the latter would affect the data subject.

Despite including regulation on information exchange with respect to terrorism, Prüm Decisions do not make any reference to classified information, although theoretically it could also be the object of exchange.

3.1 *Persons included*

According to Articles 2 and 8 of Decision 2008/615/JHA, a national DNA database shall be created to investigate criminal offences and a national dactyloscopic database – to prevent and investigate them.

There is no reference to categories of persons that shall be included or excluded from them, and it is left up to national legislation. The only supranational criteria in this regard is the case law of the ECtHR, although it does not cover all sensitive aspects.

As a general rule, in the case *Van der Velden v the Netherlands* ECtHR recognised that, "the Court further has no difficulty in accepting that the compilation and retention of a DNA profile served the legitimate aims of the prevention of crime and the protection of the rights and freedoms of others. This is not altered by the fact that DNA played no role in the investigation and trial of the offences committed by the applicant. The Court does not consider it unreasonable for the obligation to undergo DNA testing to be imposed on all persons who have been convicted of offences of a certain severity."[38]

Thus ECtHR does not insist on DNA collection and storing of DNA profiles during the investigation, but it could be done at any time when the convicted person is concerned. Nevertheless, ECtHR is not precise when DNA can be collected from other persons, for example suspects. In this

37 The same rule was established in the Prüm Treaty. See ACED FÉLEZ, Emilio, "Ejercicio y garantía del derecho a la protección de datos personales en el Convenio de Prüm", *Revista de derecho constitucional europeo*, 2007, no. 7, p. 84, 85.

38 ECtHR, *Van der Velden v the Netherlands* [2006].

respect it has been established on different occasions that there is a risk of stigmatisation[39] and:

- No systematic data retention shall be done.
- Data processing shall maintain proportion between public and private interests.
- Collected and stored data shall match its purpose, i.e. be relevant and not unreasonably excessive. Distinctions between data storage related to minor and similar offences shall be made.[40]
- Different treatment of data of convicted and non-convicted persons shall be introduced, especially taking into account data of minors.[41]

3.2 Access

As Prüm Decisions envisage rules for automated and non-automated data exchange, as a consequence different rules of access are applied.

In cases of automated data search and its double stage procedure, two types of access must be taken into account:

- At the stage of automated comparison (direct access to depersonalised data in national databases of other states), access is granted only to national contact points designated by each state. It means access very limited in terms of numbers of authorities and persons. According to Article 30(2), every state shall have a list of persons authorised to make searches and every search has to be recorded, including an entry giving its reason. National contact points make searches on requests of other national authorities responsible for crime investigation in cases of DNA search, for crime prevention and investigation in case of dactyloscopic data search and crime prevention, its investigation and maintaining public order in cases of vehicle registration data.
- At the stage of receiving data related to an automated match, first of all it is available to a national contact point that lately transmits it to the authority that has requested a comparison.

In case of non-automated data exchange, for each category of data (terrorism, public order and security) a network of contact points is also established and every data exchange shall be recorded according to Article 30(1) of Decision 2008/615/JHA. National contact points make further transmission of data to requesting authorities or in case of spontaneous data

39 ECtHR, *M. K. V France* [2013], paragraph 36; *S and Marper v United Kingdom* [2008], para 122.

40 ECtHR, *S and Marper v United Kingdom* [2008], paragraph 103.

41 ECtHR, *M. K. V France* [2013], paragraph 36, 42; *S and Marper v United Kingdom* [2008], paragraphs 22, 124.

supply – to the authority that could be interested. In these circumstances, it is very important to forward information to the right institution and to avoid any unnecessary data (including personal) diffusion. Nonetheless, this aspect is not regulated by the Prüm Decisions.

3.3 *Third Parties and onwards transmission*

Unlike the Europol Regulation, Prüm Decisions do not foresee the possibility of data transmission to third parties or onwards transmission to other than requesting institutions, to other Member States or to third parties.

Such restriction allows the identification at any time of an institution that has misused data, as the circle of subjects that process the data is very limited. It is important with respect to any data and in particular to that related to DNA.

Comparing the "destiny" of data related to terrorism and processed under Prüm Decisions and in AWF, the same data in the first case will never be transmitted onward or to the third party and in the second case – it could be.

This is one of the examples when some competent institutions would prefer to use Decision 2008/615/JHA than submit information to Europol and lose control over it.

3.4 *Data subject's access right*

Article 31 of Decision 2008/615/JHA includes a data subject's access right without unreasonable expenses, within "comprehensible" terms and "without unacceptable delays". The scope of the access right is not precisely defined, but bearing in mind the established right to obtain information about data origin and receiving authorities, it seems to be limited to the data received from other Member States; as a consequence, the data of a search and not access to data on a national database (access to this data should be regulated by national law of each country). In addition, it is not clear whether the data subject can make a general request about all processed data according to Prüm Decisions, or shall specify whether it concerns DNA, dactyloscopic or other data. Article 31 envisages an obligation to ensure effective judicial protection for data subjects whose data protection was violated.

Establishing these minimum guarantees of access right, the regulation of the whole process is left to the national law of every country, meaning that different procedures, authorities, appeal systems and reasons for denial will be applied.[42] Without any doubt, that would place the data subject in a discriminated position, and condition his or her right to access, depending on the state where the request is made.

42 See ACED FÉLEZ, Emilio, "Ejercicio y garantía del derecho...", loc. cit., p. 91.

Prüm Decisions do not foresee any rules on consultation with the states from which data was received, although as previously mentioned, the data subject has a right to know about the origin of his or her data. Thus situations where the state of the data's origin has a reason not to reveal information to the data subject (such as an ongoing investigation, public or state security) are not taken into account.

According to Article 28(2), the data subject can ask to flag his or her data when the accuracy or inaccuracy of data cannot be established.

3.5 *Supervising authorities*

Unlike Europol and Schengen acquis, Prüm Decisions do not foresee any Joint Supervision Body, leaving control to the independent national data protection or competent judicial authorities. They are authorised to perform checks of legality of data submission to other states on their own initiative, and of the legality of processing on requests of the data subject.

No existence of a central data supervision body makes sense taking into account the decentralised nature of data exchange under the Prüm Decisions and the states' responsibility for data at every stage of its processing.

4 Brief summary and evaluation

The Prüm Treaty and Prüm Decisions are very controversial instruments of information exchange. On the one hand, they establish direct access to certain national databases, creating in this way, new information exchange method and contributing to the principle of availability. On the other hand, they were adopted in such a hurry and in the process, disrespecting the applicable legislative rules of the EU that raise the question of their legality; first of all, with respect to the procedure of enhanced cooperation, deliberately omitted by seven states and then the "pushing of drafts" in record time, and without even giving enough time for the European Parliament to formulate its opinion.

New information exchange methods require at least full compatibility of national databases, legislation on minimum standards on data protection and legalisation of foreign searches, trust in searching states, authorised and trained human resources responsible for information searches and exchange. These requirements brought together technical, legal, financial and human resources problems, that states are overcoming at different paces and with varying success and until now, not all states have implemented them.

If automated searches for DNA profiles, dactyloscopics or vehicle registration data represent a new tool for competent authorities, non-automated information exchange on terrorism and major events with cross-border dimension is repetitive and brings about confusion among its users.

Despite the declaration of quantities of hits produced in automated data exchange, nobody can estimate its real added value in investigation, as no such statistics exist. In these circumstances, a question of proportionality should be raised.

In respect to proportionality of purpose, its differentiation in each category of data (only crime investigation, crime investigation and prevention, etc.) shows that both in Treaty and Decisions, it was considered carefully enough and took into account the speciality and sensitiveness of each database.

From a positive angle, strict prohibition of information transmission to other authority than requesting one should be appreciated.

Bibliography

ACED FÉLEZ, E., 2007, "Ejercicio y garantía del derecho a la protección de datos personales en el Convenio de Prüm", *Revista de derecho constitucional europeo*, no. 7; p. 65–96.

AGUILERA RUIZ, L., 2013, "La protección de datos de ADN en la Unión Europea y en España" in CABEZUDO BAJO, M. J., *Las bases de datos policiales de ADN ¿Son una herramienta realmente eficaz en la lucha contra la criminalidad grave nacional y transfronteriza?*Madrid: Dykinson, S.L., p. 27–42.

ALCOCEBA GIL, J.M., 2015, "Tratamiento y transmisión de datos genéticos con fines de la investigación penal en la UE", in COLOMER HERNÁNDEZ, I. and OUBIÑA BARBOLLA, S., *La transmisión de datos personales en el seno de la cooperación judicial penal y policial en la Unión Europea*", Navarra: Aranzadi, p. 609–652.

ASHIKMIN, S., BERDINE, S. G., MORRISSEY, M. R. et al., no date, "Effectiveness and Cost Efficiency of DNA Evidence in Volume Crime. Denver Colorado Site Summary". Available at: http://www.denverda.org/dna_documents/dnaburgrcostefficiencyreserch1.pdf (accessed October 16, 2017).

BALZACQ, T., BIGO, D., CARRERA, S. et al., 2006, "Security and the Two-Level Game: the Treaty of Prüm, the EU and the Management of Threats" (Working Document no. 234, Centre for European Policy Studies). Available at: http://www.ceps.be/book/security-and-two-level-game-treaty-prüm-eu-and-management-threats (accessed October 16, 2017).

BALZACQ, T., 2006, "From a Prüm of 7 to a Prüm of 8+: What Are the Implications?", (Briefing Paper, DG Internal Policies, Citizens Rights and Constitutional Affairs).

BELLANOVA, R., 2008, "The 'Prüm Process': The Way Forward for EU Police Cooperation and Data Exchange?", in GUILD, E., GEYER, F. (eds.); *Security versus Justice? Police and Judicial Cooperation in the European Union*, Hampshire: Ashgate Publishing Limited, p. 203–221.

CALESINI, G., 2007, *European Police Law Handbook*. Roma: Laurus Robuffo.

CÁMARA VILLAR, G., 2007, "La garantía de los derechos fundamentales afectados por la Convención de Prüm", in *Revista de Derecho Constitucional Europeo*, no 7, p. 97–118.

COUNCIL OF THE EUROPEAN UNION, 2012, "Council Decision 2008/615/JHA of 23 June 2008 on the stepping up of cross-border cooperation, particularly in combating terrorism and cross-border-crime, Council Decision 2008/616/JHA of 23 June 2008 on the implementation of Council Decision 2008/615/JHA of 23 June 2008 on the stepping up of cross-border cooperation, particularly in combating terrorism and cross-border-crime ("Prüm Decisions") – statistics and reports on automated data exchange for 2011"; 11367/12.

DE HOYOS SANCHO, M., 2013, "Obtención, registro e intercambio de perfiles de ADN de sospechosos en el espacio de libertad, seguridad y justicia", in CABEZUDO BAJO, María José, *Las bases de datos policiales de ADN ¿Son una herramienta realmente eficaz en la lucha contra la criminalidad grave nacional y transfronteriza?* Madrid: Dykinson, S.L., p. 63–94.

EUROPEAN COMMISSION, 2012, "Report from the Commission to the European Parliament and the Council on the implementation of Council Decision 2008/615/JHA of 23 June 2008 on the stepping up of cross-border cooperation, particularly in combating terrorism and cross- border crime (the 'Prüm Decision')", COM (2012) 732 final. Available at: http://eur-lex.europa.eu/LexUriServ/LexUriServ.do?uri=COM:2012:0732:FIN:EN:PDF (accessed November 21, 2017).

EUROPEAN PARLIAMENT, 2007, "Report on the initiative by the Kingdom of Belgium, the Republic of Bulgaria, the Federal Republic of Germany, the Kingdom of Spain, the French Republic, the Grand Duchy of Luxembourg, the Kingdom of the Netherlands, the Republic of Austria, the Republic of Slovenia, the Slovak Republic, the Italian Republic, the Republic of Finland, the Portuguese Republic, Romania and the Kingdom of Sweden on the stepping up of cross-border cooperation, particularly in combating terrorism and cross-border crime (6566/2007 – C6–0079/2007–2007/0804(CNS))". Available at: http://www.europarl.europa.eu/sides/getDoc.do?type=COMPARL&mode=XML&language=EN&reference=PE386.698 (accessed October 20, 2017).

FREIXES SANJUÁN, T., 2007, "Protección de datos y globalización. La Convención de Prüm", in *Revista de Derecho Constitucional Europeo*, no 7, p. 11–19.

GUILD, E., 2007, "Merging Security from Two-Level Game: Inserting the Treaty of Prüm into EU law?"; (CEPS Policy Brief, no. 124). Available at: http://ceps.be/book/merging-security-two-level-game-inserting-treaty-prüm-eu-law (accessed October 16, 2017).

GUILD, E. and GEYER, F., 2006, "Getting local: Schengen, Prüm and the dancing procession of Echternach. Three paces forward and two back for UE police and judicial cooperation in criminal matters", Commentaries, Centre for European Policy Studies. Available at: http://aei.pitt.edu/11629/ (accessed October 16, 2017).

HOUSE OF LORDS, 2007, "Prüm: an effective weapon against terrorism and crime?" (Report with Evidence). Available at: http://www.statewatch.org/news/2007/may/eu-hol-prum-report.pdf (accessed November 1, 2017).

KIETZ, D. and MAURER, A., 2017, "From Schengen to Prüm" (Comments, German Institute for International and Security Affairs, May 2006). Available at: http://www.swp-berlin.org/fileadmin/contents/products/comments/Com15_06_Ktz_Mrr_Ks.pdf (accesses November 1, 2017).

LUIF, P., 2007, "The Treaty of Prüm: A Reply of Schengen?" (deliverable of the Project within the framework EU-CONSENT "Wider Europe, Deeper Integration? Constructing Europe Network"). Available at: http://www.eu-consent.net/library/deliverables/D38c.pdf (accessed, October 16, 2017).

MARTÍNEZ PÉREZ, F. and POZA CISNEROS, M., 2013, "El Principio de Disponibilidad: Antecedentes Penales y Convenio de Prüm"; in CARMONA RUANO, M., GONZÁLES VEGA, I.U. and MORENO CATENA, V., *Cooperación Judicial Penal en Europa*, Madrid: Dykinson, p. 417–496.

MCCARTHNEY, C. I.; WILSON, T. J. and WILLIAMS, R., 2011, "Transnational Exchange of Forensic DNA: Viability, Legitimacy, and Acceptability", in *European Journal on Criminal and Research*, vol.17; no. 4, p. 305–322.

O'NEILL, M., 2010, "The Issue of Data Protection and Data Security in the (Pre-Lisbon) EU Third Pillar", in *Journal of Contemporary European Research*, vol. 6; issue 2, p. 211–235. Available at: http://www.jcer.net/index.php/jcer/article/view/264 (accessed October 16, 2017).

SOLETO MUÑOZ, H., 2009, *La identificación del imputado: Rueda, fotos, ADN… De los métodos basados en la percepción a la prueba científica*, Valencia: Tirant lo Blanch.

SOLETO MUÑOZ, H. and ALCOCEBA GIL, J. M., 2013, "Protección de datos y transferencia de perfiles de ADN", in CABEZUDO BAJO, M. J., *Las bases de datos policiales de ADN ¿Son una herramienta realmente eficaz en la lucha contra la criminalidad grave nacional y transfronteriza?*, Madrid: Dykinson, S.L., p. 325–344.

WILLIAMS, R., 2013, "Making Forensic DNA Databases: Global Themes and Local Variations" in CABEZUDO BAJO, M. J., *Las bases de datos policiales de ADN ¿Son una herramienta realmente eficaz en la lucha contra la criminalidad grave nacional y transfronteriza?*, Madrid: Dykinson, S.L., p. 359–374.

ZILLER, J., 2006, "Le traité de Prüm. Une vraie-fausse cooperation renforcée dans l'Espace de sécurité de liberté et de justice" (Working Paper, LAW No. 2006/32, European University Institute). Available at: http://cadmus.eui.eu/handle/1814/6401 (accessed October 21, 2017).

9 Passenger name record

An indispensable element of free movement of persons is the abolishment of controls on internal borders and the strengthening of external ones. As already explained, at every crossing point of the external border of the Schengen area it is obligatory to use SIS. To review its functions, it should be said that it works on the basis of alerts in relation to some categories of persons and objects.[1] That means that previous to placing an alert, a competent authority of a Member State should have information in relation to that person or object. But what to do with those crimes that remain undetected, and those persons that commit them, but do not fall under suspicion due to lack of information? In these cases, the active intelligence work of competent authorities can be more helpful; and to some extent the use of PNR, i.e. data possessed by air carriers related to bookings, carrying out the check-in process and used to control flows of passengers. In particular, it includes personal data, means of payment, passengers' meal and other preferences.

PNR use for law enforcement purposes is based on the transmission of data related to passengers from air carriers to national passenger information units, where it is evaluated on the basis of the risk criteria, and then transmitted to the competent law enforcement institution. Air carriers do not have to collect any additional data, only that which they have been collecting until now and their additional expenditures would only be related to the transmission of collected data.

As a general rule, it is applied for the processing of information of air travellers, but it does not eliminate the possibility to apply it to railway or water transport.

It can be used as a pro-active, real-time and re-active measure. Its biggest advantage would be pro-active and real-time use.[2] When it stands for re-

1 Persons wanted for extradition or surrender, sought to assist with a judicial procedure, missing persons, persons and objects for discreet and specific checks, objects for seizure or use as evidence.

2 According to the information presented by Belgium in 2009, 95 per cent of all drugs seizures in airports were made thanks to PNR data. See COM(2011) 32 final, p. 6. Nevertheless, this data is questionable by the EDPS, as at that

active measures, without denying the importance that PNR can have in some specific cases, on a large scale it would not be such an effective investigation tool as others (for example biometric data).

1 From external obligation to internal application

As the main reason for the proposal of the European PNR, the Commission took the political will expressed in the Stockholm Programme "to propose a Union measure, that ensures a high level of data protection, on PNR for the purpose of preventing, detecting, investigating and prosecuting terrorist offences and serious crime, based on an impact assessment."[3]

After the terrorist attack of September 2001 in the United States, the national legislation of some countries was supplemented by provisions that put an obligation on air carriers flying to, from or through their territory, to provide their competent authorities with access to PNR for law enforcement purposes. For example, the Aviation and Transportation Security Act from November 19, 2001 established that not providing of PNR data would mean a fine of $6000 per passenger or the loss of landing rights in territory belonging to the USA.

Under these circumstances, air carriers had two options: to agree with such an obligation or not to operate flights in those countries and as a result to see a decrease in their profits and competition capabilities. Consequently, a lot of air carriers have fulfilled this obligation.[4]

Bearing this in mind, the Commission and the Council decided to sign the agreement with these countries in order to influence (at least to some extent) data flows of EU citizens and their data protection. As noticed by Heisenberg, "Power disparities had forced the EU to accede to an agreement that did not reflect many of its fundamental demands. Even the language of negotiation was brusque on the US side."[5]

moment Belgium had not finished the implementation of systematic PNR collection scheme. See EUROPEAN DATA PROTECTION SUPERVISOR, "Opinion of the European Data Protection Supervisor on the Proposal for a Directive of the European Parliament and of the Council on the use of Passenger Name Record data for the prevention, detection, investigation and prosecution of terrorist offences and serious crime" OJ C 181, 22.6.2011, p. 25.

3 OJ C 115, 4.5.2010, p. 19.

4 See CATALINA BENAVENTE, María Ángeles, "La transmisión de datos PNR entre la Unión Europea, Estados Unidos, Canadá y Australia" in COLOMER HERNÁNDEZ, Ignacio and OUBIÑA BARBOLLA, Sabela, *La transmisión de datos personales en el seno de la cooperación judicial penal y policial en la Unión Europea*, Navarra: Aranzadi, 2015, p. 306–307.

5 HEISENBERG, Dorothee, *Negotiating Privacy: the European Union, the United States and personal data protection*, London: Lynne Rienner Publishers, Inc., 2005, p. 141.

This received a lot of reasonable criticism, as a step back from the protection of privacy and data, but looking at it from another angle, it was the best of the worst options, because laws adopted by third states would be applied anyway, both to carriers and all passengers.

In these circumstances the EU found itself in the situation when the personal data of its citizens are used for the security of third states, but not for its own. The pilot PNR project of the United Kingdom also resulted in "numerous arrests, identification of human trafficking networks and gaining of valuable intelligence in relation to terrorism."[6]

As a result, on November 6, 2007, the Commission presented a "Proposal for a Council Framework Decision on the use of Passenger Name Record (PNR) for law enforcement purposes".[7]

As Member States had not found a common agreement on this proposal until the entrance into force of the Lisbon Treaty, the Commission had had to present a new proposal according to the requirements of the new legislative procedure that was done on February 2, 2011 by presenting the "Proposal for a Directive of the European Parliament and of the Council on the use of Passenger Name Record data for the prevention, detection, investigation and prosecution of terrorist offences and serious crime".[8]

However, it took 5 years to obtain approval by the European Parliament and the Council.

In 2013, the LIBE rejected the Commission's Proposal on PNR voting 30 to 25,[9] although the Rapporteur had not proposed this in its Report.[10] The Rapporteur had proposed only 35 amendments, recognising the added value of the initiative and pointed out that the Commission had taken into

6 Ibid.
7 COM(2007) 654 final.
8 COM(2011) 32 final.
9 See EUROPEAN PARLIAMENT, "Civil Liberties Committee rejects EU Passenger Name Record proposal Fundamental rights" (Press release April 24, 2013), accessed September 2, 2017, http://www.europarl.europa.eu/sides/getDoc.do?pubRef=-%2F%2FEP%2F%2FTEXT%2BIM-PRESS%2B20130422IPR07523%2B0%2BDOC%2BXML%2BV0%2F%2FEN&language=EN.
10 EUROPEAN PARLIAMENT, Committee on Civil Liberties, Justice and Home Affairs, "Report on the proposal for a directive of the European Parliament and of the Council on the protection of individuals with regard to the processing of personal data by competent authorities for the purposes of prevention, investigation, detection or prosecution of criminal offences or the execution of criminal penalties, and the free movement of such data (COM(2012)0010 – C7–0024/2012–2012/0010(COD))", accessed September 4, 2017, http://www.europarl.europa.eu/sides/getDoc.do?pubRef=-//EP//TEXT+REPORT+A7-2013-0403+0+DOC+XML+V0//EN.

account recommendations made by the Parliament in its Resolution of November 20, 2008.

The progress was achieved with the impulse of the terrorist attacks in France in January 2015. On January 29 and 30, 2015 the Council declared its determination "to create without further delay an effective EU PNR framework in line with Council general approach and at the same time ensuring solid data protection safeguards".[11] The Rapporteur of the LIBE increased its amendments from 35 to 47 retaining the initial position, but the rest of the Members of Parliament proposed 789,800 amendments,[12] starting from the proposal to reject the initiative, proposing the inclusion of intra-EU flights, limiting the purpose to certain types of serious crimes, strengthening data protection and access provisions, and so on.[13]

The final text was approved in April 2016 as Directive (EU) 2016/681 of the European Parliament and of the Council of 27 April 2016 on the use of passenger name record (PNR) data for the prevention, detection, investigation and prosecution of terrorist offences and serious crime[14] (hereinafter – PNR Directive) with the deadline to transpose it by May 25, 2018.

According to Article 19, by May 25, 2020, the European Commission shall review all elements of the PNR data processing and in particularly:

- Fulfillment of data protection requirements,
- Proportionality and necessity of PNR data,
- Storage period,
- Effectiveness of data exchange,
- Quality of PNR data assessment,
- Necessity to oblige collection and processing of PNR data from intra-EU flights and to include not only air-carriers, but also non-carrier economic operators, such as travel agencies.

11 "Riga Joint Statement following informal meeting of Justice and Home Affairs Ministers in Riga on 29 and 30 January", accessed September 30, 2017, https://eu2015.lv/images/Kalendars/IeM/2015_01_29_jointstatement_JHA.pdf.

12 With 179 amendments only on recitals.

13 EUROPEAN PARLIAMENT, Committee on Civil Liberties, Justice and Home Affairs, "Amendments 48–329 on the proposal for a directive of the European Parliament and of the Council on the use of Passenger Name Record data for the prevention, detection, investigation and prosecution of terrorist offences and serious crime", accessed September 6, 2017, http://www.europarl.europa.eu/meetdocs/2014_2019/documents/libe/am/1058/1058388/1058388en.pdf.

14 OJ L 119, 4.5.2016, p. 132–149.

2 Scope of application

The PNR Directive regulates transfer and processing of the PNR data that, according to Article 3, is understood as "a record of each passenger's travel requirements which contains information necessary to enable reservations to be processed and controlled by the booking and participating air carriers for each journey booked by or on behalf of any person, whether it is contained in reservation systems, departure control systems used to check passengers onto flights, or equivalent systems providing the same functionalities."

According to its Article 1(2), the purpose for which PNR collection and processing can be used is prevention, detection and prosecution of terrorist offences understood as those already mentioned in the Council Framework Decision 2002/475/JHA on combating terrorism,[15] and serious crimes included in Annex II of the Directive.

The list of crimes is quite similar to the ones included as Annex I of the Regulation (EU) 2016/794 of the European Parliament and of the Council on the European Union Agency for Law Enforcement Cooperation (Europol) and replacing and repealing Council Decisions 2009/371/JHA, 2009/934/JHA, 2009/935/JHA, 2009/936/JHA and 2009/968/JHA[16] (hereinafter – Europol Regulation). However, some differences can be found.

First, Annex II of the PNR Directive excludes some serious crimes foreseen in the Europol Regulation due to the quite limited benefit of PNR data in their prevention, detection or investigation, such as: racism and xenophobia, insider dealing and financial market manipulation, racketeering and extortion, forgery of money and means of payment.

Second, supposedly for the same purpose some types of crime are narrowed and the PNR Directive refers to the trafficking of nuclear and radioactive materials, instead of crime related to these substances in general. For the purpose of proportionality it includes organised and armed robbery instead of robbery and aggravated theft.

Unlike the Europol Regulation, it foresees crimes of rape, unlawful seizure of aircrafts, sabotage and industrial espionage. If some justification for the inclusion of the first three categories of crime can be found, it is quite difficult to carry out in respect to the last category.

With regard to its territorial scope of application, only Denmark does not apply the PRN.

Article 2 of the PNR Directive envisages its application only to extra-EU flights, that means only to air carriers and air travellers and only on

15 O J L 164, 22.6.2002, p. 3.
16 OJ L 135, 24.5.2016, p. 53–114.

flights (including those with stop-overs) with origin or destination in a third country.

Member States can notify the Commission about its application to intra-EU flights (with origin and destination within the EU and without stop-overs in a third state) in general, or to certain intra-EU flights.

The PNR Directive does not foresee any special regime for intra-EU flights. The only provision directly addressed to them is in Article 8 that says "Where an extra-EU flight has one or more stop-overs at airports of the Member States, air carriers shall transfer the PNR data of all passengers to the PIUs of all the Member States concerned. This also applies where an intra-EU flight has one or more stopovers at the airports of different Member States, but only in relation to Member States which are collecting PNR data from intra-EU flights."

The EDPS considered that inclusion of all intra-EU flights would mean even bigger limitations of privacy and data protection. In 2011 the EDPS stated that "Such a widening of the scope of the PNR scheme would threaten even more the fundamental rights of individuals and should not be envisaged before any proper analysis including a comprehensive impact assessment."[17]

The question of inclusion of intra-EU brings us to significant dilemma. On the one hand, only controlling extra-EU flights does not mean the full use of the costly system for the prevention and combatting of terrorism and serious crime, as monitoring intra-EU flights can also serve for these purposes. For example, flights from the Canary Islands to Amsterdam can be more interesting to law enforcement (as a potential route of cocaine trafficking) than flights from the Canary Islands to Monaco. On the other hand, a collection of PNR data of intra-EU flights would not only mean a disproportionate limitation of privacy and data protection, but it also contradicts to the essence of free movement.

3 PNR data and its processing

PNR Directive establishes PNR data collection and processing mechanism, including: data categories that makes a content of PNR data, entities involved and their competence, storage and transmission rules.

3.1 PNR data

Data that is treated as PNR is determined in the Annex I of the PNR Directive and includes information on flight, flying person and other relevant one as it is presented in Table 9.1:

17 OJ C 181, 22.6.2011, p. 29.

Table 9.1 PNR data categories

Flight data	*Personal data*	*Other*
– Date of reservation/issue – Travel itinerary – Travel agency – Travel status (confirmation, check-in) – Ticket, seat information – Baggage information	– Names – Address, telephone, e-mail – Payment information – Information on frequent flyer – General remarks – Other travellers on the PNR	– PNR record locator – Split/divided PNR – Historical changes of all data
– Advance passenger information (both flights and personal)		

Without the existence of the field "general remarks", this list could be considered exhaustive. Although it is explained that general remarks include relevant information on unaccompanied minors, it is not limited only to such information.

Such PNR data as frequent traveller or billing address do not constitute obligatory information to be supplied about a passenger. Also, information on travel agencies is not as reliable given that the majority of reservations are made through the internet. As pointed out by Brouwer, PNR data "are less reliable, being dependent on what the traveller submitted him- or herself when making a reservation. In addition, as has been pointed out by the Association of European Airlines, with respect to the identification of passengers the PNR data are not always consistent with the persons actually on board the air carrier."[18]

Article 12 foresees that PNR data is stored in databases of relevant PIU and must be depersonalised after 6 months, although the total storage term is 5 years. Depersonalisation of personal data means masking it out. The disclosure of masked out personal data is possible only with the fulfillment of the following conditions:

a It is necessary to respond to a legal request,
b It is authorised by the judicial or other authority of requested Member State that is competent to check whether disclosure conditions are met.

18 BROUWER, Evelien, "Ignoring Decent and Legality. The EU's proposal to share the personal information of all passengers" (Paper, Centre for European Policy Studies, June 2011), p. 3, accessed July 14, 2017, http://aei.pitt.edu/32073/1/No_40_Brouwer_on_PNR_Directive.pdf.

The data is not depersonalised after 6 months if it used by a competent authority in the specific case of prevention, detection, investigation or prosecution of serious crimes or terrorism.

The result of the processing of PNR data shall be stored only "as long as necessary" to inform relevant competent authorities and the PIU of other Member States. The only exception is when the positive result of automatic assessment (matched with data bases or pre-established criteria) was denied by further non-automated individual review. In this case, depersonalisation is not used until the deadline of the deletion of these PNR data in order "to avoid future 'false' positive matches".

3.2 PNR data processing

PNR Directive envisages the following information processing scheme:

- Each Member State (or a few of them) must establish a PIU that will be responsible for receiving PNR data (on flights arriving to or departing from its territory) from the air carrier and its processing.
- Air carriers have to transmit data using the "push" method, meaning that they shall transfer it to PIU and the PIU do not have access to air carriers' databases and information other than PNR. According to Article 6(1), if the flight is co-shared between different air carriers, the airline that operates the flight has to ensure information transmission. On the one hand, it strengthens the right to privacy and data protection, but on the other hand, requires the establishment of an electronic system that would not allow air carriers to delete information on certain passengers. This observation should not be understood as general mistrust of air carries, but nobody can be sure that a person responsible for data transmission is not involved in a terrorist organisation or does not form part of a drug or human trafficking network. Therefore, there should be technical means that do not allow the manipulation by the air carrier of the received PNR.
- PNR data always has to be transmitted 24–48 hours before the scheduled departure and immediately after the flight closure.

PNR data can be processed only for the purposes established in Article 6:

- To carry out assessment of passengers in order to find out those that need further examination under suspicion of their involvement in serious crime or terrorism. In this case the data can be checked against data bases used for crime prevention, detection, investigation and prosecution, and according to the rules that regulate such data bases or against pre-established criteria of risk factors. Any automated match of data has to be individually reviewed.

- To respond to requests of competent authorities when it is related with prevention, detection, investigation of prosecution of serious crime or terrorism.
- To update or create criteria for the assessment of the PNR data.

With regard to the assessment criteria, it should be noted that PNR Directive does not establish them, but leaves it up to each Member State, foreseeing only some requirements on their establishment:

- They have to be established by the PIU with cooperation with national competent authorities (responsible for the prevention, detection, investigation or prosecution of serious crime and terrorism).
- Criteria shall be "targeted, proportionate and specific" and not based on sensitive data (a person's race or ethnic origin, political opinions, religion or philosophical beliefs, trade union membership, health, sexual life or sexual orientation).

EDPS in this respect has pointed out that "The development of such a system on a European scale, involving the collection of data on all passengers and the taking of decisions on the basis of unknown and evolving assessment criteria, raises serious transparency and proportionality issues."[19] Leaving this issue to national level also means different uses of PNR systems in Member States and is contrary to equality, non-discrimination and difficulties in the control of legality and the proportionality of use of PNR. For example, the same person traveling from Brazil to Spain or from Brazil to Germany would be the object of an application for different risk assessment criteria, even if his or her PNR data are the same (except itinerary) in both cases.

The direct access to PNR data shall have only PIU, but the aforementioned competent authorities (included in the national list) are granted with the right to request and receive it or as a result of its processing by PIU. These authorities cannot base their decisions with adverse effect on a person, only on the processing of PNR data or together with sensitive data.

3.3 PNR data exchange

PNR Directive regulates data exchange between Member States and its transmission to third countries. In case of information exchange of PNR data between Member States, the following options are foreseen:

- Obligation of PIU that has assessed PNR data and identified a person as "dangerous" to transmit his or her data, and a result of the assessment

19 EUROPEAN DATA PROTECTION SUPERVISOR, "Opinion of the European Data Protection...", *loc. cit.*, p. 26.

to the PIUs of the Member States that could be interested in these data. Receiving PIUs shall send it to their national competent authorities.
- Right of PIU to reasoned request of PNR data that is still not depersonalised[20] and kept in the database of other PIU. The deadline to provide the data is not established, it is only said that it must be "as soon as practicable".
- Right of a competent authority (in case of emergency) to request PNR data directly from PIU of another Member State, at the same time sending a copy of the request to its own PIU.
- Right of PIU (in case of specific and actual threat) to request other PIU to obtain PNR data at the same time as the latter (requested PIU) will obtain it from the air carrier. In this case, the requested PIU shall make a corresponding request to air carriers to also send data to the requesting PIU.

According to Article 10, Europol also can request PNR data or results of its processing when it is necessary to support and strengthen actions of Member States. The request must be sent through the ENU of the Member State whose PIU will be requested. Transfer to third countries is permitted only on a case-by-case basis and with the following conditions:

a It is necessary for prevention, detection, investigation or prosecution of serious crimes or terrorism.

b The requirement of data transfer to third countries established in the Directive 2016/680 of the European Parliament and of the Council of April 27, 2016 on the protection of natural persons with regard to the processing of personal data by competent authorities for the purposes of the prevention, investigation, detection or prosecution of criminal offences or the execution of criminal penalties, and on the free movement of such data, and repealing Council Framework Decision 2008/977/JHA are fulfilled (hereinafter – Data Protection Directive).

c The third country receiving PNR data could make onward transmissions to another third country only for the aforementioned purpose, and with the express authorisation of the requested Member State. Exceptions are possible only in cases where it is "essential to respond to a specific and actual threat related to terrorist offences or serious crime in a Member State or a third country and a prior consent cannot be obtained in good time". In these cases, transfer will be subject to "ex-post verification".

d The data protection officer of PIU shall be informed about each data transfer to third states (both direct and onward).

20 Personal data is such cases can be provided only with the judicial or other relevant authorisation.

As indicated by Bąkowski and Voronova, "The proposed EU PNR scheme departs from the widely accepted form of using personal data for law enforcement purposes whereby data transfer is requested [...] for a specific person, suspected of a specific crime, or at least representing a specific threat. The PNR scheme enables, on the contrary, proactive systematic checks on large sets of data concerning all passengers."[21]

4 Data protection

Unlike many of the information exchange mechanisms already analysed, PNR Directive makes direct reference to the general data protection provisions of the Framework Decision 2008/977/JHA of November 27, 2008 on the protection of personal data processed in the framework of police and judicial cooperation in criminal matters (hereinafter – Framework Decision 2008/977/JHA). It does not mention the Data Protection Directive as it was approved on the same day as the PNR Directive. But the presumption can be made that the PNR Directive refers to general data protection regimes applicable to police and judicial cooperation and as Framework Decision 2008/977/JHA was derogated by the Data Protection Directive, provisions of latter have to be applied.

PNR Directive envisages very few differences from general data protection regime in the area of police and judicial cooperation:

- Article 5 of the PNR Directive establishes that each PIU shall appoint a data protection officer who is responsible for supervising the processing of PNR, and who is a contact point to requests of data subjects.
- Article 13(4) explicitly prohibits the processing of sensitive data. Nevertheless, FRA still sees possibilities of discrimination, as the list of sensitive data included in actual PNR Directive is shorter than the one foreseen in Article 21 of the Charter.[22]
- Article 13(5) establishes the documentation which has to be maintained in every PIU.
- Article 13(6) obliges records on at least collection, consultation, disclosure and erasure of data to be kept for 5 years.

21 BĄKOWSKI, Piotr and VORONOVA, Sofija, "The Proposed EU Passenger Name Records (PNR) Directive: Revived in the New Security Context" (Briefing, European Parliamentary Research Service, April 2015), accessed July 14, 2017, http://www.europarl.europa.eu/EPRS/EPRS-Briefing-554215-The-EU-PNR-Proposal-FINAL.pdf, p. 4.

22 See EUROPEAN UNION AGENCY FOR FUNDAMENTAL RIGHTS, "Opinion of the European Union Agency for Fundamental Rights on the Proposal for a Directive on the use of Passenger Name Record (PNR) data for the prevention, detection, investigation and prosecution of terrorist offences and serious crime (COM(2011) 32 final)", p. 7, accessed September 5, 2017, http://fra.europa.eu/sites/default/files/fra_uploads/1654-FRA-PNR-Opinion-June2011.pdf.

5 Agreements between the European Union and third states on PNR

The first agreement on PNR was concluded with the United States of America in 2004 by approval of:

- Council Decision 2004/496/EC of May 17, 2004 on the conclusion of an Agreement between the European Community and the United States of America on the processing and transfer of PNR data by Air Carriers to the United States Department of Homeland Security, Bureau of Customs and Border Protection,[23]
- Commission Decision 2004/535/EC of May 14, 2004 on the adequate protection of personal data contained in the Passenger Name Record of air passengers transferred to the United States Bureau of Customs and Border Protection.[24]

Both acts were annulled by the CJEU due to the lack of Communities' competence in this field,[25] but the application of the latter Commission Decision was maintained until September 30, 2006. In the judgment of May 30, 2006, in joint Cases C-317/04 and C-318/04 brought by the European Parliament it was stated that:

- Even if primary PNR collection is made by private operators and air carriers' activities fall within the scope of Community law, the purpose of agreement is public security that is outside of the Community competence and the Commission could not base its Decision in Directive 95/46/EC that is applicable to the First Pillar.
- As the purpose of the agreement and use of PNR is public security, the Council incorrectly based its Decision in Article 95 of the Treaty Establishing the European Community that is devoted to the establishment and functioning of the internal market.

Thus the problem was related to the purpose of data (security), different from the original purpose of its collection (commercial).

In 2006, a provisional Agreement between the European Union and the United States of America on the processing and transfer of Passenger Name

23 OJ L 183, 20.5.2004, p. 83. Corrigendum at OJ L 255, 30.9.2005, p. 168.

24 OJ L 235, 6.7.2004, p. 11.

25 In the case of the Commission's Decision, the European Parliament pleaded ultra vires to Directive 95/46/EC breach of its fundamental principles, breach of fundamental rights and principle of proportionality. For annulment of the Council's Decision it pleaded incorrect choice of Article 95 of the Treaty establishing European Community for its decision, breach of its Article 300(3), Article 8 of the ECHR, principle of proportionality and statement of reasons and principle of cooperation in good faith. Nevertheless, conforming ultra vires and incorrect choice of Article 95 the CJEU did not analyse other pleas.

Record (PNR) data by air carriers to the United States Department of Homeland Security,[26] was signed and in 2007[27] replaced by another provisional agreement, finally substituted by the permanent version in 2012.[28]

In its judgment of October 6, 2015 in Case C-362/14, the CJEU stated that Decision 2000/520/EC of July 26, 2000 pursuant to Directive 95/46/EC of the European Parliament and of the Council on the adequacy of the protection provided by the safe harbour privacy principles and related frequently asked questions issued by the US Department of Commerce (notified under document number C(2000)2441)[29] is invalid, and in such a way that the evaluation of data protection level in United States as adequate was disclaimed.

Despite the complexity and sensitivity of the issue, the European Commission adopted the Commission Implementing Decision (EU) 2016/1250 of July 12, 2016 pursuant to Directive 95/46/EC of the European Parliament and of the Council on the adequacy of the protection provided by the EU-U.S. Privacy Shield[30] (hereinafter – Implementing Decision 2016/1250) in 8 months. Its Article 1 states that "For the purposes of Article 25(2) of Directive 95/46/EC, the United States ensures an adequate level of protection for personal data transferred from the Union to organisations in the United States under the EU-U.S. Privacy Shield.".

Implementing Decision 2016/1250 includes Privacy Shield Principles and Department of Commerce commitments relating to the new arbitral model to protect right to data protection.

In 2012, the new Agreement between the European Union and Australia on the processing and transfer of Passenger Name Record (PNR) data by air carriers to the Australian Customs and Border Protection Service also entered into force.[31]

On June 25, 2014, a new Agreement between Canada and the European Union on the transfer and processing of Passenger Name Records (EU – Canada agreement) was signed, but the TJUE in its Opinion 1/15 (Opinion pursuant to Article 218(11) TFEU – Draft agreement between Canada and the European Union – Transfer of Passenger Name Record data from the European Union to Canada – Appropriate legal bases – Article 16(2), point (d) of the second subparagraph of Article 82(1) and Article 87(2)(a) TFEU – Compatibility with Articles 7 and 8 and Article 52(1) of the Charter of Fundamental Rights of the European Union)[32] stated that the draft agreement is incompatible with the provisions of the Charter of Fundamental Rights of the European Union as it does not prevent transfer of sensitive data.

26 OJ L 298, 27.10.2006, p. 27–31.
27 OJ L 204, 4.8.2007, p. 16–25.
28 OJ L 215, 11.8.2012, p. 4–14.
29 OJ L 215, 25.8.2000, p. 7–47.
30 OJ L 207, 1.8.2016, p. 1–112.
31 OJ L 186, 14.7.2012, p. 4–16.
32 OJ C 138, 27.4.2015, p. 24.

All three agreements are based on Communication from the Commission on the global approach to transfers of Passenger Name Records (PNR) data to third countries.[33] The key objective of this communication was to establish, for the first time, a set of general criteria which should form the basis of future negotiations on PNR agreements with third countries. It foresees common criteria and negotiable areas concluding new agreements on PNR:

- Limitation of the use of data: fight against terrorism and serious transnational crime, clearly established key notions of these crimes.
- Scope of data: minimum, proportionate and with an exhaustive list of categories.
- Sensitive data: not used, only well-defined exceptions with appropriate safeguards and authorisation of higher authority are possible.
- Data security: appropriate legal, technical and organisational guarantees in place.
- Supervision: by independent data protection authority.
- Transparency, access, rectification, deletion, redress: information about gathering and use of PNR, access right with rectification, deletion and redress.
- Data retention: no longer than necessary for the established purpose.
- Onward transfer to other authorities or third countries: on a case-by-case basis to the third country that provides with the same data protection level as foreseen in the agreement.
- Restrictions on onward transfers to other government authorities: on a case-by-case basis, only for purposes established in agreement and with guarantees to apply the same protection level.[34]

Of course, depending on the third state involved, the results of negotiations could differ, but all negotiable agreements have the same pattern and equal primary position of the EU.

Table 9.2 presents comparisons of the main provisions of three agreements; even if the signed EU–Canada agreement shall be modified in respect to the processing of sensitive data.

From three agreements, the one with Australia has more safeguards and stricter rules on data use as establishes: prohibition of sensitive data, stricter rules on transferring to other national competent authorities and third countries, although the time of retention of personal data (without masking out) is longer than in other agreements.

The agreement with Canada has more flexible rules which are found on use, sensitive data, but stricter rules on transferring and retention than the agreement with United States.

33 COM(2010) 492 final.
34 Ibid, p. 9–10.

Table 9.2 Comparison of main provisions of EU agreements on PNR with USA, Australia and Canada.

	USA	*Australia*	*Canada*
Method used to transmit PNR data from air carries	Push	Push	Push
Use of PNR	Prevention, detection, investigation and prosecution of: – Terrorism and related crimes; – Other transnational crimes punishable by 3 years of imprisonment at least. Also may be used: – Case-by-case for the protection of vital interests of any individual (when there is obvious threat) or in case of court order. – To identify persons subject to closer examination upon arrival to or departure the US.	Prevention, detection, investigation and prosecution of: – Terrorism; – Serious transnational crime. Also may be used: – To protect the vital interests of any individual (with not exhaustive list that includes risk of death, serious injury or threat to health); – To supervise misuse of data on a case-by-case basis foreseen by Australian law.	Prevention, detection, investigation and prosecution of: – Terrorism; – Serious transnational crime. Also may be used: – To protect the vital interests of any individual (with not exhaustive list that includes risk of death, serious injury or threat to health, public health risk); – To supervise accountability of the public administration; – To fulfil court order.
Sensitive data	Use on a case-by-case basis with the approval of Department of Homeland Security senior manager in case of danger to life of an individual. As a general rule, is deleted after 30 days from the last receipt.	Prohibition of use and processing. Deletion once received.	Masked, not further processed. Exception: used not by automatic systems, but by specifically authorised officials on a case-by-case basis with the approval of Head of the Canadian Competent Authority in case of danger to life of an individual. As a general rule, it is deleted after 15 days from the last receipt.

	USA	*Australia*	*Canada*
Decision taken on PNR basis	No decision of significant adverse action based only on PNR.	No decision of significant adverse action based only on PNR. No automated processing based on sensitive data.	No decision of significant adverse action based only on PNR.
Data retention	Active period: 5 years, depersonalisation and masking after 6 months. Dormant database: 10 years.	5.5 years: years 0–3 all data, years 3–5.5 masking out personal data.	5 years: after 30 days masking out names, after 2 years masking out other personal data.
Domestic sharing	With governmental authorities only for the purpose foreseen in the agreement and to support investigation or examination, following internal laws and agreements on information exchange and ensuring the same or comparable safeguards.	With governmental authorities only for the purpose foreseen in the agreement, ensuring the same or comparable safeguards. If it is not depersonalised, only on a case-by-case basis. Before sharing the Australian Customs and Border Protection Service assesses the relevance sharing and its scope (minimum data). Further sharing by the receiving authority is prohibited without the permission of the Australian Customs and Border Protection Service.	On a case-by-case basis minimum data with governmental authorities whose functions are related to a purpose of the agreement and only for these purposes, ensuring the same or comparable safeguards. Further sharing by the receiving authority is prohibited without the permission of the Canadian Competent Authority.

	USA	*Australia*	*Canada*
Onward transfer	Following the conditions of the agreement in support of those cases under examination or investigation and informing Member State if information shared is about its citizen or resident. If it is not an urgent case an understanding agreement with proper safeguards is concluded between the US and the third state.	On case-by-case basis only to authority directly involved in prevention, detection, investigation and prosecution of terrorism and serious international crime for these purposes and that ensures the same safeguards. Before sharing the Australian Customs and Border Protection Service assesses the relevance of sharing and its scope (minimum data). If information shared is about citizen or resident of Member State, this state is informed. If it is appropriate, the passenger is informed as well. The receiving state has to agree to delete data as soon as it is not necessary for the purpose that it has been transmitted and do not make any further transmission.	Minimum data on case-by-case basis for the purpose foreseen in this agreement to authority that performs functions related to that purpose and that ensures the same safeguards as established in this agreement or applied in the EU. If information shared is about a citizen of a Member State, this state is informed.
Supervision	Department Privacy Officers; The Department of Homeland Security Office of Inspector General; The Government Accountability Office; The US Congress.	Australian Information Commissioner.	Not specified, just indicated as "an independent public authority".

6 Brief summary and evaluation

As third states had adopted laws obligating air carriers that operate flights to or from their country, to provide them with PNR data for public security reasons, it seems that the European Union had no other choice but to conclude agreements with them in order not to harm the competition of European air carriers and to some extent, protect the data of travellers.

On the other hand, once having established this agreement, the question arises, why not use it as well within the EU where stricter data protection rules can be ensured? It would be dishonest towards EU internal law enforcement authorities not to endow them with a new tool that the EU has already given to law enforcement authorities of some third states and is negotiating with others.

However, the concept of PNR processing is totally different from the processing of other data by law enforcement and judicial authorities. Although the general purpose of all law enforcement databases (including PNR) is crime prevention, detection, investigation and prosecution, other law enforcement databases include data of specific person or specific crime. PNR data is "everyday personal data"[35] collected and processed only because of the pure fact that he or she uses air transport. Comparing personal data processing in existing systems and PNR, the differences will be immense: if SIS has 1 million new records annually (and the vast majority of them are on objects and not on persons), PNR will have 500 million[36] records and this will mean mass data processing and a disproportionate limitation of the right to privacy.

A positive aspect of the approved PNR Directive could be the outlined application of general regime of data protection in the area of police and judicial cooperation, prohibition to process sensitive data (although the list of such data must coincide with Article 21 of the EU Charter) and depersonalisation of PNR data (although the period could be shorter).

By the May 25, 2020 the European Commission will have elaborated a report on the application of the PNR Directive. It has to include, among other elements, an evaluation of the necessity and proportionality of collecting and processing PNR data and, if appropriate, a new legislative proposal. It is not specified whether such a proposal could include only modifications of the current PNR system or also its derogation. If one can suppose approval of its derogation or significant limitation of its scope by the European Parliament, it is hardly imaginable on behalf of the Council.

35 MITSILEGAS, Valsamis, *EU Criminal Law*, (Portland, Bloomsbury Publishing, 2009), p. 279.

36 See EUROPEAN PARLIAMENT Directorate General for Internal Policies, "Developing an EU Internal Security Strategy, fighting terrorism and organized crime", 2011, p. 143, accessed August 13, 2017, http://www.europarl.europa.eu/document/activities/cont/201206/20120627ATT47777/20120627ATT47777EN.pdf.

Bibliography

BĄKOWSKI, P. and VORONOVA, S., 2015, "The Proposed EU Passenger Name Records (PNR) Directive: Revived in the New Security Context" (Briefing, European Parliamentary Research Service, April 2015). Available at: http://www.europarl.europa.eu/EPRS/EPRS-Briefing-554215-The-EU-PNR-Proposal-FINAL.pdf (accessed July 14, 2017).

BROUWER, E., 2015, "Ignoring Decent and Legality. The EU's proposal to share the personal information of all passengers" (Paper, Centre for European Policy Studies). Available at: http://aei.pitt.edu/32073/1/No_40_Brouwer_on_PNR_Directive.pdf (accessed July 14, 2017).

CATALINA BENAVENTE, M. A., 2015, "La transmisión de datos PNR entre la Unión Europea, Estados Unidos, Canadá y Australia" in COLOMER HERNÁNDEZ, I. and OUBIÑA BARBOLLA, S., *La transmisión de datos personales en el seno de la cooperación judicial penal y policial en la Unión Europea*, Navarra: Aranzadi, p. 301–356.

EUROPEAN COMMISSION, 2011, "Communication from the Commission on the global approach to transfer of Passenger Name Record (PNR) data to third countries", COM(2010) 492 final.

EUROPEAN DATA PROTECTION SUPERVISOR, 2011, "Opinion of the European Data Protection Supervisor on the Proposal for a Directive of the European Parliament and of the Council on the use of Passenger Name Record data for the prevention, detection, investigation and prosecution of terrorist offences and serious crime", OJ C 181, 22. 6. 2011, p. 24–30.

EUROPEAN PARLIAMENT, 2013, "Civil Liberties Committee rejects EU Passenger Name Record proposal Fundamental rights" (Press release 24 April 2013). Available at: http://www.europarl.europa.eu/sides/getDoc.do?pubRef=-%2F%2FEP%2F%2FTEXT%2BIM-PRESS%2B20130422IPR07523%2B0%2BDOC%2BXML%2BV0%2F%2FEN&language=EN (accessed September 2, 2017).

EUROPEAN PARLIAMENT, COMMITTEE ON CIVIL LIBERTIES, JUSTICE AND HOME AFFAIRS, 2013, "Report on the proposal for a directive of the European Parliament and of the Council on the protection of individuals with regard to the processing of personal data by competent authorities for the purposes of prevention, investigation, detection or prosecution of criminal offences or the execution of criminal penalties, and the free movement of such data (COM (2012)0010 – C7–0024/2012–2012/0010(COD))". Available at: http://www.europarl.europa.eu/sides/getDoc.do?pubRef=-//EP//TEXT+REPORT+A7-2013-0403+0+DOC+XML+V0//EN (accessed September 4, 2017).

EUROPEAN PARLIAMENT, COMMITTEE ON CIVIL LIBERTIES, JUSTICE AND HOME AFFAIRS, 2015, "Amendments 48–329 on the proposal for a directive of the European Parliament and of the Council on the use of Passenger Name Record data for the prevention, detection, investigation and prosecution of terrorist offences and serious crime". Available at: http://www.europarl.europa.eu/meetdocs/2014_2019/documents/libe/am/1058/1058388/1058388en.pdf (accessed September 6, 2017).

EUROPEAN PARLIAMENT, DIRECTORATE GENERAL FOR INTERNAL POLICIES; 2011, "Developing an EU Internal Security Strategy, fighting terrorism and organized crime". Available at: http://www.europarl.europa.eu/document/activities/cont/201206/20120627ATT47777/20120627ATT47777EN.pdf (accessed August 13, 2017).

EUROPEAN UNION AGENCY FOR FUNDAMENTAL RIGHTS, 2011, "Opinion of the European Union Agency for Fundamental Rights on the Proposal for a Directive on the use of Passenger Name Record (PNR) data for the prevention, detection, investigation and prosecution of terrorist offences and serious crime (COM(2011) 32 final)". Available at: http://fra.europa.eu/sites/default/files/fra_uploads/1654-FRA-PNR-Opinion-June2011.pdf (accessed September 5, 2017).

HEISENBERG, D., 2005, *Negotiating Privacy: the European Union, the United States and personal data protection*, London: Lynne Rienner Publishers, Inc.

MITSILEGAS, V., 2009, *EU Criminal Law*, Portland: Bloomsbury Publishing.

10 Projects in the pipeline

After the first decade of the century, where initiatives on information exchange were springing up like mushrooms, with the Stockholm Programme and the IMS came an attitude to first evaluate already existing cooperation possibilities and only then look for new ones. Thus in the Stockholm Programme the Council recognised "the need for coherence and consolidation in developing information management and exchange."[1]

Following this idea, it can be noticed that in last 6 or 7 years, apart from the initiatives of data protection, Europol Regulation (that were foreseen by the Lisbon Treaty and therefore obligatory) and EU PNR, only a few weighty initiatives are under consideration for the time being (1 December, 2017):

- Information Exchange Platform – a pragmatic attempt to put in order everything carried out so far in the area of police cooperation.
- Long lasting discussion on European Police Records Information (Index) System.

1 Information Exchange Platform

In 2010, following the provision of the Stockholm Programme to make better use of existing information exchange tools, the Spanish Presidency of the Council proposed to create an Information Exchange Platform. The specificity of this proposal is not in the establishment of a new information exchange mechanism or granting broader access to existing ones, but in the centralisation of all of them in one platform, as, for the time being they "are disparate in every way, displaying major differences in their nature (e.g. database, communications system, network of contact points), legal basis (e.g. international treaty, European legislation, bilateral agreement) scope

1 OJ C 115, 4.5.2010, p. 18.

(e.g. terrorism, drug trafficking, organised crime, violence in sport), technical characteristics, etc."[2]

This initiative had been included as one of the measures of the implementation of IMS and has received approval for its development from all Member States and is in line with the strategic guidelines. In addition to Spain in the development of the project, Bulgaria, Cyprus, Italy, Lithuania, Hungary, Slovakia and the Commission are participating.[3]

Proposed by the Spanish Presidency, the leadership of this action was taken by Europol that concluded that, "the establishment of the IXP will make it easier for end-users to benefit from the existing opportunities for cross-border law enforcement cooperation, while respecting the national and international processes in place."[4]

Initially it was proposed to develop at least three levels of platform:

- "Bookshop" that would contain basic information on all information exchange tools: legislation, manuals, guidelines, procedures, national contact lists and fact sheets, where necessary – national legislation, training materials, and so on. At this level the end-user would get a picture of all the possibilities of international cooperation.
- "Communications" meaning a secure e-mail system that could be used between all authorised users. Europol considered it has "huge advantages from a business perspective. It enables the user to go (in accordance with his access rights) to all relevant sources, tools and platforms."[5]
- "Queries" or "Gateways" to various databases according to existing access rules and without any type of interconnection of existing databases, if they are separated under current legislation. It was foreseen that large scale systems, such as SIS, VIS and EURODAC will not be integrated into the platform.[6] But Europol proposed at the last stage of the project, to integrate search functions across the SIS, Europol systems

2 COUNCIL OF THE EUROPEAN UNION, "Presentation of the Police Information Exchange Platform (PIEP) project", 5281/10, p. 2, accessed November 24, 2017, http://data.consilium.europa.eu/doc/document/ST-5281-2010-INIT/en/pdf.
3 COUNCIL OF THE EUROPEAN UNION, "2nd Interim Report on the Implementation of the IMS Action Lists", 13032/14, p. 4.
4 COUNCIL OF THE EUROPEAN UNION, "Business Concept for an Information Exchange Platform for Law Enforcement Agencies – (IMS Action 4)", 11117/3/10, p. 5, accessed November 24, 2017, http://data.consilium.europa.eu/doc/document/ST-11117-2010-REV-3/en/pdf.
5 COUNCIL OF THE EUROPEAN UNION, "Business concept for an Information Exchange Platform for Law Enforcement Agencies (IMS Action 4) – High level solution definition for the IXP/Draft 4", 7840/13, p. 6.
6 See COUNCIL OF THE EUROPEAN UNION, "Business concept for an Information Exchange Platform for Law Enforcement Agencies (IMS Action 4) Practical Advantages of the IXP", 7819/13, p. 2.

and Interpol databases, provided that the user in question is authorised to query these sources with a so-called *single sign-on.*[7] Such a proposal would be acceptable so far as access rules would remain the same, as it would mean only a technical solution to facilitate the daily work of the competent authorities.

As there would be three levels of platform, three categories of users are distinguished:

- The general user (every law enforcement official) with access to non-restricted data, meaning open resources of "Bookshop".
- The law enforcement officials with access to "Bookshop" and other levels if he or she has such authorisation.
- The international coordination staff that have access to all levels, but each access will depend on individual authorisations obtained for performance of his or her functions at national level, for example a person can be authorised to search in SIS, but not Europol's databases.

As Jones points out, "The idea that individual rights to privacy and data protection will be better safeguarded through the use of a single website in some ways makes sense, allowing as it does one route through which data protection authorities can monitor access and usage logs for each individual instrument. However, the technical hurdles that would need to be overcome in order for such a project to work – let alone to work securely – are vast."[8]

Bearing in mind the complexity of the project and the need for human and financial resources, a step by step approach is applied and for the time being EPE is functioning. The concept of EPE is hosting of smaller platforms dedicated to different cooperation topics, for example the Financial Crime Information Centre or the Secure Platform for Accredited Cybercrime Experts. Each platform contains a library with the relevant information (that cannot be classified or personal data), a "wiki", a calendar and communication tools for users, such as a message forum and a blog.

2 European Police Records Index System (EPRIS)

Following the initiative of the European Criminal Records Information System, in April 2007 during the Police Chiefs Task Force meeting, the German Presidency raised the idea of a European Police Records Index

7 COUNCIL OF THE EUROPEAN UNION, "Business concept for an Information…", *loc. cit.*, p. 2, 7.

8 JONES, Chris, "Implementing the 'principle of availability': The European Criminal Records Information System, The European Police Records Index System, The Information Exchange Platform for Law Enforcement Authorities" (Statewatch analysis, September 2011), p. 31, accessed October 28, 2017, http://www.statewatch.org/analyses/no-145-ecris-epris-ixp.pdf.

System that would allow access to databases run by police in performing their functions.

This initiative was taken on the agenda of different Council preparatory groups, but as to date, it has not resulted in a clear project. Some Member States were not totally convinced of its necessity, due to already existing mechanisms but finally, in the Stockholm Programme, the Commission was called to present a feasibility study in 2012.

The Commission ordered a comprehensive study that was presented in October 2012 with the main conclusion/suggestion, "If the need for a more efficient exchange of police records related information is not fully addressed by the better use of the existing systems and tools in the course of three years, then a pilot project should be initiated with the aim to evaluate the technical feasibility and impact of a new, specific EPRIS system."[9]

In December 2012, the Commission in its Communication to the European Parliament and the Council, "Strengthening law enforcement cooperation in the EU: the European Information Exchange Model (EIXM)" recognised that at that moment creation of the EPRIS was unjustified.[10]

This discussion and decision seems to be quite complicated, as to start with, there is no single or approximate understanding of what a "police record" is.

Going back to the findings of a Study on possible ways to enhance efficiency in the exchange of police records between the Member States, by setting up a European Police Records Index System EPRIS (hereinafter – Feasibility Study) made with 27 Member States[11] only 13 have a legal definition of "police record", the rest have only a functional one, or none at all.

For the sake of continuation of a Feasibility Study, it was suggested that *police record* should be understood as "any information available in the national register or registers recording data of competent authorities, for the prevention, detection, investigation and prosecution of criminal offences."[12]

In these circumstances, it is not clear at all what data and its categories would be accessible through EPRIS. Any at all? It would mean total disproportion and inequity as far as the data subject is concerned, as the police record of one Member State would include only suspects, and in another, any questioned person, witness and victims.

9 EUROPEAN COMMISSION, "Study on possible ways to enhance efficiency in the exchange of police records between the Member States by setting up a European Police Records Index System EPRIS" (Final Report, 8 October 2012), p. 2–3, accessed October 28, 2017, http://ec.europa.eu/dgs/home-affairs/e-library/documents/policies/police-cooperation/general/docs/epris-final_report_en.pdf.

10 EUROPEAN COMMISSION, "Communication from the Commission to the European Parliament and the Council Strengthening law enforcement cooperation in the EU: the European Information Exchange Model (EIXM)", COM (2012)735, p. 9, accessed November 24, 2017, http://eur-lex.europa.eu/legal-content/EN/TXT/?uri=COM:2012:0735:FIN.

11 At the time of the study, Croatia was not yet an EU Member State.

12 EUROPEAN COMMISSION, "Study on possible ways...", loc. cit., p. 38.

Thus without a clear and explicit definition of *police record*, a discussion cannot go forward as this is a key issue on which to take a decision of its necessity.

The Feasibility Study indicated that a majority of Member States would stick to inclusion of suspects and perpetrators. In this case, EPRIS would partially overlap with EIS and AWF and would have added value only in relation to those crimes that are out part of Europol's competence. But is it really worth establishing a new system for the remaining criminal offences? As was pointed out at an Expert Meeting on EPRIS, if it would be established, then the question of EIS's added value should be reconsidered.[13]

In the same Study, four technical solutions for EPRIS were proposed: no new system, decentralised (as in case of Prüm Decisions), semi-centralised, centralised system. Fourteen Member States have pronounced in favour of a semi-centralised system that would mean that all data would remain in Member States' databases, but at central level, would be in index databases.[14] That would allow optimising query, i.e. to make a single one to all Member States, and not one by one as in the case of a decentralised system. From a technical point of view, it is a complicated structure, as Member States will need to create an index system or interface and to ensure its compliance with the central one. Additionally, maintenance of the central system will be needed.

According to a very preliminary estimation, the interface at central level would cost 2,000,000 euros and the connection of national databases and data extraction from 250,000 to 1,000,000 euros for each Member State, depending on its size.[15]

As the current situation shows, there is no agreement about the content of the central system, should in include only indexes or some basic data categories as well?

In the first case, the added value of such a system can be questioned. Only two advantages of it can be identified: the single query to all Member States and the work burden for requesting Member States.

France and Finland expressed the same idea in their joint document from 2012, "It is estimated that currently 65% of the requests are not replied to at all and only 35% get a positive or negative answer. [...] However, if it is proven that information on the person in question is available from a law enforcement authority in certain Member States, a well-directed request would be made. It is most likely that a positive answer would be given to these requests and that in this respect the activities in all Member States concerned would have been worthwhile."[16]

13 See EUROPEAN COMMISSION, "Summary Report of Expert Meeting on EPRIS, 19.04.2012", p. 6, accessed October 28, 2017, http://ec.europa.eu/transparency/regexpert/index.cfm?do=groupDetail.groupDetailDoc&id=6238&no=1.

14 EUROPEAN COMMISSION, "Study on possible ways...", loc. cit., p. 28–29.

15 See EUROPEAN COMMISSION, "Summary Report of Expert...", loc. cit., p. 5.

16 COUNCIL OF THE EUROPEAN UNION, "IMS Action List No 3 EPRIS / ADEP: Automation of the data exchange process", 14944/12, p. 3.

But after the automatic index query, personal data would be received on the basis of already existing Swedish Initiative as is the case with DNA and dactyloscopic data under the Prüm Decisions. It raises a question of proportionality of creation of such a system to its practical efficiency.

In the second case a concern would be about the new legal basis and data protection. Including real data into central system, Member States would have to agree what categories of data would be included, who would be responsible for data security, deletion, and so on. This brings us to the question: what is the ratio between results that will be achieved in the fight against crime and the necessity and proportionality to limit privacy and data protection?

Although one can argue that creation of EPRIS will not mean gathering different data from an already available one, but harmonisation or at least approximation of the definition of "police record" could force some Member States to collect new categories of data. Without definition of the term *police record* again, data that could be accessed by different Member States could vary a lot. It should also be borne in mind that national information of police interest is not usually centralised and different law enforcement institutions have different access rights and their own databases.[17]

In both cases it is not clear what would be the search criteria, for instance: name and surname? ID Number? Any other criteria?

Besides, until now nobody has declared the impossibility of obtaining this information. Under current legal and technical solutions such information can be queried on the basis of the Swedish Initiative and using SIENA, or any other cooperation channel. It is true that the requesting Member State would have to ask all Member States separately, but from a technical point of view, it does not mean sending 27 separate requests, just to use one channel and send it with one mailing list as is done with other requests.

Although for the time being no clear statement on insufficiency of actual information exchange mechanisms has been made. In April 2015, the Commission committed itself to supporting the pilot project where a group of Member States would create national index systems and give access to other participating Member States for automated searches on a "hit/no hit" basis.[18]

In 2016, the EPRIS initiative was taken into consideration as one of the actions under IMS, i.e. Automation of Data Exchange Procedures dedicated

17 See DEL MORAL TORRES, Anselmo, *Cooperación policial en la Unión Europea: la necesidad de un modelo de inteligencia criminal eficiente* (Madrid: Dykinson, S.L., 2011), p. 495.

18 EUROPEAN COMMISSION, "Communication from the Commission to the European Parliament, the Council, the European Economic and Social Committee and the Committee of the Regions – The European Agenda on Security", COM(2015) 185, p. 8, accessed November 24, 2017, http://eur-lex.europa.eu/legal-content/EN/TXT/?uri=COM:2015:0185:FIN.

to the creation of index-databases with extracts of police records (family name, surname, any other names, date of birth, place of birth, gender) that would be available for consultation by other Member States on hit/no hit basis.[19]

Bibliography

COUNCIL OF THE EUROPEAN UNION, 2010, "Presentation of the Police Information Exchange Platform (PIEP) project", 5281/10. Available at: http://data.consilium.europa.eu/doc/document/ST-5281-2010-INIT/en/pdf (accessed November 24, 2017).

COUNCIL OF THE EUROPEAN UNION, 2010, "Business Concept for an Information Exchange Platform for Law Enforcement Agencies – (IMS Action 4)", 11117/3/10. Available at: http://data.consilium.europa.eu/doc/document/ST-11117-2010-REV-3/en/pdf (accessed November 24, 2017).

COUNCIL OF THE EUROPEAN UNION, 2012, "IMS Action List No 3 EPRIS / ADEP: Automation of the data exchange process", 14944/12.

COUNCIL OF THE EUROPEAN UNION, 2013, "Business concept for an Information Exchange Platform for Law Enforcement Agencies (IMS Action 4) Practical Advantages of the IXP", 7819/13.

COUNCIL OF THE EUROPEAN UNION, 2013, "Business concept for an Information Exchange Platform for Law Enforcement Agencies (IMS Action 4) – High level solution definition for the IXP / Draft 4", 7840/13.

COUNCIL OF THE EUROPEAN UNION, 2014, "2nd Interim Report on the Implementation of the IMS Action Lists", 13032/14.

COUNCIL OF THE EUROPEAN UNION, 2016, "Information Management Strategy (IMS) action No 2 – Automation of Data Exchange Processes (ADEP) – Whitepaper", 9852/16.

DEL MORAL TORRES, A., 2011, *Cooperación policial en la Unión Europea: la necesidad de un modelo de inteligencia criminal eficiente*, Madrid: Dykinson, S.L.

EUROPEAN COMMISSION, 2012, "Communication from the Commission to the European Parliament and the Council Strengthening law enforcement cooperation in the EU: the European Information Exchange Model (EIXM)"; COM(2012) 735. Available at: http://eur-lex.europa.eu/legal-content/EN/TXT/?uri=COM:2012:0735:FIN (accessed November 24, 2017).

EUROPEAN COMMISSION, 2012, "Study on possible ways to enhance efficiency in the exchange of police records between the Member States by setting up a European Police Records Index System EPRIS" (Final Report). Available at: http://ec.europa.eu/dgs/home-affairs/e-library/documents/policies/police-cooperation/general/docs/epris-final_report_en.pdf (accessed October 28, 2017).

EUROPEAN COMMISSION, 2012, "Summary Report of Expert Meeting on EPRIS, 19.04.2012". Available at: http://ec.europa.eu/transparency/regexpert/index.cfm?do=groupDetail.groupDetailDoc&id=6238&no=1 (accessed October 28, 2017).

19 COUNCIL OF THE EUROPEAN UNION, "Information Management Strategy (IMS) action No 2 – Automation of Data Exchange Processes (ADEP) – Whitepaper", 9852/16, p. 5–6.

EUROPEAN COMMISSION, 2015, "Communication from the Commission to the European Parliament, the Council, the European Economic and Social Committee and the Committee of the Regions – The European Agenda on Security", COM (2015) 185. Available at: http://eur-lex.europa.eu/legal-content/EN/TXT/?uri=COM:2015:0185:FIN (accessed November 24, 2017).

JONES, C., 2011, "Implementing the 'principle of availability': The European Criminal Records Information System, The European Police Records Index System, The Information Exchange Platform for Law Enforcement Authorities" (Statewatch analysis). Available at: http://www.statewatch.org/analyses/no-145-ecris-epris-ixp.pdf (accessed October 28, 2017).

11 Cooperation between the EU and the United Kingdom after Brexit

As mentioned in Chapter 2, Denmark, Ireland and the United Kingdom have a special position with regard to participation in the EU policy related to the area of freedom, security and justice. With the Treaty of Lisbon having entered force, Denmark has maintained an entire opt-out position, while Ireland and the United Kingdom have declared opt-in positions into new legislative proposal which are of interest to them.[1]

On the other hand, in July 2013 the United Kingdom expressed its specific position on participation in pre-Lisbon measures in this area. It notified the Council of the European Union of its decision from December 1, 2014 to apply the block opt-out from all measures and then re-joining only 35 of them (including staying in Europol, the application of the European Arrest Warrant, and so on)[2] and more recently, in 2016, also re-joining Prüm Decisions.

With the post-Lisbon measures another phenomenon has been observed recently: "Governmental concerns over the impact of participation in post-Lisbon EU criminal law in terms of the impact on domestic law in the light of judicial scrutiny by the CJEU also explains the latest tendency by the UK Government not to opt into the text of the Commission proposals, but rather to try to influence – to the extent possible – negotiations and opt in post-adoption if the adopted measure appears to be acceptable to the UK".[3]

With the United Kingdom European Union membership referendum of June 23, 2016, and the activation of the Art. 50 of the TEU on March 29, 2017, the EU and the United Kingdom face a new era of relationship that has never happened before, and where at the moment it is only clear that the

1 See as well, JIMENO-BULNES, Mar, "Brexit and the Future of European Criminal Law – a Spanish Perspective", *Criminal Law Forum*, 2017, vol. 28, issue 2, p. 327–329.

2 OJ L 345, 1.12.2014, p. 6–9.

3 MITSILEGAS, Valsamis, "European Criminal Law after Brexit", *Criminal Law Forum*, 2017, vol. 28, p. 222.

United Kingdom will leave the European Union policy and quit the organisation as from March 30, 2019 (except in the case of common agreement to postpone this deadline).

But this "re-engineering of relationship for a post-Brexit era"[4] is not so easy. From a formal point of view, the United Kingdom will just become a third state to the European Union, from a practical point of view it has much closer ties with the EU than any other third state. Additionally, even if there is no will of the United Kingdom to be bound by the policy and institutional scrutiny of the European Union, there is a will to continue strong cooperation in some areas, if possible equal or very similar to the current one. As stated in the United Kingdom's exit from and new partnership with the European Union White Paper (hereinafter – the White Paper) the goal is "Leaving the EU, not leaving Europe".[5]

1 British priorities

In 2016, the preliminary British vision of future relations between the United Kingdom and the EU encompassed four objectives: bringing back control of laws to the national Parliament; bringing back control of decisions over immigration to the United Kingdom; maintaining the strong security cooperation with the EU; establishing the freest possible market in goods and services with the European Union and the rest of the world.[6]

The White Paper has determined 12 principles of the United Kingdom's position in the Brexit process, including cooperation in the fight against crime and terrorism[7] and stressing that the United Kingdom's "pre-existing security relationship with the EU and its Member States means that we are uniquely placed to develop and sustain a mutually beneficial model of cooperation in this area from outside the Union. We are starting from a position of strong relations with EU Member States, where we have been at

4 Ibid, p. 219.

5 HM GOVERNMENT, "The United Kingdom's exit from and new partnership with the European Union", February, 2017, p. 63, accessed October 2, 2017, https://www.gov.uk/government/publications/the-united-kingdoms-exit-from-and-new-partnership-with-the-european-union-white-paper.

6 See HOUSE OF COMMONS, Parliamentary Scrutiny of Leaving the EU, 12 October 2016, vol. 615, accessed October 2, 2017, https://hansard.parliament.uk/Commons/2016-10-12/debates/F327EC64-3777-4D40-A98D-BEC2E11763A2/ParliamentaryScrutinyOfLeavingTheEU#contribution-4581E073-B39B-400F-A1ED-5098EA703726).

7 See, HM GOVERNMENT, "The United Kingdom's exit ... *loc. cit.*, p. 6. The remaining 11 principles are: providing certainty and clarity; taking control of national laws, strengthening the Union, protecting strong historic ties with Ireland and maintaining Common Travel Area, controlling immigration, securing rights for EU nationals in the UK and UK nationals in the UE, protecting workers' rights, ensuring free trade with European markets, securing new trade agreements with other countries, ensuring the United Kingdom remains the best place for science and innovation, delivering a smooth, orderly exit from the EU.

the forefront of developing a number of EU tools which encourage joint working across the continent to protect citizens and our way of life."[8]

Undoubtedly, this is the first time that the EU will face cooperation with a former Member State, but unfortunately, and as already mentioned, the Treaties do not formally foresee any special status of the ex-Member State, they only make a difference between Member States and third countries. In these circumstances, it would be quite complicated to create some kind of "enhanced cooperation of the European Union and the third country", especially taking into account that according to Article 281(11) of the TFUE, any measure or agreement could be scrutinised by the CJEU, one whose supervision the United Kingdom would prefer to avoid.[9]

What could give another perspective to this approach is the undeniable contribution of the United Kingdom to European politics in public security, development and use of its tools, as it "has been a leading protagonist in driving and shaping the nature and direction of cooperation on police".[10] On the other hand, this position is weakened by post-Lisbon "picking up" for itself only those tools that fit its own interests and not contributing to the rest of them.

As pointed out by the European Union Committee of the House of Lords, "Even with the utmost good will on both sides, it seems inevitable that there will be practical limits to how closely the UK and the EU-27 can work together on police and security matters if they are no longer accountable to, and subject to oversight and adjudication by, the same supranational institutions, notably the Court of Justice of the European Union. There is, therefore, a risk that any new arrangements that the Government and the EU-27 put in place by way of replacement when the UK leaves the EU, will be sub-optimal relative to present arrangements, possibly leaving the people of the UK – and their European neighbours – less safe."[11]

From the opt-in made in 2014, one can form an idea of the European Union security tools that the United Kingdom would like to use and have

8 Ibid, p. 61.

9 As has emphasised Steve Peers in his evidences to the House of Lords, "The EU court has jurisdiction to interpret the treaties which the EU signs with non-EU states, so the EU would be able to give interpretations of their deal with the UK. (…) Those rulings have an impact on us." See HOUSE OF LORDS, EU HOME AFFAIRS SUB-COMMITTEE, "Brexit: future UK-EU security and police cooperation inquiry. Oral and Written Evidence", December 16, 2016, p. 21, 86, accessed October 2, 2017, https://www.parliament.uk/documents/lords-committees/eu-home-affairs-subcommittee/Evidence-Brexit-Policing.pdf

10 MITSILEGAS, Valsamis, "European Criminal Law … *loc. cit.*, p. 246.

11 HOUSE OF LORDS, EU HOME AFFAIRS SUB-COMMITTEE, "Brexit: future UK-EU security and police cooperation", 7th Report of Session 2016/17, p. 2, 3, accessed October 2, 2017, https://publications.parliament.uk/pa/ld201617/ldselect/ldeucom/77/77.pdf.

access to in the future. In the case of information exchange, they would be Europol, SIS II, the Prüm Decisions and the PNR.[12]

Mitsilegas points out three possible options for the further cooperation between the EU and the United Kingdom in criminal justice "the conclusion of EU-UK agreements on various aspects of criminal justice cooperation; the conclusion of bilateral agreements between the UK and individual EU member states; and, in the absence of such agreements with the EU or member states, falling back to existing Council of Europe mechanisms of cooperation."[13]

The application of the third option to the cooperation on information exchange is unfeasible as there are no conventions in this respect. The option of bilateral agreements is possible to some extent, for example, in cases of access to national data bases or bilateral information exchange and in some circumstances this could be concluded more quickly than agreement with the EU. But on the other hand, this option means 27 different agreements (even if they were based on the same model agreement it is difficult to imagine that all of them would be equal) and it is impossible in the case of cooperation with the European Union agency (as Europol) or use of centralised databases (as SIS II).[14]

The following pages of this chapter will present a brief reflection on the possibilities of access by the United Kingdom as a third country to SIS II, Europol, Prüm Decisions and PNR.

2 Access to SIS II

By the Council implementing decision (EU) 2015/215 of February 10, 2015 on the putting into effect of the provisions of the Schengen acquis on data protection, and on the provisional putting into effect of parts of the provisions of the Schengen acquis on the Schengen Information System for the United Kingdom of Great Britain and Northern Ireland,[15] the United Kingdom was authorised to enter data to the SIS II as from April 13, 2015. As British access is limited to police cooperation and does not include the objective of border control, it does not have access to the alerts on refusing the entry of third country nationals.

In one year, more than 6,000 alerts have resulted in hits on the part of the United Kingdom, "809 people were flagged on SIS II to the UK – including 192 wanted people, 96 missing people, and 358 people believed to be involved in serious organised crime".[16] These numbers are significant and

12 See ibid, p. 2.
13 MITSILEGAS, Valsamis, "European Criminal Law ..." *loc. cit.*, p. 241.
14 HOUSE OF LORDS, EU HOME AFFAIRS SUB-COMMITTEE, "Brexit: future UK-EU security and police cooperation inquiry. Oral and Written Evidence", *loc. cit.*, p. 85.
15 OJ L 36, 12.2.2015, p. 8–10.
16 HOUSE OF LORDS, EU HOME AFFAIRS SUB-COMMITTEE, "Brexit: future UK-EU security and police cooperation", *loc. cit.*, p. 25.

certainly contribute to the increasing of security, but it also has to be taken into account that at the very beginning of use of the SIS II, or any other databases by a new member, the number of hits would be elevated due to a new stream of data (alerts and records).

The United Kingdom authorities consider that losing access to SIS II would mean some kind of informational vacuum, converting the United Kingdom into a "little island off the continent with no access to information and intelligence about who is likely to come to us and, more importantly, about what happens to our criminals when they go across to the continent."[17] or "will be the kind of Brazil of Europe (...) more attractive for criminals to come here and less easy to find them without these databases".[18]

This argument is presented as beneficiary for both the state and the European Union, as for the United Kingdom it is an important tool to ensure security and for the European Union to avoid the impunity of its criminals.

Another argument used is the vitality of package of the European arrest warrant (that the United Kingdom wishes to continue to apply) and SIS II[19] as this system allows the dissemination of alerts for wanted persons immediately in all countries that use SIS II. Without any doubt, SIS II is very useful in that it allows the insertion of photos, European arrest warrant as such, to interchange the additional information, but is not as indispensable as, until 2015, the communication on European arrest warrants between the United Kingdom and other Member States which took place out of SIS, and was still sufficient and satisfactory.

As already mentioned, the only possibility to maintain the *status quo* in respect of SIS II is an agreement between the European Union and the United Kingdom. An agreement on access to SIS/SIS II would not be a novelty as such as it has been already granted to four third states: Iceland, Liechtenstein, Norway and Switzerland. Nevertheless, the access to the SIS/SIS II is not the objective of these agreements, but the result, the compensatory measure for the abolishment of border controls between the European Union and these countries. As Steve Peers has pointed out, the United Kingdom would be "asking for something which is not normally given since we will not be joining Schengen".[20]The only states that have access to SIS II without yet having abolished their border controls are a few Members States of the European Union.

17 Ibid.

18 Ibid, p. 78.

19 See HOUSE OF LORDS, EU HOME AFFAIRS SUB-COMMITTEE, "Brexit: future UK-EU security and police cooperation", *loc. cit.*, p. 26; HOUSE OF LORDS, EU HOME AFFAIRS SUB-COMMITTEE, "Brexit: future UK-EU security and police cooperation inquiry. Oral and Written Evidence", *loc. cit.*, p. 7–8.

20 HOUSE OF LORDS, EU HOME AFFAIRS SUB-COMMITTEE, "Brexit: future UK-EU security and police cooperation", *loc. cit.*, p. 31.

Thus it could be concluded that there is no precedent of giving the access to SIS II that is neither a member of Schengen space nor a Member State. The possibility of overcoming this policy might be found within the common aim of combatting terrorism and the advantage that SIS II could give on tracking foreign fighters, both for the European Union and the United Kingdom.

3 Being part of Europol

As mentioned, the British exit from the EU also means leaving all its institutions, agencies and entities, including Europol. As a consequence of this, the United Kingdom would lose its current access to the information and intelligence processed in Europol, the possibility of entering its own data and making cross-checks and connections to SIENA (not talking about being excluded from the management of Europol in the same way as from all decision-making bodies of the EU).

The British priority in this respect is to stay in Europol. As Bill Hughes, former Director-General of the Serious Organised Crime Agency[21] has expressed, "We must remain a part of it. It was crucial right from the start that we had an intelligence unit or agency that could build on and disseminate information and coordinate that around the whole of Europe and our member state partners."[22]

It was also repeated on some occasions that it can have an effect on the United Kingdom partnership within the "Five Eyes"[23] "because sometimes they can use us as a proxy for getting work done if we are doing joint work together".[24] Although Australia, Canada and the United States have operational agreements with Europol, and the European Commission has issued decisions on the adequacy of data protection on all four states, such an argument sounds like the use of Europol potential for the interests of the multi-later alliance, and this could be considered slightly tactless and to some extent, inappropriate.

Before the entry into force of the Europol Regulation in May 2017, the relations between Europol and third countries were regulated by agreements between them. Nevertheless, Article 25 of the Europol regulation has changed this order and the exchange of personal data with third countries in the future will be carried out on the basis of the adequacy decision of the

21 Nowadays part of the National Criminal Agency.
22 HOUSE OF LORDS, EU HOME AFFAIRS SUB-COMMITTEE, "Brexit: future UK-EU security and police cooperation inquiry. Oral and Written Evidence", *loc. cit.*, p. 24.
23 Intelligence alliance of Australia, Canada, New Zealand, the United Kingdom and the United States.
24 HOUSE OF LORDS, EU HOME AFFAIRS SUB-COMMITTEE, "Brexit: future UK-EU security and police cooperation", *loc. cit.*, p. 10–11.

European Commission about the level of data protection or international agreements concluded between the EU and third states.

Nevertheless, to date, none of the operational agreements or adequacy decisions has given the third country full participation in Europol. As Mitsilegas notices, "While co-operation arrangements in the case of EU agencies are more common, existing precedents demonstrate that there are significant limitations to the position of third countries in comparison to EU member states, most notably relating to the lack of direct access to EU databases and to non-participation in the core functions of the management bodies of these agencies, with limited say or powers to shape the future direction of these agencies".[25] Third countries do not have direct access to the EIS, they are subject to additional requirements and conditions to be part of analytical work and, of course, are lacking all influence on its politics and management.

The British objective is more ambitious than such a possible position defined by Lord Condon as "second best",[26] as the United Kingdom is already a trusted and full member of Europol, contributing a significant amount of information and intelligence, Europol's activities in many fields are based on British experience, and it supposes a different starting point of negotiations from all other third countries.

In these circumstances, the feasible option would be the special, unprecedented agreement between the European Union and the United Kingdom, either related only to Europol or to all measures of freedom, security and justice that the United Kingdom would like to apply after Brexit.

However, mentioned before, such an agreement would not be free of the supervision and interpretation by the CJEU. It should be noted once more, that one of the main objectives of new legislation on Europol was to establish its effective scrutiny by the European Parliament and the CJEU, and the British vision of the participation in Europol on a higher level than third countries, but out of this scrutiny, in the words of Lord Condon might be treated as "You want to play but you do not want to abide by the rules".[27]

4 Passenger name records

The United Kingdom was the first country within the EU to establish the PNR system, and was one of the Member States strongly supporting its Europe-wide application.[28] Therefore, the British will to participate in this barely new instrument, which has to be fully applied from 2018, is not surprising. The European PNR is a decentralised system with the data

25 MITSILEGAS, Valsamis, "European Criminal Law …", *loc. cit.*, p. 242.

26 HOUSE OF LORDS, EU HOME AFFAIRS SUB-COMMITTEE, "Brexit: future UK-EU security and police cooperation inquiry. Oral and Written Evidence", *loc. cit.*, p. 28.

27 Ibid, p. 21.

28 See ibid, p. 23.

processed by the PIU of a Member State from external flights departing and arriving to its territory, and therefore a legal basis for data exchange between Member States and the United Kingdom could take the form of either bilateral agreements with all or some of them, or agreement with the EU.

In respect to agreement between the EU and the United Kingdom, it should be noted, that although there is the experience of bilateral agreements with third countries on PNR data, their content is different from the one in which the United Kingdom is interested.

The aim of the existing agreement on PNR is to create a legal basis for the PNR data transfer from European air carries to the third country, and only the PNR data of passengers travelling between the Member States and that third country where the competent authorities of the latter carries out risk assessment and processes the data.

In the case of inspiring the cooperation between the EU and the United Kingdom in provisions of the Directive (EU) 2016/681 of the European Parliament and of the Council of April 27, 2016 on the use of passenger name record (PNR) data for the prevention, detection, investigation and prosecution of terrorist offences and serious crime[29] (hereinafter – PNR Directive), the cooperation will be between PIUs of the Member States and the United Kingdom (without direct involvement of air carriers) with the possibility of transferring both PNR data and results or its risk assessments. In reference to the scope of the data, it should be noted that the goal would not only be the exchange of PNR data on flights between the United Kingdom and Member States, but about all extra-EU flights.

Depending on the time that it would take to achieve agreement with the EU, a rational option could be the concluding of bilateral agreements with the key Member States, for example, Belgium, France and Ireland because of their geographical proximity, and any other states on the basis of the assessment of potential risks derived from flights between some Member State and third countries. Nevertheless, a variety of bilateral agreements can distort the principles of the PNR data exchanges established in the PNR Directive as they give the possibility to include provisions other than those stipulated by the European legislator, for example, altering data protection rules and modifying the scope of information exchange.

5 The Prüm Decisions

As the Prüm Decisions regulate data exchange between Member States, automated access to their DNA, dactyloscopic and vehicle registration databases and rather than a central database, the options of further cooperation between the EU and the United Kingdom could be the same as for PNR data exchange, meaning: agreement between the EU and the United Kingdom or bilateral agreements with all or some Member States.

29 OJ L 119, 4.5.2016, p. 132–149.

As the alternative to bilateral agreements is also possible, and would be similar to that discussed within the framework of the participation in PNR data exchange, the focus will be on possible agreements between the EU and the United Kingdom. It should be noted that there are precedents for such agreements with third countries, for example, agreement between the European Union and Iceland and Norway on the application of certain provisions of Council Decision 2008/615/JHA on the stepping up of cross-border cooperation, particularly in combating terrorism and cross-border crime, and also Council Decision 2008/616/JHA on the implementation of Decision 2008/615/JHA on the stepping up of cross-border cooperation, particularly in combating terrorism and cross-border crime[30] (hereinafter – EU agreement with Norway and Iceland). However, one can argue that these two countries are members of the Schengen area and the United Kingdom does not have such a link. One of the recitals of the Agreement between the European Union and Iceland and Norway takes into consideration "that current relationships between the Contracting Parties, in particular the Agreement concluded by the Council of the European Union and the Republic of Iceland and the Kingdom of Norway concerning the latter's association with the implementation, application and development of the Schengen acquis, demonstrate close cooperation in the fight against crime". Nevertheless, none of the provisions of this agreement stipulate its derivation from being members of the Schengen area. It only points out that this circumstance affirms close cooperation. Thus, in the case of the United Kingdom such close cooperation could also be demonstrated. For example, as Tony Bunyan has noted, "There will be some British nationals who are suspected of crimes on the continent, or people who have a prior history in Britain whom we have data on, and it is useful for them to be able to make the request to us; plus we have a huge DNA database which I am sure is very attractive to other Member States."[31] However, it should be taken into account that the EU agreement with Iceland and Norway is applied to access national databases, but not for post-match personal data exchange. For this purpose, the Council Framework Decision 2006/960/EU of December 18, 2006 on simplifying the exchange of information and intelligence between law enforcement authorities of the Member States of the European Union (hereinafter – Swedish Initiative) has to be used and Iceland and Norway have joined it. In these circumstances, either the United Kingdom should also put among its priorities to join the Swedish Initiative, or additional provision on post-hit information exchange should be introduced into a possible agreement between the European Union and the United Kingdom.

30 OJ L 353, 31.12.2009, p. 1–8.
31 HOUSE OF LORDS, EU HOME AFFAIRS SUB-COMMITTEE, "Brexit: future UK-EU security and police cooperation", *loc. cit.*, p. 32.

6 Brief summary and evaluation

The United Kingdom among its priorities for further information exchange with the EU has pointed out four instruments: SIS II, Europol, PNR and Prüm Decisions.

Remaining part of each of these instruments has different level of difficulties:

- In the case of SIS II, there is no precedent in the EU policy of granting of permission to the state that is neither Member State nor has abolished control of its borders upon becoming a member of Schengen area. Thus, such an exceptional position would be possible only with modification of the current EU policy and wide approval by the Member States.
- Seeking full membership in Europol (more enhanced than that given to other third countries), the difficulty lies in the scrutiny of its activities by the CJEU and the European Parliament. It is not applied to third countries, but the United Kingdom would like a more favourable position in Europol than other third states and with this, it is getting closer to the scrutiny by these institutions that, on the other hand, was one of the reasons for Brexit.
- Possible agreements between the EU and the United Kingdom on PNR and application of Prüm Decisions present less political problems and consist mainly of thorough legal and technical work.

Bibliography

HM GOVERNMENT, 2017, "The United Kingdom's exit from and new partnership with the European Union". Available at: https://www.gov.uk/government/publications/the-united-kingdoms-exit-from-and-new-partnership-with-the-european-union-white-paper (accessed October 2, 2017).

HOUSE OF COMMONS, 2016, Parliamentary Scrutiny of Leaving the EU, 12 October 2016, vol. 615. Available at: https://hansard.parliament.uk/Commons/2016-10-12/debates/F327EC64-3777-4D40-A98D-BEC2E11763A2/ParliamentaryScrutinyOfLeavingTheEU#contribution-4581E073-B39B-400F-A1ED-5098EA703726) (accessed October 2, 2017).

HOUSE OF LORDS, EU HOME AFFAIRS SUB-COMMITTEE, 2016, "Brexit: future UK-EU security and police cooperation inquiry. Oral and Written Evidence". Available at: https://www.parliament.uk/documents/lords-committees/eu-home-affairs-subcommittee/Evidence-Brexit-Policing.pdf (accessed October 2, 2017).

HOUSE OF LORDS, EU HOME AFFAIRS SUB-COMMITTEE, 2016, "Brexit: future UK-EU security and police cooperation", 7th Report of Session 2016/17. Available at: https://publications.parliament.uk/pa/ld201617/ldselect/ldeucom/77/77.pdf (accessed October 2, 2017).

JIMENO-BULNES, M., 2017, "Brexit and the Future of European Criminal Law – A Spanish Perspective", *Criminal Law Forum*; vol. 28, issue 2, p. 325–347.

MITSILEGAS, V., 2017, "European Criminal Law after Brexit", *Criminal Law Forum*, vol. 28, p. 219–250.

12 Conclusions

The security of modern society is vulnerable to a range of direct threats, such as serious and organised crime and terrorism. The spill over of technological progress and facilitated cross-border mobility of recent decades has resulted not only in benefits to society, but also in the movement of criminality into virtual space and cross-border dimensions.

This has challenged a need to change, to some extent, the general perception of the limits of competence of law enforcement and judicial authorities, although their functions have, in general, been treated as an indispensable element of state sovereignty.

With respect to information exchange between law enforcement authorities, the EU took this topic onto its agenda very actively, firstly by the establishment of compensatory mechanisms for the abolition of control of internal borders, and later by opposing to intensified criminal mobility and increased terrorism threats.

In these endeavours to protect persons, ensure their safe movement and stay in the EU, different initiatives saw daylight. Many (but not all) legislative acts on information exchange were created in an atmosphere that mixes political obligation with reaction to some threat, rapid preparation of legislative draft, political and time pressure for its analysis, necessity to conciliate different and sometimes contrary positions of Member States. This resulted in some deficiencies in the created tools revealed throughout this research and summarised on the following pages.

1 Regulation of each information exchange instrument that has been analysed

Each analysed instrument has its advantages and problems, but in the light of effectiveness, precision of regulation and balance with human rights some are more successful than others. Thus:

- SIS II (and previously SIS) is a database that includes quite precisely defined categories of persons and objects. Being a centralised database it allows: quite comprehensive access control as each search (check) has to be logged, automated data deletion after the term of storage expires (if no actions on extension of storage has been taken), avoidance of storage of excessive information, collection of precise statistics.

A comprehensive *lex especialis* on data protection is applied to SIS II, including the establishment and functioning of supervising authorities.

Nevertheless, the regulation of actions on alerts on discreet or specific checks as well as Europol's and Eurojust's access to SIS are not precisely regulated, leaving possibilities to redundant intervention into a checked person's privacy in the first case, and overuse of search possibilities in the second.

- PCCC is an entity used as a general rule for the investigation of crimes in states' border areas. It does not have detailed regulation at EU level, leaving it to neighbouring Member States that establish such PCCC on their borders.

  That results in a lack of common provisions on the working scheme and on the control of data flows. On the other hand, it can be justified by the peculiarity of each EU region that provokes difficulties in establishing the same framework across the EU.
- EU regulation of liaison officers is also quite general. The two most important provisions concern the common use of the liaison officers posted abroad and prohibition to perform operational activities on the territory of a hosting country. Information exchange takes place within the limits of national law of the hosting country and of the competence of the liaison officer established by its national law. From the perspective of the dispositive nature of this instrument (Member State has freedom to post liaison officers abroad or not) and bearing in mind differences of bilateral relations that can result in more restrictive or more flexible regulation, it would be difficult, as in the case of PCCC, to establish EU level detailed rules.
- Europol is comprehensively regulated by EU legislation, with a quite precise definition of purpose of information exchange between Europol and Member States. Despite comprehensive rules on data protection, the biggest criticism is reserved for the transmission of personal data to third parties as an exception, when Europol does not have operational agreements. Regulation of onwards information transmission is even more fragmented as it has different regulations depending on the agreement concluded between Europol and the third party and in addition, exceptions to make such transmission without concluded agreement were also allowed.
- The Swedish Initiative that sets out to be a flagship of the implementation of the principle of availability, in the end merely has added value by the establishment of deadlines for reply. But even in this respect, it does

not provide the content of urgency. It is full of question marks and ambiguities, beginning with the lack of a clear definition of the purpose for which information can be exchanged, and finishing with the complicated request form that on many occasions discourages competent authorities to use it.

- Despite being brief, the regulation of FIUs and AROs is quite clear with a well-defined but narrow purpose as well as a limited list of authorities that participate in information exchange. However, with respect to data protection rules, reference to different legal acts could be confusing to competent authorities and makes the effectiveness of data protection difficult.
- As compensation for giving direct access to national databases, Prüm Decisions foresee quite extensive guarantees to their proper use, such as evaluation of each Member State before authorising access of its national contact points. By giving hit/no hit access, it is ensured that data not matching search criteria will never be seen by the searching authority and in cases of hit, personal data will be provided only after proper checks of the basis of the request.

  Provisions of non-automated data exchange on terrorism prevention and security of major events with a cross-border dimension could be considered as redundant, due to the existence of other legislative tools.
- Collection of PNR means checking the data of each passenger for security purposes, even if he or she has never been linked to any crime in any role. It converts PNR into a massive information processing system and goes far beyond the scope of data processed using other information exchange tools. Additionally, the European legislator does not establish criteria that have to be applied to the analysis of this immense quantity of data in order to reach conclusions about the level of dangerousness of a person or his or her relationship with crime, leaving it instead to the discretion of each Member State.

2 Clarity on use of totality of the EU information exchange tools

The analysis carried out has revealed that the EU pool of information exchange mechanisms is to some extent fragmented and incoherent. As a summary, it is presented in the following tables which show the purpose of each tool, data subject and data categories included, with special mention of sensitive data, possibilities of transmission to third parties or forwarding, and the data protection regime applied.

This comparison brings us to the conclusion that law enforcement authorities, as a rule, face dilemmas in which tools should be used; as for the same purpose, for example to obtain information related to a committed robbery when there are indications of involvement of nationals or residents of other

Member States, a choice between the simple use of the Swedish Initiative, PCCC, a liaison officer posted in that country or Europol, shall be made. In those cases, when it would be a single (the first and the last) request, the choice maybe will not be so important because the information could probably be obtained using any tool, and the difference could be noticed only at the time of the response. But when the possibility of further requests exists, there is no warranty that further information could be obtained using the same tool or channel. For example, primary information was obtained on the basis of an automated search in a dactyloscopic database; to get personal data, the Swedish Initiative was used; received information revealed a person's involvement in organised crime and after checking in the index system of AWF, a hit was received, the competent authority joined AWF, and further information was exchanged through Europol. Having all the pieces of data on one person received using different tools, an officer should be very careful taking decisions on possible onward transmission, transmission to a third party and use of sensitive data. And the most important question is which data protection regime must be applied to data related to one investigation, but received using different information exchange tools, in order to ensure its further effective use by obeying the requirements of the due process.

Table 12.1 Purpose of information exchange within the analysed information exchange tools

	Purpose
CISA	*SIS* – General: To ensure a high level of security in the territories of the Member States. – Special: Each category of alert has its own purpose depending on category of person or object. *PCCC* Individually established by bilateral or multilateral agreements. As a general rule should: – include prevention, detection, investigation and prosecution of petty crime committed at border area, – not interfere with the competence of central information exchange units. *Liaison officers* Individually established by bilateral or multilateral agreements or based on the national law of hosting country and competence of liaison officer established by sending country.
Europol	General objective: Prevention and combatting of serious crimes affecting two or more Member States, terrorism and other forms of crime affecting interest of the EU. The list of crimes is provided in the Annex I to the Europol Regulation. Purposes of exchange of information: – Cross-checking of data on crimes, convicted persons and those suspected of already having committed a crime or with "factual indications or reasonable grounds to believe that they will commit criminal offences". – Strategic, operational analysis and facilitating information exchange between competent authorities.
Swedish Initiative	As it is defined ambiguously, the broader provision is detection, prevention or investigation of offences.
FIUs and AROs	– FIUs: Money laundering and financing of terrorism. – AROs: Tracing and identification of crime related property for its further freezing, seizure or confiscation.
Prüm Decisions	– DNA databases: investigation of criminal offence. – Dactyloscopic databases: prevention and investigation of criminal offences. – Vehicle registration data: prevention and investigation of criminal offences, other offences under the jurisdiction of the courts or the public prosecution service of the searching Member State and for the maintenance of public security. – Non-automated data exchange: prevention of terrorism, prevention and security of major events with a cross-border dimension.
PNR	Prevention, detection, investigation and prosecution of terrorist offences and serious crime.

Table 12.2 Data subjects within the analysed information exchange tools

	Data subject
CISA	*SIS* – Wanted for surrender, i.e. prosecuted or convicted; – Missing or in need of special protection due to their physical or mental conditions; – Sought for assistance in judicial procedure; – Needed to be checked; – Not allowed to enter one of the members of the Schengen zone; – Persons whose identity is misused (with previous consent). *PCCC* Depends on bilateral and multilateral agreements. *Liaison officers* Depends on bilateral and multilateral agreements and national law of sending and hosting countries.
Europol	*Cross-checking* – Persons suspected of already committed a crime, being accomplices or, of its future commission when crime is subject to Europol's competence; – Convicted persons. *Strategic, thematic and operation analysis, facilitating of information exchange* – Persons suspected of already having committed a crime, being accomplices, or of its future commission when crime is subject to Europol's competence; – Convicted persons; – Witnesses; – Victims; – Contacts and associates of suspects; – Informers.
Swedish Initiative	Not specified.
FIUs and AROs	Not directly specified, but a conclusion can be made that they are natural, legal persons involved in money laundering or terrorism financing.
Prüm Decisions	Subject to national legislation.
PNR	All passengers of extra-EU flights, in some Member States also passengers of intra-EU flights

Table 12.3 Data categories within the analysed information exchange tools

	Data categories
CISA	*SIS* – Surname and forenames, any aliases possibly entered separately; – Any specific, objective physical characteristics not subject to change; – First letter of second forename; – Date and place of birth; – Sex; – Nationality; – Whether the persons concerned are armed and/or violent; – Reason for the alert; – Action to be taken; – Photographs; – Fingerprints; – Authority issuing the alert; – A reference to the decision giving rise to the alert; – Links to or alerts in SIS II; – The type of offence. *PCCC* Depend on bilateral and multilateral agreements. *Liaison officers* Depends on bilateral and multilateral agreements and the national law of the sending and hosting countries.
Europol	*Cross-checking* – Surname, maiden name, given names, alias, assumed name; – Date and place of birth; – Nationality; – Sex; – Where necessary other characteristics likely to assist in identification as dactyloscopic data and DNA profiles; – Place of residence and whereabouts; – Profession; – Social security numbers; – Driving licences; – Identification documents. *Strategic, thematic and operation analysis, facilitating of information exchange* General to all data subjects: – Present and former surnames (i.e. real and alias, nickname, residence, nationality, parents – if it necessary, etc.); – Physical description; – Identification means (i.e. documents, ID and other official numbers, images, fingerprints and DNA profiles, etc.). Additional data categories: Differ depending on the data subject and are provided in Chapter 5.
Swedish Initiative	Any type of information or data which is held by law enforcement authorities.

	Data categories
FIUs and AROs	*FIUs* Any available information useful for FIU for analysis and investigation of money laundering and financing of terrorism. *AROs* Any information considered necessary for the execution of the tasks of another ARO.
Prüm Decisions	– Data related to personal characteristics such as DNA and dactyloscopics; – Vehicle registration data; – All data important in prevention of terrorism; – All data important in prevention of offences and threats to the security in major events with a cross-border dimension.
PNR	– Names; – Address, telephone, e-mail; – Payment information; – Information on frequent flyer; – General remarks; – Other travellers on the PNR; – Date of reservation/issue; – Travel itinerary; – Travel agency; – Travel status (confirmation, check-in); – Ticket, seat information; – Baggage information; – PNR record locator; – Split/divided PNR; – Historical changes of all data; – Advance passenger information (both flights and personal).

Table 12.4 Possibilities to exchange sensitive data within the analysed information exchange tools

	Sensitive data
CISA	*SIS* Transmission prohibited. *PCCC* Depends on bilateral and multilateral agreements. *Liaison officers* Depends on bilateral and multilateral agreements and national law of sending and hosting countries.
Europol	– As a general rule prohibited. – Exception: strictly necessary and proportional for preventing or combating crimes and if it supplements other personal data. This exception is applied to case by case transmission of data to Member States, third countries, organisations and EU entities.
Swedish Initiative	Not specified.
FIUs and AROs	Not specified, but by the nature of purpose, not very relevant.
Prüm Decisions	Does not occur in automated data search, because in cases of dactyloscopic or vehicle registration, data is not collected and in cases of DNA, a non-coding part of DNA is used that allows identification of sex, but not any other sensitive data. Nevertheless, it is not specified for non-automated data exchange and data transmission after match (hit).
PNR	Explicitly prohibited, but the categories of sensitive data do not coincide with categories envisaged in the EU Charter.

Table 12.5 Authorities that have access to information within the analysed information exchange tools

	Accessing authorities
CISA	*SIS* – Police; – State Border Guards; – Customs; – Vehicle registration entities; – Europol and Eurojust (access limited to alerts related to their mandate); – When it is allowed by the national legislation, also judicial authorities participating an in investigation and their coordinators can be granted an access. *PCCC* As a general rule, police and customs authorities or other authorities performing their functions (i.e. State Border Guard). *Liaison officers* Not defined, depends on bilateral and multilateral agreements and the national law of sending and hosting countries.
Europol	*Cross-checking* – Duly empowered Europol staff (including the Director and his Deputies); – Liaison officers; – ENUs; – Member States can decide to give an access to EIS to other competent authorities, but it will be limited to the possibility of verifying whether requested information exists (hit/no hit). *Operational analysis* Participants of AWF after Europol's accreditation and special training. The Director, his or her Deputies, Europol staff, liaison officers and ENUs that do not participate in AWF are authorised to access only index of the AWF and make a search on hit/no hit basis.
Swedish Initiative	– Police; – Customs; – Other authorities that are authorised by national Law to detect, prevent and investigate offences or criminal activities.
FIUs and AROs	*FIUs* – FIUs; – Other authorities combating money laundering. *AROs* – AROs; – Other authorities with the competence of tracing and identification of property obtained as a result of crime.

	Accessing authorities
Prüm Decisions	At the stage of automated comparison: – National contact points designated by each state. At the stage or receiving data related to automated matches: – Firstly, is available to national contact point that lately is transmitted to the authority that has requested a comparison. In case of non-automated data exchange: – Network of contact points for each category of data (terrorism, public order and security); – National contact points make further transmission of data to requesting authority or in case of spontaneous data supply – to the authority that can be interested in it.
PNR	Direct access: relevant PIUs. Competent authorities: as a general rule on the basis of result of PNR assessment or request.

Table 12.6 Data protection regulation within the analysed information exchange tools

	Data protection regime
CISA	*SIS* Lex generalis – For all alerts except on persons not allowed to enter the Schengen zone – European Convention on Data Protection, Directive 2016/680. – For alerts on persons not allowed to enter the Schengen zone – Regulation 2016/679. Lex especialis: – Individual set of provisions established by Decision 2007/533/JHA and Regulation 1987/2006. *PCCC* – Lex generalis: Directive 2016/680. – Lex especialis: provisions of bilateral or multilateral agreements if applicable and national law of sending and hosting country. *Liaison officers* – Lex generalis: Directive 2016/680. – Lex especialis: provisions of bilateral or multilateral agreements if applicable and national law of sending and hosting country.
Europol	Individual set of provisions established by Europol Regulation.
Swedish Initiative	– Lex generalis: European Convention on Data Protection, its Protocol, Recommendation (87) 15, Directive 2016/680 and national law. – Lex especialis: rules applied to data transmission channel.

	Data protection regime
FIUs and AROs	*FIUs* – European Convention on Data Protection, its Protocol and Recommendation R(87) 15. – For AML/CFT: Regulation 2016/679. *AROs* – European Convention on Data Protection, its Protocol, Recommendation R(87) 15. – Also rules applied to Swedish Initiative (as it serves as the basis for information exchange).
Prüm Decisions	Lex especialis: Decision 2008/615/JHA and national law.
PNR	Directive 2016/680.

Table 12.7 Possibility to transmit information to third countries within the analysed information exchange tools

	Transmission to third parties
CISA	*SIS* Not permitted. Foreseen exception of data submission to the Interpol database on stolen or missing travel documents is not applied. *PCCC* Depends on bilateral or multilateral agreements. *Liaison officers* Depends on bilateral or multilateral agreements of sending and hosting Member States.
Europol	Allowed with the consent of the Member State that has provided information and on the basis of: – Agreement between Europol and Third party, – Commission's decisions on data protection adequacy, – EU agreements. Exceptions: by the decision of the Director in order to protect vital interests of data subject or another person, legitimate interest of data subject, in case of serious threat to the public security, necessity in individual cases to prevent, detect, investigate, prosecute crime.
Swedish Initiative	Not foreseen.
FIUs and AROs	Not foreseen.
Prüm Decisions	Not foreseen.
PNR	Allowed with the fulfilment of three conditions: it is for the same purpose as PNR processing in general, under transfer conditions established in the Directive 2016/680 and with notification of data protection officer of PIU.

Table 12.8 Possibilities of onward transmission and other use of information within the analysed information exchange tools

	Onward transmission, use for other purposes
CISA	*SIS* Use for other purposes is possible only to prevent serious threats to public policy or security, to national security or to prevent serious crimes. In such cases consent from the Member State that has issued the alert has to be obtained. *PCCC* Depends on bilateral or multilateral agreements that can permit so called "chain requests". *Liaison officers* Information related to serious criminal threats can be requested on behalf of other Member States or Europol that do not have their liaison officers in that country.
Europol	As a general rule onwards transmitting is prohibited, unless with prior and explicit authorisation of Europol. Operational agreements establishes different rules.
Swedish Initiative	Not foreseen.
FIUs and AROs	Not foreseen.
Prüm Decisions	Not foreseen.
PNR	For the same purpose as PNR processing in general, with the express authorisation of the requested Member State and notification of data protection officer of PIU. Exception is possible only in case when it is "essential to respond to a specific and actual threat related to terrorist offences or serious crime in a Member State or a third country and a prior consent cannot be obtained in good time".

Index

Bold pages numbers indicate tables.

For Product Safety Concerns and Information please contact our EU representative GPSR@taylorandfrancis.com
Taylor & Francis Verlag GmbH, Kaufingerstraße 24, 80331 München, Germany

www.ingramcontent.com/pod-product-compliance
Ingram Content Group UK Ltd.
Pitfield, Milton Keynes, MK11 3LW, UK
UKHW010956180926
475701UK00004B/403

* 9 7 8 0 3 6 7 5 9 0 3 9 0 *